UNCOMMON ANTHROPOLOGIST

UNCOMMON
ANTHROPOLOGIST

GLADYS REICHARD
AND WESTERN NATIVE
AMERICAN CULTURE

NANCY MATTINA

UNIVERSITY OF OKLAHOMA PRESS : NORMAN

Library of Congress Cataloging-in-Publication Data

Names: Mattina, Nancy, 1956– author.

Title: Uncommon anthropologist : Gladys Reichard and western Native
    American culture / Nancy Mattina.

Description: Norman : University of Oklahoma Press, [2019] | Includes
    bibliographical references and index.

Identifiers: LCCN 2019013749 | ISBN 978-0-8061-6429-8 (Hardcover) ISBN
978-0-8061-9007-5 (paper) Subjects: LCSH: Reichard, Gladys Amanda, 1893–1955.

Women anthropologists—Southwest, New—Biography. | Ethnology—Fieldwork
—Southwest, New. | Indians of North America—Southwest, New—Social life
and customs. | Feminist anthropology—Southwest, New—History.

Classification: LCC GN21.R438 M38 2019 | DDC 301.092 [B] —dc23
LC record available at https://lccn.loc.gov/2019013749

The paper in this book meets the guidelines for permanence and durability of
the Committee on Production Guidelines for Book Longevity of the Council on
Library Resources, Inc. ∞

CONTENTS

ILLUSTRATIONS

PREFACE

The discriminating traveler who has wandered off the highway realizes that the desert supports a people attractive, colorful, even romantic. Yet his brief contacts with them may leave him with the impression that they are so reserved as to be stolid, so patient as to be shiftless, so mobile as to be irresponsible, so acquisitive as to be beggarly or grasping.

Such impressions may seem justified by casual acquaintance but I have learned through long residence with the Navajo that these Indians are, under circumstances which they understand, actually talkative and jolly; that, toward members of their own tribe to whom obligations are well-defined, they are faithful, tolerant, dependable, and generous.

Dezba, Woman of the Desert, 1939

Gladys Reichard (1893–1955) was a maverick anthropologist, a champion of human equality and individual freedom, a master communicator, and a good sport. To aficionados of the American Southwest, she is the author of *Spider Woman* (1934) and *Navaho Religion* (1950). In the Pacific Northwest, a handful of specialists in North American Indian linguistics refer regularly to her groundbreaking studies of Salishan languages and oral literatures. A still tinier group of ethno-art historians continues to consult her *Melanesian Design* (1933) as a first step in any examination of the artistic ideas expressed in the delicate, hand-carved body ornaments known as kapkaps.

As a writer of culture, Reichard consistently matched the respect she had for objective materials with a sober acceptance of her mere humanity, though the domineering, masculine aesthetic of her day would have her don the "hard" authorial persona that gazed on "The Indian" with godlike omniscience.[1] As an anthropological linguist, she insisted on the interconnectedness of language and culture when the prevailing approach to describing unwritten North American Indian languages forbade complementary studies of meaning, usage, style, and genre in those same languages. In some circles she is remembered as stubborn or weak for her willingness to "trespass on the dangerous ground of interpretation."[2] Long residence with her writings reveals that Reichard's resolve, like her scholarly output, was of the quietly heroic, slyly transformative kind.

The extraordinary reach of Reichard's vision and competencies explains in part why more than sixty years after her death, we have not had a comprehensive biography of this pivotal figure in American anthropology until now. A passing acquaintance with Reichard's curriculum vitae gives the impression she was a nondescript Boasian, yet acknowledging that she was a student of Franz Boas gets us no closer to understanding her life or times and ignores the pervasive influence of Elsie Clews Parsons on Reichard's work. In every decade since the 1960s, a few scholars have been moved to revisit Reichard's career for their own reasons. When Clifford Geertz declared Reichard in 1970 the "most underestimated of all American anthropologists," he referred to her prescient appreciation of symbolic behavior.[3] In 1980 Gary Witherspoon invited his generation of anthropological linguists to recognize Reichard as the first champion of the then-emerging field of linguistic anthropology. (The invitation was declined.) By the 1990s, feminists looked to Reichard as a potential role model for women scholars, only to be disappointed when she didn't meet their narrow, anachronistic definition of a feminist. Through the end of the last century and into the present, the impulse to disavow the imperialistic motive in the anthropology of the past led postmoderns to sweep Reichard's legacy (back) under the rug with "fashionable critiques" that were as "insensitive to historical context" as they were "cavalier about cause and effect."[4]

Fortunately, Reichard did enough in her thirty-five years as a student of the human experience to make it impossible for her to remain a "hidden scholar" indefinitely. The quality and volume of the work Reichard accomplished, under circumstances she understood far better than we, are such that we have only to connect the scattered pieces of her story for her to emerge whole from the margins of anthropological history.

The desire to know who Gladys Reichard was, what she thought, and how she changed the thinking of others about the culture, language, art, and psychology of western Native American peoples springs from our "deeper necessity" to understand what it means to be human.[5] The approach taken here is to pay Reichard the same courtesy she paid the people she made the focus of her career: by telling her story as much as possible from her point of view and in her own words.

Reichard never took her friends and helpers for granted. I too owe a debt of gratitude to more generous people than I can list here. Several scholars kindly walked long stretches of the road to publication with me. Foremost among these are professor emerita of the University of Arizona Nancy Parezo, whose *Hidden Scholars* (1993) was my initial stimulus; Ira Jacknis, research anthropologist at the Hearst Museum; California historian and ethnogeographer Jerry Rhode; and professor emeritus of Allegheny College, my alma mater, Paul Zolbrod. Lynnika Butler, Wiyot language program manager in 2014, provided critical insight into Reichard's contributions to ongoing Wiyot language revival efforts. I thank my two readers at University of Oklahoma Press, Rosemary Levy-Zumwalt, biographer of both Parsons and Boas, and David Dinwoodie, specialist in Athabascan anthropological linguistics. I join Dr. Dinwoodie in regretting that space limitations prevent me from presenting the detailed restudy of Reichard's more famous contemporaries that appeared in an earlier version of my manuscript. The reader is directed to the extant biographies, many cited here, that explore the personalities of outstanding anthropologists who supported or were antagonistic to Reichard's progress. Not least, I thank the unerringly professional staff at University of Oklahoma Press for their guidance and vigilance.

Among the archivists, librarians, and museum administrators who went above the call of duty to assist me were Sharon Gothard (Easton Area Public Library, Pennsylvania); Kathy Tabaha (Hubbell Trading Post National Historic Site); Patricia Walker, Susan Olberding, Melissa Lawton and Elaine Hughes (Museum of Northern Arizona); Martha Tenney (Barnard Archives and Special Collections); and Beth Silbergleit (University of New Mexico Center for Southwest Research and Special Collections). Prescott College and the National Park Service provided welcome institutional support for the project. Special thanks go to two Arizonans who knew Reichard as children, Nelson Schaum Jr. of Flagstaff and Donald Wilson of Ganado, and their respective family members, Sandie Sangster and Marcie Wilson, who facilitated my interviews with their elderly parents. With the express consent of the Cornfields Chapter House council and the Navajo Nation's Natural History and Resources department, Hugh Lano, great-grandson of Maria Antonia and Miguelito of Red Point Mesa, graciously escorted me to the site of his ancestors' White Sands summer camp, which is located on his property. Laura Mogk was a total stranger until I knocked on her door to ask about the history of her Flagstaff-area neighborhood. Soon afterward she surprised me with a thick stack of papers documenting Reichard's family history back to the seventeenth century, the product of Mogk's skill at online genealogical research. Family and friends who encouraged me at crucial moments include (in alphabetical order) Shannon Bischoff, Ray Brinkman, Ivy Doak, Janice Kempster, Joe Mattina, Sarah Mattina, Bill Seaburg, and Nancy Wolin. Your every kind word or action on my behalf is deeply appreciated.

For introducing me in 1984 to the linguistic work of Gladys Reichard, the veritable first lady of Salishan linguistics, I thank my husband, Anthony Mattina. Without his multifaceted support, this book would not have been. All remaining errors of fact or interpretation not scrubbed from my manuscript during its journey are mine alone.

UNCOMMON ANTHROPOLOGIST

PROLOGUE

SPEAKING HER MIND TO AN AUDIENCE OF SLIGHTLY BEMUSED MEN was old hat for Gladys Reichard. Lately arrived at Rome's Palazzo Corsini for the 22nd International Congress of Americanists, the young delegate from the American Ethnological Society was prepared to hold her own in three idioms: art, language, and culture. Her meteoric rise from a shy classics major at Swarthmore College to confident protégé of modern anthropology's leading figure, Franz Boas, had taken less than six years. Having proved her mettle in academic papers that sparkled with warmth and wit, Reichard was chosen to fill a new faculty position at Barnard College in the only anthropology department at any women's college in the United States while still a graduate student. In 1925 she earned de facto tenure as Barnard's only anthropologist with the publication of her Columbia University dissertation on the grammar of Wiyot, the first field-based, structuralist account of a North American Indian language written by a woman. A Guggenheim Memorial Fellowship for Advanced Study Abroad soon followed, paving Reichard's way to western Europe in 1926.

After Rome her next stop was Hamburg's Museum für Völkerkunde, where she would spend a seven-month residency studying Melanesian art and acoustical linguistics. Just thirty-three years of age, Reichard was reaping the benefits of having surrendered her feminine claim to "the great soporifics—comfort and protection."[1] There was a place for her in the manly sphere of scientific inquiry, as her presence at Galileo's Accademia dei Lincei attested. Though many of her fellow *congressisti* impressed her, none frightened her. These were, after all, her people.

Missing from the multinational crowd at the Corsini mansion were Franz Boas and Reichard's principal role model and sponsor, New York activist and philanthropist, Dr. Elsie Clews Parsons. A sociologist by

training, a radical feminist by choice, Parsons had articulated more fresh
ideas on sex roles, race, marriage, war, and the chauvinistic codes of
polite society by her fifth decade than most public intellectuals manage in
a lifetime. Reichard did not need Parsons by her side to uncover with careful social science the patriarchal prejudices that had plunged "civilized"
nations into the abyss of the Great War. But defeating the stereotype of
the "primitive" mind was not so easily done by one or a hundred esteemed
scholars in Mussolini's Eternal City. By week's end, Reichard admitted to
Parsons by mail that the Congress had been less than a triumph for the
"science of Man": "The entertainment was abundant, varied & magnificent but the program was so messed up that one was unable to find the
time or the place of the very few lectures (that were worth hearing) one
most wanted to hear."[2] To Boas Reichard wrote with her usual frankness,
"I met many people I liked. As for science, it did not exist. . . . Are we all
wrong & the others all right?"[3]

Visits with a friend from Swarthmore to the open treasures of the
ancient metropolis more than compensated for temporary disappointments. "We spent one afternoon in the Forum & on the Palatine Hill. . . .
We were on the Palatine just before sunset & it is indescribable," Reichard wrote home. "Yesterday we spent the entire morning in the Sistine
Chapel, an experience I shall never forget. . . . By noon the whole place
was irradiated by a brilliance that was almost holy. Nothing that has ever
been said about it has been exaggerated; it would be impossible."[4] Moved
by masterful interiors though she was, Reichard's mind often drifted to a
landscape as empty of man-made monuments as Rome was jammed with
them: the American Southwest. A few days earlier she'd "enjoyed a little
sandstorm" outside the painted Etruscan tombs at Cerveteri.[5] Watching
the fierce meridional sun duck behind heavy clouds one afternoon, she
pictured monsoon weather ripening over the red and white escarpments
that split southwestern horizons cleanly into earth and azure sky. "If I
should not see another thing I should feel satisfied with Rome," she
recorded after marveling at Michelangelo's handiwork. "I love Italy. The
air, the light, the carefreeness remind me of the S[outh] W[est], the only
thing I have been homesick for in America."[6]

The months in Hamburg that followed deepened her private longing for her "real country."[7] Reichard could barely repress her joy as she
made her way home to New York in the spring. "I am so glad to be back

that I almost believe I would make material for Sinclair Lewis," Reichard exhaled on arrival. "I had a wonderful year but I am darn glad it is over." "My trip through Germany, France & England was very nice," she continued. "But I should be glad to get back to Indians again. Their civilization suits my taste better than the over-populated, concentrated European type." One worldly New Woman to another, Reichard asked Parsons, "Did you ever have the feeling that Europe is so awfully civilized?"[8]

CHAPTER 1

EQUALLY DESTINED
FOR LIBERTY

FRIENDS AND FOES OF GLADYS AMANDA REICHARD AGREED that she had a mind of her own. Few thought to ask her at what age she decided not to waste it. As a woman she was "courageous, receptive, ever enquiring, ever delighted with the pursuit of wisdom," possessed of the kind of open, compassionate intelligence that didn't develop overnight.[1] Born in Bangor, Pennsylvania, on July 17, 1893, Gladys was raised by Minerva and Noah Reichard to be practical, honest, generous, self-reliant, and hardworking. With her only sibling, Lilian, her elder by a year, she attended Sunday school, where she got "a great dose of Protestantism" spiked with continual warnings of hell.[2] In the Reichards's sturdy Queen Anne at 28 South First Street, Reichard wrote, the atmosphere was more that of a "stern school of loving (?) unbiased criticism," not so harsh as to break her adventurous spirit but calculated to produce backbone worthy of a daughter's highest aspirations.[3]

Reichard's small-town, Lutheran upbringing prepared her to bear the burdens of death as well as those of life. When her thirty-nine-year-old mother died on January 29, 1902, Gladys was not yet nine, but old enough to read the story "Found His Wife Dead" in the evening edition of a local newspaper. "Her husband found her on her knees beside her bed," the *Easton Express* informed the public on an inside page. "The doctor had gone downstairs a short time previous and had returned to the bed-room to learn what had delayed Mrs. Reichard in coming to breakfast."[4] The *Easton Sunday Call* noted the cause of death as heart failure, hastening to add that the doctor's wife was "possessed of many noble traits of character" without specifying any.[5] Her memorial service was held in the Reichards' front parlor, where mother and daughters had lately passed winter evenings reading and sewing by lantern and firelight. Following the service, Minerva's body was interred in the family crypt around the corner in the graveyard next to Trinity Lutheran Church.[6]

Gladys left no record of her thoughts on the signal trauma of her childhood, but her remarks in the wake of the death of Maria Antonia, the Navajo matriarch who was her frequent host in Arizona in the 1930s, revealed an intimate understanding of how it felt to lose a mother too soon. "Out of hopeful and loving expectation comes ghastly silence," Reichard wrote thirty years after her own mother's death. "Instead of natural bustling activity there is only baffling stillness. [Navajo people] do not, like us, try to 'stick it'; they simply move away, leaving the disconcerting hush to consort with the abominable quiet."[7]

What can be discovered about Minerva Jordan Reichard more than a century after her birth is found chiefly in public records about men. She began life in Riegelsville, across the county line from Bangor, to a family with deep roots in Pennsylvania that stretched back to an English immigrant, a miller named Frederick Jordan who was born in 1744. Frederick served as a sergeant in the New Jersey Line of the Continental Army during the Revolutionary War. He subsequently married Catharine Eckel, the daughter of well-to-do German-speaking immigrants whose parents had sailed from Rotterdam to reach Philadelphia in 1749, the year before Catharine was born. Over the next hundred years, Frederick and Catharine's male descendants rose to prominence in Bucks and Philadelphia counties. One of those assertive scions was Alexander Jordan, Minerva's father, who married Amanda Weikel, the younger of Gladys's two grandmothers. In 1861 Alexander Jordan graduated from the medical department of the University of Pennsylvania. During the Civil War, he served as an assistant surgeon at a Union army hospital while Amanda bore their four children, Minerva, Lillie, Alexander Hayes, and luckless Maggie, who died before her first birthday. After the war, Gladys's maternal grandparents returned to Reigelsville, where Dr. Jordan launched a medical practice deemed an eminent success until his death in 1900. Per the custom of the day, Minerva's brother received the benefit of a college education denied his sisters. After earning a master's degree at Lafayette College in Easton, the seat of Northampton County, Gladys's only uncle became a newspaper editor, a permanent resident of Easton, the father of her only first cousins, and, in 1903, the owner of the *Bucks County Weekly and Daily Republican*.[8]

Minerva, meanwhile, remained under her father's roof until June 1891, when at the age of twenty-eight she and Dr. Noah Webster Reichard were married at St. John's United Church of Christ in Riegelsville. The groom was five years older than his bride, but as both had ancestors among the seventy thousand German-speaking Lutheran and Reformed Christians who emigrated to William Penn's colony between 1681 and the mid-1700s, the sociocultural distance between them was slight. Mostly literate villagers in command of useful trades, the Palatines, as the newcomers were known on arrival, were refugees from war, famine, overtaxation, or religious intolerance.[9] Although they emigrated voluntarily, when they crossed the Atlantic under a British flag they were persecuted by English-speaking crews who subjected them to thirst, hunger, unsanitary conditions, and loss of liberty. Opportunistic sea captains took advantage of the migrants, forcing male heads of households to indenture themselves in exchange for wormy rations or medicines for their children who, with their female relatives, were listed as "whole freight" on the ship manifest. At the port of Philadelphia, the same hard men who had treated their paying customers as captives exercised their option to sell indentures at public auction. Many a proud Palatine freeman who boarded an English ship at Rotterdam or Wirtemburg set foot on American soil as another man's property.[10]

Solvent or not, some of Gladys Reichard's "Pennsylvania-Dutch" forebearers took up farming in the heavily wooded northeast corner of Northampton County known as the Minisink, a "howling wilderness," with "no human inhabitant save the red sons of the woods."[11] By the time her father was born in 1857, a new economic engine was poised to upstage the horse-drawn plow. Large slate deposits discovered in the 1830s at the base of the Blue Mountains north of Bangor would transform the area into a center of mining, commerce, and transportation by rail. Industrialized methods of extraction had been introduced to the Pennsylvania Slate Belt by Welsh mine owner Robert Jones at midcentury. With the help of Cornish, Welsh, Scots-Irish, and Huguenot craftsmen and laborers, the twenty-four-square-mile area around Bangor would come track to supply half of the national demand for roof tile, chalkboard, and structural slate by the end of the century.[12]

Noah Reichard was the son of a farmer who by the sweat of his brow made it possible for his only male heir to trade the plow for a pen. As a teen, Noah left his natal home on the outskirts of Bangor to attend Trach's Academy, a college preparatory school in Easton. One year at Trach's gained him admission to Muhlenberg College, a four-year Lutheran liberal arts school located in Allentown. After graduating from Thomas Jefferson Medical College in Philadelphia in 1888, Noah made his way back to Northampton County, where he hung his physician's shingle on Market Street in downtown Bangor by 1890.[13] His years in Pennsylvania's larger cities seemed to satisfy the thirty-three-year-old doctor that, as the Italians say, *tutto il mondo è paese*, or, "People are people everywhere." He met and proposed to Minerva Jordan; or, perhaps, his return to his home county fulfilled a prenuptial promise made in the bloom of youth. Seometime in 1891, Noah had the house on First Street built to accommodate marriage, children, and his medical practice. A few months later he settled into it for the rest of his natural life.

Noah had good reasons to stay put. His university training didn't qualify him as one of the fourteen Pennsylvania-Germans listed as "gentlemen" in the Bangor city directory, yet as one of five physicians serving a town of twenty-five hundred, his prospects were nothing but bright.[14] Open-pit quarrying of the soft, silvery stone laid down in the Ordovician period was profitable but dangerous work. Explosions, falls, dust, damp air, slides, fires, heavy lifting, and faulty equipment took their toll on the men. Child laborers, known as hillibobbers, stood in harm's way pouring water on the blocks of stone as the slaters split them.[15] Waste piles reaching one hundred feet high posed a less-immediate threat to human safety than did the huge slabs of raw stone that were hoisted from mast to mast by cable and chain over the heads of vulnerable miners. With no hospital for miles around and few competitors, Dr. Reichard was assured a steady trade in pain and disease on which to raise a family.

The trust and admiration Gladys had for women in later years suggests that the women in her small family circle, including Lilian, supplied her with the love and attention she needed to thrive in the aftermath of her mother's untimely death.[16] Noah Reichard, however, played no small part in reassuring his grieving daughters. The doctor might have followed a romantic, Victorian script that permitted him to withdraw from polite society, turn to drink, and shuffle his motherless offspring to boarding school. Instead, he hired a housekeeper to help him care for his bright young daughters at home and carried on being a model parent. Simply by practicing his profession in the family home, he provided a stabilizing moral framework for Gladys Reichard's developing character. From her earliest days, she heard the muffled sobs and groans of the sick emanating from her father's first-floor surgery. Each time the doctor was called away from the dinner table to a neighbor's sickbed, his regard for other people's lives, no matter how puny from a distance, testified to the common denominator shared by all. On days when her father returned home at dawn worn from caring for a stranger or friend, she was presented with the lesson that on the human scale, time was finite and suffering a fact of every human life. By an accident of birth, Gladys grew up surrounded by evidence that men of science like her father acted honorably when they combined compassion and skill with a disdain for fakery—real lives hung in the balance.

A pragmatist, Noah ranked personal integrity and self-sufficiency as highly as intellectual brilliance. A childhood friend of Gladys once said, "Old Doc Reichard figured his daughters ought to know a thing or two about earning a living and learning the value of money before they went to college."[17] Gladys remembered the years before she went to college as serving a more soulful purpose, saying, "My father believed you should know what you wanted to study before starting at college."[18] While both statements reveal that Noah supported his daughter's desire to train for a career at college, they also allude to the value Gladys was encouraged to place on personal responsibility, thrift as an exercise in self-restraint, and sincerity of purpose as the tools of right living. Noah put his daughters' emotional security and resilience to the test when, five years after his first wife's death, he married thirty-two-year-old widow Mary Ditchett Weiss, a Methodist from East Bangor, in the same month Gladys turned fourteen.[19] The union did not disrupt the harmony of the Reichard household, to all appearances. Both of Noah's daughters came to refer to Mary as "Mother" and Mary reciprocated by speaking of them as her daughters. The teenaged Reichards carried on with their studies at Bangor High School with an eye to becoming schoolteachers. Both graduated at sixteen and continued to live at home while saving their modest teacher's salaries for college.

On the strength of her first diploma, Gladys taught in day schools in the surrounding Washington Township School District. The area was thick with one-room schoolhouses, including one in Bangor itself. The

first two years Reichard endured a trial by fire that consisted in her super-
vising the lessons of "twenty-nine pupils and twenty-eight classes—all in
one room!"[20] At eighteen she was hired to teach at her old elementary
school, Garfield, where the children's surnames—Segatti, Dapkowitz,
Saurwine, Perinotto, Buskirk, Sandt, Harding, or Williams—spoke to
Bangor's ongoing participation in the American melting pot phenomenon.[21] When in June 1913 Lilian left Bangor to study French and Spanish
in the Paris suburb of Bourg-la-Reine, Gladys was undeterred. Her plans
for life after Bangor included by that point the desire to become a physician. Two more years as a schoolteacher would give her the financial
means to exit her hometown via the road less traveled by women of her
class and age, one that led to a university degree in medicine.

While her father's modern outlook encouraged Reichard's independent streak, life in Bangor, "town of houses," raised as many questions
for a native daughter as it answered. The business-friendly core of the
borough was a reassuring swath of the immigrant's Promised Land.
Imposing brick homes, gated gardens, and attractive storefronts lined
clean streets incised with trolley tracks laid between raised wooden
sidewalks. Allowed to roam her neighborhood with Lilian at an early age,
Gladys developed her physical confidence by playing along the banks of
Martins Creek, where baseball took precedence over less-serious games,
or at the dark green swimming hole below Flory's Dam, a magnet for
ice-skating and hockey when Bangor turned winter white. The piles of
mining waste and unlovely railyards on the outskirts of Bangor's central
grid were undoubtedly off-limits to middle-class children, but for a nickel
Reichard could ride the trolley to neighboring boroughs to attend sports
tournaments, the annual Welsh Week parade, or the Roseto Big Time, a
religious carnival held each July. With Lilian, she was free to pass a summer's evening at the Slate Belt Park pavilion, where the merry-go-round,
weekend dances, and concerts by the descendants of Venetian-born brass
bands, the East Bangor Cornet Band, or the Welsh Male Chorus effected
a sort of cultural pluralism through motion and song.[22]

The business climate in Bangor was similarly upbeat. Although Reichard's preschool years coincided with a panic on Wall Street that shook
every major industry and market in the country, the local economy made
a comeback in the late 1890s. Betting on their own grit, scores of skilled
and unskilled workers flowed into town during Reichard's youth, more

than doubling Bangor's population in a single decade. In support of a hundred slate mines operating in the vicinity, dozens of hotels and boardinghouses sprang up to serve every taste, from wealthy capitalist to eager leatherneck. The Flory Milling Company hired as many as five hundred employees to keep its customers in flour and feed. At the other end of Main Street, the Bangor Lumber Company was one of two businesses that hustled to provide wood and coal for the construction boom. In 1907, as the slate industry edged toward decline, Bangor got a shot in the arm from the opening of the Sterling Silk Mill, which paid women workers good wages while bringing much-needed economic diversity to the region.

The noise, pollution, and environmental degradation incurred by the Bangor-Portland branch of the Lackawanna and Lehigh and New England Railroad lines were easy to write off as the costs of graded prosperity for all. No one seemed to mind that slaters still spoke their native languages in addition to beginner's English. If the recent immigrants were occasionally pelted with stones and slurs as they walked to the quarries from their ethnic settlements in Roseto, East Bangor, or Pen Argyl, Bangor boosters focused primarily on the newcomers' economic value. To keep pace with the rapid, global changes afoot, social harmony in an ethnically mixed, industrialized community like theirs was a commercial imperative. A veneer of unity was not so difficult to achieve in Bangor's well-established public spaces. For Old Home Week in August 1912, all that was required to achieve the desired result was to festoon the town center with red, white, and blue banners that shouted, "Bigger, Better, Busier Bangor" in a quintessentially American idiom.[23]

Tolerant as Bangor appeared to be on its surface, Reichard's decision to attend Swarthmore College points to her having realized small-town life had intolerable limitations. Within the family fold, her sex did not count against her. Beyond the walls of her peaceful home, the rules for men and women differed. It was common practice for male teachers of her age and experience to be paid more than she was for equivalent work, as she may have discovered when she taught at her grade school. The four-year liberal arts colleges closest to her, and therefore the most economical, remained, as in Noah's day, closed to women applicants. Her father's brief stints as a chief burgess and president of the Lehigh Valley Medical Society set an example of public service. Yet the ubiquity and clout of the male fraternal orders that flourished in the Slate Belt after the Civil

War implied that civic-mindedness was the province of men only. Gladys witnessed throughout her youth that her father's membership in "various Masonic bodies" gave him a sense of belonging to and ownership in a brotherhood dedicated to individual betterment, upward social mobility, and mutual assistance.[24] As one of the six million American men who joined in the Great Fraternal Movement after the Civil War, Noah did not invent the cronyism that ensued when women and all others who were not male, white, and solvent were excluded from secret male societies.[25] But an all-white brotherhood could be abusive toward those it shunned. One male fraternity, the Improved Order of Red Men, idolized Native Americans as "the noblest type of man" yet barred living Natives from membership. Declaring the Order "the acknowledged conservators of the history, the customs of the original American people," the Red Men justified their appropriation of thousands of years of precontact history with the excuse that the "real Red Indian" had been "wiped off the face of the earth."[26]

The liberties the Improved Order of Red Men took with the collective memory of brutally exiled peoples underscored the reality that, beside injecting ritualized spectacle, romantic fantasy, elaborate costuming, and secret handshakes into the drab, industrialized existence of American men postwar, fraternal orders reflected and reinforced the view that America, if not the world, existed by and for white men.[27] As a consequence, the least educated, least gifted immigrant man of the humblest means had, strictly on the basis of sex, a greater claim on unalienable civil rights and the pursuit of happiness than did Gladys. Under the guise of promoting healthy male bonding, male fraternities made excluding women from public life respectable. To remain in Bangor permanently, Reichard would have had to content herself within the confines of the feminine sphere where she was expected to marry, bear children, keep men's secrets indefinitely, and settle for anonymity, just as her mother and grandmothers had before her.

·   ·   ·   ◈   ·   ·   ·

Swarthmore College's fidelity to William Penn's maxim "in souls there is no sex" made a four-year residence on the outskirts of the City of Brotherly Love very appealing to a student with Reichard's outlook.[28] As if the classical curriculum, a superb, mixed faculty, and a great, green

pastoral setting a short train ride away from Lilian's new apartment in
Abington weren't enough, the Quaker college had a powerful asset in
the figure of its best known co-founder, "the greatest woman of the 19th
century," Lucretia Coffin Mott.[29]

Reichard would have been hard-pressed to find a more admirable,
unflappable, and intellectually brilliant heroine. A Hicksite Quaker
minister, abolitionist, feminist, and vocal opponent of military solutions
to human problems, Mott joined with dozens of Quaker parents during
the late 1850s to create a school where, instead of learning to wage nation-
alistic or religious war, young adults of any faith or sex could receive an
education that prepared them to better society "as if building a house
we are to live in."[30] Prior to her involvement with Swarthmore College,
Mott had been "the moving spirit" behind the first women's rights convention at Seneca Falls, New York in 1848. Though known primarily as
a compelling orator, Mott left an indelible imprint on the Declaration of
Sentiments, the written charter that powered the women's emancipation
movement long past her death in 1880.[31] Elizabeth Cady Stanton, a Mott
protégé, said of meeting her mentor for the first time, "Mrs. Mott was to
me an entirely new revelation of womanhood."[32] It was Mott who ensured
that when Swarthmore's inaugural class met in November 1869, the first
great hall to grace the newborn campus was designed to permit students
of both sexes to share classrooms, a library, and a common dining room
without ceremony. Looking over the youthful heads of the school's first
cohort, Mott counted an equal number of boys and girls among the 178
pupils gathered before her. Although the faculty of four included only one
woman, Miss Susan J. Cunningham, instructor and later full professor of
Pure Mathematics, the school's board of managers had an equal number
of men and women.[33] Four years later, Swarthmore's first graduating class
demonstrated what the level playing field Mott had insisted on meant for
ambitious girls. Of the six baccalaureate degrees conferred in 1873, five
went to women. Among the first graduating class was Helen Magill (White),
who subsequently enrolled at Boston University, where four years later she
became the first woman to earn a PhD at an American university.[34]

When Gladys made her way to her dormitory room in Parrish Hall in
the fall of 1915, the egalitarian, pacifist ethos Mott championed still prevailed at Swarthmore. The war in Europe stirred debate among students
and faculty, yet an understated unity of purpose kept the sense of crisis at

bay. Initially, Gladys was preoccupied with particulars. She was four years older than the average student in her cohort, a fact that only added to her dismay at discovering that her country education had left her with catching up to do on the academic front. The toughest challenge she faced in her first semester was in learning to write formal essays. "When I went to college I had never written a composition in my life," she told a friend many years later. "I had a teacher who knew that if she gave me a failure I would be so discouraged I could never survive. Instead she gave me kindly criticism. I sweated blood through that course, but I passed it finally with a B–. I could never have done it had she not been so sympathetic. . . . I cannot fancy myself at the beginning of my freshman year doing anything but throwing the paper in the corner in sheer despair."[35]

Socially, Gladys was at the bottom of the ladder with a hundred other first-year students, a place she'd never been before. Swarthmore's reputation for attracting serious students meant Gladys was spared the acute social gamesmanship played at the snootier women's colleges she might have attended. But beside wondering if she had been wise to give up her place on the other side of the teacher's desk for life as a lowly coed, it may be assumed that she worried whether her clothes were fashionable enough, her voice too loud, her waistline insufficiently narrow, the angle of her nose too sharp—no woman had yet to step on a college campus who hadn't.[36]

Reichard wasn't required to conform to Quaker externals in speech or dress, though she did undergo compulsory Bible training and observed the campus-wide ban on tobacco products. At weekly assemblies known as Collection, she was expected to show an interest in a speaker's lofty topic, even when bored stiff. She began modestly with a first-year schedule that included Freshman Latin and Mathematics, supplemented by her enlistment in the Somerville Literary Society and the Classics Club. In her third year she served on the Executive Committee of the Women's Student Government and was elected to Phi Beta Kappa, a rare honor for a junior. Mortar Board, the senior women's honor society, inducted Reichard in her final year, together with her introverted classmate Isabel Briggs Myers, future co-creator of the Myers-Briggs personality inventory.[37] Gladys would never become one of those fast students who boasted, "As for my studies, I never let them interfere with my college education."[38] By working harder than she played, she gradually developed a reputation on campus as a woman who was going to go far. She might have appeared more often in group photos taken for the *Halcyon*, Swarthmore's aptly named yearbook, had she not also worked off-campus "babysitting and painting garages for 'poor faculty'" to defray her annual tuition bill.[39]

Issues of the *Halcyon* that documented the first half of Reichard's time at Swarthmore depict a student body barely touched by social tensions at home or the war abroad. Campus debate teams jousted abstractly over resolutions to create an international police force, institute military training at all pre- and post-secondary institutions, and reelect President Woodrow Wilson. Two-dozen enthusiasts interested in German language, literature, and customs opened a charter branch of the Deutscher Verein (Intercollegiate League of German Clubs of America), unfazed by increasing anti-German sentiment in the American general public. Intercollegiate sports occupied the lion's share of the yearbook's copy, a reflection of their importance to a majority of students. One popular faculty member observed "a certain narrowness of devotion to class, fraternity, and team, even to the college itself" among his pupils, which prompted him to remark that Swarthmore undergraduates "resemble[d] nothing so much in the world as a flock of sheep."[40] Other efforts by faculty to rouse Swarthmoreans to greater empathy with the wider world were gaily parried by student editors. Of one faculty debate on the European war that occurred at Collection, a *Halcyon* wag wrote breezily, "Dr. Breck puts the 'war' in Swarthmore, and Dr. [William] Hull takes it out; name henceforth to be 'Speacemore.'" When a German U-boat sank the *Lusitania*, killing nearly twelve hundred people including scores of Americans, the attack barely registered. The entry for May 8, 1915 in the *Halcyon*'s whimsical recap of 1915–16 read, "Germany torpedoes the Lusitania and [football coach] Dr. Martin gives the original bean feast to Football fellows and their girls." Nine months later, sports metaphors still carried water for the campus diarists: "Awful results of peace talks in Collection: Basketball men leave for the Army! Quakerism—16, Militarism—14."[41]

Reichard was a sophomore the year the United States entered the European war. Overnight, the mood on campus turned somber. Swarthmore president Joseph Swain, champion of world peace, women's suffrage, and the college's latest capital campaign, suddenly had a popular revolt on his hands. So many men withdrew to fight in France that spring that the *Halcyon* winked, "Male exodus transforms college into female seminary."[42] A year later, a petition signed by many faculty and nearly every male student demanded that on-campus military training be made compulsory. Concerned that he would lose all his male students eighteen and older unless he took action, Swain convinced the all-Quaker Board of Managers to accede to the student-faculty demand. In the fall of Reichard's senior year, the Swarthmore College branch of the Students College Army Training Corps commenced officer training and military exercises on a nearby field for every man who had not yet shipped out.

The armistice signed six weeks after the Training Corps began meant no Swarthmore trainees saw actual combat. By allowing a military presence on campus, the administration had crossed a red line nonetheless. Dismay over Swain's reluctant capitulation to militarism spread through the greater community of Friends. Pacifism was not just the cornerstone of a Swarthmore College education but a pillar of Quaker faith. A majority of students disagreed with Swain's critics. They were ready to reject Quaker tradition and embrace militarism as a necessary component of patriotism. As a result, Gladys's last two yearbooks were thick with praise for "the Swarthmore men fighting in the Service of Democracy," "their" war dead (ten in all), and those who bought war stamps, "The College Students' Way to Put The Lead Into the Kaiser." Coeds majoring in mathematics and engineering before the war were lauded for switching into the nursing program. Knitting garments for deployed classmates, raising money for the Red Cross, rolling bandages, tilling the college gardens, and staffing the clubs and student offices temporarily vacated by the men-at-arms earned women kudos for their support of the war effort.[43] The cancellation of parties, class plays, and other annual rituals wasn't rued as curtailments of Swarthmore's proud traditions; they were patriotic sacrifices that brought the waiting women closer to their absent men.

Where Gladys stood personally on world war and Swarthmore's role in it cannot be gleaned from the *Halcyon*. When she does appear in her yearbooks she fends off the spotlight. Below Gladys's junior class picture the caption written by a *Halcyon* scribe walks a fine line between admiration and mockery. "Oh I am just taking Greek and Latin so I can teach them and Math so I can teach that and Biology so I can be a Doctor," it pretends to quote her. "I hate to miss anything. I'd like to drive a locomotive, wouldn't you? (If the rest of us worked as hard as she does we wouldn't be hankering after locomotives.) Oh, no, I am not signed up

THE HALCYON OF 1919

OSBORN ROBINSON QUAYLE
2306 Delaware Avenue
WILMINGTON, DEL.
Chemical Engineering

People who see this young man wearily and slowly walking to classes are often lead to believe that such is his nature. But great is their mistake. For Quayle is merely conserving and storing away energy to be used at a later date. For what? In the spring you would never recognize him as the same man. All the accumulated energy of fall and spring is let loose in bursts of speed that carry the Garnet to victory.

GLADYS AMANDA REICHARD
BANGOR, PA.
Latin

Oh I am just taking Greek and Latin so I can teach them and Math so I can teach that and Biology so I can be a Doctor. I hate to miss anything. I'd like to drive a locomotive wouldn't you? (If the rest of us worked as hard as she does we wouldn't be hankering after locomotives.) Oh, no, I'm not signed up in Victorian Lit yet. I just go. Don't you think Miss Hogue is great? And don't you love hockey? I just think hockey is the grandest game.

HELEN HUTCHINSON REID
LANSDOWNE, PA.
History

Scarcity at Swarthmore is my specialty. You all look from the front windows and envy me my daily auto ride back and forth from Lansdowne, except when my machine gets stuck in front of Parrish in a foot or so of snow, and I need two motor-trucks to pull it out. You catch brief glimpses of me at occasional college dances, but for you to dance with me is impossible with a crowd of Lansdowners always surrounding me. You used to see me playing in class basketball games, but now I've even given up that form of exercise, and let motoring suffice.

One Hundred

Gladys Reichard at Swarthmore College, 1918. *Halcyon of 1919* (p. 100).
Courtesy Friends Historical Library of Swarthmore College.

for Victorian Lit. yet. I just go. Don't you think Miss Hogue is great? And don't you love hockey? I just think hockey is the grandest game."[44] The photograph is at odds with the cheery blurb. Expertly lit to highlight a graceful neck and downplay an everyman's nose, the black-and-white portrait shows a pleasant-looking woman with deep-set eyes above lips accustomed to concealing a small gap between the sitter's top-front teeth. While the camera found no trace of world-weariness in the twenty-four year-old's unlined brow, something in her even expression suggests she is already nobody's fool.

In her final semester, Reichard took a class from popular biology professor Spencer Trotter, M.D. Trotter's lectures on human evolution were just what Reichard needed and at the right time. Repelled by might-makes-right metaphysics by her life experience, she perked up as Trotter explained how a certain distinguished anthropologist of German origin, Franz Boas, had organized the systematic investigation of "bodily form, languages, and customs" in pursuit of an unsentimental, fact-based history of humankind.[45] He spoke of the Columbia University professor's campaign to transform anthropology from a taxonomic enterprise aimed at ranking groups of people in a race-based hierarchy into a demonstration of his conviction that all peoples, regardless of race, creed, or sex, were "equally destined for liberty."[46] Boas, Trotter informed his rapt student, didn't rule out the possibility that further scientific findings might contradict his theory. The Columbia anthropologist's brilliance as a thinker and scientist lay in placing the burden of amassing empirical proof that all but white European men were "primitive" or "inferior" humans on those who legitimized bigotry under the aegis of evolutionary science. For every biological basis the socioevolutionists used to mark whole peoples as different and unequal, Boas was prepared to conduct a systematic search for historical and cultural bases of difference that he predicted would confirm the essential unity of the human species.

Perhaps most appealing to a young woman on the verge of self-definition was the breath-taking scope of anthropology in the Boasian mold. Boas's ambition to understand "the fundamental traits of the human mind" to uncover the root causes of humanity's social problems advertised a useful as well as noble career.[47] The idea of "man as his own guinea pig, the ideal of greater objectivity, the concept of the relativity of values" all captivated Reichard as they would other earnest women of her generation.[48] Boas's mode of thinking about the human condition revealed to Gladys that society suffered from ailments a medical doctor wasn't trained to treat. "Biology is too much microscope and not enough life study," she concluded before confiding in Trotter that a graduate program in anthropology was where she belonged.[49] The biologist advised her, "Go to Franz Boas at Columbia and get the real thing—this isn't it."[50]

Without mentioning that she was the latest recipient of the coveted Lucretia Mott Fellowship for graduate study, Reichard sent a letter to Columbia University on May 18, 1919. "I expect to graduate from Swarthmore on the ninth of June and I desire to study at your University," she wrote Boas. "I should like to major in Anthropology."[51] The sixty-year-old doyen of the discipline wrote back two days later, "I shall, of course, be glad to see you here next fall."[52] In a subsequent note, Boas wondered if she meant to do a single year of graduate study for the MA or was she prepared to "devote [herself] to professional work in anthropology"? "I may say I am expecting to devote myself to professional work in anthropology," Gladys replied, adding that she hoped she could meet him in June to flesh out her course of study.[53]

Commencement Week at Swarthmore was filled with the rituals of Senior Lunch with President Swain, Last Collection, and class reunions. At graduation, senior women, decked out in shapeless, ankle-length frocks of embroidered lawn, walked arm-in-arm with men tightly buttoned into their high-necked military uniforms. For many of the graduates who donned cap and gown for the Class of 1919 picture, the festivities were a last gulp of ease before they joined a world gone mad with racial and ideological hatreds. So-called race riots, later shown to be instigated by angry white mobs, had not yet occurred in Scranton, Philadelphia, or in Darby, Swarthmore's neighboring borough. It would be July before J. Edgar Hoover, an ambitious young attorney in the U.S. Justice Department, would fan the flames of Red Summer by reporting to the attorney general, falsely, that the Chicago race riots were prompted by "Negroes" assaulting white women. Other officers of the federal government hadn't yet suggested to the public that Bolshevik agitators were prompting black militants to assassinate their own leaders. The backdrop for Gladys's final hours as an undergraduate was the campaign by Italian American anarchists to terrorize and kill wealthy industrialists and government officials with mail bombs. Rampant inflation, labor unrest, police brutality, job shortages, political fear-mongering and gridlock—the war had laid bare too many of Mankind's darkest secrets for Reichard to imagine that the urban violence that followed the War to End All Wars would subside as summer temperatures rose. Reichard's decision to become an anthropologist was no accident, but neither could she predict where her choice might lead.

•   •   •   ❖   •   •   •

The last Wednesday of September 1919 marked the day Columbia's newest graduate student in the Division of Philosophy, Psychology, and Anthropology began her journey to becoming an anthropologist. En route to Convocation in the University Gymnasium, Reichard strolled past the psychic center of her new campus, the Seth Low Memorial Library, with its grand gray pearl of a dome held high above the cascade of steps that flowed south toward Ellis and Liberty Islands. Inside the gym, she observed the stern countenance of Columbia president Nicholas Murray Butler for the first time. After leading his regalia-clad faculty in procession to the stage, Butler announced he was canceling the state of emergency he'd declared when the United States entered the Great War. In his patriotic fervor, Butler had been among the first to welcome a Student Army Training unit onto his campus. He reorganized academic departments into "Corps" in the military manner, forbade dissent on the grounds that war was no time for freedom of conscience, and, with the backing of university trustees, encouraged students to report "unpatriotic statements of Columbia faculty."[54] Not overly reassured by the Armistice of November 11, 1918, Butler felt it his duty to warn his mixed audience that the "atmosphere of danger" had passed but the "atmosphere of difficulty" had just begun. Returned veterans, ambitious civilians, and the intellectually conscripted faculty were, under Butler's command, to commit themselves in the coming year to the "whole service to our country," without regard to academic distinctions or troublesome ideals.[55]

While Butler spoke, Reichard had time to observe that women were a minority of those in the audience though far from rare. In absolute numbers, the hundreds of women enrolled in Extension and graduate programs and at Barnard and Teachers Colleges in 1919 were proof that many Columbia women had escaped sequestration in the Home Economics Department. Reichard herself was enrolled in a division where a quarter of the students seeking doctorates (at least two to three dozen individuals) were women.[56] Because Barnard seniors often attended graduate courses by permission of the instructor, on any given day women attended lectures or worked alongside men at laboratory benches without raising eyebrows. Women faculty and administrators, by contrast, were truly the exception. There had been an eight-fold increase in the number of women receiving doctorates between 1890 and 1900 nationally; Columbia alone awarded twenty-five doctorates to women between 1910 and 1920, a number equal to all those women who earned doctorates in the United States before 1890.[57] Still, the rising numbers of women with doctoral degrees hadn't translated into proportional numbers of women holding faculty or administrative posts.

At Columbia's all-women Barnard College, Dean Virginia Cocheron Gildersleeve was putting inequality on the run. Under her watchful eye, Barnard had recently acquired a slight plurality of women faculty, many of them chairs of their departments. Columbia's only female dean, Gildersleeve was easily the most powerful woman in the university administration. Since becoming dean in 1911, she put her reputation for integrity and fairness as a scholar and English literature faculty member to work broadening women's opportunities for advanced training in every academic field. Her unrelenting crusade on behalf of collegiate women brought her to the realization that women scholars had to "do better work than men" to compete favorably for jobs and prestige.[58] Accordingly, she made herself a one-woman bulwark against the charges that "women display much less intellectual enterprise and initiative than men" or that "the majority of college and university students prefer . . . the instruction of men to that of women."[59] She led by example, and if that was not pro-woman enough for her feminist critics, she thought it best to choose her battles wisely.

Had she been invited to say a few words at Convocation, Barnard's steely chief executive might have praised the college-educated women who had recently succeeded in bringing the Nineteenth Amendment to a vote in Congress. She might have pointed out that women's suffrage constituted a further repeal of the "shibboleths of social Darwinist thinking" concerning the "weaker sex" that still dogged aspiring women on the ground beneath her feet.[60] But much as he admired his protégé's fighting spirit, President Butler didn't give Dean Gildersleeve the chance to draw the crowd's attention to women's political progress on Reichard's first day as a Columbia graduate student. Yet the sight of someone like herself standing shoulder-to-shoulder with decorated men on one of the world's foremost academic stages offered Reichard solid encouragement.

Reichard surely needed the boost. It would have been extraordinary if she had not been a little intimidated by the prospect of studying with

Columbia's towering polymath, the inimitable Franz Boas. The Old Man's fierce concentration on his subject matter was legendary; the strain of trying to keep pace with his massive, omnivorous intellect filled some of his early male students with lasting self-doubt. Stories of Boas's notoriously difficult seminars on statistics and North American linguistics were passed around like lit cigarettes. Reichard's fellow student Melville Herskovits recalled, "Boas simply assumed the mathematical competence needed to grasp the development of the intricate statistical formulae he employed; in his courses on linguistics, he took an adequate knowledge of technical phonetics similarly for granted."[61] Alfred Kroeber, the first of Boas's Columbia graduates, averred that Boas taught "nothing but principles, methods, and problems, fortified by only such concrete data as were necessary for his sure and rapid mind to understand the situation."[62] "The load was wholly on the student," Kroeber noted as a man who had fallen short of Boas's expectation that students "firmly bite into a problem and suck it to the last drops."[63] Margaret Mead, who started in Columbia anthropology four years after Reichard, bridled at Boas's assumption that students entered his seminar room with a grasp of calculus, Dutch, or Danish sufficient to follow his swift train of thought. His lectures, Mead later complained, were filled with "higher-level abstractions and the unintelligible details," disorganized, and delivered in "dreadful concentration with no quarter to beginners" like herself.[64]

The initial shock of encountering Boas's greatness in person subsided fairly quickly in Reichard's case. She came to share Kroeber's opinion that Boas was "a supreme teacher for the man who would be a productive scholar in his own right."[65] Boas gave no exams in his courses and allowed students to take any courses that would support their research goals. Some said he had mellowed since boosting the careers of anthropological luminaries such as Kroeber, Edward Sapir, Pliny Earle Goddard, and Robert Lowie before the Great War, but Reichard never saw Boas as other than tolerant and generous. She discerned a tough wisdom in Boas's teaching methods that suited her independent, self-disciplining spirit perfectly. "He simply assumed that a student was a person attending college or university because he wanted to learn, that he had the ability and training to find out anything he wanted to know, and even that he had a great curiosity and therefore did want to know," she said of Boas in hindsight. "In accomplishing this he was just as successful with beginning students as with those working for the doctorate."[66]

Boas had a heroic quality that was new to the native Bangorian and it rendered his caricature-ready intensity endearing to her. Lowie aptly described Boas's appeal to idealistic students when he wrote, "He seemed to personify the very spirit of science."[67] "A scientist primarily interested in science—not in the organization of research, not in the personalities of colleagues, not in the display of his cleverness, but in the problems that sprang from his data, in the quest of truth," Boas also personified selflessness in the pursuit of knowledge, an element of his character that granted his scientific results the highest integrity. His humanitarian scruples made it impossible for him to avoid speaking truth to power when circumstance demanded he do so.

Reichard got a stark demonstration of the risks Boas was willing to take in the name of scientific honor just as her first semester at Columbia ended. In late December 1919, Boas published an editorial in the *Nation* that rebuked four unnamed anthropologists for acting as spies for the U.S. government while on a research trip to Mexico. Never one to mince words, Boas wrote, "A person . . . who uses science as a cover for political spying, who demeans himself to pose before a foreign government as an investigator and asks for assistance in his alleged researches in order to carry on, under his cloak, his political machinations, prostitutes science in an unpardonable way and forfeits the right to be classed as a scientist."[68] The executive council of the American Anthropological Association moved quickly to punish Boas for his outspokenness.[69] Before Gladys was back in Bangor for the New Year's holiday, the council voted twenty to nine to censure Boas for unpatriotic conduct. Other professional anthropological organizations he had founded or led followed suit.[70]

Though Boas soon referred to the flap over "Scientists as Spies" as "the late unpleasantness," Gladys gained important insight into the relative esteem that impartiality and intellectual independence were held in by many in her chosen field.[71] She also acquired a cardinal piece of street smarts that Gildersleeve later expressed in a memoir about her thirty-six years as the only woman on Columbia's Advisory Committee. Gildersleeve concluded after long observation of her fellow committee members in action "that men and women are far more alike than is generally supposed, and that men frequently share equally traits attributed especially

to women, such as jealousy, a fondness for gossip, and an intensity of emotion." That insight into the psyche of the self-regarding male academic
did not dispose Gildersleeve to dissuade other women from pursuing
scholarly careers. "I got a glimpse of the great structure of scholarship, of
the search for truth," Gildersleeve said of her student years at Columbia.
"I began to realize that it was built by the labor of thousands of scholars,
many very humble, working at the foundations, each providing perhaps
just one brick as a result of years, sometimes many years, of toil. I began
to realize that the most sacred obligation of any scholar, however humble,
was always to tell the truth as he found it, never to obscure it, never to
confuse the pathway for his fellows who were coming after him."[72]

As a witness to the risks involved in truth-telling among eastern elites,
Reichard may have returned to Columbia for her second semester with a
clear understanding of the difference between objectivity and neutrality.
At the very least, she was on notice that to live up to Boas's high ethical standards for anthropologists, she would often be required to take
a position dictated by her conscience and be prepared to defend her
motives with scrupulous science and unwavering courage in the face of
jealous or irate opposition.

The longer Reichard studied with Boas, the more she liked him. She
marveled that his famed "icy enthusiasm" for data collection, method,
unbiased analysis, and cautious synthesis produced humility in the man
rather than arrogance.[73] It didn't surprise her that Boas did not hoard the
spotlight. He opened his seminars to colleagues eager to share their latest
research findings and rally students to their divergent theoretical positions. Conversations begun in seminars spilled over into "anthropology
lunches" held on Tuesdays during fall and spring semesters. The informal, salon-style gatherings at a hotel across the street from the American
Museum of Natural History gave the Columbia circle of anthropologists a
venue for lively, democratic conversations that observed the same general
ban on gossip that held sway in Boas's department. Though Reichard was
more observer than participant at first, anthropology lunches helped
her integrate book knowledge with practical aspects of her new field.
Anthropology students of Reichard's generation later complained they
were offered no formal training in fieldwork logistics—how to make
appropriate contacts, negotiate with, hire, and pay interpreters, organize
fieldnotes, adapt a research design on the fly—the kind of information

typically shared in private between a don and his male protégés as a father passes the fruits of his experience on to his sons. Anthropology lunches filled that gap for Reichard, beside reassuring her from her first semester that she belonged at the table.

The midday salons were immensely important to Reichard for another reason. Without them she might not have gotten as close to Elsie Clews Parsons, eminent social scientist, and, thanks to her family's wealth, the "Department 'angel'" of Columbia anthropology.[74] Eighteen years older than Gladys, Parsons was well into her second act as an incisive, prolific cultural anthropologist. Her solo fieldwork in the Southwest before the war led to a stream of perceptive articles on the pueblo-dwelling peoples she interviewed. Her election to the presidency of the American Folklore Society in 1918 simultaneously recognized her talent for cultural analysis and her capacity for leadership. Parsons exuded a calm confidence in her own mental gifts that some of her contemporaries read as haughtiness. The aloofness in her social manner was actually unassuming intellectual poise, a self-knowing, self-correcting dimension in her character that made it possible for her to forge a partnership of equals with Boas that no woman before her had dared to imagine.

It took several tries, but by the spring of 1919, the emancipated heiress and mother of four convinced Boas to conduct fieldwork with her in the Rio Grande valley. Previously, Boas had subscribed to the notion that women were not sufficiently physically or emotionally hardy for prolonged fieldwork. He assumed as other men did that having women in field camps was a distraction for the more ambitious men and thus an inefficient use of limited research funds. Parsons's seriousness of purpose, excellence as an investigator, and impeccable professional demeanor were powerful evidence against the sexual prejudices Boas had imbibed since childhood. The month-long field trip they took together, with Parsons studying ceremonial culture and Boas collecting data on the Keresan language, marked the first time Boas had a woman field partner in his thirty-five years as an anthropologist. Bit by bit, Parsons made it impossible for Boas to continue to condone the injustice of barring women from the fieldwork that was essential to their attaining legitimacy as professional anthropologists. In demonstrating to the ultra-rational founder of modern anthropology that sex was as irrelevant in the field as it was in the classroom, Parsons changed the rules for all the women Boas supervised at Columbia over the next two decades, Reichard included.[75]

For her master's thesis, Reichard chose a library project that combined her new interests in North American Indian folklore and anthropological theory in a work titled "Literary Types and Dissemination of North American Myths." Given her tight deadline—the master's degree was normally completed in two semesters—she chose her topic wisely. She could draw on her undergraduate training in classics and mathematics to help her adopt the methodological rigor Boas had imparted to the study of folklore. The problem she chose immersed her in the theory of cultural diffusion, a mechanism of cultural change. To explain why cultural ideas did not respect boundaries of race or geography, the theory of cultural diffusion held that ideas spread or were diffused among and between disparate peoples who "borrowed" and incorporated concepts and behaviors they encountered through physical or ideological contact with other peoples. The typed thesis Reichard completed in the summer of 1920 included several hand-drawn tables on graph paper pasted neatly onto blank pages. It was forty-six pages long, excluding the endnotes and bibliography, a good fifteen pages longer than the doctoral dissertation Alfred Kroeber submitted for his PhD in 1901.[76]

Reichard drew two general lessons from executing her thesis that transferred to all her future work. First, she discovered how easy it was to devise a tentative typology from masses of suggestive data. Second, she saw the limited usefulness of such schemes, for all the sweat she might pour into them. Typologies, she discovered by creating one, were often facile and forgettable. Unless they were based on comprehensive data and ample comparative study, they rarely survived long enough to be adopted by others. At best these typologies produced new "catchwords" of dubious merit. Boas and Parsons regularly reinforced Reichard's growing suspicion concerning the "hypnotic effect" of catchwords and "the tendency to elaborate upon them"; writing her master's thesis in the register common to social scientists forced her to confront the "insidious power" of catchwords "to beguile the investigator into a vicious cycle whose pivot is his own assumption."[77]

In the end, Reichard didn't regard her results as momentous. She settled for knowing that she had pleased the two eminent scholars she most wanted to impress. Boas and Parsons, who were editor and associate editor, respectively, of the American Folklore Society's journal, indicated their satisfaction with her thesis by asking her to prepare it for immediate publication. In the first real test of her potential in anthropology, Gladys had shown them both in little more than a year that not only could she suck complex data to the last drops, she could make her results publishable.

·   ·   ·   ◆   ·   ·   ·

Throughout her first year at Columbia, Reichard supplemented the funds due her from the Mott fellowship by teaching Latin and math at Robert Louis Stevenson High School, a preparatory school for girls at Fifth Avenue and 82nd Street. At the end of the year, Boas offered her a job as his teaching assistant at Barnard, where for several years he had been giving his general anthropology course rather than at Columbia's men's college to protest President Butler's wartime crackdown on faculty free speech.[78] The Columbia assistantship allowed her to pay her own way by attending Boas's lectures at Barnard and leading weekly field trips to examine the ethnological displays at the American Museum of Natural History.

Being Boas's teaching assistant made Gladys still more appreciative of her august supervisor. Watching a relaxed master at work in Barnard Hall, Reichard saw Boas at his best, incandescently free of personal vanity and the petty disfigurements projected onto him by smaller minds, and passionately transported by the unquestioned necessity of his life's work. She later remarked, "One of the greatest pleasures of his teaching career was his Barnard class. He once told me that if he should stop teaching all classes but one, that was the one he would prefer to keep." Boas's sensitivity to and patience with his students' individual humanity had a profound impact on Reichard as an educator of women. In her memorial essay for Boas, she reported that she once spoke to him in a disgusted tone about some foolishness perpetrated by a couple of Barnard students only to hear Boas cry in their defense, *"Aber das ist ein Fehler!"* (But that is a mistake!). Chastened by his instinctive reaction to her intolerance of youthful indiscretion, Reichard interpreted his exclamation in German to contain his customary admonishment, "He is only a human being!"[79]

At the end of Reichard's second year, the composition of the Anthropology Department began to shift when Reichard's classmate, Erna Gunther, and recent Columbia graduate Leslie Spier married and moved to

Seattle.[80] The third woman in Reichard's all-female cohort, Esther Schiff (later Goldfrank), remained. Like Gunther, Schiff had earned her bachelor's in economics at Barnard before enrolling at Columbia. In the fall of 1919, she was working unhappily at a secretarial job on Wall Street when Boas wrote to ask if she would be interested in serving as his personal secretary. His strained relationship with President Butler meant Boas received no funds from the university for secretarial support, but Elsie Parsons, at Pliny Goddard's request, had offered to fund a year-round girl Friday position in his office. Schiff accepted Boas's offer, and within a few months she began to eye a career in anthropology for herself.

Months before she was on close enough terms with Boas to confer the affectionate nickname "Papa Franz" on her boss, Schiff typed a letter in which Boas wrote a colleague, "I have had a curious experience in graduate work during the last few years. All of my best students are women."[81] For Schiff, Boas's statement mirrored the warmth she'd witnessed when she traveled with Boas and family over the summer. "However tough and exacting Dr. Boas may have been with his male students, within his family circle he was warm and loving," she later wrote. "I heard no peremptory orders, no loud words, no angry arguments. . . . It was a happy and harmonious household and one in which I readily found a congenial place."[82]

Gunther's departure for Washington in the spring of 1921 reduced the size of the female cohort in Boas's department by a third but in no way disrupted the harmonious esprit de corps to which Reichard and Schiff were accustomed. The winds of change began to blow only when Ruth Fulton Benedict filled Gunther's spot in the department in the fall. An aspiring writer and poet, Benedict was converted to anthropology at New York's Free School of Political Science (later known as the New School of Social Research) under the tutelage of Parsons and others Nicholas Butler had labeled "a little bunch of disgruntled liberals."[83] With his usual disinterest in academic formalities, and possibly in light of Benedict's thirty-four years, Boas counted the year of classes she'd taken at the Free School as equivalent to a master's degree. He encouraged Benedict to begin research for a library-based dissertation at once, a proposal that assumed her deafness in one ear made intensive training in field linguistics futile.[84]

Benedict would come to admire Boas much as his best students had done before her arrival. Yet her halting, distraught manner introduced a discordant note of neediness in the department. Obviously unhappy and unsure of herself, Mrs. Benedict appeared harmless, almost defenseless, a condition that tended to evoke the sympathy of her psychologically sturdier peers at Columbia. It turned out that the practice of anthropology was a kind of psychotherapy for Benedict. Though ultimately it yielded the desired result, her female classmates would find it impossible to avoid becoming castoffs in the self-dramatizing narrative Benedict eventually constructed, with ample help from Margaret Mead, from her search for inner peace through the study of Others.[85]

Grounded as ever, Reichard had her hands full preparing for the 1921-22 academic year. Boas and Schiff were with Parsons in New Mexico until mid-October, leaving Gladys to launch the department's fall courses in their stead. Reichard agreed to meet with Boas's classes, which included his resumed "101" course at Columbia College, its equivalent at Barnard, and the seminar in Native economics. Reichard wrote Boas on September 29 that enrollments were exceptionally strong in the Barnard course because the college's Advisory Council had declared the general anthropology course "foundational." "Serious-minded" students above the freshman level had been directed to the course in record numbers as a result. Reichard had returned to campus early to prepare her lectures. "I've been studying Geography since I've been here and I am ready to meet with the Barnard class to-morrow," she wrote him. "I have located the most important tribes of Africa and marked them on an outline map, and have made a map of Melanesia & Polynesia showing their co-location with respect to the continents which I intend to use."[86]

The timing of Boas's absence from New York seemed calculated to keep the peace between Boas and his foes at the American Museum. At the invitation of the U.S. State Department, the Second International Eugenics Congress convened in Darwin Hall on September 25, with the Princeton-trained paleontologist and president of the museum Henry Fairfield Osborn presiding. The purpose of the meeting was to advocate for a host of selective-breeding policies that included compulsory sterilization of the "ill-endowed," increased taxation of "sound" but childless couples to induce them to procreate, and the summary elimination of unfit immigrants. The keynote speaker at the Congress, Major Leonard Darwin, son of Charles Darwin, called for the state to regulate marriage and reproduction by any means necessary to maintain the purity of the

"Nordics"—descendants of Irish, English, German, and Scandinavian immigrants. The tide of undesirables from southern and eastern Europe on American shores, the major claimed, polluted his country with mentally and morally inferior specimens. The event highlighted the power racist ideas commanded among prominent men of science, Alexander Graham Bell and Harvard professors William McDougall, a psychologist, and Charles Davenport, a geneticist, among them. In some quarters of anthropology, eugenics was uncontroversial enough that Czech anthropologist Ales Hrdlicka, curator of physical anthropology at the Smithsonian, referred to it as "applied anthropology."[87]

Boas had published his objections to the "Nordic nonsense" favored by eugenicists in no uncertain terms in 1916. The eugenicist's goal of eliminating the suffering caused by interpersonal and intercultural conflicts brought on by normal variations in mental capacity, personality, morals, and attitudes among individuals, Boas argued, failed to acknowledge the quintessence of the human experience: emotion. Identifying emotion with beauty, he wrote, "There is little doubt that we [scientists], at the present time, give much less weight to beauty than to logic. Shall we then try to raise a generation of logical thinkers, suppress those whose emotional life is vigorous, and try to bring it about . . . that human activities shall be performed with clock-like precision?" He applied the relativity of perspective he had championed in his own discipline when he confessed, "Personally the logical thinker may be most congenial to me, nevertheless I respect the sacred ideals of the dreamer who lives in a world of musical tones, and whose creative power is to me a marvel that surpasses understanding." To construe applied anthropology as a means to perfect human society was, in his view, to grab the wrong end of a "dangerous sword."[88]

"The Eugenics Congress has been a successful 'snob party' but it is now over," Reichard wrote Boas to conclude her September update. "They tore up the whole Museum and I am glad I didn't have classes down there while it was going on." The disruption at the museum was more than a housekeeping headache for Boas's conscientious teaching assistant. Even though Reichard belonged to the "fit" Nordic type by an accident of birth, she could read between the lines of the *New York Times* story "Want More Babies in Best Families" that ran on the opening day of the Congress. Eugenics posed a threat to the individual liberty of every woman in America. Congress attendees presumed they had the right to control women's bodies to ensure that the right vessels were available for full-time breeding. As the chief government statistician of France complained, the huge loss of potent men by injury or death in the Great War meant too many French women were gainfully employed outside the home. "But the women who work cannot be fruitful mothers," he asserted. "Feminine work will only be short-term mitigation" of the shortage in male laborers.[89] Women preparing for careers, he implied, wasted their social potential.

Reichard had been in Parsons's orbit long enough to have heard her elder's pointed observation, "The more thoroughly a woman is classified the more easily is she controlled."[90] Reichard was convinced her life's calling was to wear the title of anthropologist with the care and dignity Parsons and Boas brought to the role. The Eugenics Congress proved conclusively to Reichard that there existed a concerted effort among some male scientists to reclassify her as little more than a womb. In the closer confines of the male-dominated academy, the downward pressure on Reichard's individuality was more subtle. For every university-trained man like her father or Boas who believed in equal opportunity and liberty for women, there were many others who would wish to hold her to a second, lower class of scholars reserved for the "woman anthropologist." Unmarried and nearing thirty, Reichard reshouldered a burden that she would never escape, that of having to prove time and again that her biological sex didn't disqualify her.

· · · · · ◆ · · · · · ·

CHAPTER 2

A BREATH OF FRESH AIR

BEFORE 1919 ALMOST EVERYTHING GLADYS REICHARD KNEW about Native America was wrong. The rest was filtered through a highly ethnocentric white, European American lens. When as a teen she watched the Red Men's faux "Kickapoo Tribe" parade past her house on St. Tamina's Day dressed in feathered headgear and beaded deerskins crafted by Mohawk and Tuscarora artists, it would have been unneighborly of her to dispute their right to do so.[1] Had she read as a girl or college student that the Lenape, "ancient owners and occupants of these Northampton hills, and valleys and streams," were ousted from their homes along the Delaware River in the mid-eighteenth century by "the haughty tyranny of the Iroquois and the cupidity and double-dealing of the white man," she read also that those white historians who lamented their countrymen's treatment of the Original Peoples were in the minority.[2]

Graduate school in anthropology taught Reichard a new mental hygiene for grappling with difference and supposition. The four-field curriculum Boas insisted on acted as a firehose that aimed the scientific method at the history of language, custom, and human physiognomy in a cleansing, turbulent stream. Gladys spent countless hours in the exhibits and research collections at the American Museum of Natural History gaining an abstract sense of indigenous peoples she had yet to meet. Book-learning and museum studies were merely the prologue to fieldwork, however, and Gladys did not envision her maiden field season as a way to satisfy an "idle curiosity or fondness of adventure."[3] Her field project must satisfy an appetite she shared with Parsons for "thinking as it is done by men and women in the real world."[4] Though she passed her first three years at Columbia furthering a fascination with "primitive" art and what it revealed about the psychology of its makers, the dissertation topic she chose reflected a newly acquired taste. Boas had advised her before she set foot in his department that linguistics was "quite indispensable to thorough work in anthropology."[5] When she announced she wished to write a field-based grammar of a North American Indian language for her doctoral thesis, Reichard made plain that she had come to agree with him.

Reichard's dissertation proposal was more daring and consequential than she may have realized. The field of American Indian linguistics in the early 1920s was a bastion of male prerogative. Anthropological linguistics was assumed by men to be too analytical, theoretical, and cutting-edge for the feminine mind, a hypothesis Reichard was happy to disprove. Her plan to integrate the tiny male club responsible for classifying and systematizing unwritten American languages according to emerging structuralist standards also put Boas's commitment to equal treatment of his students to the test. Not since the death of twenty-six-year-old Herman Haeberlin in 1918 had Boas had a student as versatile, as "independent and aggressive in thought, free of narrow prejudices," and as capable of delving into symbolic behaviors that throw "light upon the relations between individual thought, feelings, and actions and social environment" as Reichard showed herself to be.[6]

Before Haeberlin, Boas's most promising student in linguistics was Edward Sapir, an intellectually brilliant but deeply insecure *enfant terrible*, who believed admitting women to the anthropological enterprise jeopardized the discipline's manly reputation.[7] Once Sapir became determined to replace Boas as the leader of North American Indian linguistics, he drove a deep wedge into the group of students and colleagues who looked to Boas to set the research agenda for language studies. Since Boas's recruitment to Columbia in 1896, dozens of men had flocked to New York to sit at his feet. Only a handful had not "washed out" of his field-based school of "scientific philology," as had Alfred Kroeber after trying half-heartedly for a decade to match Boas's propensity for wresting significant insights from the "mess" of confounding data that filled his field notebooks.[8] Given Sapir's known prejudice against women, to support Reichard's aspirations in American Indian linguistics, Boas risked being mocked by his touchy student and allies as soft, and insufficiently rigorous. Yet, to deny Reichard not only violated his egalitarian principles but ignored her obvious potential for tackling a set of research problems central to his identity as a modern anthropologist. Always a man to put his principles ahead of his reputation, Boas signaled his faith in Gladys by sending her west. He arranged a research fellowship for her at the University of California, where Kroeber chaired the Anthropology Department.

From June 1922 until the following spring, Berkeley served as Reichard's home base between solo field trips three hundred miles north to the Humboldt Bay region. A few dozen stubborn Wiyot elders continued to speak their ancestral language there; Reichard was to collect texts and write a grammatical sketch based on them for her dissertation. Before she left New York, she learned that Wiyot and a neighboring language, Yurok, were at the center of a highly charged debate about the classification of North American Indian languages. Kroeber, who had years before thrown his support behind Sapir as the rightful headman of American anthropological linguistics, predicted with his younger colleague that Reichard's results would back Sapir's claim that Wiyot and Yurok were distantly related to the Algonquian language family and not related, as was generally assumed, to neighboring Athabascan languages Hupa, Mattole, or Nongatl. The two friends viewed Reichard's residency in California through the prism of the personal resentment each bore Boas. Partly they expected Reichard's results to allow them to prevail in a bitter public fight Sapir had waged against Algonquian specialist and Boas ally Truman Michelson between 1913 and 1915. Michelson had rejected Sapir's "California Algonkin" hypothesis, unconditionally supported by Kroeber, for being based on insufficient evidence. Against Kroeber's advice, Sapir blasted Michelson in print as "illegitimate" and lacking "a liberal spirit," calling him an "amusing" man "short on ammunition."[9]

More generally, Kroeber and Sapir hoped to woo Boas's latest protégé away from the search for the phenomena that gave rise to "the history and the growth of human language" and into their camp, which stressed the importance of linguistic cognacy and historical relationships.[10] With more experience in the art of disciplinary in-fighting, Reichard might have guessed that her elder colleagues tolerated her incursion into their territory in hopes of undermining Boas's authority as a linguist. Instead, her excitement at being given a topic with such serious descriptive and theoretical import for her first attempt at fieldwork cast before her a rosy glow from coast to coast.

The letters Reichard sent Boas from California contained an amiable mix of shoptalk and personal anecdote. The four journals she kept to record the results of her field trips to Eureka were all business. The first commenced briskly: "Thurs. June 22, 1922. Left Berkeley 6:30 A.M. for Eureka. Arrived Eureka, Vance Hotel, 7:40 P.M."[11] Reichard was back on the road by nine A.M. the next day. Hoping to reach a Wiyot settlement known as Indianola, she took the automobile-stage north toward Arcata, only to be informed by a fellow passenger that she was traveling in the wrong direction.[12] That afternoon she jotted in her notebook, "Returned to Eur[eka] via same stage, took train 11:05 for Loleta, walked to Table Bluff, Schoolhouse Clark District, left of which is small [Wiyot] settlement." Using the little map she'd drawn to guide her long walk from the Loleta station to the Clark School house, she tried the door-to-door approach hoping to meet speakers of Wiyot who might work with her as linguistic informants. She didn't call it a day until a white neighbor or a curious schoolteacher explained why the Wiyot didn't answer her knock: "All away weeding, may be home Sun."[13]

Though Reichard was thousands of miles from her birthplace, Eureka had a familiar feel to it. The bayside town was bigger than Bangor at thirteen thousand inhabitants, and prettier, thanks to the pride wealthy locals took in advertising their Victorian tastes through the ostentatious Italianate or Gothic cut of their mansions. But since the felling of the first giant redwood for export in 1850, mass extraction of the area's natural resources had reorganized the landscape to suit white entrepreneurs and venture capitalists, just as mining had done long ago for Bangor. A crazy quilt of mills, dairy farms, canneries, docks, fenced homes, paved streets, and concrete sidewalks blanketed the formerly wild outpost. Ambitious immigrants to northern California had applied a single-minded energy to relieving the coastal geography of its flora and fauna, thinking both were inexhaustible. The Eureka of 1922 boasted a modern, well-lit business district that rattled and coughed with the noise of Model Ts, trucks, and wagons cautiously threading through streets clogged with two-legged traffic.

The mantle of Progress that lay over the busy California outpost was less than tightly woven, however. Just seventy-five years earlier, an unbroken marshy tidal flat had supplied the bay's first inhabitants with a rich bounty of fish, shellfish, waterfowl, seaweed, bulbs, berries, and grasses. With a bit of imagination, Reichard could envision the Wiyot's historic territory for the water world it had once been. Roughly delimited by two great rivers, the Mad and the Eel, the Wiyot homeland consisted of briny deltas, estuaries, tidal sloughs, and brackish channels that together with the fourteen-mile length of Humboldt Bay raveled out some ninety miles of canoe-worthy passage.

For background on the tribe's cultural traditions, Reichard referred to Llewellyn L. Loud's *Ethnogeography and Archeology of the Wiyot Territory*. Loud had spent four months during 1913 mapping Wiyot archeological sites for the University of California. His 1918 monograph gave the fullest account of the Wiyots' physical environment, history, and linguistic heritage publicly available. Loud observed that approximately one thousand speakers of Wiyot had occupied the 465 square miles of their ancestral homeland in 1850. The 1910 census reported "58 full blood Wiyot, 13 persons of partly Wiyot and partly other Indian blood, and 81 individuals partly Wiyot and partly of white blood" remained in the area.[14]

The reason Loud gave for the sharp decline in population was simple. On a cold night in February 1860, a large group of Wiyot were camped at Tuluwat, a village at the northern tip of a bay island within sight of Reichard's hotel, to perform their annual world renewal ceremony. While the women and children slept in their wooden houses and all able-bodied men had canoed to shore to retrieve food and supplies for the next day's proceedings, a half-dozen white vigilantes later identified as prominent white ranchers slipped onto the island prepared to slaughter the unarmed Wiyot with hatchets. "Mercilessly the hatchets descended on all alike, old and young, women and children, infants," Loud wrote. "Their skulls were cleft, their spines severed, their bodies thrust with bowie-knives. Among the children and infants killed there were a few who had white fathers. The work of destruction was finished in a few minutes, and while the dead and dying lay strewn over the ground, the fire from one of the burning cabins lit up the ghastly scene."[15] After the killing spree spread to other Wiyot encampments in the days following the Indian Island Massacre, the commander of Fort Humboldt, Major G. J. Rains, garrisoned surviving Wiyot, ostensibly for their protection. Subsequently, at least two hundred Wiyot were removed from Humboldt County to an American-style concentration camp on the Klamath River Reservation.[16]

The years of starvation and abuse the Wiyot endured at the hands of federal agents reduced their number to reportedly fewer than fifty, ten under the age of fifteen, in less than a decade.[17] The "crude" census

Reichard took in the summer of 1922 identified about a hundred people living "as Wiyot" in the Humboldt Bay area "and of those very few knew the language." Signs of language death were everywhere present. "The young people of the tribe know very little of the language; some of those between the ages of forty and fifty can understand it but not speak it." Reichard showed a sensitivity to the relative prestige of Wiyot when she added, "It is an interesting [sociolinguistic] fact that when a Wiyot marries a member of another tribe, e.g., Athapascan or Yurok, the children, if they speak any Indian language, learn the one other than Wiyot. For this reason then, and because the Wiyot are so rapidly dying off or becoming assimilated with the surrounding population, the language is fast becoming extinct."[18] The "assimilation" she referred to was accomplished in part by barring the Wiyot from the life-giving resources of the Eel River. Reichard noted in her field journal that Wiyot who used to thrive along the waterway had relocated and become wage-laborers "since the gov. forbid their fishing there." Some older Wiyot retained ancient secrets of basketry, beadwork, carving, and embroidery, but the collective memory of how to live exclusively off the land and renew the world through dance, oratory, and song dimmed with each elder's death.

Despite the small number of Wiyot speakers to be found, within the space of a week Reichard managed to locate eight who were willing to trust her to document their language. Topping the list was Mrs. Elsie Barto(w), a recently widowed dressmaker known to be highly literate in English. Her brother, Warren Brainard, was considered something of a Wiyot scholar based on his interest in recording oral histories. Mrs. Jane Searson, Della Prince, Mrs. Buckley, Amos Riley, and Jerry James and his wife Birdie rounded out the group. Each made contributions to Reichard's study in accordance with his or her unique circumstances. Mrs. Barto suffered from rheumatism and was glad of work she could do in the comfort of her Loleta living room. Della Prince would work only with her mother Miranda Berry at her side and then limited her role to giving Reichard a vocabulary for basket-making. Amos Riley "has good imagination and knows stories," but a mouthful of missing teeth hampered his speech.

Jerry James was the Wiyot speaker most accustomed to working with anthropologists. He was a principal informant for the ethnographic material on the Wiyot that later appeared in Edward S. Curtis's photographic masterwork, *The North American Indian*.[19] European American

Jerry and Birdie James, Humboldt Bay, 1910. C. Hart Merriam Collection
of Native American photographs, BANC PIC 1978.008—PIC C/3c/P1 n0.4.
Courtesy of the Bancroft Library, University of California, Berkeley.

Eurekans hailed James as a Wiyot chief and a true friend to the whites,
but among the Wiyot he stood out as the youngest survivor of the Indian
Island Massacre. The infant James was found "mixed up in blanket . . .
and thus missed by whites" by Jennie Sands, a thirteen-year-old girl who
had also survived the attack. Gladys learned of James from Jennie, then
known as Mrs. Jane Sam, who had raised James herself. "Jennie loves
her lang[uage] and the old ways," Reichard recorded on meeting her.
"She says white man's food—meat, eggs, milk, etc.—makes her sick. She
makes beautiful baskets."[20] Moved to be in Mrs. Sam's presence, Reichard

reluctantly conceded that though the septuagenarian "may be very good for ethnology," she did not speak enough English to serve as a linguistic informant.

Interviewing Wiyot speakers was both exhilarating and exhausting. Reichard wrote each Wiyot utterance phonetically on the fly. Then she checked her transcriptions with speaker after speaker to distill ideal or phonemic spellings from the raw data. The profusion of pronunciations, judgments, and skill levels shown by her informants gave her every interview a sink-or-swim urgency unlike any she'd experienced around a university seminar table. To assemble a grammatical sketch that formed a basis for others to build on, she needed to collect as much material as her time in Eureka allowed. The practical art of scientific language study called on her to subtly manipulate her informants' answers until the basic features of their language emerged from disorder. Those who collaborated with her to create a written repository of the essential facts of their native language did so in the hope that their odd exchanges with Reichard of bits and pieces of their language might extend its life to unborn generations. They may well have become bored or irritated with the apparently pointless, repeated questioning they endured for two dollars a day, but they persevered.

Traditional stories were a gold mine of linguistic and cultural information that Reichard's informants were eager to share. Birdie James stepped out of her husband's shadow to dictate several Yurok tales she told in Wiyot. For the dissertation, Reichard would ignore the cultural insights latent in the mythic stories Birdie and others told her. Similarly, she laid aside Warren Brainard's instructions for a bountiful eel harvest ("Eel basket must be placed in current with opening downstream. Eels not caught in clear water, but in muddy, baskets set on gravel riffle, sometimes as many as 8 or 10. If set in morning they would go back & get eels in the evening. Good luck would bring as many as 80 or 90 in one basket. Roasted on coals & eaten or cut & dried then peeled off skin & eaten. Most caught from 1 mi. below Fernbridge to mouth of Van Duzen.") Warren also instructed Reichard on the "worthless fellows" who refused to work in the Wiyot long ago but who were "tolerated & fed by relatives" nonetheless; murders avenged through payment to the victim's family; and divorces accomplished by returning the bride price. He no longer remembered where his people's spirits went after death but he speculated that, "they all go to the same place, regardless of whether man was good or bad."

Alongside lists of Wiyot words and phrases, Reichard's notebook eventually sported simple schematics: an eel basket, assorted hooks and snares, a drying rack, a redwood sweat house, and even a sketch of Mrs. Prince's chin tattoo. None of this material served the grammar directly, but Reichard could not bring herself to silence her informants when they warmed to their favorite topics.[21] She was constrained to write her grammatical sketch of Wiyot as Boas and other specialists in anthropological linguistics demanded of her. But her intuition that "life study" was indispensable to language study and vice versa was repeatedly affirmed in her daily meetings with her Wiyot informants.

Upbeat as Reichard was about her first three weeks in the field, Kroeber was skeptical. "There is nothing yet to report on Wiyot," Kroeber wrote Sapir two weeks into Reichard's first trip to Eureka. "Conditions among the group are not particularly favorable and it took Miss Reichard some time to make satisfactory connections among the scattered members of the group."[22] Reichard saw the groundwork she'd laid in her first trip to Eureka pay off in the second. "Dear Professor Boas," she wrote in September, "You would be about beside yourself if you were here. Because it is so easy to get informants that I work every minute."

To-morrow I will have been on the job steadily for 3 weeks. I had a chance to work with the storyteller of the tribe [Jerry James] & I have now altogether 18 tales, two of which took half a day to record. Jerry has gone hunting now, but waited 4 days longer than he intended because of me. He told me a long tale in English which I am very anxious to get & which he promised to give when he comes back. I can't do much with him on grammar, so now I am back with Mrs. Barto & she is the best I can find. She has a more "analytical type of mind" (?) & is much interested. Yesterday she expressed a desire to write [Wiyot] & we're going to try it this afternoon.

Two days later she added, "Mrs. B. is coming on with the writing. Yesterday she brot out four words she had thot of that I hadn't asked for & when I read them she was that tickled with herself! . . . Do your informants rack their brains for things you might like to know? Mrs. B. does constantly & two different times Jerry told me he got awake & studied over what he was going to tell me next day. And Mrs. B. in writing gets things I miss."[23] By the time Reichard returned from her second field trip, she had such a "mass of material" that even Kroeber was reassured. "Reichard has got some excellent texts of Wiyot and will get the language thoroughly cleaned up," he wrote Sapir.[24]

Intent on doing just that, Reichard decided she would have a complete draft of her dissertation ready by March. Such socializing as she made time for revolved around her officemates in the Department of Anthropology's Tin Shack. "Things are nice and peppy around here, the building is full most of the time & I like it much better than the funereal quiet of the summer," she confided in a chatty letter addressed to Dr. and Mrs. Boas. "I am beginning to get a little better acquainted around here now, I can almost always meet some one I know on the campus." She felt safe and welcomed on the "left" coast and wished her eastern friends to know it. "Gifford had a party & we went via 5-passenger Dodge, 7 people & 2 dogs," she wrote them.

> We had a very nice time there not at all formal as you might suppose, & I became better acquainted with our bunch. I am getting to like Nans [Lucy] Freeland very well, she and I are reading German together. I spent a Sunday at Stanford with some Swarthmore friends, had a nice time but I like the naturalness of U.C. better than the formality of Stanford. Every Tues. night our Spanish class meets for informal conversation . . . and altho it is hard work I get acquainted with some of the younger students. . . . Gif. and I had a nice time on kinship terms . . . to the disgust of all the guests except Lowie. You see you have to yell at Gif. so that no one else can think. So Lowie, Gif, & I got into a corner, Gif put on his ear trumpet & we collaborated. He was much pleased that my data corroborated his, but two elder & younger cousin terms now archaic, which I dug out of a text, gave him a bad night (Kroeber says).[25]

Reichard balanced her intellectual diet by proofing the galleys for "The Complexity of Rhythm in Decorative Art," the paper she had given at the previous year's meeting of the AAA. Her first article for *American Anthropologist* was based on 105 sketches of Thompson River Salish beadwork and embroidery and a smaller selection of embroidered coat bands made by Native Siberians. She had examined these items at the American Museum for the patterns, designs, techniques, and clues to the processes behind them they yielded. Applying Boas's "psychological-technical" theory of tribal art, which credited "the heavy weight of tradition" with constraining "the creative genius" of individual artists, Reichard asked thoughtful questions of her finite data.[26] Did the artist working in beads of glass, cactus seed, and dentalia strung or sewn with sinew, hide, or hair enjoy her work? Were silk floss, felt, velvet, and fur in the hands of Siberian seamstresses first arranged in the artist's mind by color, shade, tint, and shape or did she improvise as she stitched? Reichard's formal analysis suggested that the Native artists sought to please themselves as well as emulate their group's aesthetic by deliberately varying patterns on familiar schemes. In this regard, she offered, the Thompson Salish and Native Siberian artisans differed little from urban designers of women's hats and dresses in seeking to make something useful beautiful.

Though Reichard affirmed the Boasian principle that "purposeful departure" from Native artistic convention was rare, she was eager to emphasize that "the world's *creators* in any art could be counted on the fingers of one hand."[27] Her own touch of "play with technique" was to couch Boas's abstractions in firmly feminine imagery rarely, if ever, found in the crusty prose of the best academic journals. "The satisfaction obtained in the irregularity of a Thompson River stripe may be as great as that secured by using one shoulder band of velvet and one of flowers to support the bodice of an evening gown," she wrote. "And as long as the aim is achieved it matters little what means are used to achieve it."[28]

In December Reichard decided a third trip to the Wiyot was imperative. Finding the departmental treasury "depleted," she wrote Boas, "It seemed to me so necessary to go back to Eureka next Mar. that I thereby registered a vow that I would. With my informants able & willing, as they are, to do concentrated work & with long hours, I could do much in a week & I have decided to go either by bumming (i.e. starting to walk on the highway & getting picked up by autos) or by going on the boat which is at least half as cheap as the railroads, so that's that."[29] Alarmed, Boas requested funds for Reichard's research from his department's benefactor, Elsie Parsons. Hearing from Boas that Parsons agreed to sponsor her spring field trip, Reichard responded, "You can hardly know the ecstasy I was thrown into by the receipt of your letter. I was going to Humboldt

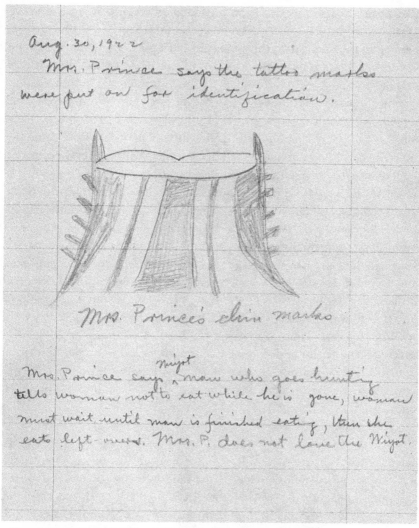

Page 168 of Gladys Reichard Wiyot Notebooks, BANC MSS 2004/111 c Box 1 (Vol. 1, pdf page 338). *Courtesy of the Bancroft Library, University of California, Berkeley.*

by hook or crook but had no hopes of staying longer than a week. Three weeks will make the job at least 50% more satisfactory, so I have written to Elsie and told her my plans & the circumstances."[30]

Tidings Reichard received from Columbia in January would have struck most aspiring academics as the best of the year. "My dear Gladys,"

Boas began in his standard form of salutation when writing to women, "Dean Gildersleeve has just informed me that the question of the appointment of an instructor in anthropology in Barnard College has passed the Committee, but has not been approved yet by the Trustees. There is very little doubt that it will go through . . . this is not an official notification of your appointment, but, as [Gildersleeve] says, merely 'to prepare your mind.'"[31] Gladys's reply was grateful but understated. "You can perhaps imagine my delight at the news you sent which reached me Sunday," she replied, adding cautiously, "I hope nothing will happen because of the Trustees to dampen my ardor."[32] The good news didn't come as a complete surprise. Boas had recommended Reichard for the position at Barnard based on her excellent performance at Columbia months before she left for California. Before that, he strengthened Gildersleeve's bid to establish an anthropology department at Barnard, the first at a women's college in the nation, by pledging to allow her appointee to teach graduate courses in his department. Though word that the labyrinthine Columbia bureaucracy had smiled on Gildersleeve's proposal for an anthropology department was certainly cheering, Reichard was more concerned with the immediate problem of meeting the highest standards with her dissertation. The extra funds from Parsons allowed her to do her best work on Wiyot. The appointment to Barnard meant she could concentrate on writing her paper instead of worrying about how she would pay her bills in the fall.

·   ·   ·   ◈   ·   ·   ·

Reichard had barely settled in Bangor for a summer of revising her thesis and preparing the new courses for the fall when she received an invitation that would alter the course of her life. Pliny Earle Goddard, assistant curator of ethnology at the American Museum of Natural History and specialist in Athabaskan languages, needed a field partner to assist him as he collected and checked texts with Navajo speakers during August and September. When he invited Reichard to fill that role, she readily consented. Reichard and Goddard knew each other from anthropology lunches and multiple interactions at the American Museum related to the field trips Gladys led on Boas's behalf for two years. As Reichard's interest in Indian languages developed, the co-founder of the *International Journal of American Linguistics* became something of a mentor to her. By the end of her residency in California, she knew Goddard well enough to send him a draft of her dissertation for his comments.

The son of a Quaker minister, Goddard came to anthropology after completing a three-year stint as a lay missionary to the Hupa of northern California. In 1900 he enrolled at the University of California, then joined the faculty where his "unprecedented" achievements as a teacher and scholar of Native Californian languages caused a rift in Kroeber's Anthropology Department.[33] Goddard wanted to make the program the first in the nation to concentrate on North American Indian linguistics. Kroeber preferred the status quo. In 1908 Goddard threatened to accept a position Boas offered him at the American Museum if Kroeber didn't budge. Kroeber called his colleague's bluff and Goddard withdrew to New York and a second career as a museum curator.[34] The move put an irreparable strain on the linguist's marriage. After returning to the east, Goddard and his wife, Alice Rockwell, eventually separated. They ruled out divorce in consideration of their five children but maintained separate households in different states for the rest of their lives.[35]

Meeting with Goddard as often as she did, Gladys discovered they had more in common than a fascination with Native languages and a revulsion for the socioevolutionary politics of Goddard's colleagues at the American Museum. Both had been raised and educated in homes of modest means located in small, provincial, but industrialized towns. Both majored in classical languages at college, taught in rural schools in early adulthood, and seized on anthropology as their true vocation as soon as they were exposed to it. Reichard's years at Swarthmore gave her a ready sympathy for the Quaker mores Goddard was raised with. Their conversations were likely free of the anxious lucubrations of the lapsed Puritans and Jews who comprised the majority in their Columbia circle. Although Kroeber never quite forgave Goddard for having a mind of his own, he described his former colleague at the University of California as "often almost shy in casual company or official relation . . . frankness itself in the contact of man to man, and then not only at ease but overflowing with playfulness and quite unusual charm."[36] Some of the students Goddard left behind in Berkeley remembered him affectionately as "Pliny, Earl of Goddam" for his colorful manner of speech.[37] Down-to-earth, quick-witted, fun-loving, and cautiously optimistic, Reichard and Goddard shared traits and tastes that mitigated their twenty-four-year age difference.

At Goddard's prompting, Parsons drew on her self-funded Southwest Society to pay Reichard's late summer expenses. "Glad to hear that you can go on the Navaho field trip," Parsons wrote Reichard from one of her country homes. "More than twice the amount of work will be done, as I have a notion you will stimulate your colleague to work harder than were he alone." Parsons made it clear that she reserved the right to influence Reichard's research agenda given that she was footing the bill. "If you are going to be near Hopi you might catch Snake or Flute ceremony," she instructed her grantee. "As far as I know the Navajo fire dance, as the Hopi call it, to me has not been described. The First Mesa people go there & dance at them, I think, as they do at the end after Night Chant ceremony, a sketch of which I enclose for you. I recall that Dr. Goddard thinks there must be a considerable unrecorded Navajo hunt ritual. Get a copy from Esther [Schiff] of her Laguna note on the hunt. I sent Goddard a list of Pueblo Indian ritual elements. Don't let it be *all* language." Enclosing a check for an additional $200 "as an emergency fund," Parsons suggested the pair add a side trip to the Rio Grande pueblos to observe ceremonies she wished she could attend herself.[38]

Once Goddard's rival for Parsons's romantic attentions, Kroeber accused his old flame of playing Cupid when he heard the news that Goddard and Reichard were teaming up. "I smiled at the Navaho expedition," he ribbed Parsons, certain that a "sincere and candidly naïve" woman like Gladys was about to be seduced. "Goddard won't clear up social organization," he volunteered. "It means handling crossed threads, and he likes sliding in a groove. Gladys is different, and I'll be interested to see how she handles something new like this. That girl is a workman." Unable to resist teasing Parsons for her sex-blind philanthropy, he added, "It looks as if the Southwest Society had the secondary aim of helping to liberate individuals."[39]

Kroeber's sense that the sun-drenched beauty of the Colorado Plateau encouraged romantic feelings between compatible colleagues proved correct. What he didn't know was the extent to which Reichard welcomed Goddard's overtures. The knowing tone of the field report Reichard sent Parsons from New Mexico suggests their affair was in full swing by early September. "Dear Dr. Parsons;—I like your Southwest," Gladys began with a flourish. She and Goddard were traveling in a Model T Ford purchased for their use by Earl Morris, an archeologist who lived and work in the Four Corners area. It was Gladys's first time behind the wheel of a car, but within a few days she fell in love with the speed and freedom of driving. In a show of affection for their sponsor, the happy couple named the car Elsie Elizabeth. "[B]ut like naming a baby, her name is appropriate in almost no respect. She is more temperamental than a movie star," Reichard bubbled, "& keeps Peggy"—the pet name Reichard derived from her lover's monogram, PEG—"busy cranking her (altho she has a self-starter)." "When she does start she goes like the wind," Reichard cheered, "we are becoming acquainted with her idiosyncrasies & she with ours." Barely able to hide her glee, Reichard added conspiratorially, "As you know, distances here are enormous & we could not get along without her."[40]

Before leaving New York, Reichard and Goddard had promised Parsons they would focus on the social and political organization of the Navajo. Together they conducted interviews and observed ceremonies where Goddard had local contacts. In Shiprock, Reichard and Goddard were barred entry to a Navajo ceremony. Stymied, they hung around outside the ceremonial hogan waiting for the open-air dance commonly known by Anglos as the "squaw dance" to begin. A disappointed Reichard reported to Parsons that the dance was "very monotonous & a mixture of old Navaho step & white man position." Told that the unsmiling girls were forced by the "old folks" in attendance to dance with the men for money, Reichard colored her report on the dance with a splash of feminist ire saying, "[I]n fact it was pathetic & a bit disgusting." Mostly the anthropologists put their noses to the grindstone. "There is no time to write," Reichard wrote Parsons at the end of her second week in Shiprock. "We work until dark & then hit the 'rocks' we are so tired."[41]

Among the many unscripted adventures she had on her first trip to the Southwest, Reichard joined Goddard at the wedding of Morris and his fiancée, the archeologist and illustrator Ann Axtell, a ceremony she hadn't packed for. "[They] are going to be married in 15 minutes," Reichard notified Parsons one Saturday morning. "We are all 'white-shirted & neck-tied' for the occasion—I have no dress." Gladys must have relished the slow smile of approval she envisioned breaking on Parsons's face as she pictured the desert wedding party in their unisex dress. But any longing to see herself at the altar with Goddard was missing from Reichard's letters. Goddard indirectly confirmed Reichard's indifference to marriage when later he alluded to his emancipated colleague in a cheeky piece for the *New Yorker.* New York's "ornamental girls with expensive habits" who worshipped the institution of marriage, he wrote, didn't hold a candle to the self-directed New Woman who "has been graduated from college, has fitted herself for a profession, or is in line for a professorship in some college." "Already earning a good salary or with one in prospect," Goddard wrote of his ideal partner, "she is under no necessity of marrying and will not do so if she must give up her work."[42]

If falling in love was a delicious passing novelty, driving, working, and camping in the Southwest permanently captivated Reichard's heart. The beauty and spaciousness of the "huge and desert Navajo country" evoked a visceral reaction from her just as it had so many white wayfarers before her. Yet it was the character of the people who called the high desert home that made the greatest impression on the young anthropologist. In the preface to her first book on Navajo society, Reichard wrote, "[T]he inhabitants of the region, white and Indian alike, have shown me untold consideration and for all the innumerable kindnesses which were granted me, I wish to express my appreciation to traders, government officials, missionaries, informants and interpreters. . . . I want everyone to know that his kindness is not forgotten or unappreciated, and I here render the highest tribute to the refreshing and generous spirit of the Southwest."[43]

The first people Reichard gave her heart to on the Navajo reservation owned and operated the Hubbell Trading Post, home to three generations of one of Arizona's most storied frontier families. Conditioned by her age, sex, and occupation, Gladys viewed the Hubbell clan at eye-level rather than from the height of the family patriarch's fame. John Lorenzo Gutierrez Hubbell, called Don Lorenzo, Nakai Sani ("Old Mexican"), or J. L. by his associates, had built a showy commercial conglomerate based on trade in Navajo textiles, sheep, wool, and a freight business that moved goods to and from railheads west and east of his Ganado post in Winslow, Arizona and Gallup, New Mexico. Hubbell was known far and wide as "the most hospitable man in the world," but by the 1920s the "old gent" was largely a romantic figurehead for a trading empire awash in debt.[44]

Visitors drunk with Hubbell lore heard "'Papa' this" and "'Papa' that" around the homestead as the trader's adult children did their best to keep the family businesses afloat.[45] Reichard was duly impressed by the self-possessed industry of all the Hubbells she encountered at the Ganado ranch, but the womanly grit she perceived beneath the masculine bravado associated with the Hubbell name made a special claim on her attention. Don Lorenzo's wife, Lina Rubí, was long dead when Reichard first visited the trading post on her return to the Southwest in the summer of 1924. Beside her "rare Spanish courtesy," Rubí left a lasting imprint on her four children as an ideal woman: honest, firm, and wise.[46] Barbara, the youngest of the Hubbells' two daughters, had been the head woman of the Hubbell households in Ganado and Albuquerque for more than a decade when Reichard and Goddard first appeared at her door. Widowed two years into her first marriage, "Auntie Bob," as Mrs. Barbara Hubbell Goodman was known in the family, was a forthright woman with "a good wide streak of humor" and a young daughter, named LaCharles for her late father, to raise.[47] Goodman's competent management of the family's ranch home meant a second generation of desert wanderers—artists, intellectuals, dignitaries, and pothunters whose appetite for authentic Mexican American hospitality couldn't be sated except by an overnight stay in the Hubbells' low-slung Ganado adobe—had kept her father's mystique alive and well. Not given to sarcasm or ingratitude, Don Lorenzo repeatedly advised his sons within hearing of LaCharles, "Barbara has more rights than anybody else."[48]

Next in line for Goodman's role was Mrs. Roman Hubbell, wife of Barbara's younger brother. In need of a teacher for the Hubbell grandchildren, aged two, six, eight, ten, and twelve in 1920, Goodman hired twenty-one-year-old Dorothy Smith sight-unseen through a mail-order agency. Smith had a teaching degree from Indiana University, a couple of years' experience working in public schools, and a hidden curiosity about life on the range. Smith's worried parents balked when she announced she wanted to accept the Ganado job, but Dorothy's aunt took her side and urged her to follow her heart. Within months of her arrival at the trading ranch, Smith and Roman Hubbell, a widower with two young children, were engaged. As soon as the sheep-buying season wrapped up at the end of June, the couple drove to Albuquerque, where they were married in a civil ceremony. Every Hubbell, including Roman's sons John and Roman Jr., was pleased that the baby of the family had chosen a life partner with a good head on her shoulders. Hubbell Sr. soon took to coaching his only daughter-in-law in the rudiments of the trading business, a sign that he, too, saw promise in the match.

Dorothy, John, and Lorenzo (Jr.) Hubbell touring near Ganado, Arizona,
c. 1930. *Courtesy National Park Service, Hubbell Trading Post National Historic Site,
photograph by Gladys Reichard, HB42/RM02/24.*

Reichard was five years older than Dorothy Smith Hubbell, better educated, and thoroughly wedded to her career as an anthropologist. That
didn't mean she didn't envy the young Mrs. Hubbell certain aspects of
her situation. When Dorothy crossed the threshold of the Hubbell home
for the first time in 1920, she seemed to shed her ho-hum urbanized life
like dead skin. "Mrs. Goodman met us at the door. She was an excellent
hostess," Dorothy recalled of that October evening,

> When she opened the door and I looked in that hall, it was as though
> I stepped into another country. I didn't know Navajo rugs at all. To my
> knowledge, I hadn't even seen any [before]. The floors were covered
> with these three very large rugs. And the walls were covered with
> paintings, oil and water-color, all originals. And the ceiling was made
> of these round cut logs [vigas] as you see it now, and the baskets on
> the ceiling. And there was a fire in the fireplace. . . . And with the
> flickering light of the fireplace on all of these Indian things that I
> didn't know before, it was as fascinating and attractive as could be.

Strange though her surroundings were, Dorothy was more awed than
afraid. "At table that night the two girls who waited on table were Hopi,"
she continued.

We had a Navajo man [Loco] cook in the kitchen and a Mexican baker. Terrones was the baker. Well, everybody had dark skin except the family. And I couldn't recognize the languages then. I didn't know a Navajo from a Mexican from a Hopi. Dinner was interesting because it was served there at the table. The [Hopi] girls brought the food on big trays from the kitchen through the open courtyard. We had two guests at the table. One of them was Earl Morris, the archaeologist who, at that time, was doing excavation at the Mummy Cave at Canyon del Muerto [in Canyon de Chelly]. Well, I was enthralled at the experiences they were having out there working on this mummy cave; I didn't know anything about archaeology either. He was telling about their finding fifty-two mummies and, of course, some old pottery and some old rope sandals and pieces of feather ropes. And I was very much interested. That made a very interesting introduction to me for life at Ganado.[49]

That Dorothy's personal choices brought her into everyday contact with her Navajo neighbors also appealed to Gladys. During her first year on the job, Dorothy was teaching in the little classroom off the kitchen when her lesson was suddenly interrupted. "I heard a very peculiar high-sounding, singsong voice that I did not recognize at all," she recalled.

But the children did. They just perked up and LaCharles said, "That's the Yeibichais coming. May I go to the kitchen?" . . . and I said "Yes." So she went to the kitchen. She came back with a loaf of bread, a can of something, something to give each child in school, a bit of food. So when we opened the door, the outside door, there were these Yeibichais, three of them. Two of them had leather masks which completely covered their heads, with holes for the mouth and for the eyes, and a feather on top. . . . [T]hey had some kind of whip in one hand, a "bull-roarer" they called it. The other one had . . . something in his hand, a rattle of some kind. All had a ruff of piñon branches around their necks and their bodies were painted white with gypsum. The third one had his head covered with a leather mask and wore a buckskin over one shoulder. He held out the sack. So when he came to the door still singing, why the children went up (they knew) and they put the food in the sack. [The Yeibichais] just nodded, turned around, and left. I made the remark to the children, "Why they didn't even say thank you." And LaCharles said, "Oh they couldn't. At the moment they represent gods and they don't speak. They couldn't. They wouldn't be allowed to."

A woman of tact and remarkable objectivity, Dorothy concluded mildly, "But you see, I didn't know that."[50]

For Dorothy's part, Gladys was part alter ego, part favorite big sister. "She was a delightful person to know," Hubbell often said of Reichard. "She was a workaholic: she worked all the time. If she was having dinner with us, and maybe it was a fifteen minute wait, she didn't just sit there and do nothing. She'd have her notebook and she'd be working. But she was lots of fun. To me she was like a breath of fresh air when she'd come [to Arizona] in the summer."[51] More prim, less forward than Gladys, Dorothy found Reichard "open and uninhibited," always ready to explore the backcountry alone or with a carload of Navajo or white friends in search of "information." "She'd go anywhere, she'd sleep anywhere," Dorothy recounted. "I mean if it meant to sleep out under a tree somewhere because she got stuck, or couldn't make it any farther, she'd do it. She'd travel with a canvas . . . with a sleeping bag."[52] Reichard cut a striking, athletic figure in the desert, a healthy woman as at home on horseback as in her desk chair. "She nearly always had her riding pants on," Dorothy said of her camera-shy friend. "She was tall. She might have been a little bit taller than I am . . . she probably weighed about 145 maybe. And she was tall. Her hair was sandy, a dark blonde I'd say."

Clad in her riding pants, Reichard favored a trusty green leather jacket for fending off extremes in desert temperatures as she roamed the range absorbed in her work. "She liked clothes," Dorothy said, "but she was not as style conscious, maybe, as some people may be." On a shopping trip in Chicago, Reichard told Dorothy's sister, "I teach at college in the East and I want a dress suitable to wear in the classroom if I want to." "She didn't want it fancy," Dorothy explained. "And so she looked at the dress and she said, 'Well, then, too, if I should be called to lunch, invited to lunch, I would like it to be suitable for a luncheon, so that I wouldn't have to change before luncheon.' And so she kept on looking. And then she said, 'Sometimes I will stay in the city all day, at the college, and I want one that I can wear out to dinner at night.' So she wanted an all-purpose dress, one that she could wear anytime." Dorothy noted with approval that Reichard's sartorial logic didn't slip as her professional prestige grew. At a conference in Hamburg, Germany in 1930, she recalled, Gladys "had to go to a banquet, which she didn't like. She didn't like to go to that kind of thing. She liked to talk to people. But not small talk. And she didn't like banquets much, but she had to go to this one. It was part of her . . . she just had to go. And I said 'Well, Gladys what did you wear, if you went to a banquet?' 'Well,' she said, 'you'd never believe it: I bought a pink silk dress that had one of these "come-follow-me Willy" capes on the back.' And I said, 'Well, what did you wear for a coat?' 'Hah!' she said, 'Why, my green leather jacket: I wasn't going to buy a coat just to wear to the dinner.'" "See," Dorothy emphasized so that the man taping her words didn't miss the point of her anecdote, "and she didn't mind. That was just all right."[53]

Reichard's attachment to the Navajo community that surrounded the Hubbell Trading Post would not develop until the 1930s. Her field project in 1924 and 1925 consisted in collecting genealogies connecting "3000 to 4000" Navajos to one another by blood and marriage per Parsons's preferred methodology. Though her research design gave her little opportunity to learn Navajo and get to know The People as individuals, a piece Reichard wrote for the annual Faculty Issue of the *Barnard Bulletin* revealed that her travels with Goddard in Navajo country stimulated her aesthetic and scientific sensibilities equally. "In the southwestern part of the United States," she wrote,

> where the day begins with turquoise and lemon, waxes into dull brown and wans in purple, rose and gold live the Navajo Indians. The children spend their days in the pine forests or on sunny mesas watching large flocks of sheep and goats which are the symbol of wealth and of sustenance. Women weave attractive rugs in the intervals of housekeeping and men fashion ornaments of turquoise and silver, or make soft moccasins. Except for their picturesque costumes taken from the Spanish the surroundings of a Navajo house are sufficiently dull. Nevertheless art has reached a high state of development. Songs are poems characterized by

delicacy of feeling, balance and skillful repetition; myths narrate wonderful exploits of supernaturals who are delightfully human.[54]

Reichard seemed especially pleased to note for her Barnard readership that Navajo women enjoyed a higher status in their society than an American woman did in hers. "The women in this tribe exercise rights which would astound the ardent feminist of our own culture," she marveled. "Although they do a great deal of the work—and where do they not?—they are economically independent. Socially their position is very high. . . . But if the position of woman is high economically, socially, religiously, and politically, it does not necessarily follow that the position of men is low. . . . Each person in the tribe is treated as an individual without regard to age or sex, but good judgment, gentleness, intelligence and wisdom are appreciated and cultivated." Though, in hindsight, these early generalizations about Navajo society were based on too little experience, they served Reichard's intention to encourage her readers to believe that, where the status of women was concerned, the Navajo were models of civilized behavior.

·   ·   ·   ❖   ·   ·   ·

Between her annual migrations to the Navajo reservation each summer, Reichard found Barnard College to be an ideal workplace. The bright start she made of the Anthropology Department gave Gildersleeve and Boas nothing to regret.[55] Reichard developed a half-dozen new courses with titles such as The Early History of Mankind, Introduction to Comparative Anthropology, The Art of Primitive Man, Traditional Literature, Primitive Social Life, and Man and the Supernatural. The heavy teaching and advising loads she took on left little time for research writing. Once the final version of her dissertation was delivered to the University of California for publication, she used her spare time to sift through the abundant genealogical data she'd collected for her Navajo study.

On her return from her second summer trip to the Navajo country, Reichard began renting the upstairs apartment of the Boas family's large, unassuming house on the banks of the Hudson in Grantwood, New Jersey. Either because of her tenancy or as a spur to it, her relationship with Boas evolved into a warm, almost jocular friendship. "She and Boas had got together like two kernels in a nut," one Columbia student who met the pair in 1930 said. "Gladys could get the sounds Papa Franz made when the rest of us could not," Ruth Underhill remembered. "I think it was a joy to Papa Franz to have her come home at night with some jokes or some question about linguistics."[56] Reichard and Boas talked shop as they rode the Fort Lee ferry to campus each weekday and continued to meet at Columbia seminars, anthropology lunches, and miscellaneous work-related meetings. At Grantwood, "Mama Franz" regularly added a plate for Reichard at the dinner table, where four of the Boas's five adult children—Frances, Helene (with her husband, Cecil Yampolsky and their twin boys), Gertrud, and Ernst—helped their parents host a visiting international scientist or two, typically men Boas was sheltering from one foreign despot or another. Because Goddard owned a house a few minutes west in Leonia, he, too, may have spent winter evenings relaxing in the Boas's parlor. Grandfather Boas entertained the group by playing an accomplished set of Beethoven sonatas on the family piano or doing puzzles with the youngest members of his congenial brood.

Reichard's seemingly unbroken run of personal success and good fortune began to sputter in late 1924, shortly after she moved to Grantwood. In the two most wretched lines Boas ever wrote, he notified Parsons on October 22, "My daughter Gertrud passed away last night after a week's illness—infantile paralysis. Please don't answer."[57] The third of the Boas's surviving children, Gertrud was a twenty-seven-year-old Barnard alumna. Engaged to be married and working as her father's assistant in the Anthropology Department, Gertrud had likely taken Reichard's survey class in anthropology; they were sisterly "campus buddies" who went to lunch and shows together in the city as time allowed. The Boases had barely begun to absorb the shock of Gertrud's death when they suffered another unthinkable tragedy. On January 26, 1925, their twenty-eight-year-old son Henry Boas was killed with his two female passengers when their "small motorcar" was struck by a high-speed train near Pokagon, Michigan.[58] The next day, Reichard's father passed away. The evening edition of the *Easton Express* reported, "Dr. Noah W. Reichard, a prominent physician of Bangor and a former chief burgess of that borough died suddenly at 9:15 this morning at his office, 28 South First Street, that place. He was sitting in a chair when he was suddenly stricken by heart trouble."[59]

Reichard missed Henry's funeral while she and Lilian met in Bangor to bury their father, settle his estate, and offer what comfort they could to his ailing widow. On her return to Grantwood, Reichard eased the pain of her losses by focusing on "work that is worth doing."[60] Foiled in his attempt to sue the railroad on behalf of his son, Boas filled the void with devotion to family, poetry by his favorite author, Goethe, and the task of completing his latest monograph, *Primitive Art*. When in the fall of 1925 Professor and Mrs. Boas sailed for Oslo to deliver the finished manuscript to the printers, Gladys automatically slipped back into the role of departmental minder. "Things seem to be going nicely," she assured Boas during his travels. "It seems to me the students in the department are nicer than usual this year." If she was feeling blue about her father's death, Reichard managed to project a cheery domestic normalcy for the elderly couple's benefit. "I sold the old car or rather have it at the agent's for sale and bought a Dodge runabout," she wrote them. "Dr. G keeps it at his garage and calls for me every morning—it took us 17 min. to come from Grantwood to Barnard to-day. . . . I drive anywhere now, in N.Y. and all." She let her friends know she was "slaving at my Navajo stuff" and getting her application ready for the "Guggenheim thing"—the new, private fellowship opportunity that could mean a full year of paid research and travel abroad if she was successful.[61]

Gladys was still recovering from a bout of influenza that made the rounds of the Boas home in the winter of 1926 when Boas seemed to project his wish for a reprieve for himself onto his tenant. He wrote Parsons, "I hope [Gladys] may [get the fellowship]. She ought to get away from here for a while."[62] It was well known in New York that the John Simon Guggenheim Memorial Fellowship for Advanced Study was born of grief. Guggenheim's parents lost their seventeen-year-old son to an acute bacterial infection of the middle ear, antibiotics not yet having been invented. Frank Aydelotte, president of Swarthmore College and American secretary to the Rhodes Trustees, was tapped to ensure the Guggenheim's grant program rivaled their British counterpart's in liberality, impact, and prestige.[63] Virginia Gildersleeve was appointed to the foundation's board and subsequently served as the only woman on the five-member Committee of Selection in the first open round of competition. The program guidelines invited men and women applicants without regard to age, marital status, "race, creed, or color," asking only that applicants propose work that would "add to the educational, literary, artistic, and scientific power" of the United States. "The announcement of the establishment of the Guggenheim fellows . . .

seemed incredible," successful applicant and future Columbia professor
Marjorie Hope Nicolson later wrote. "I am sure that many of the others
who sent in application forms [in 1926] believed as little as I did in the
possibility that a dream might come true."[64]

Some nine hundred hopefuls threw their hats in the ring along with
Reichard and Ruth Benedict. The news received in April that Reichard
was one of five women on the roster of thirty-eight awardees for the year
was a balm to the entire Grantwood tribe.[65] In early July, Reichard set sail
for Europe. Aboard the fifty-thousand-ton ocean liner on the day, she
waved good-bye to a cheerful contingent of Boas offspring, Goddard, and
Mother Reichard, who had gathered on the crowded dock to see her off.
When she finally went below deck, Gladys discovered that Dr. and Mrs.
Boas, who were by then in their country home in Connecticut for the
summer, had arranged for a folding table to be placed in her cabin. Their
kind gesture meant she would have a quiet place to write for the duration
of her first transatlantic crossing. The note she wrote them in time for the
pilot boat's run back to port said, "Just a little word to thank you greatly
not only for the nice gifts but for your very great thotfulness." "The breeze
is lovely and cool," she observed of her novel surroundings. Not one to
sink into a deck chair for long, she assured her friends, "I am going on a
tour of investigation soon."[66]

CHAPTER 3

HER HAND ON
A HIGH TRESTLE

THOUGH SHE SPENT THE SUMMER OF 1926 IN GÖTTINGEN learning
German "like a baby," Reichard's term as an anthropologist-in-train-
ing came to a close in Europe.[1] After her working Roman holiday at
the International Congress of Americanists, Reichard lived the life of
a highly educated *Wandergeselle,* or traveling journeyman, with Hamburg as her home base, until spring. The long days she put in at her
office at the Museum of Ethnology didn't keep her from frequenting
the experimental phonetics laboratory at the University of Hamburg,
then under the direction of renowned acoustical phonetician Giulio
Panconcelli-Calzia.[2] The Italian scholar graciously allowed her to spend
Saturday mornings alone in his lab, testing her ear against an updated
version of the Rousselot apparatus, a mechanical recording device
in common use by linguists interested in analyzing the properties of
human speech.[3]

Between overnight trips to museums throughout northeastern Germany, Reichard attended evening soirees at Hamburg's famed Warburg
Library. She was delighted when the library's founder and namesake,
Abraham Warburg, introduced her as "*meine collegia von der Indianern*" (my
colleague from the Indians) to library regulars neo-Kantian philosopher
Ernst Cassirer, Austrian painter and collector Carl Otto Czeschka, and art
historian Gertrud Bing, who was later instrumental in reestablishing the
library in London after the Nazis moved to close the "Jewish" research
center in 1933.[4] Wherever Gladys went in the Old World, her new contacts
availed her of "deep wells of information" on Oceanic art, aesthetic theory, or South Pacific languages. Reichard praised the *Stimmung* in her host
institutions as "perfect" for scholarship.[5] Her apprenticeship in America

had made her a world-class anthropologist. In Europe she discovered how it felt to be treated as one.

The impersonal respect paid Reichard as a Guggenheim Fellow contrasted with the unfriendly competitiveness her early accomplishments inspired in certain of her Yankee peers. Reichard's ability to convert the opportunities she was given at Barnard and the Guggenheim Foundation into tangible rewards hurt the pride of Ruth Benedict, for example. Benedict's urgent, frustrated desire for "*success*—success in writing" prompted her to construe Reichard's every forward career step as undeserved gifts from Boas.[6] Adroit at masking the full extent of her inner turmoil, Benedict succeeded at hiding her envy of Reichard, particularly of her coveted faculty position at Barnard and the license it gave the younger woman to teach at Columbia. That Reichard's facility in linguistics gave her an edge in securing grants and fellowships only added salt to Benedict's mental wounds.[7] Ever mindful of the blue blood that ran through her veins, Benedict found it in herself to excuse Boas's inexplicable fondness for a simple "farm girl" who'd managed to graduate from "a rough Pennsylvania college."[8] Reichard's audacity—that was unforgivable.

Benedict vented her frustrations over Reichard's professional progress to two other members of the Columbia circle, both inclined to displace their displeasure with Boas onto his latest protégé. One of these confidantes was Benedict's former student, Margaret Mead. The women met in the fall of 1922 when Benedict was filling in as Boas's teaching assistant while Reichard was in California. They were close enough by spring semester for Mead to comfort Benedict when the news that Reichard was to be hired at Barnard in the fall became public. Mead believed, or was led to believe, that the woman she was falling in love with had been robbed.[9] She didn't know Reichard or Boas, but she blamed them both for failing Benedict. After Benedict and Mead became lovers as well as classmates at Columbia, Mead's resentment of Reichard intensified.[10] Although Benedict revered Boas as a benevolent guardian spirit, Mead regarded Boas as rigid and hostile to new ideas.[11] Despite this, Mead craved his attention, as revealed by her charge that Boas "severely neglected" independent thinkers like herself and Benedict to instead lavish attention on "the exiled, the irresponsible, and the handicapped." "I myself did not have half a dozen conferences with [Boas] during my whole period as a student or, later, as someone doing research under his inspiration or direction," Mead recalled.[12] Boas's closer rapport with Reichard was an additional irritant. Mead was convinced that Benedict deserved special protection from enemies like Reichard, despite all evidence that Reichard "was hardly an enemy."[13]

Benedict's other key confidante early in her career was Edward Sapir. Edward needed no encouragement to criticize Boas in the flattering letters he exchanged with Ruth, and he got none from his latest conquest.[14] Reichard was a different story. Mocking Gladys behind her back was something Ruth and Edward indulged in even before Reichard misread the linguist's interest in her Wiyot work as professional respect. Determined to be her own woman in Americanist linguistics after her return from California, Reichard had innocently invited Sapir to meet to discuss a draft of her dissertation. Their June meeting went well, despite Sapir's being highly distracted. He was recovering from a broken leg. Worse, his wife Florence was in a Manhattan hospital being treated for severe physical and emotional distress.[15] Yet as a teacher he did not disappoint. "Sapir was here week before last & went over my paper with me, gave me some helpful suggestions," Gladys wrote Boas after her one-on-one with Sapir. "It is very amusing to me to hear their remarks. Michelson: 'Absolutely un-Algonkin!' Sapir: 'I don't see how anyone can look at this & say it is not Algonkin.' However I have gone over the examples [Sapir] used & found about 41% comparable. I realize of course that numbers do not mean anything in this instance as I gave every phrase equal weight. Sapir missed the reduplication of the diminutive suffix in Cree [an Algonquian language] which corresponds to Wiyot much more closely than many other things he pointed out."[16] Ultimately Reichard sided, impersonally, with Sapir's critic, Truman Michelson. "The chief objection to Sapir's [California Algonquian] thesis is that it is founded on data too meager and too little assimilated," she wrote. Reichard appealed to Sapir's own caveats about his claims when she added, "Sapir acknowledges that the cases Michelson points out are not comparable and that his chief concern is for material which will give a better understanding of the constituents of the languages in question."[17]

Assuming from Sapir's outward cordiality that he would welcome further debate related to Wiyot's classification, Reichard amassed, in consultation with Michelson, additional examples that seemed to cast doubt on the California Algonquian hypothesis. In early 1924, she sent Sapir a draft of a paper on Wiyot that she hoped to see published in Boas's *International Journal of American Linguistics*. Sapir returned her text with "highly charged" comments in the margins. He dismissed her conclusions, much as he had waved off Michelson's earlier criticisms, with barely concealed ire. "Thank you for your prompt attention to my letter and paper," Reichard replied to Sapir contritely. "I am sorry you saw in the latter a disagreeable spirit. I was unconscious that it was so until Prof. Boas brought it to my attention before your letter came and then I eliminated any remarks which might be so interpreted. I cannot help thinking your own interpretation was somewhat tinctured by your own spirit but that is neither here nor there."[18] To demonstrate that her regrets were sincere, Reichard withdrew her paper from circulation.

Widely acknowledged as a phenomenally talented "shark of the lot" by the time he was tapped for his first professorship at the University of Chicago in 1925, Sapir had a persistent chip on his shoulder.[19] Like Benedict, he felt he deserved better from the world and allowed his personal unhappiness to color his professional judgment. Like Mead, Sapir loved the limelight, which made it impossible for him to relate to Boas's selflessness.[20] Lacking his teacher's position and power in the academy, he resorted to backroom tactics to climb the ladder of success. If he used sarcastic, condescending quips to put down scholars he deemed a threat, Sapir campaigned aggressively to destroy the reputations of men who refused to submit to his will.

Sapir's assault on Pliny Goddard in the early 1920s bore a distinct resemblance to his treatment of Truman Michelson a decade before, though perhaps owing to Goddard's closer ties to Boas, Sapir preferred to malign the museum curator behind closed doors. With his superior ear and advanced training in comparative philology, Sapir uncovered serious flaws in Goddard's analysis of Navajo, which Sapir concluded employed word-level tone to signal meaning. Sapir's discoveries had important consequences for the understanding of the Athabascan family of languages as a whole. Flush with success, he began to nurse a hunch he believed would set the scholarly world on fire. "[D]o not think me an ass if I am seriously entertaining the notion of an old Indo-Chinese offshoot into N.W. America," Sapir wrote Kroeber tremulously. The presence of tonal distinctions in two languages of the Northwest coast led Sapir to posit a historical link between his Na-Dene family (consisting of

Haida, Tlingit, and Athabascan) and Tibetan.[21] To support his intuition, he sought empirical evidence that all Athabascan languages were, like Navajo, tonal. Sapir wrote Goddard to inquire about the prospects of fieldwork on Sarsi, a language spoken in southern Alberta that Goddard had studied. As Sapir told it, Goddard balked at having his territory invaded, which confirmed Sapir's suspicion that Goddard was more interested in pouring "nasty cold water . . . stolen from Boas' reservoir" on a competitor than in making scientific progress on comparative studies of Athabascan.[22]

As Sapir grew more attached to his Sino-Dene hypothesis, his disdain for Goddard's work on Athabascan turned into personal contempt. Calling Goddard "an utter groundling that does not know his own material," Sapir dismissed him as "a man of no more than average linguistic ability, completely at the mercy of his local sentimental memories."[23] When Goddard published a modest challenge to a small portion of Sapir's Na-Dene hypothesis, Sapir dismissed it as "painful balderdash" and deemed it unworthy of a public response.[24] Using the well-worn ploy of declaring himself the injured party, Sapir claimed to understand Goddard's motives better than did Kroeber or Goddard himself. "He is a queer nut," Sapir said of his latest target. "Athabaskan is not his scientific interest but a kind of private mistress. . . . I have decided that his Athabaskan is very imperfectly sublimated libido and that it would be making polyandrous innuendos for me to attempt to discuss my stuff with him." "Why," he demanded of Kroeber, "is [Goddard] so damned personal about it all? After all, nobody wants to have sexual relations with the Hupa language!"[25]

Covert psychosexual tropes had a special appeal to Kroeber, whose faith in Freudian psychoanalysis as a cure for the *Sturm und Drang* he experienced before World War I led him to open his own practice as an analyst in 1918.[26] More politic by nature than Sapir, Kroeber saw himself as "a brake on any extremists" and undeserving of the success he'd had in disguising himself as a man with "savoir faire." "I have to smile at anyone taking me to be really cool and impersonal," he once confided to Sapir, "because I have to be constantly trying to be that at all."[27] Kroeber was more open to women's participation in anthropology and less overt in demanding his due from other leading men in his field. While Sapir hid his "hide-bound" conventionality behind "Bolshevistic fanfare" Kroeber maintained a more detached air.[28] From time to time Kroeber let his Victorian slip show, however, as when he congratulated Sapir on his first marriage by writing, "I am sure Mrs. Sapir is charming, and, what is almost equally important, intelligent."[29]

Armed with the quasi-Freudian conceits in vogue during the inter-war period, Kroeber shared an argot with Sapir that rendered gossip a licit form of scholarly opining. When Sapir's conservative bent led him to complain of Reichard's insubordination in regard to Wiyot, Kroeber soothed his friend's feelings with a brotherly assessment of Boas's best "girl" steeped in pop-psychoanalytical mumbo-jumbo. "Try kidding Reichard next time. I rather liked and much admired her," Kroeber wrote Sapir. "Her work capacity is enormous. The chief fault I found was the super-impregnation with Boas, so that she neither gave nor received anything in her year with us. What she had, was el puro Boas; she wanted nothing else. She did her Wiyot the way he would approve. . . . She is hard and efficient and charmless . . . and Haeberlin's successor, almost, in his devotion. She's neither quarrelsome nor dogmatic, but argument with her is useless because she had Boas lock her mind and keep the key."[30]

Being abroad spared Reichard the ugly specifics of the charges laid against her behind her back. As a specialist in human nature, she understood that she was entitled to pick her friends but not her enemies. Midway through her stay in Hamburg, Reichard was pleased to learn that her New York supporters were unfazed by personality politics. Boas wrote to advise her he had secured a summer grant for her through the Committee on Research in Native American Languages, which Boas co-directed with Sapir and Leonard Bloomfield.[31] Reichard replied that she would like to return to California to study Yurok with informants while searching for Wiyot speakers. Boas answered tactfully, "I am not sure whether it would be best this year to take up the Yurok. . . . A particular place and tribe could, perhaps, be decided upon later."[32] Reichard read between the lines. "I got your letter about the field trip," she replied cannily. "Is Kroeber still nursing his feelings? Or does Sapir want to do Yurok himself? . . . If you get the money & want me to go I will. . . . But I haven't any feelings which have to be petted so please attend to Kroeber's and Sapir's. One thing is certain. Sapir with his keenness can never bully or intimidate me again. I have made my [phonetic] judgments & tested them with the [acoustic] machinery & they are not often wrong."[33] She left Boas an out in case the Linguistics Committee should collapse under the weight of competing male egos. "P.S. I meant to say if you don't send me to the field I shall not twiddle my thumbs this summer. It would be 'herrlich' to wipe some tasks off the slate. It might be better for me, Barnard & the Guggenheim!"

Flitting between Old World coffeehouses, castles, concert halls, and high-toned salons, Reichard filled in the corners of her education in "high culture" with her usual efficiency. Nevertheless, Germany's northern gloom left her feeling like a bear itching to emerge from its winter den. ("The only thing that can be said for Hamburg weather," she wrote Parsons, "is that sometimes it doesn't rain.")[34] "I can't begin to tell you how the country looks with Goldregen, rot Dorn, wisteria, lilacs, blossoms of every kind," she jubilated as she passed through Cologne on her way to Paris in May. Before sailing for New York, she stopped in London, where she met some of the most celebrated scholars in her discipline, including British physical anthropologist Charles Seligman, Finnish sociologist Edvard Westermarck, Polish ethnographer Bronisław Malinowksi, Sir James George Frazer of Golden Bough fame, and Elisabeth Johanna de Boys Adelsdorfer, better known as Lady (Lilly) Frazer. Relaxed and relieved to be homeward bound, she fairly glided through the last days of her farewell tour. "Will you be in N.Y. when I arrive in June? Or will you have fled?" she mused amiably to Boas. "And where are you going? And where am I going? Or am I going? All questions which will be answered in their good time."[35]

Never without a master plan, Boas framed the job he had in mind for Haeberlin's successor as a program to "take up the Cour d'Alene [sic] with the idea of getting the whole interior Salish. . . . The field that you would gradually have to cover would embrace about eight dialects; some of them fairly divergent and certainly not mutually intelligible. The country to be covered reaches from the Columbia River over to Montana, taking in a considerable part of southern interior of British Columbia. Of course the idea would be that the work would extend over a number of years. There will be no reason why the Yurok might [not] be inserted at some particular time."[36] He filled in the details of Reichard's assignment only after she accepted it. "You understand, of course, that the object of your trip this year is purely linguistic and that we expect particularly as a result a grammatical sketch of Cour d'Alene which I believe differs more from the other inland dialects than any of the others. You will, of course, collect texts and whatever else you can get."[37] He had prepared the territory by contacting a missionary in DeSmet, Idaho who knew "about interpreters and where you can stay." Then Boas wished Reichard kindest regards until fall and left to do fieldwork in California and Oregon.

· · · ◈ · · ·

Drained by the tedium of nine days at sea, Reichard landed in New York in a "scientific coma" that only a few days at home in Bangor could cure.[38] She stopped off at Columbia just long enough to hire Gene Weltfish (on Boas's recommendation) for her old job of leading class field trips at the American Museum. (There were eighty-five registrants in the fall survey course as of June 27.) Next she picked up the check and books Boas had left for her. She also bought a train ticket for her next destination, the Coeur d'Alene Indian reservation and her soon-to-be summer headquarters, De Smet, Idaho.

Luck intervened to make crossing North America again much more exciting than her recent transatlantic journey had been. "My uncle, whom I rediscovered before I went to Europe, has never had a vacation in his life & needed one," she explained to Boas from Livingston, Montana. "Just a few days before I was ready to start [west] he proposed bringing me in his Peerless 8-passenger touring car. Everybody, myself included, thot it a fine idea & the only consideration was the time for me. It was too tempting so I took it & now hope to be on the job in De Smet in a few days." The pleasure she took piloting Uncle Hayes's sleek coach along the Yellowstone Trail into the heart of the northern Rockies was unabashed. "I haven't yet regretted a moment of the trip out here," she wrote from the road, "even if in this last week all the Salish languages should have died out."[39]

The missionary settlement of De Smet lay some thirty miles southwest of the lower reaches of Lake Coeur d'Alene, a natural reservoir that stretches like a bolt of liquid lightning along the western slope of the Bitterroot Mountains separating Idaho from Montana. On a rise overlooking the rippling camas prairie, several large brick buildings—separate boarding facilities for Indian boys and girls on either side of the mission church—towered over the simple wooden homes that housed the Coeur d'Alenes on weekends ahead of Sunday Mass. Uncle Hayes dropped off his niece in front of the nearly vacant Sisters of Charity of Providence school and convent, promising to return in August on his way east. Reichard felt some guilt at being a week or two behind schedule, but not enough to curb her enthusiasm. To make up for lost time, she canceled a side trip to Portland to confer with Boas. She warned him cheekily, "You couldn't have caught me in a more playful mood & I'll have to pin myself down to Salish like a live butterfly!"

Ready or not, Gladys rolled up her sleeves for her fifth summer of field-work. A few days in, she let Boas know that she was only a human being and not a miracle worker. "I have worked only two days & cannot of course give you all details about the language yet! Don't forget you have dumped me into the middle of the Salish ocean. . . . I am gasping & gulping & hunting for shore."[40] Though it had seemed prudent to bring along a stack of papers and books on Coeur d'Alene, neighboring languages Kalispel and Spokan, and other Salishan tongues, the materials Reichard had at hand were problematic. Taken together, the sources offered conflicting information expressed in different technical idioms. Reports by Boas and Haeberlin sought to document the sounds, structures, and processes of Salishan languages on their own terms using a phonetic alphabet. The Jesuit priests modeled their reports on Latin grammar and limited them-selves to the meager set of Roman alphabet symbols for their spellings. In the event, Reichard second-guessed herself, ever mindful that Boas was counting on her to make quick work of new and old data. Through July, Reichard plied Boas by mail with more questions than answers, always with the hope that, as with Wiyot, order would nose its own way out of its opposite. By August her self-effacements acknowledged the heat of Boas's high expectations. "I don't know whether old [Fathers] Giorda & Men-garini missed the essential points, or whether Coeur d'A. is so different or whether I am so dumb. Anyway I am struggling & working with verb pre- & suff-fixes & so far seem to have a little order out of chaos, but not nearly all the order—or chaos!—there is."[41]

Success in sifting the grain from the chaff of Coeur d'Alene speech data depended on her being able to locate willing and able informants, just as it had in California. Reichard's initial contacts with Coeur d'Alene speakers didn't bode well. "I have no car & cannot chase them down. They live on their ranches 5 to 14 mi. away & come in [to De Smet] Sat. & Sun. for mass," Reichard complained to Boas. "They say they will . . . oblige you and then just simply do not show up. They have enough to live on & have a good time & don't need the money. And they do *not* like to settle down to a steady job."[42] One or two unsatisfactory sessions with less than fluent speakers made her encounter with Pascal George, a "grand interpreter," all the sweeter.[43] George was an English-speaking Spokane Indian who was adopted into the Coeur d'Alene tribe as a child. He later married a Coeur d'Alene woman before earning a position at the agency as a translator/interpreter.[44] "Pascal George is perhaps one of, if not the most enterprising on the reservation," she enthused to Boas. "He knows Kalis[pel] & Spokane & what is more analyzes many things correctly. He is like my Wiyot Mrs. Barto in that he ponders over words & finds similar examples. . . . He is really a very high grade person."[45] The self-doubt she expressed at the start of the summer seemed unworthy of her privileges, in hindsight. "I don't want you to think I was or am discouraged," she assured her sponsor. "I always have the allgone feeling, 'what if I couldn't get someone one?' But of course I know I always do."[46] Overall, her best finding of the summer was that the Coeur d'Alene language was very much alive, if held underground by the Americans in charge. The overall situation was good enough that she remarked she had never had better working conditions for linguistic fieldwork, with the usual exception. "You know how it goes," she wrote Boas. "Every time one thing gets straightened out something new & baffling turns up."[47]

Living on a federal Indian reservation for the first time was an eye-opening experience for Reichard. Unlike the Wiyot or Navajo, who had survived attempts by white immigrants and soldiers to physically exterminate them, the Coeur d'Alenes were oppressed by psychological and legal means. The psychological campaign was executed by convert-hungry Jesuit priests who wooed the Schitschu'mush ("the ones found here") away from their lives as tolerant, adroit mountain woodland dwellers, buffalo hunters, and perspicacious traders into "reductions," as Catholic Indian settlements were known in the nineteenth century. Begun in 1842, when Father Superior Pierre Jean De Smet first approached the "affable," "polite" Natives with the idea of joining the Society of Jesus as agrarian parishioners, the process of insulating the Coeur d'Alene from un-Christian influences resulted in their semi-voluntary removal from their homeland.[48] The relatively bloodless stratagems employed to separate the Coeur d'Alene from their past were typified by Father Alexander Diomedi's 1876 pledge that by relinquishing their forested homeland for the camas prairie south of the lake, the tribesmen would "become a great people." "The whites will eat with you and they will give you money; they

will buy your wood and you will be supported. But if you do not heed me,"
Fr. Diomedi averred, "your children will starve, your wives and daughters
will be unsafe; you yourselves will disappear."[49] The missionary expressed
surprise at his flock's protests. Coeur d'Alene spokesmen countered, to
no avail, "Must we leave this land, where the bones of our fathers mingle
with those of our children? these woods which have supplied us with fuel
and game? this prairie which had fed our horses? this river which has
given us trout and beaver? We are healthy; our children are fat; our wives
are comfortable in our log-houses. We are not like you; you need bread,
we have camos; you require good clothing, we are satisfied with deer-skins
and buffalo robes. We can live comfortably on what you would think poor
and wretched."[50]

Before the religious Black Robes insinuated their beliefs into the
Coeur d'Alene's mental universe, another man identifiable by his somber
habit had laid the legal groundwork for oppression. In the early 1800s,
Chief Justice of the United States Supreme Court John Marshall had
issued a series of legal judgments that reduced all Native Americans to
the status of wards without the right to vote, govern themselves in the
territories they occupied, or petition the government for redress.[51] The
Marshall Court paved the way for federal legislators to effect forced Indian
"removal," second cousin to ethnic cleansing, to federally protected reservations. Forced "assimilation," later understood as cultural dispossession,
was licensed within reservation borders pursuant to an article of Christian faith that, "Kill the Indian, and Save the man" was in everyone's best
interests.[52] In 1873 President Ulysses S. Grant signed an executive order
creating the Coeur d'Alene reservation, which led to a third "protective"
regime, symbolized by the Indian agent, to manage the Coeur d'Alenes'
present and future. "An Indian agent has absolute control of affairs on his
reservation," naturalist George Grinnell remarked near the turn of the
century, "more nearly absolute than anything else that we in this country
know of. . . . The courts protect citizens; but the Indian is not a citizen,
and nothing protects him. Congress has the sole power to order how he
shall live, and where."[53]

As a white outsider asking for the Coeur d'Alene's trust and cooperation, Reichard could not avoid the signs that with the powers vested in
them by Congress, the Office of Indian Affairs and its agents had ushered
the Coeur d'Alene into "a period of profound regression"—socially,

economically, and culturally.[54] Without intending to, she discovered that the picture Catholic missionaries and the U.S. Office of Indian Affairs painted of the Coeur d'Alene as successfully assimilated into modern white Christian culture was exaggerated, if not dishonest. Though some Natives on the reservation were relatively prosperous landowners who hired white laborers to work their farms, many others were landless and destitute. The less fortunate had sold their allotted land for quick cash to non-Indians once the reservation was opened to white settlement by the authority of the Dawes Act of Severalty of 1887. If most adults and children spoke English well, had grade-school educations, and complied with Church prohibitions on Native dress, hairstyles, and all other manner of cultural practices, the infant mortality rate on the reservation was nearly twice the U.S. average.[55]

Reichard discovered by interviewing informants away from the prying eyes of the clergy that the Coeur d'Alenes were also disproportionately plagued by life-threatening diseases including tuberculosis, pneumonia, and influenza. Trachoma, an easily transmitted eye infection that can lead to permanent scarring and blindness if left untreated, affected one in ten Coeur d'Alenes in 1927, with an 80 to 100 percent infection rate among young children.[56] Prohibition had made alcohol abuse more rather than less prevalent on the reservation. Missionaries and Indian agents enforced decrees against traditional dancing, dress, sport, pageantry, arts, and speaking in ancestral languages. Even the most devout Coeur d'Alene was rebuked or ostracized rather than comforted if she wandered from the priests' "ideas of the straight & narrow path."[57]

As it happened, Reichard's impromptu survey of life on a single western reservation coincided with the year-long investigation conducted by the Meriam Commission. Charged with investigating the so-called Indian Problem, the team of nine commissioners visited nearly one hundred Indian Office jurisdictions from coast to coast in an effort to document the actual socioeconomic conditions reservation Indians faced on a daily basis. The Commission's report, published in 1928, showed that American Indians, on average, were poorer, less healthy, and more vulnerable to predatory social and economic forces stemming from misguided federal policies and the insensitive, understaffed bureaucracies that enforced them. It charged that the government's ineffective management of tribal peoples encouraged idleness and dependency that "[broke] their pride in themselves and their Indian race," eroding "the good in the old without replacing it with compensating good from the new."[58]

Reichard was implicated in the Meriam Report as one of those "intelligent, liberal whites who find real merit in [Native American] art, music, religion, form of government, and other things which may be covered by the broad term culture." But her attentive presence on the Coeur d'Alene reservation confirmed that she did not approve of those who, "metaphorically speaking," would "enclose these Indians in a glass case to preserve them as museum specimens for future generations to study and enjoy because of the value of their culture and its picturesqueness."[59] Knowing what it meant to be patronized and constrained by unjust prejudice, Reichard tread carefully as a guest of the Church, much as the Coeur d'Alene did on a daily basis. She appreciated the daily kindnesses of the "obliging" nuns who, in their pretty "little blue & white aprons," attended to her comfort "like Mama Franz herself." At the same time, she was keenly aware that the nuns were the "jolly" emissaries of the same institution that banned the use of the Coeur d'Alene language by students in 1878.

The local priests were helpful and generous with their time, Reichard admitted, but "worse than useless as a [linguistic] help" and strangely, to her mind, uninterested in learning the mother tongues of their Indian neighbors.[60] In late August, the Archbishop of Rome paid a visit to De Smet, creating a palpable buzz bemusing to a nonbeliever. Reichard shelved her personal objections to Church doctrines regarding women and Indians and allowed herself to be "blessed" and made "safe for considerable wickedness for a while" at Mass. The longer she stayed on the reservation, the more she grasped that the restlessness that kept her guessing when or if her informants would meet with her had its roots in a rational suspicion of white do-gooders bearing blessings and promises. Ultimately, Reichard distinguished herself from the Meriam commissioners when she reassessed the "Indian Problem" in De Smet with the remark, "Catholicism is a terrible thing, gets worse the more you learn about it."[61]

•   •   •   ❖   •   •   •

On the wings of yet another successful field season, Reichard's career continued on its linear, upward path. As a novel finale to her first summer in Idaho, she had convinced Pascal George to allow himself to be x-rayed while pronouncing Coeur d'Alene speech sounds in a Spokane hospital, much to her scientific delight.[62] On her return to New York, she decided to try something new in her personal life. From a desire to offer informal evening courses in ethnography in German to the most enthusiastic students enrolled in her Barnard courses, she moved out of the Boas home in New Jersey and into an apartment next door to the college in Morningside Heights. By mid-semester, Dean Gildersleeve informed Reichard of her imminent promotion to the rank of assistant professor. Surprised or not, Reichard understood that her performance as an instructor, scholar, and chair of anthropology more than met with the dean's approval.[63]

The reception given *Social Life of the Navajo Indian*, Reichard's first monograph since her dissertation, was equally gratifying. Reichard had poured enormous energy into its production: three summers of fieldwork, travel spanning most of the eastern half of the Navajo Reservation's twenty-five thousand square-mile expanse and one year of concentrated writing in the United States. Working to complete *Social Life* in Hamburg, she oversaw the drawing of enough genealogical charts and legends to fill a seventy-five-page appendix, which she prefaced with the straight-faced observation, "They do not seem any more complex than they are."[64] Fellow anthropologist Barbara Freire Aitken praised *Social Life* as an application of the "genealogical method on the grand scale" that "will add to Miss Reichard's already high reputation in the field."[65] Elsie Parsons, the book's chief sponsor, was also complimentary. She broke her usual reserve to exclaim, "That is a fine monograph! Admirable presentation."[66]

As *Social Life* began to circulate, Reichard was free to make inroads on her Guggenheim project. Her synthesis of the trove of notes, photographs, and sketches of Melanesian bowls and body ornaments she brought back from Europe quickly outgrew the bounds of a year-end report. The paper she was preparing for the 23rd International Congress of Americanists to be held in New York in September was a stepping-stone in the direction of the two-volume work *Melanesian Design* would become. With Goddard as secretary of the planning committee for the Congress, Reichard also made time to help the busy curator enlist conference presenters and locate travel funds for European scholars, especially Professor Theodor Danzel, one of several Hamburg museum colleagues who had treated her so generously. Anticipating a cheerful reunion with Danzel and his wife in the fall, she offered to host them in her apartment for the duration of their New York stay. Between writing, teaching, tending to her many administrative duties, and lending a hand with conference arrangements, Reichard's professional life was satisfyingly full.

Through the first half of 1928, Reichard's romantic life appears to have been on a similarly happy, even keel. Though they often spent months apart while Reichard energetically pursued her career, Reichard and Goddard took pains to be discreet though not secretive about their union. Goddard not only refrained from hindering Reichard's movements, he egged her on to new adventures. One such adventure was the trip by airplane, her first, that they took together from Berlin to Munich on their way to Rome in 1926. Reichard said of her maiden flight, "It took the first hour to get hold of one's insides . . . [b]ut it was a wonderful experience. And there is no doubt it is the best way to travel in Europe."[67]

When in New York, Reichard and Goddard got in the habit of motoring up to Reichard's rustic cabin in Newtown, Connecticut to escape the spectacular congestion of the city. The woodsy charm of the Swiss chalet–style getaway made a wholesome substitute for indoor plumbing, electricity, and phone service. Gladys was a good cook and she enjoyed producing comfort-food favorites on the cabin's wood-burning stove. Winter weekends without the pressure to account for their whereabouts to anyone but themselves were a rare treat that they didn't abuse.

In late June 1928, Gladys was in Bangor grading exams and keeping Mary Reichard company when she learned Goddard had been suddenly taken ill in the city. Told the fifty-nine-year-old was vomiting violently, Reichard returned to New York the next day to find him only slightly recovered. She called Boas's eldest son Ernst, a physician, for medical advice. Ernst Boas recommended Goddard be thoroughly examined at once, but Goddard stated he would prefer a few days' rest in Newtown before submitting to a physical exam. Reichard consented and they set off for Connecticut together expecting they were in for a brief period of recuperation. Several days later Boas made the trip from his summer home in nearby Cornwall Bridge to check on Goddard's progress. He was encouraged to find Goddard "eating well and digesting," all in all, "considerably better although he looked miserably."[68]

Goddard's condition continued to improve. A few days later, Reichard packed the car for their return trip to New York. Tired but confident that he was on the mend, Goddard asked for a further delay. That evening he had another attack that prompted Gladys to call his youngest daughter Mildred, who arrived in Newtown the next day. Mildred judged that her father's condition "did not seem particularly serious." A shaken Boas later recounted to Parsons, "In the course of Thursday [July 12th] he [Goddard] suddenly became much worse and complained of severe burning of the stomach . . . and this was followed by fainting spells. Gladys called in a local doctor and also my son and another physician who had been put in charge of the case. . . . Meanwhile, however, the fainting spells increased in violence and frequency and he died evidently of heart failure about 11:30 in the evening. My son reached there about 1:30 in the morning."[69]

Within hours of his death, Goddard's body was conveyed to the city for an autopsy that revealed the cause of death to be a perforated stomach related to undiagnosed stomach cancer. Over the protests of Goddard's children, Mrs. Goddard insisted on a funeral—"a horrid ceremony on Saturday," according to Boas. Gladys did not attend. She chose to remain in Newtown, with her former classmate, Ruth Bunzel, who came up from New York as soon as she heard the bad news. By mail, Boas and Parsons pondered the ways they might help their shell-shocked friend cope with the sad turn of events. Anticipating Parsons's thought that summer fieldwork might be a welcome distraction, Boas wrote Elsie, "I had the same idea that you had, that a field trip might be best for [Gladys] and I suggested to her to go to Idaho but she does not want to. I think it may be as well because she is right in the middle of her paper on Melanesian Art and I think she will concentrate on that, which, of course, will also be a desirable distraction from troublesome thoughts."

After attending a memorial service for Goddard at the American Museum he described as "a very cold affair," Boas drafted a tribute to Goddard that captured the devotion and warm humanity of the man Gladys loved.[70] "His interest in anthropology was first fostered by personal, intimate contact with California Indians. It was not the occupation with abstract scientific problems that interested him. It was rather the human interest in their troubles, their thoughts and feelings. . . . The native never appealed to him solely as a subject to be examined and dissected, but as a man or woman who had to be understood as moulded by the culture in which he lived." That was the anthropologist talking. Past all concern that tenderness implied weakness Boas concluded, "We all miss him sorely, not the least myself to whom his personal friendship has meant much for many years—years of severe stress and years of quiet work."[71]

No stranger to loss, Gladys coped with Goddard's death by clinging ever more tightly to her vocation. She ruled out a trip west in favor of polishing her paper, "Form and Interpretation in American Art," for the Congress. Delivering it, she used her time at the podium to voice a mature, eloquent plea for the brand of uplifting, individual-centered humanism Goddard, in league with Boas and Parsons, held anthropology to by word and deed. Those who fancied themselves aficionados of truth and beauty, Reichard observed, shouldn't waste another minute theorizing about the inferiority of Native artists. Anthropologists owed it to their discipline and to society at large to use science to debunk the ethnocentric, condescending myths advanced by their predecessors. "And even if, after many art styles have been analyzed and defined, we should discover—as we have every reason to suspect we shall—that all mankind does not react in the same way, that a taste for Gothic style or for curves, points, or frets is not inborn but due to automatic habits of thinking and acting established by tradition, we shall at least have arrived at a scientific conclusion and we shall cease perpetrating a myth because it is something we like to believe. But most important of all, we shall have an intimate acquaintance with large bodies of primitive art which have real aesthetic value and which would otherwise remain unknown and unappreciated."[72]

·   ·   ·   ◈   ·   ·   ·

Through the winter, Reichard kept Goddard's memory close by continuing his Navajo work. At the request of museum president Henry Osborn, Boas named Reichard along with Parsons, Kroeber, and Sapir to a committee charged with preparing Goddard's unfinished manuscripts for publication.[73] Reichard took responsibility also for dispersing Goddard's professional library to colleagues and admirers. Although Mrs. Goddard was less than pleased with the arrangement, the sad chore brought Reichard and Parsons to a new personal understanding. Parsons had lost her husband of twenty-five years in a motorcycle accident four years earlier. Grief at the death of Goddard, one of Parsons's few close friends, opened old wounds. In a welcome gesture of solidarity, Parsons sent Reichard a check that made it possible for Gladys to purchase a portion of Goddard's library for herself. Gladys responded, "Your note received Wednesday moved me more deeply than I can say. As if you hadn't done enough for us already! . . . [I] had given up hope of having any of Dr. G's books, because of course the ones I wanted are expensive. So you can imagine—you can or you would not have thot of the most understanding thing you could do—what your note meant to me. Perhaps when you are in the wilds with no books I can do some reference work for you or send you the books [you need]."[74]

The first unfinished manuscript Reichard volunteered to edit and publish was Goddard's collection of Navajo texts. Told by Navajo storyteller Sandoval, the texts were "practically ready for the printer."[75] Although she lacked a solid grounding in Navajo linguistics, Reichard was well aware of the deficiencies of her late field partner's phonetic transcriptions.[76] She focused her efforts on illuminating the ethnographic merit of Sandoval's texts which, in her words, illustrated "the beauty of Navajo narrative." The time she spent completing *Navajo Texts* delivered a private linguistic bonus. Through the work Reichard prepared herself for the bigger task of translating and editing the "Blue Eyes" text of the Shooting Chant myth told by Sandoval to "F[ather] Berard & Goddard, paid for by Elsie" circa 1924.[77]

By spring Reichard had plans to return to the Coeur d'Alene reservation for a second lap in the sea of Salishan linguistics. The summer itinerary she laid out before she boarded her train in June seem designed to compensate for the field season she'd missed the previous year. Her route included stops in Berkeley, eastern Washington, Ganado, Santa Fe, and Chicago. At each destination she would mix anthropological business with a touch of sentimental pleasure. Traveling to Oakland on the Milwaukee line—"the best I was ever on"—with Boas's daughter, Helene, and her husband, Cecil, she wrote the Boases, "I did an awful lot of my language [work] on the way out. . . . Cecil [who] was much disgusted at my shoebox of slips, said 'Just like Papa.' Whereupon I answered, 'He made me what I am today.'"[78] By the time she left Berkeley for Spokane, she had reason to be grateful for her good standing with David Goddard, Pliny's eldest son. David, who had recently graduated with honors from the University of California, offered to smooth a sale of a group of his father's books to Father Berard Haile, an associate of Goddard's in Arizona, that his mother had blocked. "I always knew I liked him but never how much until I saw him again. . . . He has a research fellowship and hopes to get his A.M. next year," Reichard said with something akin to parental pride.[79]

The first thing Reichard did when she disembarked in Washington was buy a used car. A Chevrolet she test-drove "rattled [her] all over Spokane" before she saw "the Dodges and was lost." The Dodge she named Carry boasted a fine paint job, "a thermometer, bumpers, transmission locks, and good curtains." Thanks to Carry, Reichard could avoid the harmless but unwanted hovering of the "bleeding hearts at the Mission" by staying at the Hotel Tekoa in the little town of the same name on the Washington side of the state line. The hotel was "not so hot" but it was clean and next-door to another with a cook so adept Reichard joked, "I shall need two berths on the way home."[80]

The greatest virtue of Reichard's off-reservation lodgings was their proximity to the Antelope family allotment. Standing on a grass knoll a few minutes drive from Tekoa was the "large, airy, comfortable" home of Julia Antelope Nicodemus, Reichard's favorite Coeur d'Alene language informant. "Julia is really wonderful," Gladys wrote Boas. "I never saw her in her own setting before & her 'setting' is a high one & she a jewel with many facets. . . . She is most awfully intelligent & I am sure will be good. Besides she has great determination & loves to write." In a complete contrast with her previous stay, Gladys quickly settled into a soothing routine. "I work at a nice table while [Julia] darns, sews or whatever," Reichard wrote Boas, "She has a typewriter & her son Lawrence is typing the Eng. version of the tales." On weekends Reichard drove over to De Smet to type up her notes at the mission school while the sisters were at Mass. If she felt sad or lonely, she didn't complain. "The weather is too heavenly," she wrote home. "Temperature just cold enough for a sweater mornings, marvelous clouds & light effects, earth green with tender grain, wild roses, iris, lupine & other more western flowers, birds everywhere."[81]

The congenial work environment made Gladys and Julia allies as well as confidantes. Reichard learned that Julia was embroiled in an ongoing struggle with Father Post over her refusal to reconcile with her estranged husband, James "Jim" Nicodemus. Jim Nicodemus had deserted Julia and their sons Lawrence and Ben in 1919 for another woman. Sometime in 1928, Nicodemus *père* told Father Post that he wished to be reunited with Julia, both because his current partner had banished him from her bed and because he wanted to "get a hold of [Lawrence]" and "make something of him." The priests assumed that Julia acted out of womanly spite

Julia Antelope with sons Lawrence and Ben Nicodemus (*foreground*), c. 1920.
Museum of North Idaho, cat. no. NA 8–68.

when she ignored their order to take her husband back. Lawrence was
of the opinion that his mother refused Jim because he declined to give
up alcohol as a condition she placed on his return.[82] Reichard's sympa-
thies were further aroused when she found out that the same priests
who frowned on Julia had silenced her older brother, Morris Antelope,
when he criticized the Church's prohibitions against Indian dancing and
regalia. Additional support for the dim view Reichard had of the clergy
came from Julia's son. A star student in Greek and Latin at the Jesuit high

school, Lawrence had aspired as a teenager to become a priest himself.
As a reward for his studiousness, Lawrence was introduced to Pope Pius
XI at the Vatican in 1926. When the pontiff addressed him as "Indiano!
Indiano!" rather than by name, Lawrence's priestly ambitions abruptly
vanished. On returning to Idaho, he realigned his ambitions with those of
his mother and his uncle, who cherished their Coeur d'Alene heritage.[83]

·　·　·　◈　·　·　·

Her bags bulging with "only about 700 pages" of Coeur d'Alene texts to
study for the winter, Reichard packed Carry for the southwest leg of her
journey at the end of July. She left room for a passenger, Barnard student
Charlotte Leavitt, who had spent the summer earning her anthropologist's stripes observing a Plains Sundance ceremony in western Canada.[84]
Gladys had not been in Navajo country since her last trip there with Goddard in 1925, and August 1929 promised a series of glad homecomings in
the Southwest. At Ganado Reichard renewed her ties to the Hubbell clan
by inviting LaCharles, then a senior in anthropology at the University of
Arizona, to accompany her to the Southwest Archeological Conference,
later known as the Pecos Conference, near Santa Fe. With Charlotte and
LaCharles in tow, Reichard headed east to see for herself if the fuss made
over the debut of the Laboratory of Anthropology field school that summer was justified.

The camaraderie, scientific interest, and endlessly enchanting landscape that greeted Reichard in northern New Mexico lifted the last trace
of gloom that had clung to her since Goddard's death. At thirty-six,
Gladys was less coltish than LaCharles, who charmed the sun-kissed
"learned men" in attendance by demonstrating her facility with a yo-yo.[85]
She was less beguiling than Charlotte, against whose cool beauty the male
scientists needed "plenty of defense."[86] The satisfaction Reichard took in
the proceedings was mature and, as usual, equal parts professional and
personal. She made the acquaintance of Mary-Russell Ferrell Colton,
the acclaimed painter and co-founder of the new Museum of Northern
Arizona in Flagstaff, who she admired for creating an institution that
was "a living, growing fact in the community, not only for the storage
and exhibition of archeological material, but for the encouragement of
modern and Indian art."[87] The friendly chats Reichard had with Kroeber,
Sapir, and field school coordinator Alfred Kidder reassured her that their

attempts to deny women a role in the Rockefeller-funded anthropology lab had been thwarted, for the time being at least. Reichard forgot her irritation with Kidder for overlooking Parsons as a potential field instructor on hearing him remark that in the field "his idea of a 'good person' was one who travelled with a bedroll!"[88]

"I would have got more out of the conference had I been more conversant with Pueblo 2a 33 1/3/ xyz but there were plenty of general points which my feeble intelligence could grasp," Reichard chirped to Parsons by mail. "I should say that the outstanding feature—which I consider *very* remarkable—was the lack of emphasis on picayune details. Kroeber & Kidder made a constant effort, with complete success, to consider the summer's work only in its broad aspects. . . . The pottery bugs got together with their shoeboxes & paper bags of sherds between meetings thus sparing us the agony of their arguments." Even Sapir succumbed to the collective merriment long enough to declare the field school experiment a success. He had to admit he'd collected as much Navajo language data with six male students looking over his shoulder as he would have without them. "Sapir is intrigued by the Navajo & goes back to Crystal tomorrow to get more material with his best student [Harry Hoijer]. This on the Chicago Linguistic fund," Reichard informed Parsons placidly. Saying she'd had a fine time in good company she ended her report, "Everyone was sorry you didn't come to the conference. . . . Yours with love, Gladys."[89]

Within a month of Reichard's return to New York, the stock market crashed. October headlines shouted, "Wall Street in Panic," and "Billions Lost" above photographs of stunned investors milling around Lower Manhattan as if struck on the head. Ninety-three-year-old multimillionaire John D. Rockefeller Sr. predicted an immediate economic rebound. Gladys was not so sure. A new degree of pessimism was justified, with a vicious twist, when in late December Marie Boas, Boas's wife, was killed by a speeding motorist while crossing the street a half-block from her Grantwood home. Before the winter was over, Mary Reichard died in Bangor at the age of fifty-five.

These additional brushes with mortality, difficult as each was to accept, made it all the more necessary that Reichard push ahead with a new research design she had been mulling over since the previous summer. Synthesizing all she learned and experienced in the previous ten years, she spent the winter incubating a plan to immerse herself in the daily life of a Native family as a participant, foregoing the anthropologist's usual retreat to a distant camp or hotel at the end of each day. Living in a family encampment for weeks at a time meant she would need to learn to converse in the local language and blend into the group rather than colonize it. If executed properly, she would experience rather than merely observe the rhythms of camp life, mundane and sublime alike, though it meant suffering the indignity of becoming a novice again after having achieved an enviable status in her own society.

The contacts Reichard had in the Southwest and her love of the region made a Navajo family of weavers and chanters the natural choice for her methodological experiment, especially once Parsons agreed to sponsor the project with no strings attached. She set her plan in action by writing Father Haile to ask if he knew of a traditional Navajo family who might accept her as a pupil. To her surprise, Haile made assumptions about her proposal that ignored her qualifications as an anthropologist. "I thot he had my point of view," Reichard grumbled to Parsons. "He answers at length & with great detail showing he doesn't think I know enough even to wash behind the ears! Even mentions a nice house with curtains, easy armchair, etc. I guess except for linguistic help I can count him out."[90]

What Reichard didn't know was that since Goddard's death, Haile had allied himself and his future in anthropology with Sapir. Together, the priest and the professor decided it would be best if Reichard were to be shut out of Navajo studies. "It's all about taking the region out of the Papa Franz-Gladys combination, and I imagine that problem will be still further in the background by the time Gladys is ready to revert to Navaho again," Benedict explained to Mead after Sapir confided in her at the 1928 AAA meeting. "Father Bernard [*sic*] too is making a stand that his [Blue Eyes] manuscript, the big one Gladys was working on, should go to Edward for editorial work, not to Gladys."[91] Haile had been a willing party to Goddard's Navajo projects because they coincided with his ambition to establish himself as the leading authority on Navajo myths and ceremonies. Goddard's death created a void the Franciscan priest was not prepared to fill with a woman colleague, regardless of her abilities as an ethnologist. Orphaned early in life, Haile had spent all but the first three of his fifty-five years in the close-knit, all-male religious hierarchy of the Church. Sapir's high reputation among anthropologists and his imperious manner accommodated Haile's need for a Father Superior in the secular sphere he longed to conquer. Haile may have genuinely believed Reichard would be better off conducting interviews in a frothy Victorian parlor than in a smoke-filled hogan, though it was most convenient for him to imagine her out of the Southwest altogether.

As Haile and Sapir were joining forces against her, Reichard thought she detected a softening of Sapir's bluster. Soon after the 1928 International Congress, Sapir had sent her a "very detailed letter" explaining Navajo prosody. "I think perhaps I shall have to 'sit at his feet' before I start on a practical attack at the language," Reichard wrote Parsons sweetly. "I think it was lovely of him to think of me like that."[92] From her position outside the Benedict-Mead-Sapir clique, Reichard had no way of knowing that Sapir's general outlook on life was neither generous nor lovely. Perpetually embattled, Sapir confided to Benedict early in their friendship, "It fills me with something like horror and melancholy both to see how long and technical a road I must travel in linguistic work, how fascinating its prospect, and how damnably alone I must be."[93] The death of his first wife in 1924 did nothing to slow his nihilistic drift. "I really think I shall end life's prelude by descending into the fastnesses of a purely technical linguistic erudition," widower Sapir wrote Benedict. "There is great comfort in withdrawing from the market-place of so-called human interests and resolutely following a star (a miner's will o' the wisp) so pale, so clear, so remote it can bring neither joy nor disappointment. . . . Must everybody contribute his share toward the saving of humanity? . . . I have no desire to save or help save humanity but merely to try to keep myself as systematically busy as my innate waywardness will allow up to the moment when the demonstrator in anatomy gets tired of his demonstration."[94] Four more years of self-induced frustration led Sapir to fault "THE AGE and the piffle of mental activity" of his contemporaries for his continued disappointments. The "charm and assurance" Edward exuded in public didn't fool Reichard entirely given her rocky history with him, but nor did she doubt that she could earn his respect eventually so long as she kept "a hand on a high trestle" in all her dealings with him.[95]

Reichard's first decade as an anthropologist left no doubt in the minds of those who rooted for her that she had the intellectual brilliance, character, and emotional stamina to excel in her profession. At the 1929 Pecos Conference, she gave evidence that the trials of the past several years had served only to make the world her oyster, savoring of tears but still juicy with nourishment. But while a sense of entitlement or self-pity drew many of her highly educated peers toward cynicism and unhealthy obsession, Reichard responded to the "utterly mad, pervert universe" she lived in by deciding to edge out from under the weight of anthropological tradition and innovate.[96] Stubbornly compassionate, Reichard allowed neither personal sorrow nor generalized cosmic grief to shake her commitment to the "party of humanity."[97] Incapable of narrow-mindedness, she perceived anthropology to be large, to contain multitudes.[98] She did not intend to set a collision course with her professional competitors when she wrote Roman Hubbell in the spring of 1930 to arrange for a new kind of summer arrangement among the Navajo. Could he recommend a local family willing to host her in their camp for months at a time? Roman replied at once. He promised to introduce her to them himself when she arrived in June.

• • • • ◆ • • • • •

CHAPTER 4

WEAVING WOMAN
AT WHITE SANDS

A COMMON MISCONCEPTION OF REICHARD'S NAVAJO-FOCUSED WORK is
that she went to live at *Sai Des Gai* (White Sands Ridge) in the summer
of 1930 to learn how to weave. The charm and accessibility of her 1934
book, *Spider Woman: A Story of Navajo Weavers and Chanters*, reprinted in
each decade of her century but the 1950s, abets the error.[1] Reichard's
correspondence with Parsons makes clear Gladys set herself a bigger,
more complex problem to solve in what would become her signature style.
"I spend many hours a day weaving & the rest working on Navajo [lan-
guage]," she wrote Parsons at the end of her third week at White Sands.
"The weaving is a foil for the language study."

To get a meaningful glimpse of the "mentally-constructed universe"
shared by Navajo people, Reichard was committed to investing the time
needed to learn to speak Navajo as well as to write it.[2] Navajo religion,
Reichard had come to believe, was not only "the integrating force" of
Navajo culture; it offered all Americans a "a renewed sense of the possibilities of human nature."[3] "I have never been so intrigued by a job as by this
one for after all gathering genealogies was a bore, second to none I know
of except recording texts!" Gladys enthused to Parsons. "At suppertime I
suddenly realize I am so tired I can hardly move & it took me two weeks
to figger why. Then I realized that even at my giddiest I have never worked
12 hr. with hardly a break. But it is only a healthy weariness & the results
are a satisfaction."[4]

In June she had stepped off the train in Aztec, New Mexico, met up with
Ann (Axtell) Morris, and headed south in Jonathan, her new Ford. The
two women detoured to Gallup, where Reichard picked up the copy of the
Blue Eyes manuscript that had been mailed to her at Gallup. Returning

to camp for a few nights in northeastern Arizona, Morris spent her days painting watercolor versions of pictographs in Canyons de Chelly and del Muerto while Reichard drove over to Lukachukai to meet with "F. Berard's & Sapir's interpreter," Chic Sandoval, who was helping her translate and analyze Goddard's materials. "All this took a week & finally we landed at Ganado," she wrote. "I chose Ganado because the Hubbells have a better understanding about the 'window curtains' & such than anyone else I know. And my judgment was confirmed. We arrived—Ann left at once— on Fri. night & on Mon. at 9 A.M. I was established in my hogan. Roman knew just the family, Miguelito's, & we went up & asked them to build me a shade. But they had a storage house, bran new & unbuggy—but somehow I never think of bugs now!—which is built just like a hogan only it is dug out & has no smokehole. It is much better protection from wind & rain (if any) than a shade could be. There is lots of wind & papers do fly around. So I have all my things in this house which is only 6 mi. from Hubbell's."[5]

The encampment that would be her mental and spiritual nexus for the next seven years was nestled at the base of its namesake feature, a rise of chalky dunes that parts the surrounding swells of pale pink sand like a shy smile. Pulling up for the first time, she counted five hogans and an assortment of smaller, partially enclosed ramadas or "shades" made of pine boughs standing nearby. Low piñon pine, sage, and juniper dotted the rolling terrain in all directions. Miguelito, the male head of the family, known also as Red-Point, shared the largest hogan with his wife, Maria Antonia. Their three married daughters each had their own hogan. "There are 5 children," Reichard told Parsons—Ninaba, Yikadezba, Yikadezba's baby sister Djiba, Ben, and Dan—"varying in age from 6 mo. (this baby takes steps with help & crawls) to 10 yr. Altogether a very typical family." Pet lambs, inquisitive goats, at least one puppy, and a few well-fed saddle horses drowsed within earshot of their owners. Though Reichard was duly charmed by the pastoral scene that surrounded her, she quickly surmised that the order and tranquility of life at White Sands was not accidental. "[E]very member of this family works almost *all* the time. They have 3 very large herds & believe me, sheep make demands. Constantly, like babies, they 'have the gimmies.' Then this family has irrigated land at Ganado & the men stay away for days farming, coming back occasionally to get us water, bring the news, etc. It's a great life and well organized. Of course it is a fine family, rich, not too conservative, but correctly orthodox *& clean!*"[6]

Reichard's inclination to view Navajo women as more emancipated than westernized women was reinforced when Roman introduced her first to Maria Antonia. A master weaver of local renown, Maria Antonia wore the weight of her sixty-three years with quiet, unhurried dignity. Gladys would later learn that Maria Antonia was born in captivity at New Mexico Territory's Fort Sumner in 1868. While still an infant, Maria Antonia and her family had been released from the U.S. Army detention camp after the signing of the Treaty of Bosque Redondo officially ended the brutal exile of two thousand Navajos from their homeland. Returning to the Arizona Territory, Maria Antonia's parents stopped to rest at Fort Defiance for the winter. Maria Antonia's mother fell sick with measles. An aunt kept the baby girl alive by feeding her milk from a bottle fashioned from a sheep's throat. Four years later, the aunt died and Maria Antonia was given to her maternal grandfather, who took her, against her wishes, to live in his camp near Chinle. Maria Antonia later told her daughters, "my grandfather's wife was a very mean woman. She mistreated me all of my youth and made me herd sheep for her. She treated me like a dog, never had any compassion for me. . . . That's the way I grew up. . . . I became a woman and was able to think for myself."[7]

After marrying and bearing five children (few survived infancy) Maria Antonia worked as a cook at Fort Defiance, where she learned to weave by watching the weavers she was hired to feed. After her first husband deserted her, she met the rather rakish though promising man J. L. Hubbell named Miguelito.[8] Together they relocated to *Lok'aa kin tiel* (Wide Reed House), the place the white traders called Ganado. The couple built an ample hogan at the foot of Red Point Mesa (*Lichii Dez'aii*), close to the Colorado Pueblo wash that threaded past the Hubbell Trading Post. Maria Antonia supported the family through her weaving and working as a housekeeper for Lina Hubbell. Miguelito raised crops and studied (with Blue Eyes) to become a Navajo medicine man or chanter. Their oldest daughter, Atlnaba, earned a reputation as a master weaver by the age of five. English-speaking Marie, whose job it was to tend the sheep even as a toddler, devoted herself to weaving once she returned from the Fort Defiance boarding school as a teenager. Mrs. Ben Wilson, Maria Antonia's youngest, had primary responsibility for the health of the family herd and did not weave.

Because Reichard spoke little Navajo in 1930, Roman explained her proposal to the Red-Point women for her. The weavers were accustomed

to being paid for their expertise. Citified white people with money to
spare were common as fleas on the reservation. The chance to host one
who promised to pay for instruction in weaving without forcing religion
or tiresome interviews on them was a welcome novelty. The weavers listened in silence while Roman spoke. With the slightest of nods in Roman's
direction, Maria Antonia and daughters—for it would be Marie and Atlnaba who assumed responsibility for Reichard's progress as a weaver—the
petition of the "white woman, peculiar in many ways" was summarily
granted.[9]

Miguelito was away from home during Reichard's first visit. When he
returned to camp two days later, she could see that he held a familiar
position in the family structure. "[A]ltho the *pattern* is matrilineal the
practice gives an idea of *patriarchate*," Reichard wrote Parsons. "Peggy
[i.e., Goddard] and I had noticed it & remarked on it but staying with
it has emphasized it in my mind. The old man is looked up to by all &
sundry, surrounded by his children, his sons-in-law to take orders & do
the dirty work. He himself doesn't do any dirty work but gets it done for
himself." Miguelito's vocation often took him away from home, whether
to perform ceremonies lasting as many as nine consecutive nights or
to collect the herbs, colored stones, and feathers that were the tangible
tools of his trade. His frequent absences prompted Reichard to observe
that Navajo women were not as different from her eastern peers as she
supposed. "Nav. women are awful clinging vines!" she once sighed. "Their
husbands do many things for them, set up [a] loom at their dictation,
make all the weaving implements & do many heavy things. But, like us, if
their husbands are not home, they can do the stuff themselves, & by darn,
they do!"[10]

Finding Gladys settled in a dugout built to shield corn or hides from
the elements, Miguelito brought the white stranger into the family fold
through an ancient, socially imperative linguistic ritual. "The day after my
arrival at White-Sands, Red-Point gave me a name," Reichard recounted
in *Spider Woman*. "He has called me Weaving-Woman. I know very well the
Navajo liking for nicknames, especially names that mock at physical shortcomings, and I am pleased to have drawn one so dignified." It was equally
important that Reichard be immediately integrated in the Navajo system
of reciprocal address. "I know that the Navajo are more likely to use relationship terms than names," she explained in *Spider Woman*. "The circle

included by any one of these terms is a large one. Any woman belonging to my clan, whether blood relation or not, if she is of my generation, is a sister. . . . So it is not difficult for me to give Red-Point the most respectful term befitting his generation and mine. He is my 'maternal grandfather'; Maria Antonia, his wife, is my 'old mother,' that is my 'maternal grandmother.' But their children, Marie, Atlnaba, and Ben Wilson's wife are my contemporaries and I can hardly call them 'mother' or 'aunt.' In this free-lance sort of relationship one reserves the pleasure of inconsistency and I call them 'younger sister.' One reason they are interested in my age is to know whether to call me 'older' or 'younger sister.'"[11]

Reichard would have to make great strides in Navajo language before she discovered that the names and roles conferred on her initially were provisional, practical, social necessities drawn from the rich vocabulary Navajo speakers employ to express a panoply of "degrees of intimacy." Had she approached the Red-Point family in different circumstances, she later explained, family members might have referred to her sudden presence in their midst by asking each other the Navajo equivalent of "What in the world is that thing?" Introduced as she was by a person Red-Point and Maria Antonia "addressed as 'son,'" Reichard instead was received as "a 'person' whose credentials they were willing to inspect." "Since the stranger was to stay with them," Reichard wrote about her younger self, "she was in a position susceptible to 'favor, befriend, cooperate with, collaborate with, take sides with, become a partner to, identify self with, trust.'"[12]

While acquiring the "matter-of-fact" Navajo ideas of kith and kin was exactly the sort of information Reichard sought through indirection and inductive reasoning, it was her ethic of non-coercion that gave those methods power. Her readiness to relinquish control of the ethnographic encounter had its roots in the anti-patriarchal, feminist self-consciousness she'd absorbed from Elsie Parsons. Parsons taught that an anthropologist must make common cause with Native informants who, for their own motives, wished to record and preserve their cultural heritage with the aid of a white scientist. If tribal members risked censure or worse for working with her, Parsons believed in their right as autonomous agents to resist tribal norms. The power differential between anthropologists and their "subjects" could be compensated for, in Parsons's view, with a genuine rapport that was egalitarian, collaborative, empathetic, and mutually

Maria Antonia's granddaughter, Ninaba (*center*), and relatives
cooking near the Red Point Mesa and Hubbell ranch, c. 1935.
Museum of Northern Arizona MS22–2-10–20 Box 2.4.

respectful. "It takes something of an artist to listen to a folk-tale as well as
to tell it," Parsons wrote, "and between artists theories of social inequality
do not obtrude."[13]

Reichard broadened the extent of Parsons's positive rapport to
include intermediaries. "Why did I find an auspicious introduction to
the people upon whom I was inflicting myself?" Reichard later wrote of
her early days among the Navajo, "[O]ne is the character (personality?)
of the Navaho people and their culture . . . and the other, the character
of the white friends who introduced me to them. These friends included
anthropologists, traders, government officials, and missionaries. What
distinguished each of these individuals from others in the same category
was a willingness to view Navaho differences as legitimate and proper
without assuming the customs or habits as inferior to ours. I might have
as easily been introduced by snobs or bigots, in which case I would have
had to live down the shortcomings of my intermediaries as well as my
own."[14]

Reichard said sacrificing her presumed position of authority threw
open the doors to "one of my richest" field experiences.[15] It also gave
chance a principal role in her research methodology. "Often I did not

know what my goal was," she admitted, but in reality she seemed intent
on letting the key lessons of Navajo tradition find her.[16] Taking a selfless,
adventitious approach to ethnography made Reichard vulnerable to criticism and mockery by her hosts, whether she fumbled at weaving, speaking
Navajo, or carrying out social imperatives discovered by tripping over
them. The comedic notes she struck in *Spider Woman* derived less from
the scenes of weavers and chanters pleasantly at work she presented than
from Reichard's depictions of the cultural pratfalls she committed before
an audience of "faithful, tolerant, dependable, and generous" Navajos.[17]
In contrast to her relative ineptitude, the weavers' nonchalant capacity
for creative absorption recommended the Navajo artisans without roman-
ticizing them. "The hands of these women are so skillful that I despair
of ever competing with them in dexterity. They can even talk while they
twine and braid and loop," Reichard marveled. "They do not seem to
think about what they are doing. But let one of them make a move out of
order, the other laughingly reminds her of her mistake." "[B]y some subtle
alchemy [they] have compounded calmness and competence in a blend
whose name is accomplishment. The secret of their formula, I suspect, is
that they guard against the impurity of fussiness."[18]

Reichard's own accomplishment during her first summer at White
Sands was to regard her capacity for blunder in circumstances she barely
understood as an intellectual asset. "I probably wouldn't have learned so
much had I made fewer mistakes," she wrote home.[19] She also recognized
the limitations imposed on her "non-Navajo type of mind" in the short
space of just three months of participant-observation.[20] "I may not know
more facts about the Navajo—hardly true!—but at least I understand
them a lot better," she wrote Parsons in August. "The only thing I could
do to 'belong' more would be to be initiated, which means to belong
ceremonially. Otherwise I am theirs!"[21]

There was, as Reichard explained to Parsons, "another, purely subjective, side to the picture" of the deep play she engaged in at White Sands.
"I know you say a fieldtrip is neutral & one is neither happy or unhappy.
True only to a degree. Like research at home there comes a minus time.
But I want you to know that there is a kind of unexplainable balm about
the S.W.—you doubtless know it already. I found it last summer & needed
it even more this. There is a peace which comes to us at evening when the
air is cool & the sun sets, the mountains become purple rose & blue—we

are high in cedar & piñon country, a most comfortable setting—& night settles down with the sheep in the corral & stars & the moon & the air! Most people would hate the quiet—it *is* quiet—but I love it. It is the sort of thing some writers (a few) have gotten across, but somehow needs experiencing."[22]

The physical embodiment of Reichard's altering consciousness was her trusty, humble dugout. Weaving in it through the day, she exhausted her mind trying to profit from Marie's unhurried instruction. In the evenings, she lay prone on its roof of packed sand and surrendered her pride to the indifferent beauty of twilight. The scrupulous, striving scientist made peace with her inner artist. "Leaning against my bed roll, I have leisure to enjoy the panorama," she wrote in *Spider Woman*,

> At this, the hour of sunset, the Southwest condenses its charm. The desert addict may not know it, but this hour is the cause of his nostalgia when he is elsewhere—yes, even when he is here. My eye roves from the rose-colored sand still covered with gray-green grass because of late rains, to the hoar-green sagebrush and over the somewhat lumpy plain abundantly dotted with pine and juniper. It is too early in the season for clouds, and the clear turquoise of the sky blends with pure lemon, gold, and red. To the east, at my right, a piñon and a juniper mingle their branches so closely I am sometimes deluded into thinking the composite is a botanical freak.
>
> There's a gentle tinkling of bells from the south and east. Shouts accompany a collective thud of little feet becoming louder as it slowly approaches. A schoolgirl twirls a rattle, a tin can in which several pebbles have been enclosed, on the end of a string, causing the flock to veer toward the corral. Ninaba's red velvet shirt is a jewel in a wiggling fuzzy white setting. The approaching flock is like a mob of impolite humans. The goats belch and cough; one stops to nibble a likely sage bush; another eats the lower branches of a pinyon. Still another finds its way into my house. I think of chasing it out, but I am too comfortable to get up; and anyway there is nothing it can harm. The sheep munch digressively along, slowly as they dare, ever interrupted by their herders; a ewe calls her wandering bleating lamb, lost through curiosity. . . .

Old trite phrases come to me—"witching hour," "peace that passeth all understanding," a Navajo group I never before fully comprehended:

> *With beauty above me I lie down,*
> *With beauty below me I lie down,*
> *With beauty before me I lie down,*
> *With beauty behind me I lie down,*
> *With beauty all around me I lie down.*[23]

· · · ◈ · · ·

Reichard was not the only anthropologist of the 1930s to slip off "the rough hair shirt" of strict historical empiricism and give it an original cut.[24] In her case, she fashioned a less prickly epistemological garment from her experiential trials: learning to speak Navajo; mastering the various lengths of broomstick, reed, and peeled sticks that with the batten, comb, and spun wool were the weaver's tools; and enduring interminable nights in smoky ceremonial hogans. Holding firm to the belief that "anthropology seeks to discover rather than to change the customs of a people," Reichard aspired to avoid becoming the victim of her covert prejudices.[25]

Ruth Benedict and Margaret Mead took a different approach to humanizing their science. They set their sights on escaping the tyranny of "discrete items of behavior" in order to identify a set of universal, integrating principles by which the anthropologist could convert the "rags and tatters" of alien cultures into coherent wholes.[26] Ignoring the ethnocentric bias attendant on a heuristic that treats each culture as if it were a "personality writ large," the co-founders of the Culture and Personality school of anthropology emphasized a therapeutic goal for ethnology. By "piecing together bits from the old, sometimes vigorous, sometimes dull" ethnographies written by other anthropologists, Benedict and Mead sought to derive what Sapir called "the medicine of society."[27]

While Edward Sapir pursued his own brand of culture and personality-style inquiry, he rejected the therapeutic model of culture study for being based on a reification of culture as an entity existing independently of individual people. He viewed culture as "located not 'above' people, but 'between' them," as an open-ended dialectic between "creative personalities" interacting in real space and time.[28] Ironically, Reichard's working theory of culture as a dynamic, overdetermined phenomenon powered by less than predictable actors more closely resembled Sapir's individualistic, organic conception. In her many humbling encounters with untidy linguistic variation among speakers of a single language she seems to have concluded independently that, to paraphrase Sapir, all human-made constructs leak.[29] Importantly, Reichard rejected the "implicit elitism" of Sapir's divided culture concept, which distinguished between "genuine" or high culture and "spurious" or mob culture as determined by his personal tastes. Nor did she condone the equally elitist premise voiced by the would-be culture doctors of her day that an anthropologist was entitled to "trust her knowledge of the shape and feel of a culture of which she was recording only a small part."[30] Reichard's insistence on "participat[ing] in a living culture where she could speak the language and get to know people well as individuals" represented an alternate view of anthropology's *raison d'etre*.[31] The patterns of thought, emotion, and desire she hoped to identify through her extensive, immersive participation in Navajo society, she reasoned, should reflect as accurately as possible the Navajos' view of themselves. The simulacrum of culture armchair theorists relied on to "bound the profession that guaranteed their public identity" was of little interest to her.[32]

When speaking to supporters, Reichard summed up her Navajo research concisely saying, "[Y]ou see it is again parallel, lang., religion & rugs. I don't think [Navajo ethnography] can be done satisfactorily otherwise."[33] Her ongoing experiment at White Sands did put her on "the lonely road of her convictions," and like any explorer of the unknown, she was occasionally beset by self-doubt. [34] "I just want to tell you how much I appreciate your keeping on believing in my job & the way I am doing it," she wrote Parsons in 1932. "I say this because you & Papa Franz are about the only ones who do."[35] She also worried that by associating herself with a prosperous and harmonious Navajo family she was more susceptible to "Margaret [Mead]'s and [Bronislaw] Malinowski's problems," that of being easily tricked by her informants into mixing fact with fiction.[36]

Reichard met the greatest resistance to her research mission from the men who viewed themselves as in command of Navajo linguistics, despite her attempts to reassure them that she was interested only in a "practical attack" on the language.[37] Twice she stopped off at the University of Chicago on her way to Arizona for lessons in Navajo phonology and vocabulary from Sapir. Though she declared Sapir an excellent teacher, as an experienced second-language learner she was wise to the limitations of classroom-based, analytical language instruction. "I love the language but have to learn it blindly," she let Parsons know. "None of Sapir's stuff is available. I stopped in Chicago a mere half day & his help was out of all proportion to the time spent, but after all Nav. is a hell of a language what with length, pitch accent, verbs with a dozen principal parts,—the verbs are my Jonah—& all the rest. The F[ranciscan] F[riars'] vocabulary is very helpful but the grammar is *nil*. So I collect necessary phrases & learn them, even use them, & weeks after it dawns on me what they mean analytically. Well, perhaps that is the way to learn a language properly. . . . Do you know Sapir didn't even know the [Navajo] word for 'yes'! Erudition *can* go to seed."[38]

Conscious of her late start at Navajo, the thirty-seven-year-old anthropologist didn't dream of attaining perfect fluency—"Now I am no Polyanna"—but if weaving was a foil for language learning, aiming for competency in Navajo was her ticket to full participation in nearly every sphere of Navajo life.[39] "I like to talk," Reichard said by way of explaining her knack for attracting Navajo individuals to her cause. "The Navaho consider the ability to converse readily a desirable resource. The words that express the aptitude are so flattering that one would never use them about himself."[40]

The Navajo's appreciation of "good talk as entertainment" coincided with another "ideal" Gladys shared with them: an admiration for "expenditure of effort." Speaking of the art of chanting or weaving, Reichard observed, "If a white woman seems willing to apply herself and spend the time necessary to learn it step by step, she is probably entitled to more serious help than one who stays a few days merely asking questions. . . . If a white man seriously and unhurriedly exerts himself to grasp a part of it, and even tries to learn the language, he has demonstrated an approved attitude that should be encouraged."[41] By disdaining the shortcut, Reichard earned the place of respect and trust she was granted within the Red-Point milieu just as she had in the Columbia circle. Sustained, concerted effort had its costs. "I have a terrible time to get at writing," she once wrote Parsons half-apologetically, "because the Navs are always visiting me. But then we talk & I learn & that is what I am here for. . . . We struggle along in Navajo & it is surprising how many ideas we get across to each other. I am most proud when I get back from a trip to be able to describe the high spots to them. Of course their being *very* intelligent & good at guessing is the most important factor."[42]

As predicted, Reichard's increasing command of spoken Navajo steadily increased her privileges on the reservation. After two summers devoted to weaving and language study, Reichard began crisscrossing the rugged eastern half of Diné Biyékah to expand her understanding of family life in a wider context. Alone or with Roman Hubbell along as an interpreter, she witnessed variations in living conditions, practice, and belief that were "stacked with implications" for the comparative problems in personality and variation studies that absorbed her eastern colleagues. "You have no idea how exciting & interesting my work is this summer," she bubbled to Boas. "The possibilities are infinite."[43] Looking back on these weeks and months, Reichard would later label them an idyll. In the moment, she confessed during a rare pause in the action, "I don't know if I'm on my head or ear. But anyway it's a great life, only too short."[44]

Living and traveling in the Southwest gave Reichard the chance to build a social network of European Americans that extended beyond that of the Hubbell family. It was no accident that many of these new southwestern contacts were women. Since the early 1900s, the region had boasted dozens of women scholars, artists, reformers, writers, and adventurer-seekers who lacked the "strength of mind not to need a career."[45] These driven Anglo "daughters of the desert" included Mabel Dodge, Laura Armer, Louisa Wetherill, Mary Roberts Coolidge, and Erna Fergusson, just a few of the intrepid women whose active roles in exploring the cultural landscapes of the Southwest inspired other women to feel they could have a home there as well. The most important white woman to Reichard's progress as a specialist in Navajo studies in the early '30s was Franc Newcomb. A New Mexican trader, artist, and mother of two, Newcomb was not, initially, a familiar figure at the Hubbell Trading Post. Word had reached Reichard at Columbia that Newcomb was reproducing ceremonial sandpaintings on paper with the permission of "her" Navajo "medicine man," Hastiin Klah.[46] Unable to find Navajo youth willing to undertake the long and arduous training required to become a respected chanter, Klah had become convinced that the only hope of perpetuating the ceremonial knowledge he'd amassed over his lifetime was to create a written and pic-torial record of it. In 1917 he invited Newcomb to sketch the sandpaintings

he made during an exhibition version (without patients) of the Yeibichai
Ceremony. Watching his friend struggle to re-create the images spread
before her on the desert floor, Klah offered to personally instruct her in
the art. Newcomb brought heavy tan wrapping paper cut into twenty-inch
squares, "a water-color painting outfit," and "children's colored pencils" to
their next meeting. Together they drew and painted until Newcomb had
a sufficient grasp of the canonical figures to make accurate copies on her
own. "It took a couple of weeks of our spare time, but finally I had my first
four sketches of Navaho sand paintings, which number grew to be almost
five hundred in the next twenty years."[47]

   "I venture to say hers is the most scientific collection of sand-paint-
ings," Reichard wrote Boas of her find. "She has been working on them
for 12 yrs, & is a greater hound for accuracy than for beauty (sales value
I mean)."[48] Where others saw a frazzled trader's wife, housekeeper, and
hobbyist eager to profit from her friendship with a renown Navajo chanter,
Reichard discovered a kindred spirit trying to carve out a room of her own
against daunting odds. Newcomb had gotten her start in the Southwest
when as a young woman she left her home in Wisconsin to accept a position as a schoolteacher at Fort Defiance. She married Arthur Newcomb
in 1914 and soon afterward they opened a trading post in Nava, later
renamed Newcomb, on the eastern slopes of the Chuska Mountains.[49] At
first her interest in Navajo sacred arts developed for "the fun of collecting
even tho I never get any fame for doing so."[50]

   Newcomb's ambition to be recognized for her skills grew with the size
and quality of her sandpainting collection. Then in 1921, Boston heiress
and self-taught anthropologist Mary Cabot Wheelwright knocked at Newcomb's door asking for information about local Navajo ceremonies. The
Newcombs introduced Wheelwright to Klah, which sparked an intense
collaboration between the Bostonian and the Navajo sage that culminated
in the creation of the Museum of Navajo Ceremonial Art on Museum
Hill above Santa Fe in 1937.[51] Unfortunately, Wheelwright's fortune and
imperious nature relegated Newcomb to the role of artist-for-hire. Wheelwright wasn't interested in sponsoring Newcomb's independent work.
The money she paid Franc for driving her to sings, introducing her to
Navajo ceremonialists, and sketching sandpaintings came with the expectation that the patron and not her "liegeman" deserved the credit for her
results.[52] Franc had little experience negotiating with the moneyed set.

Before she met Reichard she had found a potential patron in Wendell Bush, a philosophy professor at Columbia, who tried to commission a series of sandpainting replicas from her by mail. Newcomb wanted the commission, but by not understanding her prospective client's requirements, she couldn't close the deal.

Foremost in Reichard's appraisal of Newcomb was the thought that, "Our information pooled is worth a lot more than twice each separate."[53] In particular she referenced her desire to publish Blue Eye's Shooting Chant myth for which Newcomb had "a marvelous & almost complete set of [sand]paintings." No one had ever before published the text of a Navajo myth together with its corresponding sandpaintings. "Now if we could get 30, 40, or 50 of [the sandpaintings that belong to] the Shooting Chant (we have Male & Female [versions]) it would be a great coup for Nav. science as well as for art," Reichard proposed to Boas. "This set of pictures which is the most complete & systematic of any (4 unduplicated) and belongs to Mrs. N. exclusively. Miss Wheelwright has nothing to do with it." Anticipating Boas's skepticism at involving an amateur in a costly art book, Reichard made it clear she viewed Newcomb as a peer. "I think Franc ought, if at all possible, get royalties. She has worked long & conscientiously; she has put a lot of her own money into getting them beside & if she gets any more it will go back the same way."[54] When Boas came through with the funds that made their partnership official, Newcomb responded to Reichard's news as no self-conscious New York hipster ever would. "I certainly feel like saying 'Oh, boy!! May I, to a college instructor?'" she effused. "This winter has almost taken the starch out of me, but I have come to life after receiving your letter. Many thanks for the check."[55]

In Reichard Newcomb found a sponsor, a mentor, and a friend rolled into one. On winter nights after her girls were asleep and her paints were put away, Franc unburdened herself to Gladys in page after page written in a looping hand. Strewn with Newcomb's favorite punctuation, the long dash, exclamation points in groups of two and three, and plenty of random quotation marks, capitals, and underlining, the letters record the anxiety created by Newcomb's beloved but expensive sideline. Franc knew Gladys understood when she complained in her cartwheel style about the ambivalence she felt after she drove to a remote ceremony from her winter house in Farmington: "my time for six days, groceries for the Sing, a dollar each day for the medicine man, besides about a dollar and a half each day spent for cigarettes for the [sand]painters. Then the afternoon that [the chanter] was at the house I gave him $3.00 and the interpreter $2.00. If I count in the expense of running the car it brings the total up to more than I can afford. So I hope there are not any more [sings] until I get back to living on the Reservation."[56] Juggling unpaid work and family with a guilty conscience took a toll on Newcomb's health. When Reichard asked how she was feeling after another hectic winter, the New Mexican replied, "I am quite alright now but am not spending all my time sitting at the table 'drawing.' Three hours a day is my schedule and that does not hurt my eyes or my 'blood pressure.'"[57]

Hard put as she was to meet the demands of her domestic life, Franc wasn't jealous of Reichard's easier circumstances. Like the Navajo weavers and chanters who were her neighbors, Newcomb had an abiding respect for Weaving Woman's tenacity. "And so you are writing on South Sea Island Art—too!!," she marveled to Reichard. "How do you do it?? You make me feel quite like a *flat* tire with the little that I do!!"[58] "Well I can't tell you how glad I am to have the privilege of knowing you," she admitted openly, "—and with what pride I say 'my friend Gladys Reichard!'"[59]

· · · ❖ · · ·

As Reichard's competency in Navajo social norms increased, she widened her sphere of inquiry to include tribal affairs. She got her first taste of Navajo self-governance beneath the rain-proof boughs of an eighty-foot fir tree, surrounded by the inviting aroma of roasting mutton and kid, on a mountain saddle above Lukachukai.[60] Stimulated by her romantic surroundings, Reichard did her best to concentrate on improving her Navajo. "They usually speak in English first," she explained to Boas, "then in Nav. & it is surprising how much I learned in the two days."[61] Mostly she gained a deeper appreciation for Roman Hubbell. "Roman knows Nav. *very well*—the Indians say he speaks without an accent—& there were many good interpreters, so I learned *a heap*." "This is *purely* incidental," she confided in Parsons, "but Roman is the handsomest man I ever knew, & is just swell to go with."[62]

Lighter moments aside, Reichard considered the systematic oppression of American Indians, referred to as "Americanization," onerous. She began to frequent Navajo council meetings where she heard evidence of

Roman Hubbell and Gladys Reichard with Navajo woman outside summer
shelter. Possibly Miguelito's Ranch, c. 1935. *Image no. 30566, Dale Bullock Photograph
Collection. Courtesy of State Archives of New Mexico.*

the moral bankruptcy of the Indian Bureau and the American business-
men from those they oppressed. As she traveled the reservation to attend
Navajo ceremonies, she listened to first-hand accounts of Navajos who
were whipped, starved, or chained to their beds at night for daring to
escape from Bureau boarding schools. Elderly chanters bent her ear with
concerns that their children were being educated for neither the white
cash economy nor for a traditional life that could sustain them physically
and spiritually. She came to realize that without widespread literacy in
Navajo and English, the Navajo were beholden in every sphere of public
life to white men who could curtail their rights with a stroke of a pen.

    The Navajo were not at the center of the first legal controversy in
Indian country to command Reichard's full attention, but she saw its
ramifications for them clearly. The case gave her the measure of Special
Commissioner of Indian Affairs Herbert Hagerman, former governor of
the New Mexico Territory and longtime factotum in southwestern Indian

affairs. In 1930 Hagerman allegedly colluded with the Atchison, Topeka and Santa Fe railroad and the Indian Bureau to push through a deal giving the railroad company title to a section of the Hualapai Reservation known as Peach Springs. The steam engines that plied the Southwest depended on the waters of the Colorado River. The Hualapai's "inherent" ownership of the Peach Springs section, whether by tradition or federal executive order, was in Hagerman's eyes the flimsiest of barriers to Progress. Hagerman's crony, U.S. Attorney John Gung'l of Arizona, attempted to block a lawsuit the Justice Department brought on the Hualapai's behalf. The Hualapai rallied fellow tribesmen, other Native groups struggling to save their land, and the Indian Rights Association to their cause.[63] Reichard let Boas know she was following these events closely. "I have the lowdown on Hagerman & the entire gang. It is all embodied in two thick volumes of Senate printing & is not my idea of entertaining reading at all. But I think I have the problem, factions, etc. well in mind now."[64]

The sordid history of land-grabbing by U.S. bureaucrats made Reichard skeptical when first-term President Franklin Delano Roosevelt gave Secretary of the Interior Harold Ickes the green light to nominate John Collier as commissioner of Indian Affairs. Collier had a reputation as an ambitious, silver-tongued crusader. To his detractors, he was a vengeful fanatic eager to embarrass his foes, many of whom had enjoyed long tenures in Congress. To his supporters, he was an honest man who couldn't be bought, and therefore an anomaly in Washington, D.C. The Hubbells settled in Collier's corner after extreme weather in the winter of 1931–32 reduced Navajo herds by more than 10 percent, leaving both Navajo and trader hungry. The Hubbells called on Collier as executive secretary of the American Indian Defense Association to lobby for federal aid. The success he had in locating funds for short-term Navajo relief marked him as a friend of the entire reservation community.[65]

In Reichard's eyes, the Hubbells' rosy regard for Collier lacked a proverbial grain of salt. By temperament, Collier was a romantic. He had first entered the fight for Indian autonomy after he and his family spent the winter of 1920 as guests of Mabel Dodge in Taos. Under Dodge's influence, Collier became convinced that the inhabitants of Taos Pueblo belonged to a race that "possessed the fundamental secret of life—the secret of building great personality through the instrumentality of social institutions."[66] Collier began writing articles that wondered if the "non-rational world-view of magic and animism and occult romanticism" didn't offer "civilized" man an alternative to Americanization, that spiritual genocide being waged "through proscription and slow killing" against all moderns in the name of Progress. If so, he argued, "tribal relationships must be conserved, encouraged and helped to make their own adaptations" as a hedge against the extinction of the human essence by the machine.[67] Remove the barriers to Indian traditions and beliefs, and "expression along many lines of literature, of the arts, of religion and philosophy will come into being. The ancient-modern Indian affirmation of the deathless man-nature relationship will flow into poetry and symbolic art of cosmic intensity, tranquility and scope." Tribal peoples, Collier would later proclaim, offered "one great message to the world": "Through his society, and only through his society, man expresses greatness; through it he unites with the universe and the God, and through it he is freed of all fear."[68]

Although Reichard had too much direct experience with too many distinct American tribes to concur with Collier's homogenous view of "the Indian," she was willing to hear him out. "The political situation is interesting if shocking & it would be amusing if one could contemplate the results with any degree of equanimity," she wrote Boas in 1933. "The Navajo Council meets next Fri. & Sat. & then I will get a slant on John Collier. My friends say he wants to do right but, as we suspected, is throttled by red tape, existing conditions & the spoils system."[69] After hearing Collier speak at the Fort Wingate council meeting, Reichard was cautiously optimistic. "I guess I'm sold on John Collier now," she said. "Has of course some crazy notions but at least he has notions & the guts to try to put them over."[70]

Collier succeeded with Reichard by proposing an evidence-based approach to solving major socioeconomic problems on the reservation. He outlined a land conservation plan for the Navajo Reservation aimed at addressing the increasing herd sizes that were tied to rapid growth in the human population. Flashing charts and graphs onstage, Collier advised that the poor, arid soil under their feet was fast eroding. Undernourished herds of sheep, goats, horses, and cattle had to be drastically reduced at once to prevent them all perishing for lack of forage. To that end Collier had convinced Congress to appropriate nearly six million dollars in support of the Indian Emergency Conservation Work bill, a good portion of which would go to pay Navajo laborers to build dams, ditches, and fences, practice erosion control, and learn to operate heavy machinery under the supervision of bureau personnel. For Navajo cooperation in his conservation program, Collier pledged to replace an icon of the bureau's worst abuses, the government boarding school, with day schools where Navajo language, dress, and manners would be welcome. He assumed no Navajo adult would mind sacrificing a few hundred thousand emaciated beasts in exchange.[71]

Most persuasive to Reichard was Collier's evident desire to represent the interests of his Native American clients over those of white profiteers and lifetime bureaucrats. "The business of doing away with incompetent whites is only too true, but when it comes right out in a meeting is a bit shocking," she conceded.[72] The commissioner's attitude toward Christian missionaries paralleled her own resentment of the toll Christian zeal took on Native communities, where denominations competed for Navajo converts using access to social services such as hospitals and schools as bait. Aggressive proselytizing of Navajos by Protestant and Catholic clergymen undermined the authority of Navajo chanters, adding to the drought in willing apprentices. Reichard sympathized with an unnamed Navajo headman interviewed by Erna Fergusson who raged, "Why don't these missionaries go home? Why do they come here? Why do they bother us? We have a good religion. It is a religion of good. It teaches good. It tells us not to bother anyone. It is the same religion for all the People. Now come these missionaries with seven religions. They all talk different. They divide our people. They make trouble among us. Why don't these missionaries go home?"[73] Her experiences on the Coeur d'Alene Reservation were front of mind when she declaimed bluntly to Boas, "I don't know if [Collier] will succeed in disgorging [the reservation missionaries] but he certainly is going to try. They commit more immoralities in a week than the Navs they are teaching do in a lifetime."[74]

As soon as Collier announced he was following Roosevelt's lead in establishing a brain trust filled with anthropologists, Reichard volunteered her services as a linguist and ethnologist versed in Navajo Reservation life as it was.[75] At the bureau's invitation, the following spring she "went to Washington to tell them in words of one syllable that the Government already had in its hands the means of recording Indian languages and had the symbols on its printing presses; they did not know this."[76] Collier, Assistant

Commissioner William Zimmerman, and bureau director of education Dr. Will Carson Ryan, a contributor to the Meriam Report, explained to Reichard that they wished to close the worst government boarding schools and open multiuse community centers where Navajo families preferred to live. Promoting literacy in Navajo among The People was their top priority. "Briefly, they intend to try to establish these community centers which will take care of adult education in a practical way before it concerns itself with children," she reported to Parsons afterward. "I think it is a swell idea if they keep the complexity out which is hardly to be hoped."[77]

The bureau's new approach to Navajo education fired Reichard's imagination. "I am so intrigued by this idea," Reichard told Newcomb in March 1934, "that I am going to have a school next summer to teach the proposed [Navajo] leaders how to write." "We are to have pencil, paper and a blackboard, otherwise the school will be like life at Miguelito's, except that we will have a cook. I am awfully thrilled about the experiment."[78] Reichard's "General Plan" had landed on Dr. Ryan's desk less than a month after her Washington meeting. Steering clear of past Indian Office educational models and practices, she insisted that it "be held on the reservation with the Indians themselves living in hogans and in no way tied up with any of the agency plants, such as use of boarding schools." Up to twenty-four students, to be selected by Reichard from employees of the Indian Service and Soil Conservation Office as well as ranchers and returned college students, would camp at or near White Sands for one or both of two four-week sessions. Government employees were to be paid their regular salary to participate; the bureau would pick up the costs of room and board for all participants, cook included.[79]

Reichard's role, she made clear, was to design the curriculum and act as a literacy trainer. Her understanding of Navajo social relationships and the ways speakers use their language to create and reinforce social boundaries and privileges was paramount. As a linguist, she was able to distinguish between the need for precision in language documentation and the equally salient objective of establishing a written tradition that Navajo learners accepted with pride of ownership. Reichard put her qualifications to Roman in layman's terms. "You need not worry about my feebleness at Navajo, the important thing is that I know how to teach them to teach themselves and me and that is far more important than [my] learning [Navajo]."[80]

The Hogan School opened at White Sands as scheduled on July 1, 1934. One hogan served as a classroom. The others, with Reichard's cozy dugout, stood ready to house students and teacher. Although the facilities lacked city amenities, Reichard saw to it that the Indian Bureau paid Miguelito rent of $25 per month for their use, a rate that pleased both landlord and tenant. After the Fourth of July festivities wound down, the group grew gradually to include a healthy cross-section of the reservation: two white staffers from the Indian Service; Adolph Bitanny, a Navajo man who was a student at the University of New Mexico; "a little boy of 10 & everything else in between."[81]

As Reichard had promised, the Hogan School didn't run in the ruts of bureau tradition. "The Navajo are born clowns," she told Parsons, "and the best student is accustomed to lie on one of the tables with his head and feet hanging down all the while writing his Navajo perfectly. He is much quicker (and more careless) than the others so he puts in his time making wisecracks which, to me at least, are not annoying. . . . All this bothers the others not at all. The school is like a Chinese one, everybody thinks out loud, but for himself, not for his neighbor."[82] Reichard delighted in the carefree informality of the school, her only concern being that everyone make strides in learning to write in Navajo. "All pedagogical, psychological & educational methods flew to the winds of heaven & having flown, how those students did learn!" she enthused. "There are three outstanding carryovers from Nav. culture: 1. their ability to concentrate. As they stay with a sing for 9 nights so they stay with a verb for 4 hr. They get bawled up, they argue, they write, they murmur, they struggle, it is dinnertime, nevertheless they persist & at last they have it! 2. their individualism: they may argue for 3 hr. about one word. If they were Italians there would be no roof left on the hogan, since they are Nav. there was quiet talk & laughter & razzing & at the end of the 3 hr. each writes his word the way he says it! 3. their eye for form: No need to teach form. The first pages of [their] notebooks are a God-awful sight but the succeeding pages come to be art. . . . Lucky we are they are like this for they do not skip by a:' as does the white! They love their γ & '."[83]

The egalitarian atmosphere at the Hogan School meant that at any given moment any participant, Reichard included, could assume the role of learner or instructor. Once they had the basic mechanics of writing in Navajo in hand, the "students" decided to produce a bilingual

newsletter to convince the broader community not only of the utility of
written Navajo but that it could be shared by Navajos of all ages with
minimal effort. Miguelito fulfilled Reichard's hopes that he would
act as a mentor to the younger students, most of whom had had their
traditional educations interrupted by lengthy, traumatizing stints at
off-reservation church or government boarding schools. In addition, the
chanter imbued the gatherings with the Navajo sense of occasion. Reichard reported, "Because he has learned much he has also taught much.
He is an excellent teacher, especially of language, for he enunciates
distinctly, carefully and slowly. He speaks classical Navajo, is intolerant of
'schoolboy' makeshifts and abbreviations. Nothing pleased him so much
as our careful worrying over a single sound. He felt we were interested in
accuracy, a major requirement of Navajo learning." Medicine man and
"a man of parts," Miguelito was also a gracious host. "Every day that Red
Point was home we found the floor cleaned and the house pervaded by
the fresh earthiness of damp sand," Reichard recalled. "Indeed one day
I was particularly touched when I arrived before he had finished [clean-
ing the floor] to find him dusting off the blackboard, the only piece of
furniture."[84]

As she was traveling the reservation in June recruiting Navajo stu-
dent-teachers, Reichard emphasized to Ryan that her project was not
perceived locally as yet another assimilationist scheme imposed from
above. "Everywhere I have encountered the greatest interest on the part
of Indians and Whites alike on behalf of my project," she told him.[85] "For
years [the Navajo] have felt the need to write their language." By the
end of July, Reichard sent her second update to Washington, this one
addressed to Collier. She enclosed a copy of the Hogan School's first bilingual newsletter, calling it a "tiny and unpretentious" sample of the group's
progress. Collier reacted by publishing the Hogan School's paper in its
entirety in the August edition of the bureau's national circular, *Indians
at Work*. "'Tiny and unpretentious' as it may be," Collier commented in
a complimentary note, "this publication represents a milestone in the
progress of the Indians toward giving modern significance and form to
their anciently-established institutions."[86]

New to the fraught history of national language policy, Collier may not
have realized that the federal government had never before underwritten
a program to teach Navajo people to read and write their native language

to meet their needs. Previously, those Navajo who learned to write in their language did so at the direction of and for the missionaries, linguists, or agents of the government, who nearly always assumed the Navajo language was better off dead. Virtually all texts published in Navajo before 1934 were of a parochial nature—Bible translations, hymnals, and catechisms.[87] The writers of the Hogan School newsletter, by contrast, addressed the Navajos' need for a new means of Navajo-centered intra-tribal communication. They were encouraged by Reichard to coin new Navajo words to keep pace with the rapid technological and conceptual changes that were affecting all generations of Diné in real time. In effect, Reichard's Hogan school curriculum challenged more than a century of federal Indian policy by quietly undermining "the present paternalism of traders, missionaries and above all of the Government."[88] The commissioner's public praise for the students' hand-lettered newsletter did appear to recognize that small, positive steps taken by Navajos on the Navajo Reservation were necessary to achieve both the cultural freedom and civic empowerment he claimed to want for them.

At the request of the bureau, in August Reichard gave a paper at Fort Wingate addressing the topic "Navajo Language and the Navajo." She offered a blueprint for local, bilingual Navajo community centers where Navajo language had pride of place in the multi-age, multi-disciplinary curriculum. She discussed the ways the Indian Office personnel might expand on the success of her pilot project, and how she would proceed were she in their shoes. "My general aim would be, by means of the community center, by which I mean an informal adult school, and the day school which I conceive as a part of it, to make the Navajo . . . a bilingually literate people. I should strive to help them become financially, economically, religiously, and if possible, politically independent." The present and future interdependence of Navajo and white worlds was a given, in her view, which meant that the centers must aim for "a constant give and take between Whites and Navajo with the fundamental purpose of helping the Navajo to help himself."[89]

Although universal, voluntary literacy in Navajo was desirable in its own right, Reichard held that widespread literacy would help heal the generational rifts in Navajo society caused by colonialism. Younger, boarding school–educated Navajos had difficulty finding their places as adults in the multi-generational households of their parents because they

were taught by government and missionary teachers to view their traditional elders as "a disgrace." Community-based literacy programs would
bring these "[English] literate, highly ambitious, thoroughly teachable"
returned students into closer contact with Reichard's second group, "the
'old men,' that is the Reservation Indians who want to learn to read and
write." "Since the Navajo standard for 'greatness' is 'intelligence' this
would be my favorite group. They know a great deal which is scientific or
pseudo-scientific but in a practical rather than a theoretical way. I should
sit at their feet. I should teach them the mechanics of reading and writing
in their medium of thought." In an atmosphere of mutual respect, the
returned students "will learn of things he never knew belonged to his
people," Reichard predicted. "He will come into his own. And if he listens
he will be given the opportunity to talk. He will, in his turn, have an
influence on the elders." English would be introduced as a second written
language "if and when the people want it."[90]

Privately, Reichard was tickled pink about her experiment at White
Sands and flirted with the idea of repeating it. "If the Navs liked the school
a quarter as well as I did—& I think they did—they liked it a lot. Never have
I had such satisfactory students," she wrote Parsons. "How I should like to
have a school for interpreters! And I am abnormal enough to want to run
the community-center-dayschool work! It is in my opinion the answer to
Indian education. With the Nav. material, the idea in perspective, it just
seems to me the most promising thing I have ever contemplated."[91] Writing these words, Reichard's pleasure was not yet spoiled by the knowledge
that Haile and Sapir had passed the summer trying to derail the Hogan
School and Reichard's cordial relationship with the Indian Bureau
behind her back. Reichard was already implementing her plans for the
Hogan School when Sapir wrote Haile to announce he had Collier's ear
concerning Reichard's upcoming project. "I was very insistent, both in
correspondence and at the [December 1933 AAAS] Conference," Sapir
informed Haile, "that this work ought, in all fairness and courtesy, to be
put in your charge, in view of your knowledge of the people and their
language and the many years of service which you have to your credit
in this field. This point of view seemed acceptable and a Committee was
appointed, with yourself as Chairman. . . . This Committee is formally to
sponsor Gladys Reichard's work and you must feel yourself at liberty to
give her instructions as you see fit."[92]

If he registered Sapir's demand for such an oversight committee, Collier chose to ignore it. Ryan didn't get wind of it until after Reichard's contract ended in August, which meant that at no time did Sapir or Haile have a bureau-sanctioned role in the design or implementation of Reichard's Hogan School. Sapir seemed to have forgotten even that Reichard had reached out to him and Haile concerning her project weeks before he imagined Haile as her supervisor. In April Gladys had sent the pair a deferential letter asking for their advice concerning the Navajo spelling symbols she planned to use at the Hogan School. "The alphabet as I have adopted from Sapir's is not complicated, it looks hard to an outsider because it is so different in its connotations," she wrote. "You understand these and it is not difficult for the Navajo to do so. . . . I earnestly request your criticism and hope we may work out such a system that we all can use. There is no sense, in my opinion, of using some system we cannot all, laymen and scientists alike, use. Especially is this true after a phonetic system has been so well and carefully done as have Navajo by the efforts of all you scholars in the field. I do not include myself. All I think I can contribute is the ability to teach the system, to put it across. I feel confident I can do that."[93] Ignoring her invitation to collaborate, Sapir replied that he had already instructed Collier on the orthography he deemed best for Navajo, one "which is gradually coming into use among the few people who are qualified to speak on the subject." He conceded that the commissioner's interest in the "business of teaching the Navajo to write their own language" was "an important idea" that might have "rather far-reaching consequences." The notes he made on Reichard's one-page list of spelling characters were categorical. Among other terse comments, Sapir affirmed one symbol with the annotation "O.K.," and vetoed another with "No!"[94]

Comfortable as Sapir's subordinate, Haile offered no comment. Prior to Goddard's death, he had viewed Reichard as a friendly supernumerary in Navajo studies. Reichard, on the other hand, treated Haile as a respected elder colleague to whom she could turn for occasional guidance. She publicly praised the reissue of the ethnological Navajo dictionary Haile had compiled with his Franciscan brothers in 1910, calling the tome "still the standard and most complete work of the Navaho Indians" and "indispensable."[95] In 1929 Haile became Sapir's eyes and ears in Navajo country after he received funding through Parsons's Southwest

Society that allowed him to join Sapir's section of the Laboratory of
Anthropology's first field school. In exchange for his exclusive loyalty,
Sapir flattered the Franciscan with long, detailed missives filled with
promises of university research appointments, together with instructions
for transcribing Navajo texts, managing the allegedly feminine whims of
two key sponsors, Parsons and Mary Cabot Wheelwright, and protecting
their scholarly territory from incursions by other men.

Not content to disparage Reichard in private, Haile published a scath-
ing review of her *Social Life of the Navajo Indians* in 1932, four years after
the book was first published.[96] Chiding Reichard for basing her analysis
of clan and kinship on too little data, he dismissed the 3,500 genealogical
ties she had methodically documented as next to nothing compared to
what he knew. Where Aitken's review had urged Reichard to be more
assertive in her conclusions, Haile deemed her too hasty. The chief
shortcoming of *Social Life*, the priest fumed, was that it wasn't as thorough
as the book he would have written if only he weren't too "exacting and
cautious."[97]

Haile's unprovoked attack on *Social Life* allowed Reichard to see that
he saw her primarily as a rival. When she brought the belated pan to Newcomb's attention, Franc waived it off as a tactical foul. "Fr. Berard certainly
did mix up his characters most remarkably," she wrote Reichard, "—If he
knew what I think of his myths he probably wouldn't care for me either—I
never had such a headache as when I tried to make sense out of his Anadje
Myth—It seems as tho he has missed the point of every incident—And I
happened to know that tale—and the whys and wherefores—so that it was
extremely exasperating to read such an aimless sort of tale—meandering
along to nowhere. . . . He told me that he had lumbago and stomach trouble so that he could not sit thru a whole ceremony—so he never tried. No
wonder that he misses the point of a 'doings' when he hasn't the faintest
idea of what medicines or charms the prophets are trying to collect. His
chief value to ethnology is the translation of 'words'–He ought to devote
his time to just that."[98]

Neither woman guessed that Sapir was behind Haile's harsh tone, if
not his pedantic cast of mind. On reading an early draft of Haile's review,
the temperamental linguist had counseled his disciple, "No doubt you
will want to be charitable but I hope that you are not so charitable as to
induce yourself to say the opposite of what you mean. After all, a little

honesty will not do our friend very much harm." Post-publication he congratulated Haile for his "restraint." "I do not think she would have the right to feel offended by your critical comments," he wrote Haile. "As a matter of fact, it seems to me that you have let Gladys off pretty easy."[99]

Sapir's elder by a decade, Haile was not the passive lieutenant Sapir supposed him to be. Long before he met Sapir, the priest became interested in studying Navajos as "human beings, intelligent, ingenious, industrious, religious, enormously so."[100] But his midlife conversion from missionary to anthropologist did not mean he abandoned his loyalty to the ideals of his Order. In particular Haile remained a staunch advocate of Catholic boarding schools as the best way to bring Navajo children into the spiritual fold, calling the government day school derisively "a happy, go-as-you-please institution."[101] When his antiquarian fascination with Navajo lore raised eyebrows among his Franciscan confreres, he had the ready retort, "Why evangelize any people unless you know something of their background, their ideology?"[102]

Through Sapir Haile received enough financial support to permit him to carry himself as an independent scholar who happened also to be a Catholic missionary. When the Great Depression reduced Sapir's hold on private research funding, Haile was again at the beck and call of his religious superiors. A monsignor based in Washington, D.C. urged Haile to share his knowledge of Navajo religious practices with Commissioner Collier in order to convince him "to give consideration to the native culture, so that that culture will be duly but not overly valued."[103] Other of Haile's brothers in Christ agreed that having one of their own in the Indian Bureau would give the Franciscans "the inner line" on the reservation ahead of their Protestant competitors.[104] Haile didn't hesitate to hedge his bet on Sapir. Anxious to secure government validation of his identity as an ethnologist, he approached the bureau directly for financial support without mentioning his petition to Sapir.

Ultimately Reichard's firm "in" with the bureau foiled Haile and Sapir's hopes of eclipsing her. Between June and December 1934, the men continued to pretend to one another that they had the upper hand. Haile reported to Sapir rather grandly in July, "I have done nothing regarding Miss Reichard's plans. . . . I am just wondering how she with her poor ear will put this over, yet she has more nerve than the ordinary person usually has. However, without a commission from the Office I can hardly follow up her work, as travelling from one point to another is more than I can stand."[105] By the end of the summer, Reichard's rivals clucked their tongues at her failure to obey the dictates of their phantom committee. "Gladys gave us no report on last summer's field work," Haile wrote Sapir in October. "At Wingate I had anxiously awaited such a report on her experiences."[106]

In response Sapir extracted a copy of Reichard's official report from Collier and forwarded it to Haile. Though the report summarized the results of a school aimed at literacy training in Navajo, Haile subsequently wrote Collier to fault Reichard for not submitting a summary of her linguistic findings. Had he been hired in Reichard's place, Haile assured the commissioner, he would never have allowed the Hogan School participants to be paid to learn to write Navajo. "The monthly allowance may induce the native to submit to the routine of a class room if this is easy money to him. But his interest must cease as soon as the allowance is discontinued." The school Haile proposed to replace the Hogan School would target children in the more tractable setting of the government boarding school at Fort Wingate. He would devote one hour per week to teaching Navajo literacy; no (white) teacher or child would be forced to attend. "Your instructor could be salaried, of course," he added. In case Collier didn't realize he was reading a job application, Haile sent copies of his proposal to progressive activist Anna Ickes, the wife of the Interior secretary, expecting her to use her influence to land him a contract with the bureau.[107]

Sapir kept their charade going by praising Haile's letter to Collier as "an excellent statement and a very dignified one." "[Reichard] is, as you know, rather self-willed about things and it may be that she has developed some inordinate ambitions of her own about the whole [Navajo] business," he wrote the priest. As Sapir's main interest lay in convincing Collier to redirect bureau funding toward his unfinished work on a technical grammar of Navajo aimed at linguists, he encouraged Haile to keep up the fight. Collier had agreed to adopt his spelling system for Navajo, the Yale-bound linguist wrote Haile, a nod that would allow them "to decide between us on all moot questions of orthography," and "finally legislate, as it were, on recommended procedures."[108] He couldn't fathom why Reichard's Hogan School was so highly regarded at the bureau. "I suppose that the best we can do about [Reichard] is to think as little about her and her ambitions as possible and let things take their natural course," Sapir advised Haile.[109]

Yet Sapir could no more be passive than impassive. Although Reichard had delivered on her promises and been recognized by the bureau for doing so, Sapir made one more play to undermine her standing with Collier. "At the risk of appearing conceited," Sapir wrote the commissioner in November, "I may say, for instance, that the primary reason why [Reichard] has had as much success as she has had with the Navaho is that she was given adequate and simplified methods of writing Navaho in all its essentials before she had learned the first thing about its phonetic or grammatical system. Of this there is not a hint [in her final report]. The point is, perhaps, not very important in itself but it does seem to me to reveal something of the heady and confused psychology of Dr. Reichard."[110]

Two months before Collier skimmed Sapir's uninvited note, Dr. Reichard concluded that life in the public sector was not for her. "I do like to work with the Navs," she wrote Parsons in her usual September wrap-up. "I never had much to do with the educated [Navajos] before & they are the ones that need help & can use it. They are interesting too . . . but the personnel on which the whole thing depends is certainly sketchy. And the colossus of Gov. machinery. I should be in a stew ¾ of the time."[111] As the big wheels at the Indian Bureau had turned over her proposal for the Hogan School the previous winter, Reichard remarked to Dorothy Hubbell that the gridlock in Washington worried her. "It was only John Collier's persuasiveness that let me in for this anyway and now I ask myself why I allowed myself to get mixed up in it."[112] Dr. Ryan, Gladys noted, was "a person of whom it may be said 'She couldn't say 'Yes.' She couldn't say 'No'!'"

Reichard didn't suffer from chronic ambivalence. Her decision to relinquish her temporary title of supervisor of Navajo language instruction at the end of August was made easier when the Navajo rejected Collier's signature piece of legislation, the Indian Reorganization Act of 1934, at the polls. "It grieves me beyond measure to say that our hopes of John Collier's administration were in vain," she confided to Parsons. "The administration of the ideas is a complete failure which fact once more makes Papa Franz right. . . . The people who have the fat jobs are largely

Collier family and retainers, the usual thing in spite of all the talk about taking politics out of it. That would be all right if they were worth a darn but they ain't!"[113]

Because she objected to bureau politics and not progress on Navajo literacy or in Athabascan linguistics, Reichard volunteered to teach "Navajo phonetics for whites at Crownpoint [N.Mex.]" without pay during the first weeks of September. "Twenty attend regularly & there were more than 30 altogether," she reported evenly before catching a last-minute train home. "I am doing this just to show the whites how to help the Navs. & the reverse. I do not believe all the effort is wasted."[114]

CHAPTER 5

NEITHER FISH NOR FOWL

THE GREAT DEPRESSION WAS EARNING ITS CAPITAL LETTERS when Reichard asked Parsons, "Do you wonder I like the work I am doing?"[1] With Americans of every hue and class, Reichard spoke of work with renewed reverence. In Manhattan, women without extraordinary means returned to making do for themselves and their families a vocation. They stretched recipes to their limits, did their own sewing and laundry and, often over the protests of their husbands, took low-paying jobs as domestics, waitresses, and piece workers to provide the family's only cash income. Black working-class women in Harlem gave haircuts and perms in their kitchens, or took in lodgers to replace the wages they lost as white labor supplanted them in the workforce.[2] As historian Susan Ware observed tartly, "no housewife lost her job in the Depression." But working for pay as men did didn't improve a woman's social standing. Oddly, the worst hard times served to "reinforce traditional gender roles, not subvert them."[3]

For women like Reichard "who [had] no men to work for them," having a well-paying, recession-proof job filled with travel, adventure, and intellectual stimulation was the height of luxury.[4] Among unmarried, middle-aged, urban woman, her rare position as a university professor spared Reichard the humiliation of dependency or homelessness, a plight many single women faced during the Depression. College enrollment held steady at Ivy League schools. Wealthy philanthropists continued to support research and educational initiatives, albeit at lower levels and with more strings attached. Barnard and Columbia deans agreed to freeze faculty salaries rather than cut them, as was done at small colleges and high schools, where educated women were most likely to be employed as faculty. Through a combination of hard work and luck, Reichard was lousy with opportunities to bear "the agony of producing creative work" in the

1930s.[5] Yet, day-to-day, she was immersed in the atmosphere of scarcity
with nearly everyone else. She painted for Parsons a Chaplinesque scene
of life at the Boas home in Grantwood, where she was once again a tenant.
"You really ought to be here in these historical times," Reichard wrote
Parsons, who spent the early years of the Depression traveling abroad.
"We are all alike."

> Nobody has any money at all except of course the bankers and
> brokers who knew this was coming for three weeks and nicely
> attended to themselves. But those who have large bills such as a $20
> (very large now) can't buy anything because there is no change. He
> who has only a dollar or maybe four is the best off. With us it is a
> matter of ferry fares and we pile the whole family into my little car
> (25 cents each way; the [George Washington] Bridge is out) and all
> come together. We see to it to[o] that we all go back together. The
> psychology at least around here is delightfully Indian. All about
> one is asked, "Have you enough money? Can you eat?" Of course
> we who are sedentary can charge even our meals at the Faculty
> Club or at Barnard. As is usual the poor ducks who pay cash are
> the ones who get it in the neck. They have no credit.
>
> When we took account of all our assets Cecil was found to have
> 78 cents in a pocket he knew nothing of, and Robert, one of the
> twins, remarked with glowing eyes, "And we have $2.03 in pennies."
> He also decided to call in his outstanding debts to the sum of 10
> cents, but today shows his attempt was unsuccessful. So far it is
> amusing; I hope it will not go beyond that point.[6]

Because Reichard didn't have a husband, children, or elderly parents
to help through the crisis, she filled her waking hours with scholarly
pastimes and the joys of photography. Dorothy Hubbell's use of the word
"workaholic" to describe her favorite anthropologist would have been apt
had Reichard not glowed with satisfaction when she spoke of her many
labors of love. Gladys thought of her diligence as "bloodsweating" rather
than "brilliance" because any discoveries she made "took work, and
brilliancy never does. It just comes!"[7] In her "winter" months, October
through May, she concentrated in equal measure on teaching college
students and writing books. On campus her "passionate absorption in her
special field," paired with an unexpectedly casual manner, kept the flame

Gladys Reichard at Barnard College, c. 1935. *Barnard College Archives.*

of humanistic scholarship burning brightly despite the general gloom. As one anthropology major wrote in the *Barnard College Quarterly*, "Miss Reichard's students, certainly, would wish to pay a tribute to her informality, to her relationship of easy equality with them. Professors who take their students skiing and talk to them about clothes and cooking and the more mundane aspects of living definitely do not grow on every bush."[8]

> You can say that Miss Reichard is a scholar, par excellence. That is true. A person who frequently and enthusiastically spends ten hours at a stretch in the analysis of the intricacies of Navajo grammar can hardly be called other than scholarly. If you wish to

apply the designation "scholar" to [her], however, you must divest it of all its stuffy and aloof connotations. Then again you might emphasize the diverseness of her interests and the incredible number of activities in which she is engaged. Once more you would be literally correct. She can talk with equal ardor on the wisdom of certain aspects of Navajo child psychology or on the importance of sane automobile driving. . . . At one time she may be engaged in subjects as varied as a course on the cinema, a semi-novel on Indian life, and the compilation of a Navajo grammar. . . . Numberless are the people who, regarding her impressive list of publications, have exclaimed helplessly: "But, Miss Reichard (or, more likely, 'But Gladys') how do you do it?"[9]

The book that had Reichard burning the midnight oil through the winters of 1930 and 1931 was *Melanesian Design*. She had completed the research phase of the project in the fall of 1929 with a week-long stop at the Field Museum in Chicago on her way home from the Pecos Conference. The visit proved necessary, by her standards, once she discovered in Europe that "the best supply" of the types of objects she was analyzing had been collected or curated by A. B. Lewis, an American trained by Boas before he was hired at the Field Museum.[10] Museum personnel allowed her to "[p]leasantly . . . make a nuisance of [herself]" nosing through storerooms taking rubbings and photographs of the carefully documented artifacts.[11] On her return to New York, she took possession of the wax rubbings Boas had made for her in Berlin during what turned out to be his final trip to Germany with his wife. The wish list Reichard sent Boas before he sailed included images of "unusual" Tami and Admiralty Islands bowls, kapkaps—intricately carved body ornaments worn chiefly by men—tortoise-shell hair pins, and rings from the Carolines made of the "light yellow bellypart" of sea turtles. "You can see now how very greedy I am & if you can't swing all of this just never mind about it," she had replied to Boas's offer of help. "If you *do* get rubbings perhaps you better get them all nice & ready for publication as they might not let us go digging into them again."[12]

Composing *Melanesian Design*, Reichard took Boas's "germinal suggestions and brought them to fruition in her own way."[13] Since 1922, when he gave his lectures on Native American art in Oslo that formed the basis of his 1927 tome, *Primitive Art*, Boas had fully distilled his ideas concerning the universal principles of artistic expression: the pervasive nature of the aesthetic impulse; the multi-dimensionality of the creative and aesthetic process; the standardization of meaning and technique by tradition and their susceptibility to personal reinterpretations that erased or obscured their origins; the existence of an inevitable tension between innovation (borrowed or spontaneous) and resistance to change.[14] Reichard's point of departure from *Primitive Art*—and the quality that would make *Melanesian Design* an original and enduring contribution to ethno-art history—was the value she placed on the beauty and style of the artifacts she examined. "The objects chosen must be beautiful from my own point of view," she wrote in her introduction.[15] They appealed to her not just as complex data useful in documenting the development of the mental processes associated with human creativity, but as art for art's sake. "None of these techniques: woodcarving, tortoiseshell carving with polished shellwork, and pyrography, is primitive," she advised her reader, "[they] belong to the realm of sophisticated art," their "grace achieved through virtuosity and fineness of feeling which are of course indescribable." Anticipating the criticism that she had done no fieldwork to supplement her findings, Reichard explained that her study focused neither on the origins or evolution of art nor its symbolic or religious significance. "The rewards of objective analyses are inherent in art itself. They consist in formulating the principles underlying the art style; the definition of elements, their combination into an organic whole; attitudes toward zones and fields, toward filling spaces; preference for regularity, symmetry or asymmetry, or rhythmic repetition. Almost every style furnishes surprises. In the Tami style an astonishing result is the possibility of establishing schools of influence, another is a feeling of acquaintanceship with individual artists which comes from familiarity with their work."[16]

Reichard finished her art history manuscript in the fall of 1932. Boas scared up $2,400 from Columbia and other scholarly coffers, making it possible for Reichard's third book to appear in a deluxe edition, printed in Germany. As the book went to press, it was likely Boas who alerted the New York Academy of Sciences to the imminent publication of an important report by one of its younger members. The Academy's A. Cressy Morrison Prize Committee selected *Melanesian Design* as their honoree in the

natural science category for 1933. Celebrated alongside Reichard at the
academy's December banquet at the American Museum were the three
male authors whose paper on the stimulation of plant roots by carbon
monoxide gas earned the year's Morrison Prize for Experimental Biology.[17] No one appeared to question whether a rigorous examination of the
purely aesthetic aspect of Native handicraft qualified as natural, empirical
science. Even those who viewed humankind as divisible into "primitive"
or "civilized" types greeted Reichard's opus appreciatively. One leading
figure of the socioevolutionary old guard lauded the award-winning
book for "open[ing] a new approach" to the study of non-western art with
"great skill" and "sane skepticism."[18]

Reichard's receipt of the Morrison Prize was front page, above-the-
fold news at Barnard. A *Barnard Bulletin* reporter turned up at Reichard's
Milbank Hall office as soon as spring semester was underway. Thumbing
through a dummy copy of *Melanesian Design*, the student pronounced the
cover art Reichard had designed, a stylized angelfish outlined in white on
black cloth, "decidedly modernistic." The text presented to the Morrison
Prize committee in the fall had been supplemented with 650 indexed
images arranged in 151 plates in a second volume. What, the reporter
wanted to know, motivated the six-year "pilgrimage" Reichard undertook
to produce a tour de force about a little-known group of nameless artists?
"My idea was to study compositional ideas and differences in detail,"
Reichard replied mildly. "And I found plenty."[19]

"Plenty" didn't begin to describe the cornucopia of ideas Reichard
had for books and articles concerning the Navajo. After the awards ceremony at the museum, she'd spent two uninterrupted weeks finishing
a manuscript she referred to simply as "NAVAJO WEAVER."[20] "I never
had so much fun doing anything," Reichard said of her at-home writing
retreat. She doubted that with teaching, two sets of galley proofs to correct, and the usual hodge-podge of administrative duties on her plate she
could get back to the Navajo book before June.[21] Time was always short for
writing, but she felt a certain urgency about this project. Other specialists
in southwestern studies were waiting to hear what she had to report on
Navajo weavers and weaving. One who had said so in print was Charles
Avery Amsden, a pot-hunter and aspiring anthropologist Reichard met
at the Pecos Conference in 1929, Amsden published *Navaho Weaving:
Its Technic and History* in 1932. His survey of the changing industry led

him to conclude that a contemporary Navajo woman wove "when she has nothing better to do" thanks to the volatility of the market for lambs and raw wool. "How long will Navaho women consent to toil at the loom for a wage of five cents an hour?" he asked. "The tribe is getting royalties on oil produced on the reservation (discovered only in 1923), and if affluence comes the old ways will vanish like snow in spring. Surely the end [of Navajo civilization] is clearly in view."[22] He hoped Reichard would prove him wrong. "Dr. Gladys Reichard has in preparation a study of Navajo weaving from the subjective, i.e. the weaver's point of view, which may throw some valuable light on this point," Amsden wrote in a footnote. "I commend her work to my readers in any event, both for the high authority of Dr. Reichard and as covering a phase of the subject upon which I have not touched—weaving as the weaver sees it."

Early in her 1933 field season, Reichard wrote Boas that the "Nav. Book" was "dominant in my mind now."[23] Dramatic developments in the Red-Point family circle that summer would lead her to reformulate the plans she had for it. In mid-July Reichard returned to White Sands from one of her many desert forays to attend a sing organized for Maria Antonia's benefit. The "dear old soul" Reichard loved as she had her own grandmother had a bad cough and more than the usual aches and pains. Pneumonia seemed the likeliest culprit. Miguelito conducted a restorative ceremony over his wife; when that failed to produce the desired result, a Knife Chanter was sent for. Reichard watched with "grim fatalism" as the ailing sixty-three-year-old was made to bathe and wash her long hair in the cold wind of a late, overcast afternoon. Determined to facilitate her own cure, the patient sat upright throughout these preliminaries despite a high fever and stabbing chest pain. "The sing must be done properly, if at all; the details of it are no more cruel than the surgeon's scalpel," Reichard argued with herself.[24]

Watching Maria Antonia's voluntary suffering, Reichard shuddered at the memory of another woefully ill woman she'd met the previous year at a divination ceremony she attended with Roman. It was obvious to Dr. Noah Reichard's daughter that last year's patient had advanced breast cancer. She wrote in her field journal, "Her breast is in a frightful shape & she can hardly sit up, but had to have her hair washed in yucca [suds]. The whole atmosphere is one of terrible depression, suffering & desperation. This is Nav. med. at its worst & shows trad[ition] gone to seed."[25]

Reichard wouldn't allow the distress she felt about Maria Antonia's treatment to permit her to interfere with the family's joint decisions. She left White Sands for a research trip willing herself to believe Maria Antonia had the strength to rebound. While Reichard was away on business, Maria Antonia's condition worsened. The sick weaver agreed to let Roman drive her to the mission hospital, but only once she lost all hope of surviving her illness. She died there before Reichard could return. Afterward Marie tried to comfort Gladys by telling her, "The morning before [Maria Antonia] died she asked for you."[26] Sometime after that, Reichard's "Navajo Weaver" took shape as a story of intercultural friendship, joy, and loss. The tale of learning to weave, suffer, and heal as Navajos did became a kind of instructional scaffolding for overly sophisticated readers.

The draft out of which *Spider Woman* eventually emerged blossomed on the page so quickly that not even Reichard knew what she had when she pitched it to Macmillan Publishing in the fall of 1933. "One thing I find amusing is that none of the readers [at Macmillan] discovered it was a book on weaving," she wondered to Parsons. "Am I so dumb or are they?"[27] From the craft point of view, Reichard's manuscript delivered a master class in style. After four years of mulling over her White Sands experiences, Reichard achieved a voice that allowed her to write frankly about the art of her science in service to one of her foremost passions, the science of art. As Parsons had before her, Reichard chose an unapologetic, sympathetic woman as her writing persona. She wooed her reader to her side as a trusted confidante might, shunning the pretensions of an omniscient narrator and the social distance they create between an ethnographer and her surroundings.

In the first quarter of the twentieth century Parsons had pioneered the practice of stepping into the frame of her verbal snapshots of ordinary people, a practice that humanized her "subjects" without recourse to sentimentality. Essentially democratizing, Parsons's writing style encouraged her white audience to encounter Native interlocutors as living, breathing, purposeful individuals rather than as stony tokens of the incomprehensible.[28] Through close contact with Parsons and her ethnographic writings, Reichard learned she could animate dry ethnographic writing by showing "the anthropologist" in conversation with her Natives associates, negotiating in plain sight, as it were, the terms of their relationship to one another. Parsons's innovations eventually led to dialogic ethnography becoming commonplace in anthropology. Decades before anthropology made the "reflexive turn" that revealed ethnographers as equal subjects of their prosaic field accounts, Reichard built on Parsons's advances. In Reichard's hands, ethnography became a vehicle for depicting the universal human comedy from a postcolonial perspective.[29]

At the time of *Spider Woman*'s writing, the American public had a taste for a tragic view of Navajo civilization. In 1929 Harvard-trained anthropologist Oliver La Farge won a Pulitzer Prize for a tale of two star-crossed Navajo protagonists. Set in "a less corrupted, purer era," *Laughing Boy* presented a mass audience with a fateful love affair that dramatized the chasm between Navajo and European American worldviews. La Farge's aim, he made clear, was entertainment, not ethnography. "This story is meant neither to instruct nor to prove a point, but to amuse," he informed readers in the preface to the first edition.[30] When Reichard reviewed *Laughing Boy* she ignored the author's stated motive and focused on his results. "There is no task so intriguing as to try to fictionalize ethnology," she wrote. "Few tasks are so frequently doomed to failure. In the desire to combine fiction and ethnology the literary artist and the scientist are one. The former appreciates the setting and the novelty of the native group but does not know the culture. He all too frequently projects his own reactions into the alien culture and his art fails because it is not true. The ethnologist realizes that he has the stuff of which romance is made but rarely can he write." La Farge seemed to Reichard to be the exception that proved the rule. "He has captured the glint on silver, the silhouette of the lone horseman at sunset, the rich change of light on mesa and canyon, the drama of native life," she said in praise. "Not only are the ethnological observations accurate, but they are portrayed for the most part with a feeling which approximates the attitude of the Navajo."[31]

When it was Reichard's turn to balance feeling with fact in her representation of Navajo people, she rejected the doom and gloom of La Farge's dramatic arc and the English-patois he invented to simulate Navajo speech as stylistic models. Instead she drew inspiration from English country novelist Sheila Kaye-Smith, author of the 1921 international hit *Joanna Godden*. Master of the homely detail that authenticates local color and the lilt of a little dialect, Kaye-Smith brought a new kind of heroine to the printed page, a bumptious but unsinkable Kentish shepherdess who bestrode a seeming continent of marshland defying village gender norms by refusing to marry.[32]

To depict humorous or poignant moments of mental confluence and transformation in *Spider Woman*, Reichard looked to Shakespeare, Pagan folklore, and Christian scripture for telling turns of phrase. Ultimately naive understatement, "the art," as Reichard described it, "of furnishing a dénouement in a single sentence," became Reichard's favorite literary tactic.[33] She first admired the style in the English conversations she had with Navajo speakers. Early in her first summer at White Sands, she had asked Marie's husband, Tom Curley, if to wash their wool for spinning they had to leave their waterless camp and drive the two miles to the well at Sage Springs. Curley replied with a straight face, "Yes, we usually do our washing there because there's more water." "Tom's remark even to this day draws from me an inward smile," Reichard admitted. "The reason is so obvious, my inexperience so blatant, the joke not on him but on me." Understatement in this vein was also well-suited to pathos, as in the narrative style of Chona, the subject of Ruth Underhill's *An Autobiography of a Papago Indian Woman*. Calling Chona's story "a triumph of the anti-climactic," Reichard noted how Chona compressed her emotional pain over the death of her first husband into the fewest possible words: "It was as if we had been children in the same house. I had grown fond of him. We had starved so much together." At puberty Chona had imagined the sound of love flutes she heard night and day as the product of crystals that had been ceremonially removed from her body when she was a child. "These hallucinations she did not lay to the fire of sex awakening in her," Reichard observed. "Her explanation was simple and satisfactory, 'I thought my crystals were growing again.'"[34]

Reichard's stylistic choices produced a type of ethnographic magic better suited to a postmodern reader than a pre–Vietnam War era one. There was no established market for decentered ethnographic reports exhibiting frank subjectivity, self-directed irony, and exacting detail in the 1930s. Reichard had a solution to that problem, too. "[I]t is now, yes, going to be twins again!" she informed Parsons in early 1934. In response to Macmillan's puzzlement, Reichard "figgered out a plan whereby there should be the bedtime story part, the first 175 pages continued for a whole book and including a lot more than weaving, this to be called SPIDER WOMAN."[35] The balance of her manuscript, which offered detailed instructions from the Navajo weaver's perspective on how to weave a proper Navajo rug, would follow in a separate volume. Reichard's editors weren't worried about competition from Amsden's book and neither was she. "Charlie's book is a great disappointment," she wrote Parsons in confidence. "It answers, or rather corroborates, about two things which I doubted. . . . I am grateful that [the history of the blanket] is gathered together. Otherwise he reprints the old stuff including the old errors and illustrations."[36]

Since becoming a published author, Reichard had come to share her sister Lilian's love of photography. On the summer cruises Lilian took to Europe and South America from time to time and during vacations out west with Gladys nearly always in the driver's seat, Lilian's camera led the way. Gradually, with Lilian's blessing, Gladys absorbed enough of her sister's technique to feel confident taking and developing her own pictures for her publications. Gladys and Lilian both contributed photographs to *Spider Woman*. By 1936, when *Spider Woman*'s twin, *Navajo Shepherd and Weaver*, was published, Gladys was more accomplished and confident in all phases of the art. Reichard fully appreciated photography's special appeal to modern readers. But the sixty-two photographs and thirty-five commissioned line drawings she included in *Navajo Shepherd* caused "a number of commercial publishers," including Macmillan, to turn her down "because they are afraid of the [cost of] the illustrations."[37]

Academic publishers balked for less practical reasons. Leslie Spier, then editor of *American Anthropologist*, took a pass on the manuscript, saying it was not technical enough for the AAA's monograph or "Memoir" series. Not wishing to offend his one-time classmate, Spier equivocated, "It seems to me that the book ought to appeal widely for use in classes in textiles, to the public interested in the Southwest, and to anthropologists for its detail on the Navajo—I, for one would want a copy."[38] Reichard deflected Spier's shaky logic using a favorite adage from her childhood. "[I]t seems the book is neither fish, nor fowl, nor good red herring," she remarked to Parsons. "I realize that it is alarming to contemplate an anthropologist opening a [AAA] Memoir and finding it interesting!"[39]

In the end, it was *Spider Woman* rather than any of the technical pieces Reichard published before 1935 that secured her reputation as a reliable observer of contemporary Native life. Helped by prominent ads like the full-page one in the *Barnard Alumna* that claimed "It makes ethnology as gripping as romance," Macmillan sold more than eleven hundred copies of *Spider Woman* within the first six months of publication.[40] Reichard thought that "not too bad for a book of that kind," particularly during a worldwide depression.[41] Charles Amsden was the first to finger the secret of *Spider Woman*'s crossover appeal. "The literature of the American Indian can be divided broadly into two classes, the scientific and the sentimental," he wrote in his review for *AA*. "Dr. Reichard has kept to the middle ground, giving her reader both instruction and understanding in the guise of a day-to-day narrative of Navaho life. 'Spider woman' should be judged primarily as literature, for the author has worked conscientiously to make it that. . . . To say that it is [ethnology] disguised with human interest would be unjust; rather it is completed by re-creation of its living, human setting, as ethnology deserves."[42] Historian Lillian Fischer of the Oklahoma College for Women praised *Spider Woman* for sounding a social-justice theme Amsden missed. Beside creating a "fascinating" tale of Navajo chanters and weavers, she wrote in her review, Reichard had "clearly shown the fine qualities of the Navajo people," and "thoroughly disproved the common idea that they are lazy, untrustworthy, and unfriendly."[43]

．　．　．　◈　．　．　．

Women who made names for themselves in anthropology before World War II did not regard themselves as inventing feminist ethnography. For the most part, they were reluctant to even identify as feminists. The all-hands-on-deck battle for women's suffrage was all but won by the time Reichard arrived in New York in 1919. Between the ratification of the Nineteenth Amendment in 1920 and the onset of the Great Depression, a decade typically considered "devoid of feminist activity," New Women like Reichard who had supported the mass "woman movement" in spirit channeled their pro-woman activism into smaller, less inclusive, less organized campaigns.[44] Feminism as class struggle harbored a worrisome paradox that made Reichard, along with most other professionally prominent women, uncomfortable with the label "feminist." To deliberately align herself with the cause of First Wave feminists, Reichard would have been obliged to acknowledge that women differed fundamentally from men, an admission that ran counter to her egalitarian precepts. Surveying her options, Reichard sympathized more with radicals like Parsons who aimed to fulfill "'not just our female selves, but our whole big human selves.'"[45]

By the late 1920s Reichard had bucked conventional sexual stereotypes by becoming a gainfully employed, self-actualized career woman who answered first to herself. She declined to join the National Women's Party or any other group constituting "a declared feminist elite."[46] More to her taste was the International Federation of University Women, co-founded by Virginia Gildersleeve before the war, where she could help promote women who were preparing to compete head-to-head with men based on their merits as individuals. As a member of the IFUW's Committee on Fellowships after 1935 (she became the committee's convener in 1947), Reichard worked to give aspiring women scholars access to the same kind of high-quality graduate education she was privileged to receive at Columbia. Claiming to be a feminist seemed to invite a charge of special pleading. As a self-made, intrinsically motivated, nationally recognized scholar, Reichard chose to remain unapologetically independent from labeled social movements.

For that reason, Reichard didn't contradict herself when she declared Ruth Benedict's hiring as an assistant professor at Columbia in 1931 "a grand scoop for feminism!" after dismissing as "nonsense" the suggestion that women scientists were discriminated against at the International Congress she attended in Hamburg the previous year.[47] Her separate remarks reflected her appreciation of the particulars of the distinct contexts of the two events. Of Benedict's promotion from adjunct to faculty member, Reichard knew that Boas had been trying for years to regularize Benedict's appointment in the face of an administration intent on thwarting his departmental ambitions.[48] Reichard was also aware that Benedict's lack of success at grant-writing and her unwillingness to relocate to accept a faculty position outside the city contributed to her professional situation.[49]

Furthermore, it was no secret in her circle that before the Depression, Boas's top staffing priority was to bring Sapir to Columbia to lead a program in North American Indian linguistics. After Sapir accepted a faculty post at the University of Chicago in 1925, Boas continued to hope that he could hire Sapir away. Boas was "almost dumbfounded" when he learned within a year of the stock-market crash that his department had been allotted funds for new faculty on the condition that he step down as chair.[50] He approached Sapir, who was being courted by Yale University, and Kroeber, who had found his angle of repose in the Bay Area and would not budge. Reichard gave Parsons an unsentimental account of the double rebuff: "Well, Sapir turned it down on the grounds—not expressed quite the same way but equivalent in meaning—that he would not here be the largest frog in the pool as he would at Yale. My opinion is that all this is going to be an awful wear & tear on the egos of these two men; Kroeber can stand it, I think, better than Sapir. The latter has a sweeping offer of everything he wants at Yale (which he accepted), Chicago matched Yale & lost & then Columbia 'called' him. It's a pretty big strain on the modesty of a person who never had any."[51]

Pleased as she was that some good had come of Boas's sacrifice, Reichard did not agree with Sapir that hiring Benedict was "a modest and criminally belated acknowledgement of [her] services."[52] Yet she took Benedict's side when she learned that Benedict used her promotion as a means to finally separate from her unfaithful husband. News of the break appeared to "upset Papa Franz a lot." "I certainly can't see why," Reichard huffed to Parsons. "It seems to me bad enough to get 'het up' over one's own affairs . . . without going into other people's emotions."[53]

Reichard had long since conditioned herself to hold her personal feelings in check in the workplace. As a result, her relations with Benedict were always cordial, although a mutually guarded quality had crept into their interactions since graduate school days. Gladys's elder by six years, Ruth's awkward manner was laced with a subtle hauteur that Reichard chalked up to her persistent unhappiness. By her own assessment, Benedict was a "human being cruelly tortured" long past her twenties.[54] Dissatisfied with her passionless, childless marriage and unable to "prove [herself] by writing," Benedict at forty epitomized a divided self. She wore a public mask of dutifulness over "the self I love," a confident alter ego who wrote pages filled with the "unwavering, ringing belief that the Me within them is of untold worth and importance."[55] Reichard thought it proof of good character that Benedict was willing to "suffer in harness" on Boas's idealistic scientific team.[56] Who Benedict loved, hated, or slept with was none of her concern.

Reichard accepted Benedict's performance as an ethnographer with equanimity, at least until the International Congress of Americanist came to New York in 1928. Benedict's paper, "Psychological Types in the Cultures of the Southwest," announced that she had come to view the "Pueblo Indians" through the lens of Nietzsche's two "diametrically different ways of arriving at the values of existence," the Dionysian and Apollonian personality types. This perspective, Benedict claimed, made sense of the "baffl[ing]" cultural history of the region. She thought that overemphasizing the kinds of objective materials Reichard had spoken about moments before—basketry, prayer sticks, pottery, dance, song, myths, and legends—rendered the "cultural dynamics of the region . . . unintelligible." As only the highly perceptive anthropologist had the necessary preparation to illuminate the "fundamental psychological set" of a tribe's traditions, it followed, Benedict implied, that the individual Native's view of his culture was less valuable than the ethnographer's.[57] Only the latter could describe it using metaphors the European American reader could easily interpret.

"She can't realize that her brief visits need not give the final word," Reichard scribbled on her conference program for Parsons, who was seated beside her as Benedict spoke. She added, "She was always kinda tacitly scornful of Peggy's method & mine of going about [fieldwork]."[58] Parsons rose to her feet during the question-and-answer period to object to Benedict's self-serving arguments, but the roomful of men took Benedict's side.[59]

Benedict's "Psychological Types" revealed critical differences between Reichard's and Benedict's theories of anthropology, differences that were also played out in the way they expressed their relationship to the cause of feminism. Benedict's feminism reflected a broader "'therapeutic' morality of personal health and self-development, in which the secular self [is] the ultimate value, an end in itself."[60] Since becoming an anthropologist in the 1920s, she had used the disciplines of anthropology and feminism as means to bind her personal psychological wounds and assert herself in both arenas.

Despite being an individualist morally obligated to seek self-improvement, Reichard saw it as an equal duty to place her accumulated self-knowledge at the service of others. Not a joiner by nature, she nevertheless grasped the power of group solidarity in the face of injustice. Where women's equality was concerned, Reichard was not content to view her personal success as a stand-in for the progress of womankind, as if all women defined liberty, opportunity, and fulfillment in the same way. As her reputation in American letters grew, Reichard felt a greater duty to lift up other aspiring professional women, that is, to become less selfish rather than more self-focused in the fulfillment of her whole big human self through anthropology.

Reichard's tacit feminism prompted her to take full advantage of her faculty position at a premier women's college to build up the next generation of college-educated women. Between her heavy teaching load at Barnard and the graduate seminars she taught and audited at Columbia, Reichard influenced, encouraged, and advocated for scores of university women throughout every academic year. Unlike her male colleagues on ivy league faculties, she had no power to place women scholars like Ruth Bunzel, "one of the best among the younger people," in full-time positions at other colleges and universities.[61] But when in 1927 a self-possessed twenty-one-year-old Bryn Mawr graduate named Frederica de Laguna entered the Columbia graduate program, Reichard stood out for the "kindness and devotion to Anthropology" she showed when students "imposed" on her for help with unfamiliar material.[62] The daughter of two Bryn Mawr professors, de Laguna didn't arrive feeling she was intellectually or physically inferior to men, but she did recognize that it was "harder for girls" to get ahead in academic life.[63] Reichard was the ideal role model for determined hopefuls like de Laguna. "[O]ur teacher was uncompromising in showing us what we ought to know," the student Gladys later addressed as "Freddy" said of professor Reichard, "she brought to us, in the classroom and in informal settings, her own enthusiasm, and the virus was contagious."[64]

A woman student more than twice de Laguna's age also benefited from Reichard's open-door policy toward Columbia's female graduate students. Forty-six-year-old Ruth Underhill enrolled at Columbia in 1930. She was a Phi Beta Kappa out of Vassar College whose well-regarded feminist novel, failed marriage, and fifteen-year career in social work had left her with a hidden hole in her self-esteem. Underhill later claimed she was drawn to anthropology because it taught "what you needed to know about human nature in order to get along with human nature."[65] In Underhill's second year, Reichard prevented her from dropping out of Columbia by hiring her as a teaching assistant at Barnard. Then Reichard, ten years Underhill's junior, convinced her timid elder to apply to Boas for summer research funding after she was turned down by the Laboratory of Anthropology field school in its third year. The following summer, Reichard invited Underhill to shadow her in Navajo country, after which they tacked on two weeks in Gallup studying Papago and Navajo language with a multilingual elder.

Writing her memoirs in the 1970s and '80s, Underhill's didn't mention that Reichard got her appointed to her first position with the Indian
Bureau. The summer job Reichard arranged for Underhill in 1934 translated into fourteen years of employment with federal agencies charged
with reservation management. Nor did the Columbia graduate credit
Reichard with the hearty, sisterly push she gave Underhill's first popular
book, *First Penthouse Dwellers of America*, which was loaded with photographs taken by Lilian Reichard.[66] Though the details had faded with
time, well into her nineties Underhill remembered the welcome warmth
of Reichard's support. "Gladys Reichard was a glorious person. . . . What
a companion," she said of her former mentor. "I, swimming uncertainly
in new waters, was touched to the heart by her generosity toward me."[67]

Making no demands on their personal loyalty, Reichard cradled
careers as diverse as those of Zora Neale Hurston, Thelma Adamson, Ruth
Landes, Gene Weltfish, May Edelman, Marian Smith, and Kate Peck Kent.
For their sake she squeezed her departmental budget to create jobs they
had only to cross Broadway to accept. While Benedict cultivated a small
group of male students willing to treat her as an "ageless priestess Cumaean
Sibyl," her "aura of lesbianism" serving as proof of her feminism, Reichard
challenged every woman student in her orbit to make her own luck.[68] Kent
summed up Reichard's special appeal to budding women anthropologists,
dark horses all, when she remarked, "She assumed you had a brain. She
was so bright. Her mind worked so fast you couldn't keep up with it."[69]
Another student described Reichard as "one of those rare professors who
always seem to know just how much work you are really able to do justice to
. . . her brusque manner conceals a heart of academic gold."[70]

There was a physically demanding side to being an anthropologist
that Reichard didn't teach so much as model. Her stamina as a "lusty day-
by-day worker" could not be faked.[71] She did not need to tell her students
that she considered fieldwork the most demanding and rewarding aspect
of being a serious anthropologist. Direct and sustained contact with
unfamiliar modes of existence required quick thinking and fellow-feeling
in addition to deep wells of patience and book knowledge. Reichard's
hardiness also conveyed the message that going to the field was a hard-
won privilege for women in a society that continued to regard marriage
and child-bearing as a woman's lot. For men, extended solo fieldwork
was a normal phase of life as a professional anthropologist; for aspiring

women anthropologists of the 1930s, it was yet a political statement. Even Benedict, who characterized library-based research as "a kind of field work where I don't have to go around to feasts or lay myself out to stupid old women," advised other women to perform field studies if they had any desire to be taken seriously by the men.[72]

Allergic to snobbery, Reichard invited undergraduate students to scholarly pursuits with equal vigor. Fully aware that the greater part of the Barnard student body dreamed of a making a quick trip to the altar as soon as they graduated, Reichard rarely missed an opportunity to teach her younger students "to have a good time with their minds."[73] She was less concerned with turning pupils into anthropologists than in fostering "a willingness, even an eagerness, to anticipate and to understand new or at least varied ideas and viewpoints." Her stated goal was to teach her "girls" to develop "a receptive mind [that] can tolerate with sympathy the peasant's pride in his cattle and sheep, as compared with its own preoccupation with plumbing."[74] To that end Reichard enticed non-majors to love language learning in an experimental course, "Language and Thought," that she "designed to show the relationship between language and daily experience" using texts in English, Spanish, German, and French.[75] As often as possible she followed a progressive pedagogy partly inspired by Navajo educational techniques she observed at White Sands, ones that valued experiential, trial-and-error learning over the "oral moralizing" most American teachers did in their classrooms. Thinking was a craft like any other, in her view. "Learning a craft imposes its own discipline as anyone who pursues one can attest," Reichard wrote in her chapter on social life in *General Anthropology*. "A badly spun string will tear, a granny knot will slip, a cut in wood deeper than necessary cannot be uncut, a fish weir loosely fastened will be washed downstream. Consequently art and industry need no human coercion, for nature, by her laws, takes its place."[76]

To counteract the years of "moral suasion" that rendered too many of her "city-bred" middle- and upper-class students "blissfully unconscious" of "the inevitable facts of nature," Reichard prescribed practical work to complement book-learning.[77] Under her light supervision, Barnard anthropology majors sorted, typed, collated, and interpreted the file slips and transcribed texts she brought back from the field each October. She also encouraged them to write their own papers for publication if they showed an interest in analysis or interpretation. To promote civic engagement over apathy, Reichard wrote articles for the *Barnard Bulletin* that invited students to join her campaign to solve the city-wide nuisance of ride stealing, the dangerous practice engaged in by young men who jumped on the back bumper of an unsuspecting motorist for a free ride uptown. She exposed this and other popular "auto rackets" with a rousing call to action: "[N]o evil exists which cannot be broken up if enough people wish to have it discontinued."[78]

Refusing to be put on a pedestal or deemed a stern taskmaster, Reichard remained approachable. She could deliver sparkling lectures on the semiotics of religion in the morning and spend her late afternoons engaged in student-faculty tennikoit (also called ring tennis) matches, which she usually won. She served as a panelist at a "stump the faculty" forum, lent one of her baby pictures to be displayed as part of a fundraiser for the Spanish Department (a "stream of student spectators" paid to see Dr. Reichard with a nautical tam-o'-shanter perched on her long childish curls), and wove a Navajo-style rug for the faculty talent show, also a fundraiser.[79] The student who remarked "Miss Reichard is impossible to pigeonhole in any neat little categorical description" noted that her professor's common touch was rare among Columbia faculty.[80] To most everyone else, she was simply "our favorite anthropologist."[81]

Reichard demonstrated her willingness to stand with women writers outside the academy who were reflexively put down as amateurs by men. Harvard professor Alfred Tozzer, the reigning authority on Mesoamerican archeology and longtime Boas confidante, contacted Reichard in early 1933 regarding a controversial story about the Navajo published in *Scribner's Magazine* the previous summer. Told to a journalist by former trader Hilda Faunce Wetherill, "Death of a Medicine Man" was a lurid tale of mayhem and murder perpetrated against an incompetent chanter. For months *Scribner's* was "flooded with letters from Navajo Indians and those connected with them, saying that the article was entirely false,—that the Navajos never were as there represented." Finally, *Scribner's* editor, Maxwell Perkins, asked Tozzer if the story were "authentic."[82] Tozzer included a letter sent him by Philip Johnston, a Navajo-speaking missionary's son who had served as a language interpreter for President Theodore Roosevelt when he was but nine years old.[83] Johnston decried the "misstatements" in Wetherill's story as so egregious as to constitute a "libelous canard."[84]

Saying, "[M]y Navajo information is thirty years old. It exists only as a memory," Tozzer asked Reichard to step in and render a verdict.[85]

Reichard's communication with Perkins was a model of restraint. The story was damaging to the image of the Navajo, she allowed, but it was best to think of it as an unfortunate consequence of the non-Indian reader's appetite for spectacle. "My interpretation of the situation is the following," Reichard wrote the editor. "There are good stories extant. Certain versions of the stories are misleading, even misrepresentative. They are the ones that have 'news value.' So if upon occasion a person identifies herself (or himself) with the stories and writes them up in a sensational manner, he is only doing what he has been taught to do. The important thing is to get publicity and acceptance; truth is of very minor importance."[86] Regarding the question of the story's historical accuracy, Reichard noted a faint resemblance between some scenes in Wetherill's story and a little-known atrocity story Navajo storytellers told Goddard about the cruelty of their ancient enemies, the Utes. "The usual way is for a [Navajo] medicine man to lose his practice gradually if he is not successful," she reported from her own experience, "but I do not believe the Navajo would tolerate violence believing that its evil would in turn revert upon those who performed it." Wetherill was guilty of being gullible. That did not mean she should be blacklisted. "The article stands as published," Reichard concluded, "but I hope that any future articles written by Mrs. Wetherill which you contemplate printing will be scrutinized with special care."[87] Perkins pulled "Death of a Medicine Man" from a compilation volume his magazine was about to publish. Wetherill, none the wiser for Reichard's intervention, went on to find less-dubious literary success with her 1934 novel *Desert Wife*.

That Reichard's democratic, boots-on-the-ground support for rising women contrasted with Benedict's more abstract feminist creed was underscored by their contrasting reactions to the murder of twenty-two year-old Columbia anthropology student Henrietta Schmerler. In July 1931 Schmerler was found lifeless at the bottom of a ravine on the White River Apache Reservation three days after she was reported missing. Schmerler was soloing in Arizona because she had been turned down for a place at the Laboratory of Anthropology summer field school being taught by Benedict in New Mexico.[88] With nearly two years of graduate study in anthropology to her credit, Schmerler thought herself ready to imitate Mead's studies of romance, sex, and gender in tribal life in the American West. She turned to Benedict for advice; Benedict sent Schmerler to Boas to apply for a small grant to conduct fieldwork at a site of her choice. Boas acceded, on Benedict's recommendation, and Schmerler bought herself a train ticket to Arizona as soon as classes were out.

On the train west Schmerler happened to speak with a James Stewart of the Indian Office about her plans for the summer. Stewart considered Schmerler dangerously ill-prepared for the task ahead and told her so. A press report divulged, "She told him, Stewart said, that she intended to leave white civilization behind to adopt native dress and, if possible, make her home with an Indian family in order to establish confidence and break down reserves."[89] On arriving in White River, Schmerler dispensed with the fieldwork norm of enlisting local authorities to formally introduce her to Apache interpreters. Instead, she avoided the local Indian agent and installed herself in an unused cabin four miles from reservation headquarters. When her body was found on July 23, conflicting reports of her demise were front-page news from coast to coast. Schmerler had been strangled, bludgeoned to death with a rock, or stabbed in the neck and head with her own knife. There had been multiple assailants or a lone Apache man. Perhaps the killer was a local white man she had praised in a letter home. Newspapermen were too prim to use the word "rape" in print. They identified the assailant variously as a "brave," a herdsman, or a range-rider. Once they depicted Schmerler as a brilliant young woman scholar clad in her good dress for the Saturday night dance, sexual assault was presumed.[90]

Stopping in at the Hubbell Trading Post one evening, Reichard learned of the murder when she was handed a two-day-old newspaper by Auntie Bob. As the shock subsided and sympathy for Henrietta and her family took its place, Reichard's thoughts turned to Boas, who was traveling in Europe. She called Benedict in New Mexico but the line was bad. Ringing off none the wiser, she wired Columbia and the Indian agent investigating the case in Arizona. Neither had answers for her except that arrests had been made. She wrote Boas, "Before this you will have heard of this most incredible tragedy of Henrietta Schmerler which to me is still incomprehensible no matter how hard I try to visualize or realize it. . . . The only way I can explain it all is on the basis of H's naivete," she wrote Boas. "I told you she was a babe in arms but I was thinking only of a contest with a physical environment. But she trusted everyone & I can almost understand how she would not sense trouble behind the scenes. Of course I know nothing except these newspaper reports, & they may be dead wrong."[91]

Mingled with her horror was the thought of the murder's effect on women anthropologists generally. "When I think of my own situation— every moment of my time is accounted for by my Indian family & the Hubbells. . . . I simply *cannot* think of Henrietta," she told Boas. "And I keep thinking of her family & confreres in N.Y. & the terrible responsibility on your Department. . . . You know that if there is anything on earth you should want me to do I should be glad to do it. Do let me hear from you. With all my love & sympathy, Gladys."[92]

Claiming illness, Benedict stayed put in New Mexico when Arizona authorities notified her that Schmerler was missing. Rather than cable Boas, she contacted Mead. Once murder was confirmed, the pair decided to keep Boas in the dark as long as possible. With rumors swirling in national newspapers that Schmerler had provoked the attack by mixing romance, sex, and drink with the wrong people, the pair reasoned that making a "martyr" of Schmerler would prevent Boas from becoming "the butt of an Arizona murder trial that has carte blanche to play up the motifs of sex and race!"[93] The murder became a national news sensation, which forced Benedict to switch tactics. Columbia settled out-of-court with Schmerler's father, but a spring trial date was set to decide the fate of the accused murderer, a twenty-one-year-old Apache, Mac "Golney" Seymour.

Benedict next prevailed on Ruth Bryan, the departmental secretary, to dissuade Boas from testifying at trial. But Boas had taken Schmerler's death as hard as Reichard feared he might. In January he suffered an embolism that left him bedridden. His doctors ruled out a long train trip west for any reason for at least six months. Called on to testify in court as Boas's surrogate, Benedict wrote a letter to the Indian Bureau blaming the tragedy on Schmerler's refusal to follow her instructions. She proposed that Underhill, a student who idolized Benedict as much for her physical beauty as for her intellect, represent the Columbia faculty perspective in the courtroom. Let off the hook, Benedict threw an "excellent and convivial" party where she and a few of her closest friends broke "open a bottle of Cointreau that had been part of a bet as to who would have to go [to the trial]."[94]

Uninterested as Benedict was in the outcome of Seymour's trial, she guessed its tenor correctly. With the accused's coerced confession top of mind, defense attorney J. P. Dougherty built a case most likely to spare his client the hangman's noose. Dougherty opened by saying that his client was a remorseful man "whose credulity and child-like mind had been exploited by a woman who was his mental and emotional superior and that he killed by accident and in self-defense."[95] Pointing to Seymour, Dougherty attacked Schmerler's character as bluntly as he dared. "[S]he tantalized and teased this poor savage. She played the part of a temptress," he lectured the all-white, all-male jury. "I hope you are not fooled into believing all women sent to the reservation by a great university are angels. I hope you gentlemen are not so bamboozled by college students as to believe they never take a drink. She was out on a lark. But give her the benefit of the doubt—say she did everything proper. She was a canary released from a cage, seeking refuge in the paws of a domestic cat. Would you kill the cat because it could not resist its instincts?"[96]

With so many questions left unanswered by the trial, Reichard accepted the life sentence given to Seymour with a heavy heart. She had refused to take part in Benedict's quixotic effort to hoodwink Boas, choosing instead to hold out hope that "the Indian may be saved" and a trial avoided.[97] When it was clear Seymour would be tried and possibly hanged, she sent an unsolicited letter to the court vouching for Henrietta's good character and pointing out the many factors that muddied the case for first-degree murder. As she feared, Schmerler's killing ruined not one family but two. The *Spokesman Review* reported on Seymour's transfer to McNeil Island Penitentiary in Washington state within days of the guilty verdict. "As Seymour walked from the jail he was greeted by his aged father and mother, his 6-year old brother, and his wife and their infant child. Tears streamed down the dusky, copper-hued faces of the little group as the manacled prisoner was led away."[98]

Reichard was rattled enough that in June she drove to White River from Ganado with a Navajo friend, John Curley, eager for closure. "We had a long talk with Donner, the Agent at Whiteriver & it seems all our excuses of Henrietta were gratuitous," she wrote Parsons afterward. "Even the distribution of whiskey was true & proved because she was friendly with (euphemism) the bootlegger maildriver who has since been convicted (privately). There were other proofs which make my theory of the rape all wrong & the motive for killing (as well as of her resistance) was probably pure drunkenness on the part of both."[99] Satisfied that the tragedy arose from plain human weakness rather than a clash of incompatible cultural patterns, Reichard took some comfort in a growing consensus among her Navajo associates concerning the trial's outcome. "The Indians [on the Navajo reservation] are in a good mood & are satisfied that no matter what the provocation no one can go around killing people & that drink is no excuse."[100]

If the personal tension between Reichard and Benedict never surfaced in public, it was because the hard feelings ran in only one direction. Reichard rarely mentions Benedict or Mead in her preserved correspondence, but she was often a target in theirs.[101] Episodes like the one that occurred in 1933, when Benedict was named one of three women selected as "a notable scientist" in a directory known as *American Men of Science*, serve as an example. Although her book, *Patterns of Culture*, did not appear until 1934, Benedict's appointment at Columbia and the buzz surrounding her un-Boasian theory of psychological types brought her to the attention of psychology professor James McKeen Cattell, formerly of Columbia. As editor of *AMS*, Cattell instituted the tradition of adding a star beside the names of those scientists he selected for the honor in his annual listing. Though it was common knowledge that outstanding men and women scientists went unstarred without rhyme or reason year after year, American scientists craved Cattell's stars just the same. Women scientists were grievously underrepresented in general, but a woman's marital status, the number of women nominees relative to the number of men nominated, and simple cronyism were among the rogue criteria Cattell applied at will.[102]

Benedict's selection as a recipient of a coveted star made her the third woman anthropologist since the directory's inception in 1903 to be so honored.[103] To console Mead, who was also nominated but was denied a star, Benedict assured her that the *AMS* stars represented "an age-group classification" that should be regarded as "pretty silly."[104] When it came to Reichard and fellow nominee Ruth Bunzel not receiving a star, Benedict reacted differently. She gloated to Mead that Reichard was "as sore as the corn on your toe" about being passed over.[105] Reichard's correspondence with Boas, who nominated her for the *AMS* list, and Parsons, her confidante in all professional matters, gives no hint that Gladys ever pined for Cattell's star.

Other signs point to Reichard's disinterest in the arbitrary kudo. During the Depression, Reichard and Boas developed a type of friendship for which the English language lacks a precise term. Squeamish about using the word "love" to characterize the emotional connection Boas and a few of his students shared, historiographers of anthropology have often relied on the relatively impoverished and situationally inappropriate lexicon of kin terms to interpret the interpersonal dynamics of the Columbia circle.[106] Ruth Underhill broke with tradition when she recalled of the pair, "Dr. Boas loved her for her German and her integrity. Also her simple idea of humor chimed with his." In the moments when neither was immersed in "the struggle for freedom from prejudice," they enjoyed one another's company not because they were teacher and student but in spite of it.[107]

Because she lived upstairs from him, taught on the same campus, and drove him across the Hudson and back most days of the week, Reichard was more aware than most of the burdens Boas placed on himself after the personal tragedies that befell him in the 1920s, particularly the death of his wife in 1929. Work was the only lasting solace he allowed himself, no matter how "terrible, small . . . and really ill" he became after the heart attacks he suffered in 1932 and 1936.[108] Despite recurrent physical ailments, Boas gave public lectures and founded new organizations dedicated to exposing and ameliorating inequalities of income, education, and food supply in the United States and abroad. He argued for civil and individual liberties in venues ranging from the Chamber of Commerce in the state of New York and the halls of the U.S. Congress (where he protested those chambers' growing animosity to freedom of dissent) to the pages of *The Nation* and *The Atlantic*. He coolly blasted the repressive, racist regimes consuming Spain, Cuba, Italy, and Germany.

Boas's activism was so thorough in its scope and vigor during his seventies and eighties that many of his colleagues in anthropology viewed what Parsons called his "ardor in combating the scientific fallacies which bolster up social injustices" as a betrayal.[109] Benedict spoke for many of her peers when she exclaimed, "He has given up science for good works. Such a waste!"[110] Reichard, by contrast, greatly admired Boas's indefatigable pursuit of knowledge just as she did his humanitarianism. "[H]e learned to take movies last winter," Reichard told Parsons in 1931, "took, 46 films & less than three whole ones were unsuccessful. He is really too remarkable."[111]

The mutual affection Reichard and Boas had for one another provoked interpersonal, professional competition and, inevitably, jealousy
among Boas's associates. Anyone who came in contact with Boas knew
immediately his high regard was not for sale at any price. One of Boas's
older students, Robert Lowie, observed that Boas's determination to take
a rational point of view sometimes "clashed with the disciple's emotional
urges." "He was wont to survey the chessboard of anthropological jobs
and figure out how science could be best served. . . . His judgment was
usually right, but then some men and women resented the impersonality
of his strategy."[112] For the men and women who were inclined to displace
their resentment of Boas onto Reichard, the falsehood "Papa Franz gave
Gladys every scholastic plum until she got her PhD," suited them better
than the truth.[113]

Reichard didn't patronize Boas either. She made no secret that she
found some of his eccentricities irritating. "[W]hen there is anything
requiring physical strength he insists on overdoing," she said of one sign
of his "senility." "My automobile is primarily used for a moving van here
as in the Southwest. We no sooner get our books here than they (it may
really be others!) must be hauled to the office or vice versa. But this winter
there can be no question of weight. The suitcase or carrier must be so
full you can't budge it from the floor before it is considered eligible for
the rumbleseat. Papa F. won't even let the elevator man touch it."[114] She
acknowledged that his mind was very good until the end, but occasionally,
when he lost track of some galley proofs or drafts she'd sent him, she
didn't hesitate to issue a mild scolding. Ever sensible, Reichard counted
on Boas's having "an awful lot of females buzzing around" at home and
at the office who allowed him to hold out against old age.[115] Far from
co-dependent, they met their separate challenges in life independently.
Reichard had her all-important work to do and Boas had his. They occasionally helped one another. *AMS* star or no star, they were birds of a
feather in every way that mattered to either of them.

CHAPTER 6

"SINGS, DARLING, SINGS!"

"THE POOR WEAVING!" REICHARD GROANED IN JULY 1932.[1] No loom had hung in her White Sands dugout since the end of the previous summer; her steamer trunk was often absent as well. Weaving technique in every phase, from care of the wool on the hoof, to dye-making, through crafting a textile "worth its corner tassels" had occupied one channel of her mind for the previous two years; it would continue to do so for four more.[2] But once Reichard got word that Red-Point was preparing to sing the nine-day Shooting Chant over Marie, her concern for her friend was mitigated by her intense excitement at the prospect of participating in the imminent ceremony. Marie had suffered from headaches, sleeplessness, and leg pain for more than a year. A white doctor in Los Angeles, where Marie and Tom worked on a cattle ranch over the winter, advised her to have all her teeth pulled as a remedy. Refusing that, Marie put her trust in her father, who unlike most Navajo chanters was willing to sing over his own family members. Marie assured Reichard that there was no need for a second opinion on which was the appropriate ceremony. "[M]y father knows this is the right one. You see when I was at school at the Mission, it was struck by lightning. That is why I am sick. The Shooting Chant is the cure for diseases caused by lightening, snakes, and arrows."[3]

Marie's assurances were unnecessary in the face of Reichard's high esteem for the widely respected chanter. Since her first summer at White Sands, Red-Point, usually referred to as Miguelito by his white neighbors, had been her most articulate guide to Navajo language and worldview. What Reichard knew of Red-Point's personal history directly was supplemented by stories of the chanter's past she had picked up at the Hubbells' trading post: his first years living near the post with Maria Antonia and her young daughter Adjiiba in the 1890s; his work as a ranch hand and foreman at the Hubbells' before he decided to study with Blue Eyes to become a Navajo singer; his subsequent work as a demonstrator for Fred Harvey Company's Indian Department in Albuquerque until he quit them for a life as a full-time chanter and family man.

Through her sources Reichard gradually discovered Miguelito was no stranger to failure. "Before supervision by white Government officials became strict," Reichard later explained, a Navajo man's "second wife was provided by the first, particularly if the first was an older woman with a daughter." Following custom, Miguelito married Adjiiba soon after she reached puberty. The family was in Albuquerque when Adjiiba went into labor with her first child. "Although he had had many contacts with whites, Miguelito had not accepted any of their treatments for illness or any of their religious beliefs," Reichard continued. "In fact, until the day of his death, he remained firm in his own faith in spite of the unrelenting pressure of missionaries. Consequently he did what was natural for him to do. He took his young wife to an isolated place on the Rio Grande where he built a shade for her and sang as the Navajo used to do to aid childbirth. His efforts were however unavailing and the girl died." With "the Navajo fear of the dead and a possible feeling of guilt," Miguelito turned to representatives of the Harvey Indian Department to arrange for Adjiiba's burial, which none of her immediate family members were expected to attend. Miguelito showed his love and respect for the girl in the Navajo way by sending all of her silver and turquoise for burial with her body.[4]

Knowing something of the physical dangers of childbirth for teens, Reichard judged Miguelito less by his failure than by his response to it. "Although in his youth he sowed his share of wild oats," she wrote of the chanter, "Miguelito had the qualities which make for leadership and authority by our—as well as Navajo—definition. Above all he was intelligent, the Navajo proof of his intelligence being the vast amount of ceremonial knowledge he was able to acquire, retain and use satisfactorily. . . . His mind was also curious and questioning. He was always wondering about things, putting two and two together, and arriving at astonishing conclusions, which often seemed quite reasonable, based of course upon the assumptions and logic of his own culture. The conflict between his tendency to reason and the requirements of his dogma led occasionally, as is natural, to rationalization which in some circumstances might be called social intelligence."

Navajo chanter Miguelito (also known in English as Red-Point) at White Sands, c. 1933. *Museum of Northern Arizona MS22–2-3–31, Box 1.10.*

Reichard believed Miguelito's "bravery and honesty, and his willingness to face facts" led him to atone for his early overconfidence. After Adjiiba's death, he redoubled his study of "his faith and the processes it prescribed to remove such harm as might ensue." Saying, "That which is most dangerous according to Navajo tenet is the unknown error. Known and acknowledged mistakes can be removed by ceremonial properly conducted," Reichard admired the mature medicine man for being "relentless in the detection of error" in his craft.[5]

In the run-up to Marie's sing, Miguelito expressed his eagerness to use the occasion to advance Reichard's training in Navajo ceremonial arts. Reichard's field notebook records his promise to her, along with her response: "'And I am going to tell you everything & you will have to watch

& be exact about everything I tell you. I start before sunrise & I am going
to make you get up.' All this with me saying nothing in secret elation."[6]
As preparations began, the chanter refused Reichard's offer to help him
gather the materials he needed for the medicines and the sandpaintings
he would make to effect a cure. Her role, he insisted gently, was to help the
patients, Marie and Ninaba, Marie's niece. There would be no charge for
Gladys or Roman Hubbell to attend the sing because Miguelito thought
of them both as close family. Other white people would have to pay a
dollar each to attend. "White people make us pay for everything, and
they ought to pay, too," Red-Point volunteered.[7] Once the sing was underway, Reichard surmised that Marie was expected to pay her father for
the nine-day ceremony, per the objective formalities that distinguished
patients from chanters.[8]

Reichard's written record of her first Shooting Chant balanced the
immediacy of a fully engaged participant with the exactitude of a practiced observer. Punctuating the pages of field notes that detail the work of
Red-Point and his assistants step-by-step are "Remarks" that capture the
generalizations Reichard made as events unfolded. "A chant cannot be
understood from a single point of view except perhaps that of the singer,"
she noted after the first day of intensive activity inside and outside the ceremonial hogan. "If you're a patient you can't see the workers sometimes. If
you are in the hogan you can't see what's going on outside & the reverse.
The way to do [it] is to be lucky to have Mig. let you look on all you want to,
then to be a patient & finally a singer." At first she entered the ceremonial
hogan armed with the tools of her trade, paper and pencil, even though
the low lighting in the hogan, filled with the smoke of the ceremonial
fire along with its wilting heat, was hardly conducive to note-taking. Then
there was the engrossing, often hypnotic nature of the ceremony itself.
While "efficiency with seriousness" characterized the actions of one evening's performance, long periods of waiting for ceremonial potions to
boil or "dragged out" hands-on treatment of patients with ceremonial
implements filled others. Slow passages induced sleep in most white participants, including Roman. The strain of daily fasting, sleep deprivation,
and the constant inhalation of heavy woodsmoke forced Reichard to draw
on every ounce of self-control she possessed to remain alert throughout.[9]

By the fourth night of the sing, Reichard was asked through an inter-
mediary to leave her notebook in her dugout. When she appeared early

one morning outside the ceremonial hogan expecting to watch the men create one of the forty-seven sandpaintings that belong to the chant, she was turned away. Asked later that morning why she could not record and see everything as he had promised, Red-Point explained, "[W]e never have even our own women in the hogan when the painting is being laid. . . . We have always been taught that way. It is in the story. So you must not feel sorry because you cannot come in." Marie allayed Reichard's suspicion that the men believed women contaminated the sandpainting process by their presence. She told her that once a woman had been sung over, the sandpaintings made for her were no longer off limits. She could watch them being laid the next time they were used for another patient. Nor had Red-Point banned her note-taking because one of his assistants complained he thought Reichard would write a book that earned her money. Miguelito worried only that her bringing paper and pencil into the hogan might not be good for his patients. "[M]y father says you are his child and he would not refuse to have his own child [at a sing]," Marie conveyed to Reichard in English. "Besides, he says his teacher [Blue Eyes] told him if outsiders want to be sung over, he should do it. Once there was a Hopi who asked him to sing, and he did; then there was a white man at Chinlee; and of course he always sings for Old-Mexican's-Son when he wants him." "And I will sing over you sometime too," Red-Point chimed in, "let the Navajo say what they will!"[10]

A feat of physical endurance and mental concentration, the Shooting Chant ceremony also tested Reichard's commitment to the craft of ethnography. To understand why the Navajo practice an art as demanding as the chant, she knew she had to experience it herself. After the ceremony concluded at five A.M. on the morning of the ninth day, Reichard asked, "Can it be that the satisfaction (mine perhaps only) lies in having carried a complicated, fatiguing, nerve-ending ritual out to an end[?]" Finding "the atmosphere of the peace today . . . quite impossible to describe," she noted, "Part of it is due to the uncanny peculiarity of time. I have however a feeling of restoration."[11] Writing about the "communion of suffering" she experienced in the darkened hogan, Reichard eventually did find the words to convey the ceremony's cumulative effect on her. "Certainly I have never before felt this sort of oneness with other individuals. Can I ever make anyone understand how utterly inoffensive and unobjectionable this barbaric-sounding rite appears?"[12]

Before the summer was out, Miguelito kept his promise to sing over his white granddaughter. If the private rewards of the five-day "blessing for travelers" the chanter performed over Reichard were more pronounced than she experienced during the Shooting Chant, so too were the rigors. As before, she vigilantly observed each of Red-Point's directives, including when to strip to the waist for ritual bathing. Following a thorough sprinkling with dry medicines, Reichard "was made to undress very hastily & wash hair in the [foamed soaproot] suds. There the ♀ went into a huddle with the blankets & M[arie] washed my back & poured the whole business over me, me gasping at the coldness."[13] When the purification phase of the ritual called for deliberate vomiting, Reichard gave herself a "violent headache" trying to comply. After the sing she paid Miguelito "$35 and a $12 bracelet" plus "food and 2 sheep" for his work. She was satisfied that he had taken no shortcuts on her behalf. Smoking a cigarette together at the sing's "post-mortem," the chanter instructed Reichard on the prohibitions she would have to observe henceforth, as well as the protections she had gained from the hardships endured.[14]

Being "the one sung over" conferred a special street credibility on Reichard from the perspective of her white peers, particularly southwesterners who had met the demands of the Navajo sing themselves. Franc Newcomb was one of those who could appreciate the ordeal from direct experience. She was already well pleased with Reichard for, among other things, brokering a deal with Columbia philosophy professor Wendell Bush, a collector of religious art, who wished to commission Newcomb to make a large set of sandpainting drawings. Newcomb's growing reputation as a scientific illustrator hadn't yet translated into her being recognized as a scholar. Franc confided to Gladys that an illustrated article on sandpaintings she'd submitted to *National Geographic* was returned "without thanks—with the advise [*sic*] to send it to the Bureau of Ethnology—ahem!! Guess I am simply a *dud* on the writing end of it—because I know the pictures were O.K. Oh! Well!"[15] Reichard offered to level the playing field by reviewing Newcomb's future manuscripts before she sent them off. "I wouldn't offer to [critique your writing] if I thot it were for nothing," Reichard wrote Newcomb with feeling. "You have the dope. You have not had the training to write it up yourself and the result is likely to be that most of it will be swiped from you. Since you are intelligent is there any reason why you should not leap your only hurdle and get it done yourself. . . . So don't lets waste any more time on arguing."[16]

Still, the two had no trouble dividing the labor for their joint book, *Sandpaintings of the Navajo Shooting Chant.* Reichard was to author the text in an anthropological vein. Newcomb's task was to provide the multicolored illustrations. Reichard's respect for Newcomb as a partner was genuine. She credited her with taking up her studies "out of an appreciation of art, a natural ability to get along with Indians, and a sense of appalling futility at the realization that here was a field untouched by, practically unknown to, artist or scientist."[17] Yet Newcomb's slower pace inevitably became a problem. In the six years since they first met, Reichard had churned out four separate books and a dozen journal articles or reviews, founded and led the Hogan School, steered Barnard's one-person Anthropology Department through the worst of the Depression, and been elected president of the American Ethnological Society. She'd bought herself a trailer, in essence a rolling plywood box sturdy enough to withstand monsoon rains at altitude, that she named "El Camellito" in honor of the long intervals she could spend traveling the high desert in it away from "civilization."[18]

In the meantime, Newcomb struggled to eke out a few hours per day to draw and paint while seated at the family hearth. In 1936 she suffered a run of bad luck. She spent the winter in California undergoing surgery and treatment for a mysterious illness Reichard feared was cancer. The good news that Newcomb had severe anemia rather than cancer was followed by stories that reached Reichard through the Hubbells that Newcomb's trading post, house, and barn had burned down. After weeks without hearing from Newcomb, Reichard was relieved to learn that rumors saying Newcomb's entire sandpainting collection was destroyed were false. "I can never get [Franc] to be definite in a letter," Reichard told Boas, "but she lost some 40 unfinished sketches of the sandpaintings [in the fire] & saved some 200 which is far better than I had anticipated."[19] Hoping to speed Newcomb's progress, Reichard sent her harried collaborator fresh copies of some of the reference books that had been destroyed in the house fire.

The patience Reichard showed Newcomb amounted to more than chummy indulgence. In the academic sphere, Reichard's growing reputation in Navajo studies had begun to attract negative attention from her male rivals. Collaborating with Newcomb became less and less a choice as

the men began to squeeze Reichard out of "their" territory by ignoring her
results. Leading the clique of male anthropologists focused on the Navajo
was Clyde Kluckhohn. Scion of a privileged midwestern family, Kluckhohn
spent his adolescence roaming the New Mexican desert for health reasons
before he elected to become an anthropologist. Intelligent, ambitious,
and well-connected, Kluckhohn rose through the academic ranks with a
speed that seemed calculated to put him in charge of all Navajo studies
under the aegis of the Peabody Museum and Harvard University, where
he earned his PhD and an appointment to the faculty in 1936. By the
time the thirty-one-year-old Harvard instructor paid Reichard a courtesy
call, his mind was made up that all previous ethnographic studies of the
Navajo were "flat," "one-dimensional" treatments that missed the "basic
patterns" and "cultural dynamics" of the group over time.[20]

Of the course-corrections Kluckhohn proposed for Navajo studies,
one was the development of a taxonomy of Navajo "song ceremonials"
to supplant the lists of chants made by the Franciscan Fathers and other
amateur scholars years before. Teamed with Leland Wyman, a Boston
University zoologist turned medical anthropologist, Kluckhohn enlisted
the help of Edward Sapir for linguistic matters, Berard Haile for his collection of Navajo sacred texts and connections to Navajo medicine men,
and Reichard, as a potential co-author. Reichard thought it scientifically
prudent to involve Newcomb for her knowledge of Navajo chants and
chanters, especially Hastiin Klah.

When Reichard forwarded to Newcomb the working list of ceremonies
Kluckhohn and Wyman were intent on classifying, Newcomb brushed it
off as the blinkered work of two self-important greenhorns. "I don't think
much (not anything at all) of Clyde Kluckhohn as an ethnologist—and
not too much of Wyman," she responded. She accused the men of taking
the word of younger medicine men "who will mix up anything they happen to see or hear just in order to hold a ceremony and get the money."[21]
Moreover, their approach lacked the sociohistorical perspective she was
better qualified to contribute after her years of close contact with the
older generation of medicine men. "All the major ceremonies started with
nine days," she wrote, "the first four being hochonje and the next four
hozhonje and the last the big finale. Well medicine-men, who for some
reason, could not learn the whole ceremony began to split it up–singing
the first four days in combination with the last day—making a five day

hochonje ceremony with the name of the mother chant attached. Or else they took the last five days and sang a Hozhonje. Then sometimes half of it was lost and so those ceremonies become known as being nothing but one or the other. The Star [chant] is supposed to be pure Hochonje but I am ready to bet that when it was sung nine days there was a 'blessing' part to it." The neat classificatory system Kluckhohn and Wyman set out to record as fact looked to her like a figment of their overeducated imaginations.

Kluckhohn's pet idea that some ceremonies centered on sorcery and witchcraft got under Newcomb's skin and stayed there. "I get perfectly *furious* over the word 'witch,'" she fumed, "—There is never an attempt to 'bewitch' anyone and that word 'life' chant gets a *rise* out of me too—*every* large ceremony has a restoration ceremony—goodness! [Washington] Matthews was better than either W- or K- will ever be. A nahtoie-anadje [Male Shooting Chant] is simply a grand mixture. Some of [the chants] that Kluckhohn lists as separate ceremonies are just minor sings that may be included in the [chant] if certain circumstances arise that require it. . . . This makes a great deal of confusion in getting a cut-and-dried-list."[22] Newcomb took issue, too, with separate work Wyman did on a Navajo "listening rite." She judged that in trying to satisfy Wyman's request for information, the informant had "mixed this rite with that of the [S]tar], probably because he did not know much about the listening rite."[23]

Though she was more sanguine about Kluckhohn and Wyman's abilities than Newcomb was, Reichard agreed that her colleagues' research design was flawed. Her own experience with Navajo chanters, pooled with Newcomb's, taught her that individual Navajo medicine men were specialists in particular ceremonies, and highly pragmatic ones at that. Their years of apprenticeship under elderly masters did not require them to grasp the totality of Navajo ritualism in order to become able practitioners. Each singer devoted himself or herself to learning subparts of the entire "mythic body" acquired slowly and deliberately from a mentor who himself controlled only parts of the religious dogma. Because ceremonial knowledge was vested in individuals rather than in a superorganic canon, as the number of elder chanters and apprentices declined in the interwar years, large quantities of ritualistic information were permanently lost to living memory. Klah's decision to devote the last years of his life to recording as much of his unwritten store of Navajo religion as he could with Wheelright and Newcomb's help was symptomatic of his historical moment. Even Klah never claimed to control the superstructure of Navajo ceremony that Kluckhohn and Wyman believed they could discern by interviewing individual practitioners.

From her systematic testing of vegetal dye-making techniques, Reichard reached the conclusion, "You never know what you are going to get. . . . It is impossible to control conditions. When the supply of materials is as uncertain and as scattered as this, when the method of concoction so crude, one can never be sure of exactly duplicating the circumstances."[24] She believed chanters exhibited a similar lack of fussiness in their art. Differing in their grasp of mythic lore, they improvised according to their specific tastes and location, though not without carefully reconciling their innovations with tradition after the fact. "My view," Reichard wrote a colleague a decade later, "is that every singer took a look around from where he practiced (maybe this ought to be in the present tense) and fixed up his worldview from his front door, so to speak. He makes it jibe with tradition and there he is."[25]

Reichard was concerned also that Kluckhohn and Wyman's methodology was ripe for observational bias. While they claimed their methodology illuminated how the Navajo medicine men understood the relationships between the ceremonies they performed, Reichard thought they ignored the fact that the Navajo rationalized and ordered their universe just as westernized Americans did.[26] "In order to make a study [of Navajo systems] satisfactory a realization of Navajo methods of classification is indispensable," she claimed in "Navajo Classification of Natural Objects," "Navajo categories are inclusive, complementary, analogous, rather than distinctive, exclusive and homologous—they are more religious than scientific. They must, therefore, be approached in a way to which taxonomists are unaccustomed."[27] Kluckhohn and Wyman clung stubbornly to the idea that they could extract a "distinctive, exclusive and homologous" taxonomy from what chanters said and did in their presence. They applied no safeguards to handle contrastive categories, negative evidence, secondary rationalizations, or "spoofing" that Reichard could see. "Clyde and I have deliberately, with malice aforethought, painfully, tediously, and I can assure you with no particular pleasure, recorded every twitch of the eyelids, in short every bit of objective behavior that we could observe, just in case it might be useful in the future," Wyman replied indignantly when she questioned their methodology in private.[28] It was certainly less time-consuming to bring Navajo ceremonialism to heel in the terms most familiar and convenient to the investigators, but Reichard saw no point in that. "I never feel a compulsion to reduce complicated material to a unity which satisfies a mere sense of neatness," she later wrote, to which all of her publications, before and after she met Kluckhohn and Wyman, testify.[29]

In theoretical terms, Reichard recognized that Navajo ceremonial practice was dynamic in a sense that Kluckhohn and Wyman missed. In her experience, Navajo chanters delighted in speculating about the interpretation and function of the constituent parts of their ceremonies. They engaged in conversations with anthropologists and one another so probing and uninhibited that their oral scholarship was itself a distinctive feature of Navajo religious practice, particularly when compared to the secretive and orthodox habits of pueblo-dwelling peoples of the Rio Grande region. Underlying their eagerness to debate ceremonial matters under the right circumstances was their love of their native language. Through learning Navajo "by ear" rather than from a book, Reichard came to appreciate that Navajo speakers feared "no diminution" or corruption of their language owing to diversification, variation, and innovation. "On the contrary," Reichard said of the language, "it may look forward to unlimited enrichment which, though the despair of the learner, is a perpetual satisfaction to the users who appreciate its genius."[30]

Unable to influence Kluckhohn and Wyman's thinking about Navajo ceremonials, Reichard dropped out of the project. Her "active cooperation" was duly noted in the introduction to *Navaho Classification of Their Song and Ceremonials* when it was published as an AAA Memoir in 1938. Haile, with Sapir, who by then was recuperating from the near-fatal heart attack he had suffered the previous summer, came in for more emphatic thanks.[31] In spirit, Kluckhohn and Wyman's classification owed more to Haile's fusty certitude than Sapir's bold impressionism, though neither man approved of the pair's work.

Dry as well as pedestrian, *Navaho Classification* lacked the sensitive multidimensionality that Reichard brought to Navajo ethnography by including Native women's voices. Kluckhohn and Wyman asserted that ceremonial knowledge was not safeguarded by Navajo women, who coincidentally played no role in validating the authors' results. The men's arrangement of ceremonies was systematic on its face but vulnerable to charges that it isolated myth from ritual to the detriment of both. They demonstrated that the warrant for their taxonomic decisions hinged on quantity rather than quality of data with their claim that "the adult male Navaho over fifty probably knows at least fifty percent of the facts" presented in their paper.[32] In the end, neither Kluckhohn nor Wyman were fully convinced that their classification or the theories that informed it comprised the final word on the topic, though neither ever conceded that Reichard's critique of their methodology had merit.[33]

· · · ◈ · · ·

In the fall of 1936, Reichard was at Barnard feeling "full of prunes about the Southwest."[34] Heading her list of delightful topics was the plan the publisher of *Navajo Shepherd and Weaver*, J. J. Augustin, had to launch a new series on Southwest ethnology for her type of audience. Then a letter from Roman Hubbell reached her desk on October 13 containing bad news. Miguelito was dead. Three days earlier Roman had stopped at White Sands to find the old chanter alone, looking "awful bad, weak," and "breathing very hard and fast." He left to collect Miguelito's daughters and sons-in-law from their winter camp near the trading post, Roman recounted, then, leaving them with their ailing parent, set off to find a white doctor. It was too late. By the time Roman reached White Sands for the third time in one morning, the family turned to him for help with burial arrangements. The trader saw to it that their mutual friend and elder was buried "with his saddle, buffalo robe, quirt, buckskins, saddle blanket." "I gave them a quilt and Pendleton robe to wrap him in. They killed his sorrel horse at White Sands. We buried Miguelito at Ganado next to his wife. . . . That is the sad story—the medicine man's last hours. . . . I will miss him and so will the Navajos."[35]

Reichard replied immediately. "I am sorta numb still from the shock of your letter. . . . [Miguelito's death] marks the end of an epoch with me, really I shall have to start all over psychologically and I am doubtful so far as to how I shall do it. . . . It is too unbelievable and sudden to be able to get any perspective." Yet grief was no excuse for ingratitude. "Right here I want to say again what I tried to say feebly in the Preface of Shepherd and Weaver and I don't seem to have any fancy words in which to say it, but it is simply that the experience with Mig's family was an event in my life and if you had not sent me to him I should have missed all that richness."[36]

Roman's offer to find Reichard another chanter to help her with the Shooting Chant lore proved unnecessary. Newcomb, knowing Reichard had plans to spend her winter break in the Southwest working with her on the sandpainting book, arranged for the anthropologist to spend three weeks studying with her good friend and teacher Hastiin Klah.[37] All of the personal attributes Reichard treasured in Miguelito were evident in Klah, who, if anything, set a still higher bar for self-collected individuality. Described variously as a hermaphrodite, transvestite, berdache, or man-woman by his white contemporaries, Klah occupied a narrow ledge in Navajo society as both medicine man and weaver. Local lore told of his being castrated as a baby by Utes who attacked his family on the trail home from Fort Sumner. Beyond that, Klah's Navajo and white friends took little note of his sexuality. "[T]here was nothing feminine about him unless an indescribable gentleness be so called," Reichard later wrote of Klah. He invested his entire being in the practice of his faith, through chanting, weaving, and teaching.

On whether it was Klah's cosmology or his personality that contributed more to his appeal Reichard did not hazard a guess. Instead, she described him as a man who belonged to that rare class of open-minded scholars. "He was a person with many facets," she wrote of Klah. "One became instantly acquainted with him, one constantly found in him depths not easily plumbed, uncanny intuition, capacity for quiet and bubbling humor, a sure stability, and, at the same time, a wide and even experimental tolerance. His voice was gentle and low, though interesting, his actions never impulsive but energetic and swift, his principles and convictions unshakable. . . . His was an intuitive, speculative, imaginative mind, far from conservative, though he remained orthodox. He was always ready to examine new ideas, he harbored certain notions probably held by no other Navajo, unless taught by him."[38]

The three weeks Reichard spent under Klah's tutelage in January 1937 steadied her.[39] When the seventy-two-year-old chanter died in March she found a slim silver lining in being able to share Newcomb's genuine sorrow at losing him.[40] Reichard's determination to carry on with her work in spite of the deaths of Red-Point and Klah was tested further when Atlnaba died in the spring.[41] Of the Red-Point family Reichard wrote gloomily in April, "There is now really no head left in any sense to the family."[42] She was wrong, as she was glad to discover in summer watching Marie take her older sister's place in the ritual cleansing of her father's medicine bundle. "While Miguelito lived I had sometimes asked Marie the why of a rite or ceremony and often she answered, 'I don't know,'" Reichard observed as hope returned. "Now I discovered that Marie's former 'I-don't-knows' were due, not to lack of interest, as I had supposed, or to real lack of knowledge, but rather to the fact that [her] seniors were authority and she was not. After the death of her sister she was the head of the house, and when I asked her how she knew all this [ceremonial knowledge], she said, 'My father taught me.'"[43]

"Am glad you got your helper for the summer," Newcomb wrote Reichard ahead of her return to the Southwest that year. "It will probably speed up collecting but I can't see that you needed any extra speeding—."[44] The helper Franc referred to was Adolph Bitanny, one of the young Navajo men who'd participated in Reichard's Hogan School. Orphaned at a young age, Bitanny developed into a quirky, inquisitive young man with college ambitions. The grandmother who raised him was a traditionalist with a passion for Navajo language. She delighted in "drill[ing] her grandson in 'classical' Navaho" and "play[ing] games with forms and meanings," games that instilled a love of linguistics in Bitanny before he knew the science by name.[45] Though Bitanny's fascination with oral and written traditions was ill-served by the fragmented, largely vocational education he'd received in a succession of boarding schools, he dreamed of becoming a bilingual writer, teacher, and community leader. At their first meeting, Bitanny casually responded to Reichard's observation that tribal council members and white bureau employees always seemed to talk past one another. "Yes, they don't have the proper psychological weapons for understanding," he remarked. "He is a philosopher," Reichard liked to say of Adolph, a youth inclined to ask, "How did that come about?" and "How do you explain that?" when other returned students stayed mum.[46]

After the Hogan School, Bitanny had returned to the University of New Mexico, where his grades in all subjects were unimpressive. His behavior at college gave signs of the apathy that the forced dependency of reservation life often produced in young Navajos. Bitanny was cavalier about his own and other people's money. Keeping appointments, completing homework assignments, and filling out paperwork on time were a challenge for him. He received some encouragement from members of the Anthropology Department, but his prospects for graduation were dim. As soon as Reichard offered him a summer job as her assistant in 1937, however, he snapped out of his doldrums.

With Bitanny in the jump seat, Reichard flew past the milestones she'd laid out for the summer of 1937. "I have been in the Southwest 3 weeks & have done as much as many do in 3 months," she wrote Parsons. "I have gone over the notes on the Shooting Chant & the myth & it is nothing short of remarkable the way they jibe."[47] Bitanny's youthful zest fueled Reichard's own. Adolph was wonderfully keen and "clicks faster than I can write," she wrote Parsons, "he writes insatiably himself & we are so excited an 8-hr. day like today goes like a twinkling."[48] To Boas she effused, "[Adolph] has great files of the Nav. verbs all written out in conjugations, he is working on the prefixes & he roams up & down giving me lectures" on possible connections between Navajo language and worldview. "He brot out a drawing representing the Nav. idea of man, his relation to the earth & the universe based on *post-positions*. It is as neat & original piece of business as you could ask for. . . . Everyday he presents me with new surprises, works all day & all night, for fear he won't live long enough to get it all down!"[49] By summer's end Reichard had arranged the funding for Bitanny to attend Columbia. He could finish his degree at Columbia College while acting as her winter research assistant. No one assumed it would be easy for Bitanny to adjust to big-city life, yet Gladys was certain she could mentor Adolph in New York just as she had supervised Lawrence Nicodemus's studies at Columbia during the previous year.[50] By November Reichard's optimism seemed justified. She wrote Roman Hubbell, "Adolph seems to be very happy here. He is learning a lot and displays none of the disagreeable sides which we noted—I am sure they were a product of his social situation out there."[51]

The small edition of *Sandpaintings of the Navajo Shooting Chant* J. J. Augustin issued in time for the holiday shopping season sold out quickly. Newcomb's deft line drawings and brightly colored paintings on handmade Japanese paper delivered the visual feast Reichard had envisioned from the start. Her eighty-seven pages of text tickled the reader's imagination with vivid passages such as this one: "When [the Chanter] gets to the painting of the feet I almost shiver, but the patient sits immoveable even when the Chanter covers her big toenail with paint to represent the head of a snake and also when he carries the paint down under part of the first joint to designate the tongue. This patient is a Stoic. I have gone through this twice myself and I know it is possible to remain quiet, but it stirs me to see someone else do so."[52]

For the specialist and layman alike, Reichard supplied a condensed, English-language version of the Shooting Chant legend told by Blue Eyes, followed by chapters that analyzed the form, content, and meaning of sandpainting art for non-Navajos. "It is then with a relatively small assortment of artistic devices, with subtle and balanced use of color; with outline and contrast; with conventionalized and largely inarticulate proportions; with rhythm and motion, these based upon the ritualism of the number four and a subsidiary variant, five; that the Navajo attain effects which have the permanent charm of unity, variety, and with few stereotyped exceptions, consistency," she explained. "The secret of the effect is the originality in the choice of device, the subtlety in its use, the imagination with which the simplest devices are combined, the surprise which is constantly created, in short, a demonstration of naivete and great knowingness combined with the most extreme simplicity.[53]

Perhaps because *Sandpaintings* was received as an art object in its own right, no anthropologist acknowledged it in print as an addition to "the permanent literature on the subject of the Navajo."[54] Reichard herself greeted her first co-authored book with a touch of chagrin. Newcomb had demanded many last-minute changes to the galley proofs, which produced significant cost overruns for Augustin. With her better understanding of Augustin's burdens, Reichard took her favorite publisher's side in the conflict. An exasperated Reichard confided to Dorothy Hubbell, "I am just lucky as hell to be finished with Franc without anything having happened to upset it. Mary Wheelwright and she are having a lawsuit about the sandpaintings and she has abused J.J. shamefully. I think it a great accomplishment to have wangled her, but this is of course my conceit." The incident did not spoil the women's friendship, but Reichard's wish to co-author books with Newcomb came to an end. "The smart thing to do will be to be ready with another [sandpainting book]," she noted looking ahead rather than back. "And I very much fear that it will not be Franc who will collaborate on the next one."[55]

In 1938 Reichard's stunning productivity, combined with a slight improvement in Barnard's finances, yielded the sweet tender of a sabbatical.

For the first three of her eight months of liberty from teaching and advising she retired to an Edenic cabin on the densely forested slopes of Lake Coeur d'Alene. She had passed the summer of 1936 finishing her grammar of Coeur d'Alene for the *Handbook of American Indian Languages* at the same location. Salish language work, frequent dips in the "lovely and cold" lake water, and word from Adolph that he was making excellent progress with the Navajo texts they had collected the previous year kept her from fretting about "the only fly in my ointment" in Idaho, "that the time here is too short."[56] Somehow she finished her ethnographic novel, *Dezba, Woman of the Desert*, which she brushed off as "the little book I had promised Augustin."[57]

Once back in Arizona for the fall, she went "'on the hoof' just like the Navs." "So as of Aug. 27 I arrived here and have been at it ever since," she crowed to Parsons. "What is 'it'? Sings, darling, sings!"[58] In the first six weeks she attended enough Navajo chants and rituals to keep herself and Bitanny busy analyzing texts for years to come. "Every sandpainting I saw but one was new to me & I have seen many collections," she told Boas. "My system—the only satisfactory one that I know—is to follow the whole damn [ceremony] thru from beginning to end & this I do for those [chants] I am working with. . . . One can't do everything."[59]

Not that Reichard found anything damnable in the ceremonies. It was the constant demand for haste and efficiency in the white man's terms—her terms as a working anthropologist—that weighed heavily on her as she sought to synchronize her actions and moods with Navajo rhythms. "In nothing that the Navajo undertake is the question of time important as it is to us," she noted in *Sandpaintings of the Navajo Shooting Chant*.[60] When teaching, chanters and weavers did not "condemn a person because he was deliberate, no matter how long he might take at a task. Accuracy and finish are the ideals and if they can be attained in three days better than in one, by all means take three." Reichard rejected the idea that the Navajo lacked a concept of time, as the linguist Benjamin Whorf suggested the Hopi did. She did allow that Navajos valued time differently. They didn't worship, commodify, and fetishize it as European Americans did. When Reichard joked to Boas near the start of her sabbatical, "Who said 8 months was a long time to work?" she voiced a most "un-Navajo" plaint: Not enough time.[61]

Reichard took great pride in meeting the challenges of flash floods, washed-out roads, and threading her bulky camper through rough

terrain. Best of all, her first protracted stay on the Navajo Reservation confirmed the "marvelous" sense of inclusion and faith afforded her by the
commitments of time, effort, and responsibility she'd made to the Navajo
at White Sands. She articulated this solidarity first as she earned her
"degree in weaving" from Marie and Atlnaba, who worried only, "'What
if we shouldn't be able to teach her?'" rather than whether she planned
to put them out of business.[62] After Miguelito died, Gladys discovered
to her joy that her education as a chanter was to continue unimpeded,
out of respect for her teacher. "It's all right!" a chanter she knew cried to
someone protesting her presence as sandpaintings were being drawn for
a ceremony. "She is the granddaughter of Red-Point, recently deceased.
He was teaching her to sing. He can't do it now anymore, but we have to
do for her what he would do if he were living."[63]

The social obligations that bound individuals dead or alive into the
social cooperative were not symptomatic of crass cronyism, in Reichard's
view, because they were executed impersonally. The fact of her apprenticeship with Red-Point marked her as trustworthy and dedicated, traits
that outweighed the force of a negative reaction any single Navajo might
have to her presence at a sing. A similar objectivity applied when Reichard
pointed out an omission in a large sandpainting she observed being laid.
She was prepared to have to soothe the feelings of the painters because
in her culture an individual generally identified an error in his work with
himself. "I was nonplussed when the crowd of thirty painters shook my
hand and thanked me for pointing out the error. . . . I am quite sure,
too, that they were all impressed because the criticism was based on the
Navaho word 'zigzag lighting' which they were not accustomed to hear
used by a white person." Reichard analyzed the chanter's lack of defensiveness as owing to their respect for greater knowledge, which easily
trumped personal pride. "Knowledge is power," she understood the men
to believe, "a little knowledge is a recommendation for gaining more."[64]

To Elsie she wrote, "I do think the Navs come as near being an objective people as any I know. For that reason they also seem to step over
all the sensitivities and emotions of the white man, and I suspect that
is where the difficulty most people have getting along with them lies."[65]
Seen through a romantic lens, Reichard found her "real country" among
the wisest men and women of the Navajo people.[66] In her more pragmatic
view, she was simply their perpetual student. "The Indians take very good

care of me . . . now they take me very casually & as one of them, so that I am constantly filling in gaps and hearing things. I understand almost all the ceremonial talk now."[67] She was not yet worthy of the title "woman chanter." Still, it was indescribably gratifying to her to overhear the old sages explaining to new arrivals that she was "not like other white people," and hadn't been for a good long while.[68]

· · · ◈ · · ·

Adding an upscale coda to her first sabbatical, Reichard made an overnight stop in Kansas City on her way east. There she met Minnie Harvey Huckel, daughter of Fred Harvey and widow of John Frederick Huckel, co-owner and director of the Fred Harvey Company. A year earlier, Harvey Company representative Herman Schweizer approached Newcomb on Mrs. Huckel's behalf with a proposal. Huckel wanted to commission a book on Navajo sandpainting in honor of her late husband, a collector of Indian "curios" who many years earlier had commissioned a set of sandpainting pictures from Miguelito. "Hurray!! And Hurray!!" Newcomb wrote Reichard with the news.[69] "We are going to help with the assembling of material and publishing another Sand-painting book." Newcomb assumed the role of writer-coordinator and assigned Reichard a minor role.

> Well!! Thank Something!!. That we did not use very many of Mig's in ours. So out of the forty-nine or fifty, there were ten that we listed as doing in black and white because they were duplicates of those already published. . . . Their own artist is to make the copies all of one size on the same paper that I was using before—thinks he can get them done sometime in Jan. Is that all right? Mr. Switzer [sic] and Mrs. Huckel will prepare the preface that tells of Mr. Huckel's interest in collecting Navajo sand-paintings. Also about their work with Mig. (They have some excellent pictures) Then comes you, to give it an ethnological standing—as much space as you need—Then comes the myth that Switzer took from Mig, and the sand-paintings with descriptions, Then I have a chapter on the Symbols of the various paintings, and then there are the notes which you and I will see fit to use for explanation. . . . If you are coming to Albu- anytime I will get the manuscript up here and we will try to thresh [. . . it] out.[70]

Reichard was on sabbatical by the time Newcomb conceded, "I'm not a good writer," and dropped out of the project altogether.[71] She urged Reichard to make time to "write a couple of chapters" for Huckel over the winter. "You asked just what I wanted you to do about [the Huckel book]—in four words—"Take charge of it"—tell me what to do and I will follow on to the best of my ability."

Reichard's skepticism about the Huckel book gave way to a sense of duty tinged with curiosity. Since Miguelito's death, she had been discussing with Roman Hubbell a book that would memorialize their favorite chanter. If she agreed to accept the Harvey commission, she could pay tribute to Miguelito and have a chance to work with a private collection of his watercolor sandpaintings. She tested the waters by making Schweizer an offer to write the entire "script" of the book without interference from Harvey staff. Reichard named a fee of one thousand dollars plus research expenses for herself. Augustin, her first choice of publisher, was to be reimbursed for all publication expenses for the costly limited edition. Sounding more disinterested than she felt, Reichard let it be known that if her terms were not acceptable she would not be offended. "I am very eager to see the Huckel Collection put into a form which can be used by the public interested in such things, and if I should be the one chosen to do it. . . . I should do all in my power to make the work a worthy one."[72]

By mid-December she had her answer. The Harvey people thought her fee modest and her plan for the text sound.[73] Reichard promptly informed Boas, "[A]fter a lot of balling up by Franc Newcomb, the Fred Harveys are going to let me write up their sandpainting collection. . . . I'm dying to see [it]."[74] Her trip home to New York in February would include unscheduled stops in Kansas City and Chicago to ink a deal that met all her terms. When she met Huckel, her Chicago lawyer, and Fred Geary, their in-house artist, they were as impressed with her as she was with them.[75] Someone let slip that they were relieved to have Newcomb off the job, as Geary was known to be "temperamental" and needed a cool-headed, organized partner to keep his nose to the grindstone.[76]

Reichard's path may have been "covered with Fred Harvey flowers from Albuquerque to Chicago" at the start of her contract, but by the time *Navajo Medicine Man Sandpaintings* came out in the fall of 1939, relations had soured.[77] Huckel's last-minute objections to the proofs and plates ballooned Augustin's expenses. When the company refused to cover the cost overruns he incurred, Reichard watched in dismay while her friend was "almost ruined." Although writer and patron had been on a first-name basis throughout the project, Huckel never contacted Reichard to acknowledge her contribution once the book was published. Harvey Company press releases promoting the volume to wealthy collectors omitted mention of Reichard as the author of the text. "I must say that the Huckel outfit is one of the hardest I ever had to contend with," Reichard complained in response. "I hope I am finished with them, and as far as I am concerned I have no kick, for I have lost nothing except more of my faith in human beings and I suppose that does not matter much since I had so little left."[78]

Newcomb's reaction to the Harvey book was no less puzzling to Reichard. She had called on Franc on her way to Kansas to make sure the artist did not regret her decision to withdraw from the project. "We had a very nice visit," Reichard reported to Dorothy Hubbell. "[Franc] is in fine fettle & there are a great many pleasant things about her. I feel much better about the affair from having seen her."[79] Yet, in an interview for the *Albuquerque Journal*, Newcomb took credit for *Medicine Man*, though her name didn't appear on the book's title page. "You know I hope that this does not make any difference to me at all, because the people who ought to know do know and those who do not know don't matter," Reichard vented to Dorothy. "So I would just laugh at this if I did not think it indicates even more abnormality than I had accredited to Franc."[80]

All five hundred copies of the book sold for the princely sum of thirty-six dollars apiece within two months of issue. The fuss that attended its publication remained a private matter. Writing to ask where she should send the drawings still in her possession, Reichard told Huckel's lawyer, "The only place where the book has had a cool reception is in Kansas City. You might like to know that here [New York] and also in New Mexico— Franc Newcomb included—it has been received with the same effect as that of an exceptional music program where people are too overwhelmed to clap for some minutes. Objectively and as far as the most discriminating public is concerned it is an unqualified success."[81]

Once more, university anthropologists took a pass on reviewing a "picture book" not sanctioned by their academic traditions. Writer Erna Fergusson was less meek. The author of *Our Southwest* made clear Reichard was no wealthy white transplant to her region intent on exploiting Native artists for political or financial gain. Writing for the *New York Herald Tribune*, Fergusson called *Navajo Medicine Man Sandpaintings* "a volume of distinguished beauty" destined for "important public and college libraries." Miguelito's sandpaintings were "works of art" of "extraordinary loveliness in their balanced design and delicate color" and Reichard's essays contextualized them with "no hint of condescension or of invidious comparison."

Fergusson declared the book's overarching value its potential to accelerate "the white man's changing attitude toward primitive peoples and their beliefs and ceremonies," a judgment that harmonized perfectly with Reichard's intentions. *Medicine Man*, the native New Mexican wrote, opened her eyes to Navajo ideas that serious students of Native history and myth like herself had not understood before. "One is struck throughout by the foreignness of Navajo concepts," she wrote. "Unlike Egyptian, Greek, or even Oriental arts and religions which have been filtering into our culture for centuries, Navajo painting and literature are so strange to us that they appear like a distant view through a newly opened window. They have not yet even begun to enter our stream of consciousness through our own arts. So far Navajo lore is meaningless to most of us, even though we can see the beauty of a sand painting and enjoy the imagination and the humorous knowledge of human nature that enlivens the legends."[82]

Taking a page from the Navajo, Reichard set aside her ruffled feelings. "I got the Huckel business figgered out now," she told Dorothy. "It is *their* book & they aim to keep it *theirs*. . . . They probably won't be able to avoid the library listing but they will keep it Huckel in all public ways." Huckel and Newcomb had taken her for granted, but she had little else to complain about. As always, publication allowed her, if only momentarily, to be heard above the din of romantic nonsense about the Navajo. "Although I bellyache . . . about all I have to do," she once wrote the Hubbells, "I seem to keep getting on. I wouldn't like it if nobody noticed me."[83] Hobnobbing briefly with the captains of industry for a good cause did no lasting harm to Reichard's ego or integrity. "Well I suppose that is all right," she said to Dorothy of the Harvey dust-up. "They paid me didn't they? Just like buying a sack of wool. You pays your money & you takes your wool! So we may as well forget it. And after we have done so, the book remains 'a thing of beauty & a joy as long as it lasts.'"[84]

CHAPTER 7

COOPERATION

MOBILITY WAS A CONSTANT THEME OF REICHARD'S LIFE in the Dirty
Thirties. Despite the great black blizzards of topsoil that choked anything
that breathed in the American heartland, she moved as freely between
wintry New York and sunny Arizona as she did between Grantwood and
Manhattan Island. Fellow travelers might find her silently marking up
galley proofs in a Fred Harvey–style lounge car or chatting amiably with
a westbound stranger, the now familiar landscapes thundering past the
windows at speed. Others glimpsed Reichard as she ran through the gears
of the faithful Ford she named Jonathan, determined to reach Gallup or
Grants or Albuquerque by nightfall. Friends and family out East stopped
being astonished to receive letters postmarked in Idaho, Montana, California, New Mexico, and Arizona in a single summer. As she headed back
to New York one fall, she remarked, "A train certainly seems like a cage
after my summer."[1] Relatively speaking, she wasn't exaggerating. From
the thousands of lineal miles of hardpan, gravel, asphalt, and steel that
zigzagged across her wounded nation, Reichard fashioned an office the
size of a continent.

   The innocuous social lubricants she'd learned growing up in a small
town—friendliness, respect for others, sensitivity to needs beyond her
own—served her in every social circumstance. "I can never understand
why people are so nice to me," Gladys wrote the Hubbells, but as her
closest allies in the Southwest, Dorothy and Roman were not surprised
that doors opened to their learned friend wherever she went.[2] The key
to the welcome Reichard received was her genuine interest in people
and places. By midcareer, Reichard had joined the profound simplicity
of the Golden Rule to the Navajo facility for "adaptations to persons."
"The Navaho judge persons as individuals and approve or reject them

as such rather than as members of a group," she wrote in 1954. "This attitude is basic as a factor of Navajo individuality."[3] Because to most of her nervous American readership an individualist was one who set herself apart from society by focusing on her radical self-interest or personal pride, Reichard had to explain in *Navajo Religion* (1950) that "individualism" was a relative concept, subject to varied interpretation by groups as well as by individuals within them. "The Navaho has always been recognized as an individualist. Since his inherited membership in a clan and a clan group imposes on him rigid restrictions, as well as obligations to a great many people, and his acquiescence in his religious system requires the strictest sort of discipline, one might well inquire wherein his individualism lies."

> Doubtless the most important factor is that [a Navajo] does not feel bound. He retains his individualistic attitude because of the system rather than in spite of it. Since his membership in a clan and clan-group and an additional relationship to his father's clan and clan-group make it possible for him to consider a great many persons obligated to him, he emphasizes his privileges rather than his duties. . . . If Tall Navaho decides to have a Mountain Chant sung, he calls upon Shorty to donate a sheep and invites him to attend the performance. Shorty considers the request an honor, for has he not upon several occasions borrowed small sums from Tall Navaho which he has not yet returned? . . .
>
> When Tall Navaho's wife enters the hogan or ceremonial enclosure, unmindful of ritualistic requirements other than knowing that women sit at the north side of the hogan, she may stalk casually to the right of the fire, since that is the shortest way to the place she is bound for. The chanter or someone else will say, "Go around the fire," meaning "move in a clockwise direction." She reverses, goes the roundabout way, and takes her place. She does not interpret the request as depriving her of her individuality any more than Shorty does if the chanter tells him to wind a string around a withe in a clockwise direction when he has unthinkingly started to wind it counterclockwise. The homogeneity of belief interprets [religious] dogma as protecting individualism rather than impinging on it.[4]

In the act of exploring the "great river delta" of Navajo social philosophy, Reichard came face-to-face with an alternate conception of the individual in relation to society.[5] Navajo-style individualism, she observed, gave a Navajo person entry to her society instead of isolating her from it. "A good Navaho is, therefore, an individual who can and may make his own decisions, but he is most stable if he has social corroboration. . . . Ideally, the 'good' individual should be industrious, dependable, tractable, skillful, good-humored. He should be able to live with others without friction, for social relations are a part of the universal scheme which demands harmony for right living."[6] The wellspring of the Navajo's "democratic, untrammeled way of life," in her view, was not an innate restlessness peculiar to semi-nomadic peoples but an emotion common to all humans: loneliness.[7] "I consider solitude the basic reason for Navaho development of and insistence upon self-reliance. . . . The co-operation that extends from the individual, on the one hand to family and all residential relationships, and on the other to clan members, father's clan relatives, clan-group members, and finally, to strangers, seems to be due to the fight against loneliness. . . . [H]elp [is] a primary ideal which gives the lonely individual security in his broad and often unfriendly terrain." If watching Navajos be raised "to act independently from earliest childhood" reminded Reichard of her own upbringing, she was also able to appreciate "the privilege a Navaho individual values in his personal subordination to the group." Such subordination as was required of a Navajo individual was amply rewarded, she knew, by "his extreme pleasure in any group activity, be it harvesting, building a dam, or attending a council meeting, rodeo, ceremony, or Christmas party.[8]

Reichard's personal integrity didn't allow her to pretend to be a Navajo woman with well-defined clan and kinship obligations. To "go Native"—that is, "to achieve complete identification" with the Navajo worldview—would have meant surrendering her hard-won identity as a free-thinking, university-trained anthropologist.[9] The best she could do to transcend her ethno-cultural boundaries was to attempt to belong to multiple "tribes" simultaneously, each with conventions and privileges established by the weight of distinct histories and traditions. Her rights and responsibilities at Barnard were distinct from those she incurred on the reservation or in the exclusive anthropological establishment. The challenge often came down to her figuring out how to behave in ways that expressed the high value Navajos placed on efficacy, imperturbability, and self-restraint in mainstream settings where efficiency, precipitancy, and going-it-alone were extolled.[10] Reichard's concern with being a fair-minded, "objective" anthropologist under every circumstance didn't leave much time for social gamesmanship or romantic intrigue. When Reichard wrote Boas, "I really have no private life," she merely acknowledged the "what you see is what you get" attitude she had with respect to her personality.[11] She had little need to "cultivat[e] [her] soul" for ego's sake.[12] As a public intellectual her character was a matter of public record.

Despite being an avid consumer of print and radio news, Reichard was, like most Americans, slow to grasp the seriousness of the political trends occurring in western Europe during the 1930s. In mid-1934 she knew so little about Germany's newly elected chancellor in mid-1934 that she asked Boas, "What is Hitler about? Can & will his power be busted up?"[13] By the end of her first sabbatical, resurgent hostility toward immigrants and rising nativist paranoia on Main Street and in Washington, D.C. prompted Reichard to concede that "the whole world ha[s] changed since I left [New York]" and it was high time she "g[o]t used to it as it is."[14] She was far from alone in thinking mass-media reports were false, for they often were. Excitable journalists conjectured without facts about the material dangers posed by Hitler's militarism. Wealthy industrialists and their congressional toadies herded public opinion in one direction while the Roosevelt administration and allies steered popular support, without loss of power, in another.

Even with the facts in constant dispute, Reichard knew enough by the end of 1938 to act against "the present outrages in Germany." She was one of just four Barnard faculty to join 1,284 scientists from 167 universities in signing an anti-fascist manifesto pledging signatories to "educate American people against all false and unscientific doctrines, such as the racial nonsense of the Nazis."[15] Reichard quietly made cash donations to national organizations for "Jewish relief." She also offered to resettle her Hamburg friends, African art specialist Theodor Danzel and family, in her Newtown cabin should they choose to seek permanent asylum in the United States.[16] Once committed to asserting her global citizenship, Reichard became an anti-Nazi standard-bearer on her campus. In December 1939, as Nazis were ramping up mass "mercy killings" of undesirables. Reichard was asked by students to answer the fraught question, "What is race?"

The answer she gave to a large, mixed crowd at Barnard's Brinkerhoff Theatre was a subtle justification for the study and celebration of human differences. "Contrary to popular belief," Reichard repeated patiently, "all tests devised show no provable connection between bodily form and mental ability." Racial prejudices were "inculcated during childhood," she said, and those with the means to free themselves of harmful bias must resist demagogues who instigated "religious, imperialistic, and political conflict" grounded in racial or physical differences.[17]

A year later, Reichard wrote an invited editorial for the *Barnard Bulletin* that tactfully exposed the dangers of "America First" isolationism in the face of the Nazi "juggernaut." She took a wide-angled view of the unfolding crisis to argue that human progress was less a steady upward climb toward perfection than a tale of "recurrent succession." Calling "our social confusion" part of "man's necessary environment," she recast progress as "the speed[y] boomerang our culture has made for us and at the same time hurled against us." She recommended deliberation and courage as the tools needed to "reassemble and synthesize" America's social order "into a new pattern." Time was of the essence. "A new solution will therefore not be allowed a slow growth. It must spring up and attain maturity over night, and must be as strong as the thread of a bridge cable, as practical as a bombsight."[18]

Reichard's position on U.S. entry into the war against Hitler was less clear-cut. Antiwar sentiment had run high at Columbia since the early 1930s. In response to the atrocity of the Great War, the Anti-War Committee became a fixture of Columbia's extracurricular life. By 1933 the Committee had passed resolutions urging students, faculty, and staff members to pledge themselves to "NON-COOPERATION WITH THE WAR OFFICE in any of [the] ways in which they might be useful in case of war." President Nicholas Butler and others criticized their position on war and peace as "immature" and tantamount to a pledge to "sabotage" their country's ability to defend its territory, people, and democratic way of life.[19] There was too much emphasis on antiwar proclamations and pledges, moderates said. The young were missing the opportunity to agitate for a rational peace-seeking agenda in Washington, D.C., they warned, where American prejudice against collective, international arbitration through the League of Nations and the World Court had hamstrung more than one administration's efforts to engage constructively with other nation-states.

Anti-War Committee member Franz Boas, on the other hand, defended the younger generation of activists. He agreed with students that the "attack on civil liberties" being waged domestically by the Dies Committee of Congress, forerunner of the House Un-American Committee, against Communists, Russian "plants" on college campuses, labor unionists, peace activists, and other subversives was "an important step in the drive to involve the U.S. in the war" against the will of most Americans.[20] As much as Boas hated fascism, by 1940 the eighty-two-year-old freedom-loving pacifist was spotted wearing a large button on his lapel that read, "Roosevelt is a warmonger."[21]

At Barnard, isolationist, antiwar rhetoric was less strident, thanks in large part to Dean Gildersleeve's open sympathy for President Roosevelt and America's western allies. After the fall of Denmark, Norway, the Lowlands, and France and the trauma of the Battle of Britain, few Barnardites could maintain the pretense of the Nazi campaign as a wholly foreign affair. Since the end of World War I, Gildersleeve had evolved into a globetrotting internationalist who articulated the need for a league of nations months before former president Woodrow Wilson had. As totalitarian regimes gained strength abroad, Gildersleeve launched a sweeping campaign from the Barnard deanery designed to mobilize university women in the fight against "the powers of hate and violence" embedded in "Nazi philosophy."[22] Fortunately for Reichard, her dean deemed free inquiry into the nature of humankind to be as patriotic as teaching the National Service courses in civil defense, map reading, and first aid that Gildersleeve added to the Barnard curriculum with lightning speed.

As a ranking "officer" in Gildersleeve's "War of the Trained Brains," Reichard was able to acquit herself as a committed pacifist might, armed only with books and liberal, democratic ideals. Her bulwark against racial prejudice was the biennial survey course, which in the late 1930s enrolled as many as 135 students per year drawn from "practically every department . . . at Barnard."[23] She championed minority peoples and the psychic unity of humankind from the lectern in each of her elective courses as well. In 1940 Reichard published an essay in the *Barnard Quarterly* that gave students and alumnae a glimpse of a Native American worldview aimed at peace rather than war. "The Navajo believes that only by keeping himself in complete harmony with all things with which he is acquainted, both material and spiritual, can he expect to succeed in his earthly undertakings," Barnard's anthropologist wrote. "The ideal of his worldly and even other-worldly relationships is to 'be at one with them.'"[24] This sensible, life-loving human, she explained, employed ritual, repetition, magic, and song to drive off evil and correct the imbalances introduced by human error into the "essential harmony" of his universe. "But although the Navajo considers ritual or ceremonial as a cure for all ills—of nature, of the flesh or of the spirit—he uses song for pleasure, for company, for protection." Judging many of her readers to be too frightened, apathetic, or numb for a change of perspective, she ended by reminding them that human differences were only skin deep. "As an airman pilots his course on a beam of light so the Navajo, straying or lost in the fog of doubt, confusion or error, or happy and content in a golden shower of sunset, pilots his life 'on the beam of a song.'"[25]

Early in 1942, President Roosevelt held sixty-one million map-wielding listeners spellbound as he "explain[ed] to the people something about geography," in a fireside radio chat.[26] With other Barnard faculty, Reichard sensed the broadcast created a teachable moment for college students as well. She teamed with several other Barnard science faculty to mount a series of exhibitions of rare maps of historical, anthropological, linguistic, geological, and mineralogical importance in Milbank Hall. Students reportedly "gathered in such large numbers" to view the exhibitions that they "blocked traffic" in the campus's main classroom building.[27] The following year Reichard joined faculty from the departments of speech and four modern languages in a series of round tables on comparative phonetics. She gave a lecture to the Classical Club on "The Relationship Between Language and Thought," and continued to draw steady enrollments in her popular elective courses Language and Thought, Religion in Primitive Society, The Art of Primitive Man, and The Study of Folklore.[28]

The *Barnard Bulletin* announced in 1944 that Reichard would be teaching a summer class called Problems of Race. Reichard had begun to prepare the new course months before the U.S. Education Office urged all colleges to "inaugurate as part of the regular curriculum the scientific study of the Negro and other races and their contribution to American and world culture" for the purpose of eliminating "race as a disruptive element in the American nation."[29] Student interest in the course was stirred by "The Negro: Viewed by an Anthropologist," an interview

Reichard gave to the *Barnard Bulletin*. Unafraid of reprisal, she had noted
the discriminatory nature of Barnard's entrance exam and its failure to
accommodate "inequalities of the social environment" common to African American hopefuls. Segregation, discrimination, and patronage, she
made clear, were the instruments of power used to keep individual black
Americans from fulfilling their human potential.[30]

Reichard's outspokenness about race and discrimination suggests she
achieved social corroboration at Barnard without loss of individuality
under Gildersleeve's enlightened command. Just before the war broke,
Dean Gildersleeve acknowledged Reichard's willingness to be a team
player for democracy by promoting her anthropologist to the rank of
associate professor.[31] During the war, Reichard's campus-based gratifica-
tions came largely from her students. She took comfort in the fact that
the anthropological perspective she deemed so important for the young
to adopt seemed finally to have achieved relevance in the minds of her
students. Rather than skip class to meet up with their "GIs" on shore leave,
patriotic Barnardites brought their boyfriends to class. Others got in the
habit of writing their men about what they were learning of South Seas
cultures in their anthropology classes so that the soldiers enjoyed a free
"correspondence course in anthropology," with Reichard's full blessing.[32]

In the spring of 1945 Gildersleeve was appointed the lone woman
member of the U.S. delegation to the San Francisco Conference where
the Charter of the United Nations was to be written and signed. The
nine weeks she spent drafting a "Charter for a Broken World" alongside
hundreds of foreign and domestic dignitaries made her briefly "the most
conspicuous woman in the United States" as well as a key asset in the
postwar effort to legally "bind the wounds of the world."[33] Before she
retired from Barnard in June 1947, Gildersleeve was not so distracted by
affairs of state that she forgot to thank Reichard for "carrying on the great
tradition of Franz Boas" through good times and bad.[34] Among her last
budgetary decisions as dean, she granted Reichard her second sabbatical.

•   •   •   ❖   •   •   •

With her instinct for trusting her own eyes over what she was told was
true, Reichard recognized that Americanization—the process of imposing idealized socioeconomic and psychological norms on Americans of
every ethnicity, creed, and religion—adversely affected everyone in the

reservation's orbit. The days when J. L. Hubbell could impress a credu-
lous eastern listener by describing the white trader as the "de facto czar
of the domain over which he presides" ended more than a decade before
the trader's death in 1931.[35]

Though it had been scarcely apparent to the casual visitor who viewed
reservation life as an obligation of Manifest Destiny, the interdependence
of traders and their Native clients was plain to see in the wake of the collapse of the world economy in 1929. Sheep and goats, the "chief source of
wealth among Navajos," had once produced "a quarter of a million dollars
a year in wool and hides alone" in trade, without which Hubbell might
never have made a name for himself in Navajo blankets, Arizona politics,
or as the head of a dignified and generous American family. Focusing on
"Work and Economy," J. L.'s heirs succeeded in keeping the family business alive by observing the tacit Navajo wisdom of "what is good for the
individual is good for everyone else, and what is good for everybody is also
good for the individual."[36] Yet the Hubbells were no more safe from the
pitfalls of laissez-faire capitalism than were the Navajo. As the younger
generation of Hubbell traders fought to keep from becoming the last,
Reichard didn't blame them personally for being in the thrall of a heart-
less economic system. She sympathized with them in their struggle for
financial security, just as she supported the Navajo in their incremental
steps toward tribal sovereignty.

During Reichard's early days at White Sands, the Hubbells' "faculty
of spreading balm on the wounds of my discouragement" created in
her a sense of inextinguishable debt.[37] She repaid their kindnesses at
first with gifts of books, magazine subscriptions, hard-to-find items she
brought from New York, and a hundred small gestures that reinforced the
individual bonds of friendship she developed with each family member.
Reichard's first major opportunity to repay Dorothy and Roman Hubbell
arrived when their youngest son, John, prepared to leave home for college. John was book smart from a love of reading inculcated in him by his
first teacher, Dorothy, and seconded by the rest of his well-read clan. After
he was diagnosed with an enlarged, leaky heart, it became clear that the
pale and underweight teen wasn't destined to follow the men in the family
into a life on the open range. Jack, as Reichard often referred to him,
spoke Spanish and Navajo in addition to English. Reichard encouraged
him to apply to study modern languages at Columbia University, then

helped him test out of his freshman year to enter Columbia College as a sophomore on a full scholarship.

Acting *in loco parentis* in New York, Reichard did more than take John to lunch occasionally so she could report on his weight and mood to his worried mother. She introduced him to other faculty, her students, and Boas's grandsons. When she spent weekends with friends at her cabin in Newtown, she took John along. In his first semester she tutored him in German in her office and commiserated with him about the outdated standard of language instruction he encountered in the French department. Occasionally John's teenaged mind misread that of his Columbian guardian angel. After he imagined Reichard expected him to reciprocate her invitations to lunch and social events, she groaned to his mother, "I could bite the tongue from out of my head! If I ever meant that. . . . As if all such debts were not prepaid long before he was born!"[38] After graduating in May 1939, John thanked her in "four large long pages" for all she had done for him. Reichard beamed with satisfaction. "I spend my life for young people but I am not much accustomed to having them realize that anyone but themselves exist or have any effect on the world," Reichard wrote Dorothy, "and when such does come out it surprises and I need not say, pleases me."[39]

In 1937 Reichard leapt at the chance to help promote the Hubbells' latest business venture, Roman Hubbell Navajo Tours. In keeping with the times, the tours were designed to capitalize on Roman's intimate knowledge of the land and customs of his birthplace, his movie-star good looks, ability to speak Navajo, and longstanding friendships with Navajo, Hopi, and Zuni in the region. "I am as interested in these tours as if they were my own," Reichard wrote a friend, "because I always felt there was a need for them, and they are organized in the best manner."[40] Reichard believed Roman's Tours presented an opportunity for the education of travelers that was far superior to the passive voyeurism offered by Indian Detours and its parent company, the Fred Harvey outfit. Instead of gawking at Indian artisans in a darkened salesroom at the Grand Canyon's Hopi House or in a painted stall at a World's Fair, the tourists in Roman's cars would, Reichard was confident, meet and interact with Native persons on something closer to Native terms. She had high hopes that the tours would promote admiration of the Navajos' best qualities in addition to directing cash to Navajo host families and artisans who lived in rarely visited corners of the reservation. Believing "that all people have a right to their own ways," she expected that when citified whites met Navajos in their camps, they would reject the stereotypes promoted by assimilationists and return to their cities "with a different state of mind."[41] The mental "detours" from the cares of modern city life that the Harvey Company peddled to casual tourists could not hold a candle as far as Reichard was concerned to the direct, unstaged experiences Roman was capable of facilitating.

To help the Hubbells on their way, Reichard talked up the tours with everyone she knew. She personally invited Dean Gildersleeve, who shared a vacation home in Tucson with her partner, retired University of London professor Caroline Spurgeon, to consider booking a tours trip for her winter break in Arizona.[42] Judging the brochure Roman designed informative but visually boring, Gladys gave the Hubbells the use of photographs that she and Lilian took on their Southwest travels to make the flyer more appealing.[43] In the winter of 1939, Reichard touted the tours in "Fifty Thousand Sign Posts," an article she wrote for *New Mexico* magazine, and supplied all eight black-and-white photographs that illustrated it. Freeing herself once again from the strictures of scientific writing, Reichard evoked the terrifying grandeur of the landscape surrounding Gallup, the "mingled fragrance of cedar smoke and boiling coffee" along the Tours' typical route, the "eerie" notes of a solitary Navajo rider absorbed in his song, and the reassuring forthcomingness of fifty thousand Navajo individuals, "not stereotyped or readable . . . but human." She stressed that destinations featured in Navajo Tours were "not just curious places through which one wanders . . . saying 'how quaint!'" but locales where tourists could participate in "something different, something surprising, something new."[44]

Reichard continued to act as the Hubbells' proxy in New York after she returned from her first sabbatical. When she met with executives at the New York American Express office to describe Navajo Tours, Reichard's pitch was infectious enough that they invited her to write a script publicizing the annual Gallup Ceremonial and the Tours for radio broadcast on WNYC, a non-commercial station. Navajo Tours, the Gallup Chamber of Commerce, and Gallup's Inter-Tribal Ceremonial Association chipped in fifty dollars each for national distribution of the script, which resulted in its being read by broadcasters at 281 stations nationwide.[45] Reichard also made inquiries at movie and sound recording firms in New York on the Hubbells' behalf. She and Roman explored the commercial possibilities of making sound recordings of Navajo chants that might be used for soundtracks or sound effects in radio. They also discussed making a film about the Navajo that was culturally accurate rather than rife with Hollywood clichés. As a step in that direction, she audited a class in scenario or screenwriting primarily as a way to learn about the motion picture industry. "Our movie is going to be deep!" she wrote Roman conspiratorially after her screenwriting "prof" assured her she had "the most marvelous material" on which to base a screenplay.[46]

Gradually Reichard began to suspect she was overdoing. "You would not think I was anything but a journalist the way my life is running these days. Every weekend seems to be a race to beat a deadline," Reichard complained to Roman.[47] Fond as she was of the enterprising trader, her support for his commercial agenda threatened to compromise her scholarly one. She'd long known that Roman's self-interest was never far behind his outgoing, agreeable manner. Though he'd backed her ethnographic research as well as new sidelines in photography, script writing, and sound engineering, he'd nixed her idea of writing a biography of his father and nagged her about other projects he thought more interesting. Once, she had had to counter Roman's charge that she wasn't doing all she could for others as a scholar. "Where you say I live a self-centered, selfish life could it be that I have tried to build up a defense against having a load like the Navajo on my back?" she replied. "I might say too that I have not succeeded in this defense."[48]

It wasn't until Reichard's script-writing teacher and a reader of her *Dezba* manuscript commented that she placed too much emphasis on ethnographic accuracy in her stories that the seeds of doubt she had about chasing a popular following finally sprouted. "I give my audience too heavy a diet [of cultural background]," she told Dorothy Hubbell. "I am not good at diluting."[49] Unlike novelist Oliver La Farge, Reichard was less interested in delighting her audiences than in teaching them something they didn't already know. When René d'Harnoncourt, host of the radio program Art in America, head of the New Deal's Indian Arts and Crafts Board, and an enthusiastic fan of *Dezba* tried to encourage her to see that anthropologists "could do science but must present ballyhoo," she remained skeptical.[50] Reichard's moral compass pointed her back to her scholarly purpose: "After all, I am highly trained to do something which I am conceited enuf to think no one else can do."[51] She resolved to "do the best I can in my own field and let the Olivers go."[52]

Reichard's commitments to Barnard and the Hubbells didn't exhaust her sense of responsibility to others. Chief among her other reciprocal interests in the immediate prewar years was the career of Adolph Bitanny. Under her wing at Columbia for the 1937–38 academic year, Adolph made swift progress in his ability to do phonetic transcription, linguistic analysis, and cultural interpretation per Reichard's instructions. Reichard's sabbatical in the fall of 1938 prompted Adolph to return to the University of New Mexico for the 1938–39 academic year in a final attempt to complete his college degree. From Albuquerque he wrote Reichard long, technical letters on the interaction of grammatical categories including person, mode, aspect, and voice. The excitement Bitanny expressed over the intricacies of Navajo grammar must have reminded Reichard of her own early enthusiasm for linguistics. "Another thing that I'm doing is to go over the active stems by using optative mode," he told her. "I've found that I've had to do likewise with the prefixes. I dare say that the optative mode affects both but how far I can not yet determine. I do know that optative plays 'heck' with prefixes and stems. Big nut to crack!"[53]

Reichard was understandably proud of her star student. His facility with formal linguistics confirmed he had the potential to become a leading teacher-scholar among his people. "We have an awful good time now," she said of their teamwork, "because we have the ground work laid so we can play with theory. [Adolph] loves theory more than anything else but I wouldn't let him touch it until he had learned something of method. His previous education had been almost entirely theoretical with nothing to base theory on."[54] Helpful as Bitanny was to Reichard in unpacking the niceties of Navajo grammar, their long conversations about meaning, religion, and attitude informed her ideas on the interactions among culture, personality, and cultural changes specific to the Navajo as a people. Bitanny regularly expressed a desire to apply his expertise in Navajo linguistics to improve his society and the outside world's perception of it. Reichard created the character of John Silversmith in *Dezba* to convey Bitanny's unique voice through the novel. "There are many things I would like to do that I think I can do," Silversmith tells an unnamed white auditor in *Dezba*. "I think that the Navajo social system works better than the system you have. But I don't think the white people understand it, and I should like to investigate it and write it up so they would. And then there is the religion! There is so much I want to do about that! I want to get the ideas of the old men down in their own words, and show what they really think, for their religion is not nonsense. It contains all their artistic life, art, music, poetry."[55]

Bitanny/Silversmith wanted also to convince Navajo medicine men to "adopt certain medical principles" that would put patients suffering from pneumonia or pleurisy at less risk during long, physically demanding sings. "I would not do as others who have become Christians have done, tell them everything they do is wrong and they ought to cut out all the sings. The Navajo believe in them and get a great deal of comfort and pleasure out of them. If I had a chance, I would not be in a hurry to change. . . . One has to be patient and do a lot of talking and work things out gradually. . . . [E]verything you tell them that science has worked out they already know."[56]

Adolph, in turn, took great pride in being Reichard's student and assistant. At a seminar at the University of New Mexico, one of Sapir's former students, W. W. "Nibs" Hill, asked Bitanny what he thought of Reichard's command of Navajo compared to Father Berard Haile's. Bitanny replied, "I think F. Berard may use the language better, but for scientific purposes he is not as useful because he cannot analyze & Dr. R. can."[57] Bitanny also had warm praise for Reichard's experimental novel. "About Dezba (the book)," he wrote his Columbia mentor, "It's queer how I can read the book so quickly. Good work and congratulations! I find nothing wrong with the whole work—except in one or two cases which I am sure were unintentional." "The book is a great piece of work," he continued, "and I thank you for portraying the Navajo typically. A person reads your book and begins to feel for more! I don't care what characters incidents and episodes occur in a literary work like this but to portray them as simple people who seek simplicity, happiness, security, beauty and religion, knowledge and wisdom, progeny and unity with universal forces in an environment such as theirs is really something that I believe is a magnificent achievement. Furthermore, your way of portraying cultural conflict (social, political, and academic) in this 'ding-dangest' complicated heterogenous and dog-eat-dog type of the 20th century civilization among Indians such as the Navajo should make anyone proud of your social work."[58]

Bitanny's departure from New York for New Mexico made it difficult for Reichard to supervise her assistant's work; Dorothy and Roman Hubbell volunteered to help. For Roman, seeing that Bitanny was paid and supplied with the equipment he needed for his transcription work was modest recompense for Reichard's generous contributions to the family interests. Having watched her books on the Navajo pile up over the course of a decade, the trader teased her with a mix of pride and stifled envy. "Now don't swell up and burst!" he cautioned Reichard after hearing J. J. Augustin, by then a mutual friend, enthuse about *Dezba.* "That's just another book my guests are just going to have to read."[59] "Don't worry that I will swell up and burst," Reichard shot back. "I just don't have time!"[60] Dorothy understood Reichard's relentless productivity as the labor of love. "Gladys, your letters have been swell," she wrote her friend with unabashed affection, "so full of things and such enthusiasm, so full of life! We have loved getting them."[61]

· · · ◈ · · ·

Elsie Parsons found it easier as a rule to get closer to men than women, but Reichard was a notable exception. By the mid-1930s, the two women's intellectual interests and professional characters were so thoroughly intertwined that they were de facto partners in the liberal wing of the anthropological establishment. One born "into circumstances that practically demanded she live the life of a debutante," the other raised in middle-class comfort across the fence from working-class neighbors, as anthropologists they found many more reasons to pool their knowledge than to compete with one another.[62] Gladys had an upbeat and outgoing personality, while Elsie's outward manner was more reserved, almost to the point of seeming aloof. Yet differences of personality meant little to Reichard in estimating her colleague's true character. "She was above all a respecter of evidence," Reichard said of Parsons, "and never did she skew it to bolster some preconceived or later deduced theory of her own."[63] Reviewing Parsons's ethnography of a Mexican village, *Mitla, Town of Souls*, Reichard hailed the author's conscientious technique, "[S]he indulges in no great color splurges or in bold brush work, but builds a mosaic bit by bit. Each minute stone is cut and fitted so nicely that gradually out of the welter of details comes the finished picture, and the little town and its poised citizens fairly glitter, so sharply are they done. This is the kind of documented book which a lay reader feels *must* be relied upon."[64]

Reichard would have none of the gossip that accused Parsons of manipulating her associates for financial or other motives. "If one trait of her sturdy character were to be stressed more than another it must be her absolute regard for the truth," Reichard said of Parsons. "She had her ethical ideals, other people had theirs. She could understand and tolerate such differences, but the overlap, the sine qua non was the demand for honesty, of which the greatest part was self-honesty. She could face any fact, no matter how damaging it was to self-complacency."[65] Parsons's "innate simplicity," an enlightened candor shared by Reichard, prevented her from playing the part of queen bee despite her mounting professional authority. The credit Reichard gave Parsons allowed them to laugh at themselves together, share confidences about their respective families, and exchange lively letters they could be sure would remain private. Reichard could write Parsons with open affection, "I like to look at you at lunch if I don't get a chance to talk to you!" knowing her words wouldn't be read as flattery.[66] When Parsons invited Reichard to stay with her in one of her country mansions, or gave her the occasional use of the family opera box in New York, she trusted Reichard to view these gestures as the acts of a close friend, not a patron. In sum, behind "the hard shell" of their public personas, Reichard and Parsons were two intellectually brilliant, liberated women "whose idea of complete comfort was to have *at the same time* a cigarette, a cup of coffee, and an open fire," especially "among Indians."[67]

After Parsons bought her first apartment in Manhattan in 1935, Parsons and Reichard spent more time together in New York than their busy schedules had previously allowed. Though Parsons's main motive for making the city her home base was to be closer to her three sons, she settled happily into the life of a full-time urban scholar.[68] Reichard liked having the New Yorker with her "twinkling" sense of humor closer to hand, particularly once Boas announced his intention to retire. If Reichard thought the less said on the topic of Boas's retirement the better, Parsons worried that her "immediate world in anthropology" was about to "crash."[69] Columbia's President Butler naturally refused Parsons a role in the matter of Boas's replacement, despite her high stature in anthropology and the steady financial support she'd provided to the department since World War I. As Parsons feared, Butler appointed a search committee antagonistic to the anti-nationalist, humanitarian spirit of Boas's forty-year tenure, setting the scene for a reactionary departmental order to flourish.

From the sidelines, Parsons viewed Boas's vocal support for Ruth Benedict as the next chair of Anthropology with some dismay. Their philosophical differences aside, Parsons had concerns about Benedict's capacity as an administrator, concerns that Margaret Mead shared.[70] Ralph Linton's eventual appointment to succeed Boas realized everyone's worst fears. Benedict maintained Linton was chosen over her strictly on the basis of her sex. Before and after Linton replaced her as interim chair, Benedict treated the newcomer to regal condescension laced with chilly, disapproving silences. Linton countered Benedict's passive aggression with strident threats and slights that divided their graduate students into "his and hers." The little civility that survived the changing of the guard evaporated once Linton did Butler's bidding by firing a number of Boas's year-to-year appointees. "He is a swine," the soft-spoken Benedict said to Mead in private. "I may have to wallop Linton hard in public someday."[71]

In the end the brouhaha at Columbia Anthropology had little impact on Reichard's or Parsons's anthropological ambitions. Each remained dedicated to multiple projects independent of Columbia's personnel or resources. Within a few years, Reichard discovered Flagstaff's Museum of Northern Arizona to be a properly civilized institution in a location that she loved. By the end of the decade the "Mountain Town" and its friendlier intellectual climate became her primary summer destination. Reichard took a copy of Parsons's twelve-hundred-page *Pueblo Indian Religion* with her to Flagstaff in 1939 intending to make a start on her own book on Navajo religion during her first summer-long stay. Reading Parsons's massive tome on the train, Reichard wrote her colleague, "I want to thank you and to say [*Pueblo*] is going to be <u>most</u> useful."[72]

Reichard was in a comparative frame of mind as she pondered Parsons's results but Parsons's subsequent suggestion that they write a book together on prayer sticks was nearly too much of a good thing. "But <u>why</u> oh <u>why</u> do you get me steamed up about <u>another</u> book!" Reichard replied.

"Four started now, and two all planned out in the mind and no time for
the pencil and paper, or so little time. . . . Of course we must do it."[73] The
wind *Pueblo Indian Religion* blew into Reichard's sails was evident a few
days later when Reichard wrote the Hubbells, "Yesterday was a red-letter
day. I started to write the Navajo Religion and wrote 15 pages out of the
possible 1000. But it is a start which I had hoped to make last June . . . so
I feel real proud."[74]

Reichard and Parsons had shared a warm regard for the American Folklore Society almost since the beginning of their relationship.
Through the Depression, Parsons had outdone herself in the effort to
keep the AFS solvent and relevant. Her tenure at the Folklore Society
dated to 1918 when Boas, then editor of the society's *Journal of American
Folklore* (*JAF*), made her an assistant editor. She was elected president of
the organization in 1919, the year Reichard first enrolled at Columbia.
However, Parsons did not replace Boas as editor of the journal and monograph series known as Memoirs when he stepped down from the post in
1924. The editorship went instead to Benedict, at Boas's insistence. Parsons contented herself with being a permanent member of the society's
executive council, an associate editor, and a major donor. It would later
be revealed that between 1918 and 1943 Parsons donated in excess of a
half-million dollars to the society to ensure the regular publication of
the journal and the printing of sixteen of the twenty-six Memoirs issued
in that period.[75]

Once Reichard became AFS secretary-treasurer in 1924, she helped
Parsons keep the low profile she sought as a philanthropist. When the
heiress was forced to reduce the amount of her support for her favorite
cause in the 1930s, Reichard made sure "the large amount of help and
interest" Parsons gave the perennially low-budget enterprise was publicly
recognized.[76] Privately she thanked Parsons for having "slung us a lifeline
as long as you have."[77]

Neither woman believed that money alone could keep "the dear old
folklore society" afloat indefinitely.[78] In 1934 Parsons tried, and failed, to
convince Benedict, whose salary she paid, to allow Reichard to take her
place as editor.[79] Reichard wrote Boas in 1936, "They have (Elsie now)
been devilling me to take the editorship of the Folk-Lore again and again
I am not at all interested."[80] The effort to dislodge Benedict had its origins
in behavioral patterns not fully recognized until 1940. As Reichard later

explained to Parsons, "The old technique seems to be that an ms. arrives for RB at Columbia; then [Ruth] Bryan [the departmental secretary] writes a note to the effect that it has been received & will be referred to RB. Then when she returns RB tucks it away somewhere like a packrat & goes on about her own affairs sublimely & maddeningly ignoring it."[81] Better noted by the AFS executive was that the society's publications were typically behind schedule during Benedict's fifteen-year tenure.[82] Benedict's foot-dragging called to mind Parsons's unpleasant experience with the *JAF* editor in the role of Southwest Society grantee. In 1923 Boas pressed Parsons to hire Benedict to compile and publish a concordance of Southwest mythology. A decade later, the manuscript was "an outrageous mess" that Parsons refused to publish despite the small fortune she had invested in it.[83]

Parsons tolerated Benedict's poor performance longer than she might have if the dire state of international relations in the late 1930s hadn't excused some publication delays. No reasonable administrator could lay blame for the naval blockades that interrupted the flow of communications and shipments between the AFS and its European printers on Benedict. Careful not to abuse her position, Parsons waited until the end of 1939 to voice her concerns about the journal's management to the AFS executive council. Benedict was on her first sabbatical leave, in California, when the council voted to relieve her of her editorship in absentia. They resolved to install a new editor as part of a slate of reforms meant to repair a defect in internal relations some members attributed to the journal having "run too far in the direction of publishing 'indigestible' chunk[s] of data" owing to Boasian dominance.[84] Within weeks of the December council meeting, Reichard was elected to a one-year term as editor of *JAF*.[85] In February, Reichard received her marching orders from Parsons, along with a check described as the first of two payments of $150 for the "heavy work [that] will come these next two months."[86]

The quarterly journal was a year behind schedule; three of four issues in production were in disarray. Three manuscripts were slated to appear as Memoirs that year: Parsons's *Taos Tales*, H. T. Wheeler's eight-hundred-page *Tales from Jalisco Mexico*, and Morris Opler's *Myth and Legends of the Lipan Apache*.[87] Looking into the status of each, Reichard discovered that Wheeler's manuscript had languished untouched by Benedict for eight years. More surprising still, Wheeler hadn't offered so much as a murmur of protest. Reichard expressed wonder at "how little it is possible to find out about the folklore business, unless one does by accident," adding, "I thot the affaire Wheeler was so bad it was humorous."[88] Unsurprisingly, Reichard dived into her new role as a problem solver. Though she voiced her frustrations from time to time to Parsons, she did not criticize Benedict in public. After months of concentrating her energies on moving from the "great confusion" in the society's publications arm to "a firm base on which to build a more flexible and marketable *Journal of American Folklore*," Reichard told Parsons with satisfaction, "I am now in a position to consult Ruth and you would be surprised to know how many times, practically unanimous, we come to the same conclusions."[89]

Reichard and Parsons shared a similar ability to immerse themselves in numerous projects simultaneously without shortchanging friends, family, or their own peace of mind. Tending several open fires at once, they bantered by mail during their frequent separations. From her cabin on the outskirts of Flagstaff, a contented Reichard sent Parsons a large manuscript to proof for an upcoming AFS Memoir with the note, "I would like to have the proof as soon as you can, but don't miss a good day for sailing or anything on account of it. I'm past that! As the famous sinologist said, 'Pekin Man has been there half a million years, I guess he can wait 3 months longer!'"[90]

Parsons repaid Reichard's cheerful good humor by helping her make sense of the personalities and motives of mutual associates. In the summer of 1941, one of those under the microscope was J. J. Augustin. After the German publisher announced he was opening a New York office, Reichard and Parsons invested one thousand dollars each in his new firm. Because the Folklore Society was looking for a U.S.-based publisher at about the same time, Parsons proposed Augustin as a replacement. The AFS committee on policy gladly followed Parsons's recommendation, especially because Augustin was the son of their former publisher. But near the end of Reichard's term as editor, the committee voted to terminate Augustin's contract for being too costly. Although Reichard was not personally involved in Augustin's dismissal, the German reacted to the termination by cutting off all communication with Reichard just as *Dezba* was due to be published. Reichard tried not to take the botched rollout of *Dezba* too hard, but Augustin's assumption that she had betrayed him stung. "You are a great comfort to me," Reichard told Parsons as she chalked up the sudden rupture between herself and Augustin to male "madness."[91]

Both women had bigger fish to fry. After being held at the periphery of the anthropological establishment as a wealthy eccentric, Parsons was riding a wave of critical attention from a group of "Young Turks," those frisky male comers who'd discovered her early feminist writings in the wake of *Mitla* and *Pueblo Indian Religion*. Their acclaim for Parsons's work catapulted her into the presidency of the American Anthropological Association in December 1940. Reichard plowed ahead on *Navaho Religion* in spite of the extra distractions the job at AFS had created in her life. Busy with her goal of building a strong, enlightened audience for Navajo studies, she couldn't think of anyone more deserving than Parsons to be the first woman to hold the AAA's top post.

·   ·   ·   ◈   ·   ·   ·

The least well-documented personal relationship of those Reichard held most dear was her bond with her sister, Lilian. One basis for the evidentiary gap is the absence of any letters exchanged by the sisters. What can be gleaned from public records and inferred from references to Lilian in Gladys's surviving correspondence is that, like her father before her, Lilian trained for a profession in her youth and then settled permanently into a cozy rut doing work she loved. Unlike her father, Lilian never married. A high school language teacher by profession, Lilian's only known passion aside from teaching and travel was for photography.

In a show of support for her sister's artistic interests, Gladys arranged for Lilian to test herself as a commercial freelance photographer with a paid commission. J. J. Augustin needed photographs to illustrate Ruth "Jill" Underhill's *First Penthouse Dwellers of America* and Lilian's naturalistic style fit the bill. Facilitating the collaboration between Lilian, Augustin, and Underhill was less than easy. "Without me [*Penthouse Dwellers*] would never have been!" Reichard assured Dorothy and Roman Hubbell. "My suggestion in the first place, steering Lilian through it, then when Jill [Underhill] fell down on the job completely I held up the life raft—built it even—& administered oxygen for weeks."[92] Naturally, the reading public saw only an attractive finished product. All smiles, Roman Hubbell wrote Reichard in 1938, "Received Jill's book and I am crazy about the set up—I

Lilian Reichard at a Southwest campsite, c. 1940.
Museum of Northern Arizona MS22–2-5–196, Box 15.

like the vein it is written in. And the photographs . . . are so inspiring."[93] Although others joined Gladys and the Hubbells in admiring Lilian's color and black-and-white photography, Lilian remained a hobbyist, taking and developing pictures to share with students and friends. She took a photography class now and then and submitted a photo or two to contests—further than that she showed no desire to go.

What the relationship between the Reichard sisters lacked in drama it made up for in a simple companionability. Though they regularly indulged in good-natured ribbing, they respected one another's careers, spent winter holidays and weekends together when possible, and, after 1930, made a joint three-week summer vacation driving, camping, and photographing their way around the American West an annual event. Occasionally Lilian invited Gladys to be a guest speaker at her school in the Philadelphia suburbs, Abington High. After one such visit, a reporter for the *Abingtonian* raved about Gladys, saying, "It isn't often that one has the pleasure of talking with a woman who combines so delightfully keen intelligence, sense of humor, love of outdoor life, and a jolly friendliness and informality of manner. . . . She is a delightful talker and made her audience see the desert, the mired auto, the Indians who helped get it out—all so vivid and real. But this realistic quality of description is one of Dr. Reichard's chief charms. No matter what questions were asked, her replies always ended with a story and a laugh."[94]

Lilian had an athletic independent streak of her own but to all appearances she was as content with reflected glory as she was with her unique lot in life. The stories and facts Gladys shared with her about the desert, Navajo culture, and American Indian languages never lit a competitive fire in her only sibling. Though Lilian would have read her more famous sister's popular books along with the general public, the scientific and philosophical aspects of anthropology and linguistics that fascinated Gladys were never Lilian's cup of tea.

There is some evidence to suggest that Gladys deliberately shielded Lilian from, "[t]he atmosphere of greed and envy and jealousy" that came to hang over Gladys's elite profession as Boas's influence waned.[95] Hints of Reichard's protective attitude toward her older sister surface in Gladys's correspondence with the Hubbells. In May 1940 Reichard had major surgery, almost certainly a hysterectomy, at Harkness Pavilion Presbyterian Hospital in New York. Afterward she told the Hubbells that through the previous winter she had wakened in the night with a numbness in half her body that "scared the pants off me." Not wanting to alarm anyone, including her closest living relative, Reichard waited to tell Lilian about her condition until the operation was over and pronounced a success. A month later Gladys traveled by train alone to Flagstaff, where she had rented a cabin at Hidden Hollow ranch for a second season. "So I will be a lady of leisure & someone else will—to my regret—have to haul the saddle & chop the wood," she promised the Hubbells.[96]

That "someone else" was not, as might have been expected, Lilian. Gladys seems always to have felt responsible for "duding" Lilian around the West. Yet any time Gladys spent with Lilian ending up being a welcome respite from the turmoil of the ivory tower and the loneliness that Gladys sometimes experienced during fieldwork. Judging from Lilian's ignorance of the prevailing disciplinary politics in anthropology at the time of her sister's death, the sisters did not misspend their vacations together analyzing the psychology of their respective colleagues, plotting their next career moves, or bemoaning the latest work-related indignity chance had thrown their way. Each had fulfilling lives apart from her workplace. Neither seemed to demand more of the other's attention and patience than her sister could reasonably spare. The daughters of Minerva and Noah Reichard didn't need a "family" of anthropologists or coworkers as a substitute for the real thing. Alone in the world together, they remained securely attached to one another by the more reliable bond of actual kinship.

CHAPTER 8

GHASTLY STUFF

THE DEATH OF EDWARD SAPIR IN EARLY 1939 surprised no one who knew him well. Two summers before, he suffered a heart attack so severe it seemed unlikely he would live long enough to have his "full say."[1] When Reichard heard from Boas that the fifty-four-year-old had had a relapse in late 1938, she replied simply, "I am very sorry to hear about Sapir. I suppose he undertook too much."[2] She floated a pet theory about those who "always worked too hard" as "most worth-while people" did: "Then they overdo, and they die young."[3] She believed untimely deaths were sad enough if the person died "doing what she wanted to do." But in the case of Sapir, who according to Ruth Benedict "poured vitriol continually upon the whole earth" on his deathbed, Reichard declared his early undoing "Very tragic."[4] She had the good sense to recognize that her would-be nemesis had "many a vulnerable spot." "I tell you he is so obvious that he is not as dangerous as some more placid souls," she reassured Parsons in 1935, "at least he can be fought."[5] Despite knowing with Mead that Sapir "never really counted [women anthropologists] for gain," Reichard nonetheless joined the anthropological community in recognizing the late linguist as intellectually "the best of his generation."[6]

Far more difficult to bear for Reichard was the unexpected death of Elsie Parsons twelve days after the Japanese attack on Pearl Harbor. In November 1941, Parsons had returned to New York from a month-long field trip to Ecuador "in excellent spirits" and "apparent good health."[7] All serene, the reunited friends attended the council meeting of the American Ethnological Society together on December 10. The next day, Parsons checked into New York Hospital with symptoms of appendicitis. With her children and Reichard often by her bedside, Parsons spent the week in hospital recuperating from surgery. To pass the time, the patient refined the speech she was scheduled to deliver as outgoing president at the imminent AAA meeting. In the early morning hours of December 19, Parsons succumbed to undiagnosed kidney disease and "simply slept away."[8] Though her four children were left to cope with Parsons's mother's Spartan burial instructions ("no religious services whatsoever" and cremation "if convenient . . . ashes left at the crematory"), their decision to appoint Reichard their late mother's literary executor was an easy one. Reichard tamped down the emotions unleashed by the loss by writing Alfred Kroeber a clearheaded account of Elsie's last days and hours. Allowing herself one muted protest, "She seemed to be doing extraordinarily well," Gladys proposed a way to honor Parsons without offending her unsentimental dignity. "She had her presidential speech ready," Reichard wrote Kroeber, "—I have it now—& and I think it ought to be read, don't you?"[9]

On December 29, Reichard read Parsons's presidential address, "Anthropology and Prediction," to a throng of fellow anthropologists mightily distracted by the United States' entry into the Second World War. Lucid, tactful, and dryly humorous, Parsons's speech reaffirmed the moral charter set by Boas for anthropology nearly a half-century before. Using a technique she mastered in her days as a propagandist for pacifism and universal human rights, Parsons drew revealing parallels between the mental habits of lettered and unlettered peoples confined to one lonely planet. She acknowledged that the rising tide of global war increased pressure on anthropologists to deliver "the goods" their societies coveted—"foreknowledge," a glimpse of the future, certainty if possible—in exchange for social privileges they would be wise to resist: fame, prestige, and, most coveted of all, the power to control the human herd.[10]

Parsons did not use the word "patriarchy" to encapsulate the weakness that passes for strength in modern states. She warned, however, that anthropologists should be wary of appointing themselves their brothers' keepers based strictly on their self-regard as scientists. "A world directed by anthropological science," Reichard read aloud, "will be a conceptually revolutionized world; actually the changes will have to come so slowly that they will never be recognized as revolutionary. I venture to say that in this world of tomorrow prediction, or better say, foresight will come of itself through increase of knowledge almost without our knowing it, whereas predictive formulas which are directed to immediate social ends, even slow and patient searches for social laws may easily smack of divination which according to our definition is concerned not with process but with particular interests and that are callous to scientific control."[11]

Boas, too ill to visit Parsons in the hospital earlier in the month, had rallied to attend the AAA meeting in Andover, Massachusetts. Listening to Parsons speak truth to power through Reichard, the Old Man of anthropology must have been greatly moved. In his 1938 editorial, "An Anthropologist's Credo," he too called on anthropologists to lead by example rather than through force of personality or will to power. "The one outstanding fact" of human culture Boas wrote, "is that every human society has two distinct ethical standards, one for the in-group, the other for the out-group." Double-standards, applied with ever-shifting, illogical rationalizations to serve the in-group's perceived interests, were used to justify everything from mass murder to lying as long as the victims were classed as outsiders. "War, restrictions of migration, economic barriers, class conflicts are evidences of the persistence of" imagined social hierarchies, he warned. Sadly, he concluded, "We do not observe any progress in the [ethical] standards of human society," despite the increase in scientific knowledge accumulated over many centuries. Real progress in the ethical realm must stem from free individuals consciously choosing to adopt and enact the tenets of genuine democracy. Every individual in every nation must decide to avoid the "unpardonable error" of overgeneralization made by the architects of Nazi Germany. Humanistic education, not coercion, Boas advised, was the key to producing an inclusive, liberal social order. Only once individuals in their millions were free of the "intolerable egotism" around which elitist groups of every stripe have always coalesced could a just society be achieved.[12]

After the AAA meeting, Reichard wrote Herbert Parsons Jr. that his mother's words were "very well received" but unlikely to recruit her excited colleagues to the "unselfish devotion to science" Elsie Parsons exemplified.[13] As proof, Reichard told Parsons's oldest son that the day after she'd read Parsons's speech, her fellow AAA members had debated and passed a resolution placing the association "and its resources and the specialized skills and knowledge of its members at the disposal of the country in the successful prosecution of the war."[14] Reichard did not explain to Herbert Jr. why she described the speeches made by the impassioned nationalists behind the resolution as flag-waving "slop." But as an insider, Reichard might have noted that at least two repressed ideological currents prevailed at the AAA meeting and weaponized anthropology before her very eyes. One expressed the anxiety of younger anthropologists frustrated with the slow pace of Boas and Parsons's cumulative, self-correcting model of anthropology and the meager financial support it attracted. The late Edward Sapir had had far greater success raising funds in the private sector with his combative, impressionistic style of scientific work. Thanks to the war, the U.S. government was in immediate need of thousands of men and women trained to non-violently extract secrets from alien peoples. The breaking global crisis represented a potential jobs bonanza for perennially underemployed junior anthropologists. In the heat of the moment, none had to resort to Bolshevistic fanfare to alter the AAA's ruling ethos to their advantage.

The other elephant in the room was a perspective espoused by Margaret Mead that she later named the "generation gap."[15] Mead had never troubled to hide her longstanding conviction that the greater physical vitality (and sex appeal) of the young signaled their greater fitness to lead. An exception was made for the silver-haired Ruth Benedict, who Mead declared ageless, but the biological age of others always figured in her estimation of her colleagues' value. "We have to realize that no other generation will ever experience what we have experienced," a sixty-nine year-old Mead would write in 1970. "In this sense we have no descendants and our children have no forebearers." Each new generation upstaged the previous one as the sheer passage of time rendered elders impotent. "Today," the icon of 1960s counterculture asserted, "[t]here are no elders who know what those who have been reared within the last twenty years know about the world into which they were born."[16] Mead's view that perception and knowledge were radically discontinuous from generation to generation dovetailed nicely with the self-interest of those younger AAA members in need of an excuse to usher themselves into positions of influence after driving their elders out.

Only eight years older than Mead, Reichard knew from Mead's indifference to her work that she was on the wrong side of the Mead's age divide; Reichard had always been an old soul who sought wisdom rather than fame through anthropology. She may not have realized to what extent the sociocultural anthropologist mocked her as conventional and boring behind her back, but Reichard refrained from calling attention to their stark philosophical differences in public.[17] The subtext of Mead's argument in favor of war work, that the scientific results of one generation were incommensurate with those of the next, was a prescription for tunnel vision and dogmatism, in Reichard's view. The history of science could never be for her the story of lone heroes who prevailed by disdaining the past as an enemy of the future. Reichard was no traditionalist, but she admired any person of any age who adapted to changing environmental and social conditions by collaborating with the best minds available to them in their moment. She joined Nobel Peace Laureate Jane Addams in rejecting "the insufferable assumption that the older generation is *per se* wiser."[18] "After all it is not so much that different generations are hostile to each other as that they find each other irrelevant" Addams wrote in 1930. In the struggle for a more just society, Addams observed, "What we want is not mere argument, certainly not suppression of any sort, but the release of energy and the evocation of new powers in common action."[19] The social philosopher and activist voiced Reichard's anthropological credo in a nutshell.

With Parsons gone, Reichard felt no little responsibility to fill the gap the New Yorker's death opened in Boas's life. Boas was in his eighties, and he was less interested in disciplinary politics than ever. Many of the same cool climbers who had expressed admiration for Parsons in her final years took advantage of Boas's partial retreat from Columbia to distort his legacy. Leslie White, for example, had inveighed against Boas at the 1939 AAA annual meeting, accusing him of doing more harm than good to the science of anthropology. Boas led his flock utterly astray by "destroying theory in American anthropology," White railed. Esther Goldfrank described White's in-person denouncement of Boas for his anti-evolutionary humanitarianism as "strident" and "intemperate."[20]

Yet the respect paid to White's diatribe suggested that an emerging norm in AAA's culture equated vehemence with validity. Boas's decision to make himself a political lightning rod in the anti-Communist storm that had settled over the country contributed to his waning prestige. Esther (Schiff) Goldfrank faulted her former teacher and employer for associating with known Communists, expressing his skepticism about the sincerity of British and French democracies, and for failing to criticize the evils of Stalin and the Soviet Union to her satisfaction. She later wrote that she was personally offended by Boas's refusal to toe the establishment line "in two periods of his life—1914 to 1919 and 1933 to 1942," when his political activism seemed to her "in contradiction to his own scientific standards and core beliefs."[21] Other AAA members were no more able to distinguish moral from methodological principles than Goldfrank was at the start of World War II than they had been when Boas was censored for "Scientist as Spies" at the end of World War I.

Reichard remained close to the entire Boas family in spite of her long absences from New York. After returning from Flagstaff in the fall of 1942, she moved out of the apartment she had occupied at Grantwood for most of two decades. Her former executive assistant, Marian Smith, had finished her degree at Columbia and suggested Reichard take her first-floor apartment across the street from Barnard at 600 115th St. Reichard saw no reason to refuse the offer as the raise from her recent promotion made renting in the city feasible. She planned to sell her car and do without for the winter. Boas busied himself at home most weekdays, and when he didn't he rode with Helene to campus, where they worked together in his old office. Grantwood was a far quieter place than it had been during the Depression. The twins were students at Columbia. One of Boas's widowed sisters had emigrated from Germany and was living out her days under her older brother's roof. As for Boas, the man others insisted on elevating to mythic status, Reichard regarded him as having outlived his body. "Papa Franz is smaller and weaker every minute," she wrote the Hubbells from her new apartment, "really he is heart-breaking." "Don't ever pity the people who die young."[22]

One year and ten days after Parsons breathed her last, Boas suffered a killing stroke at a luncheon held at the Columbia Faculty Club. While exhorting his guests to fight the "monstrous error or impudent lie" of racial entitlement, Boas fell dead into the arms of French anthropologist Claude Levi-Strauss.[23] Whether Reichard witnessed Boas's end or not, the emotional shock of her friend's demise must have been great.[24] Nevertheless, she didn't allow the historic moment to budge her commitment to "the individual and variability within groups" that had anchored Boas's scientific work to the humanities. Ruth Bunzel wrote of Reichard, "Above all in the field she never forgot that she was a human being working with subjects who were also human beings and with whom she shared a common humanity."[25] Reichard understood her best teachers had shaped her for this purpose. The deaths of Parsons and Boas opened to her a still lonelier path forward in anthropology. Fortunately, thanks to the wisdom passed on by her elders, she knew the way.

. . . ◈ . . .

The emphasis the Culture and Personality school of anthropology placed on identifying individuals as "abnormals," "deviants," or conformists in relation to idealized behavioral norms specific to their group never caught on with Reichard.[26] She expected individuals to be unique in any group, given the huge number of variables affecting any one person's existence, even within small, insular groups. Assuming, as Benedict and Mead did, that "A culture, like an individual, is a more or less consistent pattern of thought and action" seemed wrong on all counts.[27] In wartime, Benedict and Mead began to identify the culture-as-personality concept with "national character." The conceptual shift only increased Reichard's aversion to stereotyping as an aim of ethnology. Because the members of a cultural group shared linguistic, artistic, and social traditions, they might be referred to conveniently as "The Navajo." Yet the full story of a people could not be told without reference to the variations in the behaviors of individuals within the group. Reichard's pluralistic view of culture was strengthened by her close contact with Adolph Bitanny.

Viewed as an oddball and a misfit by whites and Navajos alike, Bitanny dropped out of the University of New Mexico at the end of fall semester 1939. His habit of working hard at just those things he enjoyed did nothing to endear him to the rigid academic set. He didn't show the proper deference to their medieval traditions in the classroom or their superior academic credentials.[28] It upset Reichard that he borrowed money from New Yorkers she'd introduced him to without paying them back. Reichard was chary of patronizing her would-be protégé during his year at Columbia, but she could see that Adolph needed and wanted the steadying hand of an elder mentor to help him navigate two distinctive cultures. She stood by him after he left Columbia no closer to earning his degree. Then a final dispiriting semester in Albuquerque prompted Bitanny to write her, "I'm as unstable as the wind and I detest the fact as much as my own people would."[29]

Two weeks into 1940, it looked as though Reichard's investment in Bitanny might be a bust. Sounding torn, she asked the Hubbells to stop advancing Adolph money for the transcription work he agreed to do for her. "The arrangement was very disappointing to me because I did not get what I thot he could give," Reichard complained. "I still think he *could* give but he doesn't. But I may have shot too wide of the mark. The funny thing is that I have done [the transcribing] myself and can continue without him easily. I wonder what he will do after that." Bitanny's surrender put Reichard in a funk about Navajo studies generally. "I think I have worked on the Navajo too long and too continuously so that I am now deliberately giving it up for a short time to recover my perspective if any. It is an awful grind and I know it makes me cranky." Disheartening as Bitanny's failure to "crash thru" was, Reichard sought to put it in a broader perspective until it sorted itself out. "Awfully sorry he bothered you," she wrote Dorothy Hubbell. "But you know Indians and after all he is more Indian than anything else."[30]

Bitanny's response to Reichard's tough love was to be contrite and disarmingly vague. "I regret very much that I have been a chronic problem to you," he wrote Reichard. "I am so eager to find out your plans for research work this summer. I can judge that there are some unfinished business on what we already started."[31] Convinced that his lack of a college degree didn't spell doom for a career as a linguist, Bitanny landed a job as a cultural assistant at the Navajo Agency in Window Rock. He was assigned to reworking Navajo legends into a script for a pageant at the annual Navajo Fair, interpretive work that put him on the fringes of the agency's efforts to revive the Navajo literacy program Reichard had piloted in 1934.

For serious linguistic work, the bureau deployed two white men with college degrees to Window Rock: Columbia graduate Edward Kennard and former University of New Mexico student Robert Young. Young had dropped out of New Mexico's graduate program in anthropology to work at the Southwestern Range and Sheepbreeding Laboratory at Fort Wingate. There he met Navajo speaker William Morgan. The two men developed a practical orthography of Navajo based on the advice of J. P. Harrington, an obsessive recorder of North American Indian languages and a contract employee of the Indian Office. Oliver La Farge, by then John Collier's anthropologist-in-chief, took a shine to Young and his orthography and pitched the Young-Morgan alphabet to Collier as the most workable spelling system for Navajo yet devised. Per Collier's orders, Kennard and Young were to begin the difficult task of uniting under a single standard (misnamed the La Farge-Harrington alphabet) the various white and Navajo factions that had been at cross-purposes over written Navajo for decades.[32]

When Bitanny showed up for his new job at the agency in April 1940, the bureau linguists had barely started their work. "Dear Dr. Reichard," Bitanny wrote his erstwhile employer, "This is a smoke signal to let you know that I'm alive. Things are fine out here. I have worked under education department so far,—and confidentially, I don't like it for various reasons: 1, Department is not too encouraging; 2, personnel are always strangers to one another; 3, Poorest department in the Navajo Service." Mindful of his low status in the agency and perhaps a bit envious of Young's higher position, Bitanny assured Reichard that he was keeping his "mouth shut on questions of any sort having to do with the Navajos—I'm humble-like and neutral." Modesty didn't keep Bitanny from privately voicing his opinion of the language work being done at the agency. "So many linguist out here who don't know anything about any one language—i.e. people talk a lot out here on Navajo language don't know anything about it. Not even their own—seems," he wrote Reichard. "J.P. Harrington is well thot of out here as *the* linguist on Athapascans. (In my mind—it's a Phooey). Too, the service is putting out small books pre-primer, primer, Reader, etc = Nav.-Engl Bi-Lingual Readers. Published at Phoenix Indian School. One thing tho—none of the authors of any idea seem to agree once & for all. Too, a fellar (Mr) Robert W. Young (formerly University of New Mexico) one I told you about in connection with the Nav. language is now Harrington's best man—and he has most of my ideas on Nav. language before I began working for you."[33]

Down but not out, Bitanny didn't intend to keep to the sidelines indefinitely. "Do you think that I will be able to become an associate research worker in ethnology for Carnegie, or Rockefeller Foundation, or Smithsonian Inst.?" he wrote Reichard from Window Rock. "How may one get in touch with responsible people? I believe you and Dr. Boas may know more about it. Reasons: I think I will serve many people by working on things of ethnologic interest rather than being told what never to do as an Indian Service employee. What thinks thou? I like and am going to do some writing and sell to publishers. . . . I still do study what I have on the southwestern ethnology. I'm simply dying for literatures of all sorts on anthropology—and I hope to God that either you or Dr. Boas have some literatures or books to through away—and I hope I find them somehow."

In a postscript he wondered if she needed a hand. "If you need some help send *SOS*–and I'll try as I'm now able to help to the best of my ability."[34]

By fall, Young cleared his former classmate to work for Reichard on the agency's dime. "So we are on our way again," a relieved Reichard wrote Parsons. "I was always on mine, but [Adolph] got into the quick sands up to his nose." Her new long-distance arrangement with Bitanny meant she was free of political wrangling at the agency and safely out of the bureaucratic mire. "The interpreters [at the agency] say Adolph can't speak Nav," Reichard noted, but she had too good a grasp on the sociolinguistic dynamic at work in the group to accept their criticism. "[O]ne time," Reichard explained to Parsons, "in front of a bunch of old men, real old timers, AB said, among other things *xwiyisá*. The regulars say *xazá*. It all has to do with the law: *xazá* means 'it is the law.' The regulars said right out loud 'you are always *yis*-ing and *xwiyis*-ing when you talk. Why can't you say, *xazá?*' Whereupon AB was highly embarrassed, in fact stunned into silence when an old man popped up, 'Didn't you learn your xwi's & yi's when you learned to talk? We say *xwiyisá* [laws made repeatedly] when we mean that. It doesn't mean the same as *xazá*.'" Adolph's defender scolded the others, "You seem never to have learned these things!" Without an elder who knew the older forms of the language present to vouch for him, Adolph's youth made him an easy target for the jealous bickering that had plagued the language program from its start.[35]

Bitanny continued to report to work at the agency, where he fancied himself Reichard's eyes and ears. Saying he was "deeply interested" in the literacy work led by Young, he sent her the names of the members of the Language Committee on Navajo recently convened by tribal chairman J. C. Morgan. He described each member of the all-male committee in terms of his "staunchly conservative" or "ultra-liberal" take on a practical orthography for Navajo. "Have you any comparative analysis or comparison of systems of writing Navajo readily at hand?" he asked her. "I have to educate all Navajos named above quickly." To assure Reichard he was turning a new leaf, he promised her, "I'll do my utmost to keep up with you. . . . Waiting for your smoke signals; where are we?"[36]

The war and not Bitanny's real or imagined shortcomings brought an end to the young man's career in Navajo linguistics. Less than a month after Pearl Harbor, Bitanny's Selective Service number was called and he vanished into the ranks of Roosevelt's fresh-faced army of a million and a half young men. Reichard heard nothing from him until October 1942, when he wrote her from the Army Materiel Center at Fort Smith, Arkansas. "Dear Gladys," he wrote, "Here's that Indian again."

> I'm not to tell about what I do. Anyway, this army life is giving the works far beyond my patience . . . seems. Just became a lieutenant in the Air Corps on the 16th of Sept. This is indeed fortunate, as far as it goes, for me to be far removed from the frontiers of the theatres of war. Perhaps some of my ancestors would turn green with shame if they really hear me say that. Any how, my function has to do with the production end of the Air Corps. I had learned how to fly a plane and also became an efficient gunner on fly fortress but seems like I won't see foreign service after all . . . as much as I wanted to. Few strands of my philosophy has been changed by the circumstances attending war and severe confinement to duties.
>
> These days are relieving because I find more time at my own disposal during evenings and Sundays. Of course during the week days there's that confinement to duties. I have not gotten furlough yet. I aim to apply for one when I thought best . . . but where to go if I do get one is still not clear in my mind. I'm afraid I'm still a will-o-the-wisp (yet) and I let come what may. My attitude towards humanity became rather reckless lately . . .
>
> Yours truly,
> Lt. Adolph D. Bitanny
>
> P.S. I received your card. And thanks a lot. I hope your Nav. Religion is ready (about). My hope was to try to help on it but I suppose you needed no help.[37]

Reichard's empathy for Bitanny's marginal status in two worlds may have stemmed from her own experience as a rare woman thought to have overstepped her station by becoming both an ethnographer and a linguist. The number of women ethnographers rose steadily in the first half of the twentieth century, but women linguists who specialized in American Indian languages before 1940 could be counted on one hand.[38] The Linguistic Society of America, founded when Reichard was still in graduate school, did nothing to address the shortage of women with her particular interests in their midst. Intent on becoming "the preponderant expression of American linguistics," the LSA was firmly committed to the maxim "structure is the object of our search."[39] As such it was hostile to suggestions that linguistics had a role to play in cultural investigations and vice versa, on the grounds that cultural information or the referential meaning of linguistic elements contaminated the purity of formal procedures devised to reveal linguistic structures. Initially, the LSA had invited "All persons, whether men or women," to join the society, be they schoolteachers or amateur language buffs. "Very quickly," a historian of the LSA writes, "there arose a movement to define linguistics narrowly . . . to withdraw from philological study of written texts and their cultural context, and to exclude the nonprofessional."[40]

A concomitant of the LSA's emphasis on the study of unwritten languages via mechanistic, synchronic procedures was the sense that an exemplary member was a firebrand, a scientific revolutionary who exhibited "contempt for how languages were studied at the time" and permitted himself to "disregard any previous scholarly work."[41] Women linguists didn't fit this description generally, by choice or by attribution, and for Reichard the arrogance implied by these attitudes was intolerable. Accomplished university-trained linguists like E. Adelaide Hahn (a founding member of the LSA and the society's first woman president) and Mary Haas eventually held high office in the Linguistics Society, but not until after World War II.[42] Reflecting on the years she spent patiently climbing the LSA ranks, Haas recalled, "I remember once [Sapir] mentioned Adelaide Hahn. . . . She was sort of made fun of by the men. . . . One time Sapir was talking to me and perhaps forgot himself and spoke of Adelaide as being a "femme savante," and I could tell that was a derogatory term."[43] Front office politics at the LSA reflected acceptable "locker room" prejudices. Women were appointed to neither the Standing Committee on Research, begun in 1933, nor the Committee on Publications during Reichard's lifetime.[44]

The grammar of Coeur d'Alene Salish Reichard wrote for the 1938 *Handbook of American Indian Languages*, edited by Boas, was thus easily waved off by LSA member Charles Hockett. The self-appointed pitchman for structuralizing formalism adopted the "eclipsing stance" toward linguistic theory then fashionable to dismiss all five grammars in the volume for having been written to meet Boas's outmoded, pre-1930 expectations.[45] As far as Hockett was concerned, the only "satisfactory guide to linguistic analysis" was Bloomfield's 1933 textbook *Language*; all other presentations of linguistic data fell short. Though he dribbled faint praise on the three grammars written by men and made only glancing mention of Ruth Bunzel's pedestrian description of Zuni, Hockett singled Reichard out for "deficiency in phonetic description." He asserted that her section on morphology was "difficult to grasp because the material is organized on the basis of contrast of ideas rather than contrasts of form," labeled her section on syntax "confused," and staked his claim that her translations of Coeur d'Alene were "frequently" unintelligible on a single gloss he disliked. "One feels," Hockett sniffed in a final snub, "except in the case of [Manuel] Andrade, a lack of methodological stringency which is so admirable a characteristic of the volume's editor and of his best students."[46]

University of Washington professor and Northwest specialist Melville Jacobs effected a partial rescue of Reichard's reputation as a linguist in a fairer review. Jacobs acknowledged *Coeur d'Alene* as "the first full length portrait of a Salishan language" to appear in the fifty years since Boas began a systematic survey of the language family. He welcomed Reichard's second major contribution to North American Indian linguistics as establishing "the foundation upon which most future field researches and analyses of Salishan languages may be conducted." It was modest praise for a first-of-its kind description of a language as yet steeped in mystery. Still, Reichard had to be thankful that Jacobs gave her more credit for her years of work on the grammar than he gave the two Coeur d'Alene speakers who she'd warmly acknowledged in her introduction. Jacobs avoided referring to Lawrence Nicodemus by name when he identified Reichard's informant as a "young man visiting New York in 1935 and 1936." He made no mention of Julia Antelope's role in the grammar whatsoever.[47]

· · · ◈ · · ·

Not the sorry trifecta of Bitanny's disappearance and the deaths of Parsons and Boas but the war itself brought Reichard to a crossroads as she neared fifty. The "ghastly stuff" she heard on the radio every night—bloody-minded nationalism, nativist panic, reports on the rising toll of blood and treasure—seemed to mock her life's work.[48] Tuned to the Navajo medicine man's dictum, "One who knows how to keep things in order has the key to life's problems," Reichard had done more than most as an anthropologist to advocate for social renewal through education and collaboration rather than violence.[49] Yet the "careless" men who specialized in sowing disorder disguised as virtue swept her into their war as briskly as they had Bitanny.[50] With millions of other Americans she met the "equality of sacrifice" imposed on her in large and small ways.[51] Air raid drills, nightly blackouts, inflated prices, and rationing of staples and dry goods affected her whether she was in New York or Arizona.

The disruptions she liked least were related to driving. In February 1942 the president issued an executive order severely restricting the sale of automobile tires; rationing of gasoline was soon to follow. Before the war Reichard wrote Parsons from Arizona, "rolling over these great prairies & deserts of ours—that's when I become patriotic! And I think best on wheels!"[52] A year later it was difficult to avoid the sight of war posters depicting armed soldiers cruising in a military jeep below the slogan, "They've got more important places to go than you!"[53]

No corner of Reichard's nation was too remote to be spared the disordering effects of mobilization. Flagstaff was brought into the fight practically overnight once the War Department announced plans in early 1942 to construct the Navajo Ordnance Depot ten miles west of town on Volunteer Prairie. At a cost of thirty million dollars, the arsenal for democracy would come to cover close to thirty thousand contiguous acres with three and a half-million square feet of storage capacity for war materiel in eight hundred concrete igloos, 150 warehouses, magazines, garages, and above-ground shelters, and more than two hundred miles of roads. At the north edge of the compound close to Route 66, clapboard housing units were raised in the whites-only Victory Village. Three miles away stood the tents and hogans erected for the inhabitants of Indian Village.[54] A boon to the local economy, the depot significantly increased the dysfunction in Indian-white relations across the region.

Thousands of Navajo and other Native peoples of the Southwest migrated from their reservation homes seeking wage-work for as long as it lasted. After ten years of federally mandated livestock reduction, Navajo shepherds and weavers had few other options. Over the objections of the herdsmen, Navajo women in particular, livestock reduction was normalized on the reservation after a disastrous start in 1933.[55] The ingrained cruelty of the program quickly grew casual. White and Navajo range riders sometimes shot sheep and freshly dismounted saddle horses by the side of the road, leaving the carcasses to rot in the sun while the shepherds, frequently small children, ran home on foot. John Collier's apologists argued that livestock owners were usually paid for the animals, but no amount of money could compensate for the depraved actions of some of the bureau's employees. "Our subsistence, our sheep and horses, had been in our hearts," Navajo elder Curly Mustache told an interviewer in the 1970s. "But all this just turned into smoke." Men who protested or disobeyed were jailed, while their livestock were killed in their absence. The goat that Navajo mothers had relied on for centuries for meat and milk in times of famine or drought was demonized as the greatest threat to Navajo survival. For a majority of Diné, "Livestock is an evil thing to have" was Collier's primary message, the commissioner's betrayal of their early trust unforgiveable.[56]

While the senseless slaughter of Navajo livestock continued, the federally funded job training and educational opportunities Reichard once supported failed to materialize. The nearly two million dollars the federal government spent on wages and public works on the Navajo Reservation during the Depression served to make younger Navajos wage slaves. Their children were sentenced to poorly staffed schools and community centers where they were taught to waltz but not to read.[57] Employment at the Navajo Ordnance Depot was forced assimilation of Navajos into the wartime economy by another name. Shift work at the depot disrupted their traditional seasonal rhythms and made the days of preparation for and execution of their culturally essential restorative ceremonies impossible. Banned from Flagstaff public schools, non-English-speaking Navajo children attended the Bellemont Day School in Indian Village. The white teacher was charged explicitly with making the youngsters proficient in English and tacitly with convincing them that their futures depended on the extinction of their culture as the elders practiced it. As their fathers and uncles shouldered tons of missiles and heavy munitions and their mothers and aunts inspected and packed hand grenades by the bushel, the Native children took to the schoolyard for games, including "cowboys-and-Indians." One former pupil at the Bellemont Day School recalled that the "Indians" were routinely on the losing end of such play.[58]

Thousands of miles away from Arizona's War Town, eastern elites spent the first year of the war building a virtual monument to war hysteria in Washington, D.C. Reichard's regard for the anthropological establishment deteriorated rapidly as the majority of her peers flocked to the U.S. capital, the nerve center of the Allied Forces, to offer their services as "applied anthropologists." More committed to "Win the war first!" than to justice and liberty for all, war anthropologists were in demand in the national security sector for their skill at gathering cultural intelligence. The specialized knowledge of foreign languages, cultures, and geographies they possessed was urgently needed to manage allies and enemies through propaganda campaigns or outright psychological warfare. Anthropologists sympathetic to culture-and-personality ethnography were the sharks of the lot. Claiming that they could psychoanalyze their targets at a distance through a process Mead referred to as "culture cracking," they took up positions behind desks at the Office of Strategic Services and the Foreign Morale Analysis Division of the War Information Office.[59] By the end of 1942, AAA spokesman Fred Eggan boasted, "over one-half of the professional anthropologists in this country are directly concerned with the war effort, and most of the rest are doing part-time war work." "By mid-1943," a student of the period writes, "virtually every wartime agency had an anthropologist or two on staff."[60]

The rapid transformation of anthropologists into "'technicians for hire to the highest bidder" gave birth to a new association, the Society for Applied Anthropology. Fifty-four like-minded anthropologists including Mead, Benedict, and Clyde Kluckhohn helped launch the action-oriented club, which they conceived of as "a means whereby social change could be engineered for desirable ends . . . desirable implicitly" to "elites striving for more control" over the masses. The SFAA "did not champion increased democracy; it championed increased management of people, regardless of their free desires or intentions."[61]

Aside from its narrow self-interest, the most troubling aspect of the AAA's effective surrender to militarism was the low priority given racial justice in their in-house deliberations. As the resolution to commit to the war was being debated in 1941, Esther Goldfrank tried to inject concern about the unequal treatment of black men in the military into the discussion. Following a nervous silence, Mead, who chaired the session, ruled Goldfrank out of order for raising the issue.[62] Melville Jacobs was granted more time to plead for a statement by the AAA protesting the probable forced "evacuation" of Japanese Americans from his state of Washington and three others. The AAA declined to draft a formal resolution on the matter. Two months later, President Roosevelt reluctantly signed Executive

Order 9033 into law, initiating the incarceration of civilians of Japanese descent, children and U.S. citizens included, by the tens of thousands.[63] Instead of protesting the internments, scores of applied anthropologists on the payroll of Collier's Bureau of Indian Affairs, the University of California, or the U.S. War Relocation Authority fanned out across the nation to interrogate captive Japanese Americans. The approach and scope of ethnography conducted in the camps ranged from benign attempts to improve life behind barbed wire to the chillingly illiberal task of convincing detainees to inform on one another.[64]

If the newfound military-industrial loyalty sworn to by her discipline's top professional organization forced Reichard into the role of a conscientious objector, she refused to stand down in the face of the bellicose men who sought her retreat from the field of North American Indian linguistics. The battle lines meant to keep women out of anthropological linguistics were drawn for Reichard by Sapir back in 1924. The linguist's fervent disciples held their fire until after his death in 1939. In 1940 Reichard wrote "a peach of an article on Navajo" grammar with Bitanny. She was unusually proud of the findings they presented in "Agentive and Causative Elements in Navajo." "All of this is so simple" she exulted to Boas as she wrote the paper, "that I go around hugging myself at the brilliancy of my discovery." It crossed her mind to submit the article to the Sapirians who were preparing a festschrift in their late leader's honor. "Since the article refutes every idea that Sapir sprung [about Navajo]," Reichard decided against the notion "as a matter of taste."[65]

Because Sapir's aggression had conditioned her to expect an emotional rather than rational response from defensive Athabascanists, she was careful to credit Sapir in her article with giving "liberally of his time and information to make Navajo available to me." She also explained that as no single, authoritative alphabet had yet been established for Navajo, she retained Sapir's 1934 orthography, with minor tweaks, as a convenience to those familiar with that system. Poker-faced, Reichard summarized her motives for publishing her results in anticipation of claims of trespass. "There is a demand for a grammar of the Navajo language. This work differs greatly from Sapir's in approach and conclusions arrived at. The results of his vast labor on the subject are not available."[66]

By naming Bitanny as a co-author, Reichard imbued the paper with an important subtext. Although she had written the paper herself, Bitanny's

keen insights into the meaning of the grammatical elements they analyzed allowed them to interpret the Navajo textual material examined "as
felt and dictated by the natives."[67] Reichard and Bitanny's partnership,
unequal because of their differences of training and experience with
structural linguistics, differed significantly from the relationships that
obtained between Sapir and his Navajo-language consultants. Sapir let it
be known that he was dissatisfied with Chic Sandoval's ability to transcribe
or analyze his own language, skills Sandoval never fully mastered. During
Sapir's only field trip among the Navajo, in 1929, he ignored attempts
by other Navajo consultants to contextualize or critique the social and
linguistic features of the stories they told him. Sapir reportedly stopped
informants from straying from the "genuine stuff," lore that conformed
to Sapir's preconceived idea of authentic material.[68] Although in writing
"Agentive and Causative Elements" Reichard applied the key tenets of
structuralist linguistics to the data, she implicitly challenged the idea that
the non-Native linguist's intuition was superior to that of her informant,
usually stereotyped as obliging but insensible. With her first formal paper
on Navajo grammar, Reichard illustrated how a sensitive, intelligent
Native linguist, properly trained in the latest analytical techniques, might
provide important contributions to the analysis when he was treated less
as a sponge to be wrung dry of "stuff" than as an active partner in the
scholarly enterprise.

Reichard's first choice would have been to see the paper published in
the *International Journal of American Linguistics*. Unfortunately, *IJAL* was
on hiatus until Boas recovered his health or named his successor.[69] When
University of New Mexico professor and Anthropology chair Donald D.
Brand asked Reichard to submit the "Agentive and Causative Elements"
to the *New Mexican Anthropologist*, she jumped at the chance. Brand asked
Harry Hoijer, Sapir's handpicked heir in Navajo and southern Athabascan linguistics, and Clyde Kluckhohn to conduct the peer review. Hoijer
flatly rejected the manuscript. Kluckhohn, who spoke some Navajo but
made no claims to be a linguist, was in favor of publication. Brand turned
to Berard Haile to break the tie. When Haile voted with Hoijer, Brand
notified Reichard he would not publish the paper. Reichard smelled a rat
and said so, though her complaint was more tame than she made out. She
told Parsons she'd sent a "red hot" letter to the university's publications
committee protesting her treatment, yet her message was reasonable

enough that they didn't dismiss it out of hand. "One of them voted to reconsider," Reichard reported after the committee met, "but they voted that down so as not to set a precedent (right I think)." She thought Brand "an ass" but brightened when Kluckhohn shared with her that Brand said of the affair, "[H]ad the readers been other than they were [the paper] would have been received even with acclaim."[70]

In rejecting "Agentive and Causative Elements," Hoijer signaled that he intended to continue Sapir's campaign to end or undermine Reichard's research in Navajo linguistics. Reichard's junior by less than a dozen years, Hoijer had come of age as a linguist listening to Sapir disparaging women scholars generally and Reichard in particular. Thus indoctrinated, and with extreme territoriality, Hoijer proceeded to condemn everything Reichard wrote related to Navajo linguistics as if the very fact that she published was an insult to his master's memory. Hoijer, like Haile, fancied himself a purist. As Sapir's literary executor, Hoijer felt it his duty to protect Athabascan linguistics from contamination by the riffraff, that is, those linguists who refused to bow to Sapir's supremacy in American linguistics. Hoijer's chief, unending gripe about Reichard's work concerned the spelling system she used for writing Navajo. It didn't matter that the orthography or analyses Sapirians advocated remained buried in unpublished papers or that they themselves deviated from Sapir's frequent revisions over time. Hoijer repeatedly called Reichard to account in print for failing to adopt an orthographic standard for Navajo that was constantly in flux, thanks to revisions Hoijer, Haile, and Sapir felt entitled to make at will.[71]

Hoijer's carping over Reichard's spelling and typography became so insistent that Reichard finally addressed it head-on in 1947. She replied to Hoijer's laundry list of critical comments about her hand-typed *The Story of the Navajo Hail Chant* by dividing his charges into two categories, those bearing on the writing or labeling of linguistic elements and those dependent on "personal taste." She demonstrated first where her analysis of the Navajo linguistic facts differed from Hoijer's (and Sapir's) analysis, in effect reclassifying putative mistakes as differences of informed opinion. Second, Reichard repeated that Hoijer's objections to her orthographic choices, in Navajo and English, were built on personal bias. It was common knowledge among specialists in Navajo studies that each used his or her own phonetic spelling system and Reichard merely pointed to this fact, saying, "As the situation now stands in working with Navaho material it is necessary to use at least five major [spelling] systems and several minor ones, two of which are used by Hoijer." On the trivial topic of the spelling of the non-Native name for the Diné and their language, she responded, "As for 'Navajo,' I have explained my reason (p. x of text) for the spelling. I do not think it makes a bit of difference which way it is spelled and a perusal of any bibliography exclusive of entries under my name will establish the futility of standardization."[72]

Reichard was clearly fed up with Hoijer's arbitrary dismissals and appealed to fairness when she wrote,

> There was a long period (1930–7) of my work on the Navajo religion during which I relied on Sapir and Hoijer for the linguistic material, expecting its publication yearly. The Story of the Navajo Hail Chant was recorded during this time when I had no means of checking it. Not until 1937 when it seemed that my need of a grammar and dictionary was overwhelming and that theirs was not forthcoming did I start seriously to work independently on the language. I had the text here discussed lithoprinted under a sense of pressure about its ceremonial and literary value, since [Klah], the narrator, had died and it was unlikely that I would be able to record as full a text of the myth again. I did not then and do not now consider it very good as linguistic material except insofar as it may be suggestive. If I had waited to give all the explanations Hoijer demands and which I agree would be desirable, the text would still be in four notebooks in a file. On the other hand, if I were using material primarily to present and confirm linguistic questions I should not use this text but rather others I have which are phonetically more reliable, or even Sapir's and Father Berard's which are now available.
>
> I make this protest because the tenets laid down in Hoijer's work seem dogmatic and therefore final. Navajo is a living, growing representative of a great linguistic family, a language which, because of its diversity and changing form, may lead us to the solution of many Athabaskan problems. It should therefore be open for discussion and the findings, when different from the dogma, should be freely admitted so that new rules may be formulated and new insights exploited.[73]

"Your answer to Hoijer is put convincingly and with restraint," Kluckhohn wrote Reichard on reading an advance copy of her rebuttal. "There are a few points I would disagree with you about but for the most part you—so far as *I* can judge—have the advantage of the argument."[74]

Kluckhohn, Reichard discovered reluctantly, was a stealthier foe than Hoijer. Any support the Harvard anthropologist voiced for her work turned out to be a disarming ploy to allow him to control the direction and funding of a unified program in Navajo studies under his aegis. In the 1930s, Reichard hadn't resented Kluckhohn as an *arriviste* as Franc Newcomb did, possibly because she assumed he would eventually outgrow his conceited manner. Also, she fell for his personal charm. "However Clyde may be regarding his scientific work he is certainly nice to work with," Reichard wrote Parsons in 1940.[75] She added, "Clyde is using my Nav. language work and says the examples check with his old men 100 percent which is too high. Furthermore he is improving in his Nav. something terrific since he has had it to use." The respect and professional courtesy Kluckhohn showered on Reichard made her protective of him. "You know Sapir said he is no good," she mentioned casually to Parsons. "Roman Hubbell who is hypercritical in a practical way says Clyde speaks [Navajo] very well, and that is what we really need."[76]

Reichard viewed Kluckhohn as a friend first and a rival second, but Sapir knew a cunning player when he saw one. Once Kluckhohn and Wyman published their *Navaho Classification* in the *AA* Memoir series, Haile complained to Sapir that the men had stolen his ideas and left him with barely more than a pat on the head. Haile also alleged that Kluckhohn had maneuvered behind the scenes to block the publication of an article he'd written criticizing *Navaho Classification*. Sapir responded by dismissing the Memoir out of hand. "[M]y dear boy," he wrote Haile airily, "I don't think it's any worse in the violence it does native concepts and terminology than 90% of the supposedly authoritative stuff published by anthropologists who have not a proper control of linguistic analysis." Wyman was a nobody in Sapir's book, but Kluckhohn bore watching. "He is intelligent and interested, but not as able as some people think," he warned Haile. "Moreover, his ambition strikes me as somewhat pathological in character." As to Kluckhohn's willingness to manipulate *AA* editors to do his bidding, Sapir observed cryptically, "He's quite capable of doing far worse, judging from certain facts I happen to know."[77]

Reichard was forced to come to terms with Kluckhohn's duplicitous nature after she learned he had worked behind the scenes to draw her into a fruitless squabble in the pages of *American Anthropologist*. Her "brief communication" of 1942, "The Translation of Two Navaho Chant Words," was a concise, pointed application of her meaning-based approach to Navajo language. She hoped that by presenting her technique she might "clear up linguistic confusion" and be "helpful and suggestive in further revising the classification of myth and ritual" she judged to be "ably introduced" by Kluckhohn and Wyman in their classification of Navajo ceremony.[78] Reichard's note harkened back to statements she had made in a review of Haile's *Origin Legend of the Navaho Enemy Way*, a book published by Yale University with Sapir's help. "The work is especially illuminating to the student of Navajo," she had written of Haile's text collection, "who depends on linguistic evidence as the ultimate means of interpretation of belief as strange as that of the Navajo."[79] Haile had repaid her courteous review by helping to quash "Agentive and Causative Elements" the following year. The collegial tone of "Two Navaho Chant Words" showed Reichard bore the prickly cleric no hard feelings. Reasonable people could disagree, she implied, without personalizing the scholarly debate.[80]

It is unclear if the *AA* editors intentionally tried to fuel a controversy by running Reichard's article alongside one Haile had written offering alternate translations for the same chant names. Haile preferred "Upward Reaching Way" to Reichard's "Chant of Waning Endurance." Kluckhohn pounced on the opportunity to stir the pot. Because he did not have the reputation in Navajo linguistics to challenge Reichard himself, he wrote Haile to say, "I think that damned 'Waning Endurance' should be publicly debunked so that no serious professionals will pay any attention to it. . . . I do hope you'll write the Anthropologist showing the error of Reichard's ways!"[81] Accustomed to following orders, Haile obliged. *AA* editor Ralph Linton ran Haile's retort the following spring. In it, Haile waved off Reichard's analysis of the words in question as "unwarranted speculation" that added to the confusion over Navajo chant words rather than resolving it. Unintentionally, Haile gave credence to Reichard's formal approach to translation by responding to her short note with an onslaught of alternate terminology and phonetic spellings that no typical reader of *AA*, Linton included, could evaluate on its merits. Satisfied with his verbal blitzkrieg, Haile expressed the sarcastic hope that Reichard "can persuade herself to understand certain linguistics points of Navaho," as if his acid tone throughout had not already insinuated that she was unfit to publish on Navajo alongside the men who knew better—himself, Sapir, Hoijer, and the "Way Boys," Kluckhohn and Wyman.[82]

Kluckhohn's motive for prompting Haile's attack may have had less to do with Navajo chant words than Haile realized. In the same issue that featured the paper Haile condemned, Reichard's review of *Language, Culture and Personality: Essays in Memory of Edward Sapir* appeared. Though Reichard praised the thick volume generally and many papers individually, including one by Mary Haas, she showed less enthusiasm for several. Harry Hoijer's failure to do more than rehash Sapir's arguments pertaining to linguistic classification disappointed her.[83] Papers she thought conveyed a methodological rigidity that presupposed patterns marked by "extreme neatness" included ones by George Trager and Clyde Kluckhohn. "Pattern does of course exist," Reichard wrote of Kluckhohn's thesis, "but the most difficult thing in the world—more difficult even than the discovery of essential pattern—is to resist the temptation to gather those facts which fit into the scheme while at the same time ignoring, or not discovering the others." Trager's paper struck Reichard as naive prescriptivism disguised as theoretical exactness. "It, like other rigorous terminologies and classifications, does not consider that, illogical as all culture is, language is perhaps its most illogical phase. Each language has something which might be called its own logic, but it is so divergent from our conception of logic that it ought to be called something else. Perhaps pattern, order, mode, trait, or configuration would do, but not logic."[84]

Reichard closed her measured review with a general call to Sapirians to raise their game. She pointed to the paper by Benjamin Whorf, "The Relational Habit of Thought and Behavior to Language," as a shining example of intellectual courage. Whorf dared to tackle broad problems of language and cognition at the risk of exposing himself to "the most savage criticism" from smaller minds, she wrote. "No language is devoid of interesting ideas, but those developed by the American Indians, numerous and unusual as they are, are of the most vital significance in the history of the development of language." "What, for instance, do languages find it necessary to express?" she asked. "What generalized concepts do they have in contrast to specific?" The intriguing questions "poor Whorf" chose to dwell on before his untimely death in 1941 addressed "the most challenging of all linguistic problems"—why do languages have the properties they have and not others?[85] And while Whorf's paper was a fitting salute to Sapir's lightning intellect, it served to highlight what went missing in the tribute volume on the whole. Sapir had shown anthropological linguists "the rich uses to which linguistic studies may contribute in illuminating ethnology," Reichard noted. "It is rather a pity that no one [in *Language, Culture, and Personality*] has gone into them."[86]

Kluckhohn's hidden resentment of Reichard's critique surfaces in a series of letters they exchanged after Gladys discovered through the grapevine that Clyde had set her up. Kluckhohn's reply to Reichard's request for an explanation of his behavior in regards to "Two Navaho Chant Words" clarified his attitude toward Reichard, once and for all. He couldn't resist stealing a page from Sapir's playbook when he told her he acted in poor brother Haile's defense. "I have always, genuinely and deeply liked you as a person and I continue to," Kluckhohn wrote. "But when it comes to Navaho studies I have slowly and regretfully come to the conclusion that your views and mine as to what constitutes evidence, your views and mine as to the basic canons of scientific logic were so far apart that agreement was not to be hoped for. With occasional and usually utterly minor qualifications it has been my experience that Wyman, [W.W.] Hill, Father Berard and I saw pretty much eye to eye on Navaho questions." He continued, "I am as sure as I can ever be of anything that you are dead wrong and he is right. . . . In my opinion, your attitude toward [Haile] and his work is based upon an understandable but regrettable emotionally based resistance. . . . This tendency toward idiosyncratic separatism—proper enough in personal but not in scientific life, in my judgment—I find reflected in other details."[87]

Struck by disbelief, Reichard sought a sympathetic ear in Wyman. Clyde's sidekick, however, stood by his man. He advised Reichard to accept Kluckhohn's conclusions as well-intentioned, dispassionate, and correct. When Reichard reached out to Wyman a second time, her disappointment in Kluckhohn had turned to righteous indignation. "I think it would have been decent of Linton and Clyde at least to have shown me F.B.'s paper and asked my opinion," she wrote her colleague. "Instead Clyde passes on it and says OK Reichard all wet—and whatever he *said* that was the effect—and then writes me 'Of course I don't know anything about the linguistic side of the matter.' This, my dear boy, is science and method and anything else isn't. It is obvious I think that there is really nothing to discuss because this is all on a plane where discussion is impossible. And then *I* am emotional and I have not written a word for publication which has anything like the content 'F B knows more than anyone about the Navajo language.' What has that got to do with a specific discussion?" Reichard saw too well that Kluckhohn's betrayal turned on her sex, and most shamefully, on his crass desire to disqualify his competition. "Of course Father B knows more than anyone," she groaned in frustration, "but does he know the things I want to know. Or if he does, and by this time you will know that I have used his stuff for all it is worth, is there any reason I should not try to find out more using his stuff as a foundation?"[88]

In the event, Reichard lost her innocence about Kluckhohn without losing her head. Turning the page, she told Wyman, "Don't do any more about [Kluckhohn] or me, but let's just go on as we planned if you are still interested. Until I find out to the contrary I shall not depend on Clyde's word and I always used to. . . . Thank you no end for your interest in this affair and don't worry, I hold each person individually responsible for his own sins, not for those of others."[89] Between letters to Wyman, Reichard typed a brisk reply to Kluckhohn calling out his "naked honesty" as a sham used to condemn her "without a trial." "I am naturally very sorry that you feel as you do; I don't know anything to do about it," she wrote him. "I thought I had presented evidence for my attitudes but since you, not having read it, do not think so I have no basis for discussion." She signed the typed reply in pencil, "Yours, nice person, lousy scientist! Gladys."[90]

Though Reichard didn't send her final word on the conflict to Kluckhohn, she saved her letter. As the sole example of an unsent letter in Reichard's collected papers, the fact of its survival in her papers suggests she embued it with special powers. She withstood the sexism and territoriality she encountered in Navajo studies by refusing to yield to feelings of inferiority. When dealing with the mean-spirited scheming that Kluckhohn and company introduced into her career in the 1940s,

Reichard may well have drawn courage from lessons she learned in the company of her Navajo teachers during the 1930s. After Miguelito sang the Male Shooting Chant over her in 1932, he presented Gladys with a medicine bead she greatly treasured. Handing her the bit of turquoise tied to an olivella shell, the singer told her, "After this if you are out in a thunderstorm shake this bead at them (that is, the thunders) and they will stop."[91] If Reichard saved her draft letter to Kluckhohn as a tangible token of a particularly disheartening episode, who could blame her if it crossed her mind that by safeguarding those thin typed pages she might ward off the next attack?

· · · · · ◈ · · · · ·

CHAPTER 9

UNDERSTANDING

AT THE CONVOCATION CEREMONY REICHARD ATTENDED on her first day as a student at Columbia, she was presented with dramatically different views of a university. President Butler had implied that day that Columbia was an instrument of the state, a perspective that by 1945 was prevalent in polite society. John Erskine, English professor and author of the essay "The Moral Obligation to be Intelligent," had taken the stage after Butler to offer a contrasting vision. "It is our inspiration to think of society as one," Erskine said in 1919, "to dream of the worker as intellectually master of the whole plan in which he builds a section; to conceive of mankind at their tasks as differing only as to the tools and materials not at all to the dignity nor the value of the labor; to conceive of mankind at play as differing only in their talents but all alike trained artisans of happiness and beauty; and to imagine the community, at work or at play, finding its unity, its communion, in the university. This is a dream, but it will begin to come true when the university says to us, 'Whatever you do, whether for use or for pleasure, can be done beautifully. I am here to show you the way. Whatever you do has meaning also. I am here to tell you what it means. That I am here at all, after the centuries, is a sign that those long dead, who bade me say this to you, touched the work of the hour with the enduring mind.'"[1] Attuned to the Quaker ideal of a university as the place where scholars learned to build a house for all to live in together, there can be no doubt which speech Reichard found the more inspiring.

World War II, which saw Young Turks and white-haired college dons cavorting unapologetically with generals and spies, forced Reichard to reevaluate her professional allegiances. The American Folklore Society had been the first scholarly club she'd joined as a graduate student. As she turned away in disgust from the AAA, the LSA, and the Society for Applied

Anthropology, she realized the AFS was her logical guild.[2] Though they held their annual meetings together and had overlapping memberships, the Folklore Society's culture had always been distinct from that of the AAA. Historically dominated by men, the AAA cultivated a reputation for admiring muscular scholarship accentuated with hints of derring-do. The Folklore Society, by contrast, was like folklore itself, perceived as a quaint, artistic, feminine collective. On the question of femininity, the Folklore Society stood guilty as charged. Its long tradition of employing women as executive officers, editors, and book reviewers was irrefutable evidence that women played a major, even dominant role in building an organization that valued the enduring mind above the sex of its members.

When Reichard was elected president of the American Folklore Society at the end of 1942, she was the fifth woman to lead the society since 1888.[3] Her tenure was an unqualified success. By the time she handed off the president's gavel in January 1944, overall membership was up more than 20 percent. With the last of Parsons's bequest added to a nine-hundred-dollar return on war bonds for the year, the society's receipts were more than double those of the previous year's, enough to finally bring out Wheeler's long-delayed *Tales of Jalisco, Mexico*. Working with other executive members, Reichard updated membership and governance policies, instituted a modest annual budget for secretarial assistance to the editor, and initiated a review of the society's constitution and bylaws in order to promote greater transparency for its growing membership. With Reichard's hands-on help, journal editor Erminie Voegelin met the quarterly publication goals (319 pages in four numbers) and published two lengthy Memoirs.[4]

Rather than rally the growing membership around the cheap bauble of nationalism, Reichard continued to direct her AFS colleagues to attend lovingly to their chosen craft, whether they were story-loving literary folklorists or pattern-seeking anthropologists. She'd never made a secret of her admiration for Navajos as "motor-minded people." "There is not a single person among them who is not able to do something with his hands," she told a student reporter in 1933, "and what is more they apply the crafts they know to other crafts."[5] Versatility was a trait she deemed eminently worthy of emulation, even by scholars. As *JAF* editor, Reichard had highlighted other "artisans of happiness and beauty" in a review of *Shaker Furniture, The Craftmanship of an American Communal Sect*. The tastefully illustrated book, Reichard wrote, demonstrated that Shaker artisans "carried their faith in 'purity, simplicity, and utility' into every possible phase of daily life." She thought authors Edward and Faith Andrews beautifully conveyed the information that Shaker craftsmen learned to do many things well from a young age, so that their natural energy and ambition were directed "toward only one purpose, the good of the community." One member of the sect might be an expert "clocksmith, cabinetmaker, tailor, farmer, mason, blacksmith and teacher," Reichard noted, adding for emphasis, "A person intimately acquainted with so many phases of his environment brings enough viewpoints to his craft to make a permanent contribution." As a parable for the modernist craftsman who wielded only a pen in his trade, *Shaker Furniture* offered humanists and scientists "a model which might be used by more workers in the collection of material objects, all of which are more than things, since they are closely coordinated with the social, religious, economic and psychological background of their owners."[6]

True to her word, Reichard led by example. In the space of her presidency she published five papers and three book reviews, each lit by the spirit of liberal humanism and, in the case of her tributes to Parsons and Boas, love and repect. The book she wrote in 1943 was the groundbreaking *Prayer the Compulsive Word*, the first study of Navajo verbal art to qualify as a formal ethnopoetics.[7] In fewer than one hundred pages, Reichard accomplished the feat of being thoroughly original and scientifically rigorous at once. Her originality lay in her approach, which she summarized as the "use [of] language as a tool to get at meaning, an analysis of meaning to interpret thought and through it, ritual."[8] Her eclecticism allowed her to probe the subconscious of a Navajo at prayer in a forthright and testable way, bringing out the underlying rhetorical patterns in twenty-five hand-drawn figures collected at the end of the book. While *Prayer* was a highly technical treatment meant for specialists, Reichard emphasized that her work in Navajo oral literature was preliminary rather than the final say. "[I]nvestigators of Navajo lore have come to realize that because materials used and their treatment are different as we compare one informant, locality or ritualistic complex with another, we are not justified in considering any informant 'wrong' rather than right," she wrote. "Many of us now realize that the very inconsistencies we find may be our best clues to enlightenment about the whole."[9]

Reichard's startling productivity during this period shared the back-drop of dread and helplessness the mothers and wives she knew experienced. She was spared the agony of losing a husband, son, or a brother to the battlefront, but she was haunted by the absence of the young men she'd helped raise. Dorothy and Roman Hubbell's oldest son, Roman Jr., known as Monnie, joined the army after graduating from Palo Alto Military Academy. Stationed at Fort Bliss Military Reserve with his wife and child before the United States entered the war, Monnie, an officer, shipped out after Pearl Harbor to a series of undisclosed locations. Younger brother John was kept out of the army by his heart condition during the first years of the war. With Reichard's backing, he won one of twelve Roosevelt Fellowships, which took him to Buenos Aires for eighteen months of language and cultural studies at multiple universities. On his return, John's multilingualism landed him a desk job as an intelligence officer, where and for how long he wasn't allowed to say. Boas's grandsons, Robert and Philip Yampolsky, were drafted within months of graduating from Columbia, in time for their grandfather to see them off to war. If Reichard kept in touch with them by mail as she did Bitanny, she greatly multiplied the time she spent hoping against hope all would be spared.

The lowest point of the war for Reichard personally occurred in April 1944. The news probably reached her by phone that a few weeks before, Captain Roman D. Hubbell, 7th Regiment, 1st Cavalry Division, was killed in the Admiralty Islands during the campaign to retake Manus Island from the Japanese. As was customary for soldiers who lost their lives half a world away from home, Monnie's body was interred with military honors at Fort William McKinley in the Philippines. With no body to bury next to Monnie's grandparents on Hubbell Hill, Roman Sr. simply put on a brave face. Writing to his niece and sometime ranch hand LaCharles, he mused, "It seems hard to write this letter at this time for Monny would have been a grand help in the business. But we must not forget that John is too much of a Hubbell to let things slide. I believe that when he comes back he will be willing to get into harness and go along with us."[10] Hoping to lighten the Hubbells' load while she could, Reichard offered to run their remote Piñon Trading Post for the summer. Before she headed west she typed a 155-page proof of the legend associated with the Navajo Hail Chant given to her by Klah. Paper and pressmen were in short supply, she reasoned. Why shouldn't scholars do the manual work of publishing their results themselves in times of scarcity? She circulated a flyer to "Anyone interested in using linguistic text" until all two hundred copies she had printed were in the hands of people who knew what to do with them.[11] It was hardly business as usual, but she would not quit being an active humanist out of personal pride or despair.

For LaCharles, Monnie's death was the worst of many heartbreaks she'd faced as the mother of three young sons and the wife of a geologist the war had turned into a roving intelligence officer. In 1929 she had been the yo-yo-toting University of Arizona coed Reichard drove to the Pecos Conference in the hope that her passenger would decide to become an anthropologist. LaCharles, or "Cha" as she was known in the family, chose romance and cozy domesticity when she married her college sweetheart as soon as she graduated. The war separated Don Lorenzo's only granddaughter conclusively from an idyllic childhood she longed to re-create for her energetic brood. She woke up one day to find herself a de facto single parent, a shoulder for her uncle to lean on in his grief, and a live-in caregiver to her mother, Auntie Bob, who suffered from Parkinson's disease. Through the end of 1944 as the tide turned in favor of the Allies, LaCharles sometimes caught her mother listening in tears to the "good" war news on the radio in their Denver home. Raised a Hubbell, she hung on. She had enough kick left to complain to her Aunt Dorothy, "I'm sick—but I have [had] a headache for *four* years!!" She was unimpressed that Reichard's candidate had won a fourth term in the White House in November's election. "I guess the American dopes wanted Frankie—and they've got him. All we can hope now is that he doesn't die or something and we wind up with Truman."[12]

·   ·   ·   ◈   ·   ·   ·

The price of victory in the Pacific Theater was extraordinarily high, far higher than anyone outside the atomic weapons industry dared to imagine. Pulitzer prize-winning science writer William L. Laurence filed a story on August 9, 1945 that might have prompted buyer's remorse had it not achieved an inhumane beauty. Attempts to document the carnage on the ground were to be vigorously repressed by U.S. censors for months to come, but the War Department was too proud of the unnatural weather it planned to unleash over Japan to refuse Laurence a seat in the belly of *The Great Artiste*, the B-29 Superfort deployed in the attack on Nagasaki.

The *New York Times* reporter marveled in anticipation as the warhead was loaded onto a waiting plane. "Never before had so much brain-power been concentrated on a single problem," he wrote. Detonated, the weapon approached the sublime. "Observers in the tail of our ship saw a giant ball of fire rise as though from the bowels of the earth, belching forth enormous white smoke rings. Next they saw a giant pillar of purple fire, 10,000 feet high shooting skyward with enormous speed. . . . It was a living thing, a new species of being, born right before our incredulous eyes . . . the entity assumed the form of a giant square totem pole. . . . Its bottom was brown, its center was amber, its top white. But it was a living totem pole, its face carved with many grotesque masks grimacing at the earth . . . the mushroom top was even more alive than the pillar, seething and boiling in a white fury of creamy foam." "Does anyone feel any pity or compassion for the poor devils about to die?" Laurence wondered as he watched white and rose-colored petals of death bloom at 60,000 feet. His answer echoed the thoughts of a frightened people united in hatred of their enemies. "Not when one thinks of Pearl Harbor and of the death march on Bataan."[13]

Not long afterward, when Laurence's story was lining birdcages in Upper West Side apartments, Reichard sat for her official portrait for the Barnard yearbook. The 1945 photo records the face of a serene and dignified woman still in her prime. Her neutral gaze betrays neither the losses she'd suffered in the conflict nor the depth of character she'd gained by surviving them. A journalist named Elsie McIlroy stopped by Milbank Hall to interview Reichard at about the same time the picture was taken. McIlroy seemed surprised that her interviewee wasn't a dry, stern academic. "Meeting her, you see a woman who smiles easily and you are struck by the warm enthusiasm in her voice and expression as she talks about Anthropology in general, primitive cultures, and the Navajo in particular."[14] Seated at her desk, Reichard was "a pleasant, vigorous-looking person . . . dressed simply in a softly coloured tweed suit. The silver and turquoise brooch at her throat pointed up her lively gray-blue eyes. Her gray hair is turning white where it frames her face; it is cut short but gives an impression of simplicity rather than severity."

McIlroy continued, "It is not hard to imagine Dr. Reichard living the life of the Navajo and sleeping under the Arizona stars through the summer nights. Now in her early fifties, her face is unlined and full of vitality and even seated in her office she seems to be surrounded by fresh air." When asked how long it took her to learn to speak Navajo, Reichard chuckled softly in response. "You can just write down 1923 with a dash after it. . . . I still don't feel I've learned it." Impressed with Reichard's description of anthropology, McIlroy declared the field a "fascinating tapestry of interwoven sciences." "It's all one world," she exclaimed, "if we only took the trouble to understand one another we could surely all live together in peace!" McIlroy thought spreading the anthropological perspective more widely might help people shed "any feeling of superiority and uniqueness" they had in exchange for "a feeling of kinship with peoples [they] used to consider inferior." Reichard smiled "kindly and a little wearily" before replying, "Of course that's so. Boas said so in 1908 and repeated it with variations until he died in 1942."[15]

The hint of weariness McIlroy detected in her subject was actually a gracious, forgiving resilience. Reichard could never rationalize the sacrifice of tens of thousands of Japanese mothers, children, munitions workers, soldiers, and old men as Mead did when she called the August bombings "a mercy" that "dramatise[d] for [American] people that a new era has begun."[16] Reichard wouldn't detach the cold, abstract art others saw in Laurence's word picture for the *Times* from its meaning. The debut of the Atomic Age put Reichard firmly on a trail of beauty prescribed by neither Navajo dogma nor the high cult of Science and Technology. Just as she had rebuffed war work of every kind throughout the conflict, she would not now presume to solve "the problem of peace" through social engineering dressed up as anthropological science.[17]

Without Reichard's support, applied anthropology had made a good number of anthropologists into national celebrities. Mead was Exhibit A. Her visibility as a war worker in Washington, D.C., her regular columns in ladies' journals, and most especially the success of her 1942 love letter to white Anglo-Saxon Protestant Americans, *And Keep Your Powder Dry*, gained her a devoted mass audience. At war's end, Mead worried, briefly, that taking her case for culture-and-personality studies as a cure for international conflict directly to the public had damaged her standing in the scientific community. She predicted she would face "punishments" on her return to the American Museum by people like Reichard, "who stayed on in their jobs and did nothing during the war."[18] Far from being penalized, Mead and other war anthropologists were showered with job

opportunities and research grants "as a sort pelf befitting victors."[19] The
Office of Strategic Services that had paid many an anthropologist to wage
war from a desk chair was dissolved, only to be replaced by the Central
Intelligence Agency. The new agency didn't open until 1947, but when
it did it created new career tracks for any anthropologist comfortable
with "the hitching of science to warfare under conditions of secrecy."[20]
However enticing these developments seemed to war-and-peace anthropologists, they only deepened Reichard's resolve to resist them.

Accordingly, Reichard didn't volunteer her services at the Research
in Contemporary Cultures center the Office of Naval Research opened
at Columbia in 1946. Ruth Benedict, as the principal investigator, hired
her live-in partner, the psychologist Ruth Valentine, along with Mead
and Ruth Bunzel to help run the multiyear project. Ruling out fieldwork
as impractical, the project leaders engaged scores of social scientists to
conduct interviews with foreign nationals in New York City to replicate
the culture-at-a-distance papers Benedict wrote for the military while stationed in D.C.[21] Had Reichard been interested in joining a well-funded,
woman-led research program, she wasn't invited to do so. Mead said the
research center brought together "all the gifted people who had somehow
managed in wartime but who did not fit into the peacetime mold—the
aberrant, the unsystemic [sic], the people with work habits too irregular
ever to hold regular jobs." They were also trusted personal allies. "We
never looked for a member of a discipline as such—for a 'psychologist'
or 'sociologist,'" Mead noted, "but worked with those with whom some
one of us had already worked for years in some other enterprise—so
we knew each other's potentialities—or with those who came asking to
participate."[22] Benedict liked to think of the research center as the triumph of highly sensitive cultural outsiders over the conformist mob.[23] As
attested by the huge commercial success of her 1934 *Patterns of Culture* and
her postwar study of Japanese culture, *The Chrysanthemum and the Sword*;
generous funding from the U.S. military after 1941; and her election as
AAA president in 1946, Benedict was hardly an outsider.[24]

The humanistic project that occupied Reichard for most of 1946
was the writing of *An Analysis of Coeur d'Alene Indian Myths*. She'd always
planned to publish the stories the Coeur d'Alene told her in the late
1920s, and as a change of pace from her Navajo books, she took them up
again. Her motive was partly preservationist. "If this type of knowledge is

to remain implicit only," Reichard wrote in the introduction, "it is likely
to be lost entirely."[25] The Coeur d'Alenes had effected something of a
cultural renaissance in the intervening years, but Reichard was not convinced they had attained the respect they deserved. "That [culture] which
the Indians now have is neither white nor Indian but a doubtful residue of
both," Reichard noted. "The Indians own large ranches which they rent
to Whites; they live in houses like those of white men, dress like them,
eat their kind of food and perform their religious rituals, in short, try
to behave as Whites. The most apparent difference is social. The Whites
for the most part consider the Indian a subject for exploitation, use him
accordingly and scorn him by every conceivable means in their power.
The Indian on the other hand defends himself by apparent stoicism,
stolidity and passive resistance. He realizes that he is being exploited but
is defenseless. His only compensation is the privilege of pointing out the
mistakes of the Whites and gloating over their absurd conceits."[26]

With its sensitive discussion of the dramatic arts of body language,
gesture, sound effects, song, pitch, tone, and cadence so critical to the
vitality of Coeur d'Alene storytelling, *Coeur d'Alene Indian Myths* introduced the forty-eight texts in the volume as literature no less worthy
for being an oral, performed art. Unlike in *Prayer the Compulsive Word*,
where Reichard proposed a formalism aimed at uncovering the structure
and functions of Navajo ritual speech, the author of *Coeur d'Alene Indian
Myths* approached the texts as would a folklorist who is sympathetic to the
humanist's imperative: to discover in cultural expressions "what it means
to be human . . . to discover the basis of our common humanity."[27] The
literary character of greatest interest to a Coeur d'Alene audience (and
therefore to Reichard) was the enigmatic figure of Coyote. "Above all Coyote is versatile," Reichard wrote of America's original literary anti-hero.
"He is greedy, sly, impudent, impatient, impulsive, stupid, suspicious,
ignorant, imitative, cruel, ungrateful, interfering, boastful, vain, clever,
and rarely, compassionate. The Coeur d'Alene admire his slyness, fear
his power and trickery, distrust his promises and even his success and
above all, despise him. Nevertheless they, like the mythical animals, are
curious to see what he will do next." In the immortal trickster, Reichard
thought she glimpsed the hem of humanity's pleated skirt. "One of the
most universal traits of man is his inconsistency," she ventured. "The
Coeur d'Alene are no exception. They are not only cruel but they are

proud of it and, on the other hand they are compassionate. . . . Although one must always consider myth clues suggestive rather than conclusive there is ample evidence that they define attitudes toward the culture and ideals which delineate the more subtle and deeply rooted ethics of human behavior."[28]

The obvious pleasure Reichard took in working up the Coeur d'Alene stories prompted her to tell a story of her own about a Coeur d'Alene woman she observed in 1929. Taking a page-long detour from her analysis of the interrelationships between Coeur d'Alene story and culture, Gladys drew the reader's attention to the character of eighty-year-old Susan Antelope, Julia Antelope's mother, who she'd watched prepare a traditional treat of baked camas for friends and family in 1929. Reichard told how Susan labored for nearly a month to gather and clean camas bulbs and wild onions and locate and stockpile the special leaves, firewood, grass, and bark for the baking pit. Once everything she needed was close at hand, Antelope spent two-and-a-half days continuously tending the fire in strong winds to get the desired result. "It is not difficult to understand the satisfaction the Indians take in a job of this kind well done, but it is not easy to describe," Reichard noted placidly as she returned to her main theme.[29] The culture doctors in the ascendant at the AAA held the study of "personality" to be more central to their craft than "character." The folklorists who awarded Reichard the 1947 Chicago Folklore Prize for *Coeur d'Alene Indian Myths* sided with Reichard.

Because she had not stopped working on her Navajo materials to go to war, Reichard's insight into Navajo cosmology and how it differed from Judeo-Christian and Pueblo conceptions of the universe grew steadily through the decade. To work out how to do justice to Navajo philosophy and psychology in print for an English-speaking audience attuned to Judeo-Christian frequencies, Reichard published a half-dozen original, imaginative, and meticulously researched journal articles about Navajo artistry, language, thought, and values en route to completing her 1950 masterwork, *Navaho Religion: A Study in Symbolism.* Of the many strands she would gather together in *Navaho Religion,* her understanding of female and male gender concepts among the Navajo stood out. From long residence with the Navajo and their literature, she concluded that the prerogatives of Navajo individualism were not apportioned differently depending on a person's sex. In biological terms, male chanters told her,

women are assumed to be born with a mental weakness corresponding
to their weaker physical strength relative to men. A woman's biological
inferiority, however, could be erased through experience, specifically
religious practice aimed at strengthening a woman's mind and spirit to
"withstand anything a man can." Reichard discovered that the protection
ritual confers on a woman "is quantitative rather than qualitative—she
needs more than a man but the character of the prophylactic or defensive
measures is the same." Though to the non-Navajo observer, tribal women
appeared to be ill-used by their husbands, the premium Navajos placed
on the sanctity of the individual meant that Navajo women as individuals
were capable of achieving a social position "in the home, in the economic,
social, even political life . . . equal to that of the men."[30]

Intensive language study taught Reichard that Navajo thought "classi-
fies potency, mobility, energy, bigness, and dominance as male; and gen-
erative capacity, passive power, endurance, smallness, and compliance as
female." Reichard found the clearest expression of "female" versus "male"
ideation in the figure and story of Changing Woman, "the most fascinating of many appealing characters conjured up by the Navaho imagination." Reichard surmised in *Navaho Religion*, "Sun [Changing Woman's
husband] is attractive, his character obvious and clear. Changing Woman
is Woman with a sphinxlike quality. No matter how much we know about
her the total is a great question mark. She is the mystery of reproduction,
of life springing from nothing, of the last hope of the world, a riddle
perpetually solved and perennially springing up anew."[31]

No mere fertility goddess, Changing Woman is also Promethean.
"Many of Changing Woman's gifts are rites or ceremonies. . . . Her decrees
are kind. She gave man many songs, created the horse, decreed fertility
and sterility. . . . Her presence at an assembly of the gods is pointed out
with special respect; other gods bow their heads when she comes in." Her
husband and many children seek her advice and obey it; at times she has
charge of the rain and vegetation, at other times she is portrayed as the
Earth itself. Said to have first appeared on the slope of a sacred mountain
as "the first and ideal baby," a creature without blemish and beholden to
no one, Changing Woman was raised on pollen "moistened with game
broth and the dew of flowers." As a young woman she exposed herself to
sunlight and water to quench her ripening sexual desire. She took Sun
as her lover and gave birth to Monster Slayer and Child-of-the-water as

well as many daughters. Sun eventually persuaded Changing Woman to relocate in the west, where he promised to visit her each evening. Torn by competing desires for privacy and companionship, Changing Woman built a new home on the western horizon before she "created new people and directed them how to reach their relatives in the east." And while Sun exhibited a brash but volatile charisma, Changing Woman exuded harmony. "Although she had borne the children destined to kill the monsters, which feats made them the chief war gods with power against all foreign dangers, Changing Woman stood for peace."[32]

During the war Reichard wrote, "Navajo dogma connects all things, natural and experienced, from man's skeleton to universal destiny, which encompasses even inconceivable space in a closely interlocked unity which omits nothing, no matter how small or how stupendous."[33] Her goal as she composed *Navaho Religion* in the war's wake was to craft a monument to the interconnectedness of a living belief system with its inconsistencies, contradictions, and awe-inspiring complexity intact. This aspiration differed from the wartime vogue of "essentializing" or stereotyping non-western cultures into discrete units that social scientists might then fit into a harmonious postwar geopolitical order. The paragon of the technocratic ethos Reichard resisted as the Cold War set in was none other than her calculating competitor in Navajo studies, Clyde Kluckhohn. Kluckhohn's war work brought him immense professional prestige and no little fame, which translated into his being put in charge of applying the "psycho-cultural" approach to containment of the Soviet Union as the head of the Harvard Russian Research Center.[34] Confident she could contain Kluckhohn by maintaining her professional objectivity, Reichard calmly reviewed Kluckhohn's 1946 monograph (with Dorothea Leighton) *The Navaho*. She observed that the book met "a longfelt need" for a comprehensive ethnography of a striking people. She noted also that while the authors' "main interest" was the applied anthropologist's concern with "the effect of white culture on the Navaho and what to do about it," they did well to communicate regret for past injustices perpetrated against the Navajo that had contributed to their current difficulties.[35]

Knowing what Kluckhohn was capable of when riled, Reichard kept quiet about the authors' simplistic approach to "getting the Navaho viewpoint."[36] Where intimate acquaintance with Navajo language and religion were key to Reichard's methodology, Kluckhohn asserted that anyone "who wants to know Navahos" could do so with "a few days of intelligent study" of the language.[37] Claiming "speaking of 'Navaho religion' does violence to the viewpoint of The People" (in the full knowledge that Reichard's major book on the subject would bear that title), he described the "Navaho view of life" in strictly behavioral terms as an entirely secular social heritage driven by fear of the uncontrollable.[38] To "understand fully the Navaho 'philosophy of life,'" Kluckhohn advised readers to adopt his "premises of Navaho life and thought." One norm among the Navajo, he wrote, was to be subconsciously guided by the premise "Life is very, very dangerous." The "formula" the typical Navajo applied in novel situations was best captured in Kluckhohn's words by the maxim, "When in a new and dangerous situation, do nothing," a response in marked contrast to the average American's impulse to "*do* something."[39] Reichard's experience with individual Navajos over twenty years led her to a more positive generalization about Navajo thinking: "Accept what you encounter." "Expressed this way," she pointed out in an unpublished paper, "the white American form of thought and behavior become negative: 'Do not accept what you find, try to change it, no matter how difficult it may be.'"[40]

While in private Reichard blamed the ethnocentric speculations that marred *The Navaho* on Kluckhohn's weak methodology, it was the condescending attitude he expressed toward women in his 1947 paper, "What the Modern Parent Can Learn from the Navaho," that most offended her. Though Kluckhohn bemoaned the lack of objective evidence linking childcare practices such as breastfeeding, weaning, toilet training, and swaddling to healthy personality formation in adults, he recommended that American women be more permissive toward their infants as he claimed Navajo mothers were toward theirs. For Kluckhohn, Navajo mothers' permissiveness consisted in their allowing infants to breastfeed scores of times per day rather than per the strict schedule modern white women were instructed to maintain. Reichard knew from sleeping in Navajo camps that on-demand breastfeeding was less an indulgence than a result of the mother's need to keep her infant quiet overnight in communal sleeping quarters, supply the entirety of the child's diet in the absence of baby food or formula, or counter the lower nutritional value of milk from her frequently malnourished body.

"The data [on breastfeeding] suggest that those who train white American children must make their own judgments about 'scheduling' consistent with their own needs," Reichard argued in defense of urban mothers. "A woman, especially if she happens to be a career mother, or if she wants to participate in activities outside her home, must take into account the fact that she herself is scheduled."[41] On the issue of infant swaddling, Kluckhohn was all for it. While not permissive on its face, he admitted, swaddling "probably has good psychological effect" because all newborns wish to be immobilized in a cradleboard following their nine-month tenure in the tight confines of the womb. "The logic of this conclusion is somewhat difficult to reconcile with the fact that the [Navajo] baby is not placed in the cradleboard until a month or longer after birth," Reichard dead-panned. "Our hypothetical [white] mother must decide whether the psychological value, if it exists, compensates for the child's physical development in view of her own modern notions of sanitation and the child's physical enjoyment of exercise."[42]

Far from embittered that Kluckhohn, Mead, and Benedict had become the public face of anthropology, Reichard took Parsons's advice to "see man's motives and understand his psychological drives, but . . . tolerate the anthropoid."[43] In anticipation of her 1947 sabbatical, she resigned from the executive council of the Folklore Society (to be replaced by Mary Haas). At Barnard, she chaired a pair of forums on racial prejudice and discrimination sponsored by Barnard's Liberal Club in honor of American Brotherhood Month and National Negro History Week. A *Bulletin* reporter noted that Reichard "deplored" the need to set aside a few days a year to promote racial tolerance when, obviously, it was necessary to promote tolerance every day.[44] The next month she shared a sample or two of the Navajo-style rugs she'd woven in her apartment for the Interfaith Council's Faculty Hobby Show.[45] At the request of Katherine Harvey, Minnie Harvey Huckel's niece, she appraised the Huckel collection of sandpaintings, soon to be donated to the Taylor Museum at the Colorado Springs Fine Arts Center. Harvey wrote Reichard, "As you are the top authority on this subject I would appreciate it greatly if you would be willing to give me your estimate of the one hundred and eleven paintings. I am convinced that the Government would accept your estimate as correct [for tax purposes]."[46]

In late May, as Reichard packed her bags and books for another eight-month stay in Arizona, she received a long letter that brought a welcome if poignant closure to her personal experience of World War II. His written

Adolph Dodge Bitanny (known as Adee Dodge after 1941), c. 1947. Adee Dodge
Papers. *Yale Collection of Western Americana, Beinecke Rare Book and Manuscript Library.*

English showed some rust, but Adolph Bitanny was pleased to inform
her he was making his way back to the Navajo country. "Dear Grandma,"
Adolph began, "Here is your surprise. Hello. I'm right over here where I
am. Been here about a week now. Transferred here for release from active
duty and I'm just marking time with such patience impatiently. . . . I don't
know whether or not you're there. I hope you are so I could hear you."
Bitanny was due to be released from the Mobile Air Technical Service

Command at Brookley Field in Alabama. "I'm on my way out from army now and it's about time. Too much strain & mental stress—the causes of which is apparently cumulative over past 5 years. My wife and others tell me I'm *pretty* nervous, easily upset, pensive, moody and so on. I can't seem to stop doing things—I've got to be busy—doing anything. Lately I've given more thoughts as to what I may plan on doing—but just seem unable to muster expert decisions. So many factors to be considered." The recent death of Bitanny's octogenarian grandfather, Chee Dodge, cast a shadow over the soldier's return to a reservation still under siege. "[Friends] . . . tell me Navajos are worse off now. Navajo Service appropriations being chopped down to the minimum seems to make everybody there worry. Seems to me it would be inopportune time to get out to go back to Navajo Service—and I doubt if opportunities would be incentive or even encouraging."

Bitanny's priorities had been changed by active duty; there would be no restart to his career in linguistics. "I believe I've learned a little bit more so I can shift by self," he confided in her,

> I'm not decided: I'm married, yet I want to go on to further schooling—and if I can in study of Law, I hear a fellow can complete full courses in half the time it used to require. At the same time, I've got to make money on the side. I may do some writing and I think I can do it (If I can arrange with Columbia Univ. it'll be swell). How are the possibilities from your look-out window?
>
> I do want to rest up this summer—in fact I've got to. Presently my Jeanie is in New Orleans, La. at our former apartment. She's working and doesn't want to come over here, & it's going to be a short time (at end of this month) before I get out. I went back up there for the weekend and she's doing fine. Just a little scared to stay by self at nites but otherwise safe. I'm glad she's a good sport. Many people ask her why she doesn't become a model—& I'm proud of her . . .
>
> I've read about Clyde Kluckhohn and his contributions to science—papers raved about him for awhile. I always like the Doc. 'cause I knew he'd make good. Haven't heard about Leland Wyman anymore.
>
> I'm gonna close. Hope to hear from you soon as dawn.

I couldn't tell the whole experience & nightmares I've gone thru in the past 5 or six years in short while—so I'll let it ride. Any way it was pretty daggone tough and shocking. I did what I can for Uncle Sam in his trying hours and now I feel satisfied—

> With best regards,
> A.D. Bitanny, Capt. A.C.
> and Jeanie Bitanny[47]

· · · ◈ · · ·

"My friends in New York think I am living in a Navajo hogan," Reichard told an Arizona reporter near the end of her second sabbatical. "I can't convince them that I have a doll-house of a cottage in Flagstaff that has all the refinements of their steam-heated apartments."[48] She was in Phoenix poised to give an invited lecture on Navajo religion at the Heard Museum, and as always she was happy to allude to her happy scholar's second home at the Museum of Northern Arizona. Since 1939, when Reichard first began renting a cabin on or near the museum grounds every summer, she had lost none of her enthusiasm for life at seven thousand feet above sea level. "I don't know why anyone living at Flag should go anywhere," Reichard had written the Hubbells as early as 1940. "I just can't bear to think of leaving."[49] The presence of the little museum on Fort Valley Road had cemented her bond to an alluring place. The scientists, artists, patrons, and National Park Service employees who met for tea and conversation on summer afternoons at the home of Harold and Mary-Russell Ferrell Colton were eclectics like herself. Residents of Flagstaff since 1926, the Coltons and the regional salon they founded in 1928 represented intellectual concerns that didn't slide in a groove but branched and twined like desert washes across the Colorado Plateau.

Reichard's friendship with Harold Colton seems to have begun after she sent him a copy of *Dezba* for the museum library. "I have been reading [*Dezba*] the last three evenings and find it quite absorbing," he wrote her. "I think it fills a great need, to present the Navajo problem in a popular form, giving the necessary background." As a biologist-turned-archeologist and museum director, Colton approved of more than Reichard's literary style. "The Indians in the family that you are portraying are very real people to us; we can almost duplicate them among our friends in

Gladys Reichard in an article published in the *Arizona Times*, November 11, 1947,
"snapped as she was giving a translation of an Indian prayer" at the opening
lecture of the Heard Museum's Sidelights Series. *Courtesy of State of Arizona Library.*

the Wapatki Basin. It rings very true."[50] Thereafter Reichard and Colton
kept in touch by mail as she gradually became a fixture in the museum's
summer roster of guest speakers and research associates.

Reichard's contacts with Mary-Russell Colton are undocumented,
largely because by the 1940s Mrs. Colton began to recuse herself from
all but essential public functions related to the museum. The art and
ethnological departments she ran between 1928 and 1939 continued to
"stimulate the best in Indian arts and crafts" and "encourage the artistic presentation of scientific subjects" for a popular audience long after
her retreat from public life. The art department Mary-Russell inspired
offered Reichard an unparalleled opportunity to pursue the complementary aim of presenting artistic subjects scientifically.[51] For the last art
exhibit of 1944, Mary-Russell and staff displayed the silk-screen prints of

sandpaintings from *Where the Two Came to Their Father: A Navaho War Cere-monial*, a portfolio of colored plates documenting the wartime revival of a Navajo ceremony meant to "fortify the modern young [Navajo] man and make him able to withstand malaria, German and Japanese attacks."[52] Reichard donated the volume to the museum after she reviewed it for the *New York Tribune*. The beauty of the sandpaintings Maud Oakes pre-sented and the interpretive essay American mythologist Joseph Campbell wrote to accompany them gave Reichard grounds for warm praise. "The pictures and the ideology behind them are completely fascinating and artistically they vie with some of the best art of the world," she enthused.

Eager as she was to finish *Navaho Religion* and her reference grammar of Navajo, Reichard spent part of her sabbatical traveling around the Southwest. On one trip, she met with John Adair, the University of New Mexico's first doctoral candidate in anthropology. Adair had written an appreciative review of *Dezba* for *AA* before the war temporarily interrupted his career. He called *Dezba* "both readable and accurate" as a picture of Navaho family life, "a phase of Navaho culture which has been slighted in other books on the Navaho, of both popular and scientific nature."[53] Responding to remarks Reichard had made at a recent conference, the affable thirty-five-year-old took a shine to his refreshingly candid elder. "I agreed with what you had to say in your paper about Anthropology and Education, agreed with you 100 percent," Adair wrote Reichard from Zuni, New Mexico. "Anthropologists have been so busy studying every-one else that they haven't gotten around as yet to studying themselves. (It would certainly make a worthwhile project for the anthropologist from Mars to study the social organization of a meeting of the AAA . . .) And one thing that is lacking, which you so well pointed out is a sense of humility."[54]

Reichard's trips to the Navajo Reservation brought to her attention the impact of demobilization on her erstwhile neighbors. The Navajo had accommodated themselves to wage-work since 1941, and the loss of those jobs when hostilities ceased hurt. Returning veterans and muni-tions workers who witnessed the economic might of the wider world during the war years recognized that livestock could no longer provide them and their families with everything they needed in life. No grazing land of any lasting value was available to them, in any case. When the bilingual, skilled laborers, and soldiers came home, they soon realized they lacked the basic prerequisites for starting anew. War heroes though they might have been, they had no sheep, no jobs, and no political voice at the state and federal levels. The reservation's infrastructure was in a shambles. Public schools, medical facilities, and roads were so inadequate that Navajo parents reversed course on boarding schools and were glad to send their children to off-reservation sites, even though it meant putting their children's identities as Navajo at stake.[55]

Reichard's fall visits to the reservation coincided with a fresh crisis that turned out to be a tipping point for the tribe. Severe early snowstorms hit northern New Mexico and Arizona in late 1947, cutting off the most impoverished Navajos from their supplies of food, fuel, clothing, and medical care. Given credible reports that four to ten thousand Navajo could starve, freeze, or succumb to disease by the end of the winter, dozens of local and national charitable organizations mobilized to head off the impending "national disgrace."[56] President Truman tried to put through a major relief bill in time for the holidays. The crisis validated complaints by the Navajo Tribal Council that the Indian Bureau needed immediate and sweeping reform. Truman responded by announcing plans to "prevent a serious collapse in Navajo community life."[57]

Peter Yazza, president of the Returned Indian Students Association and a veteran, refused to sit silently by. Yazza made clear in a lengthy editorial published in the Gallup Independent on December 30 that he and other English-speaking Navajo activists would not tolerate being treated like laboratory animals by federal bureaucrats. On behalf of other younger, literate Navajos, Yazza called for the Indian Bureau to be eliminated or reformed "top down" to rid it of the "petrified policies of John Collier and W. Zimmerman"; for states to govern the Navajo as part of "We the People" in place of the federal government; for the radical reorganization of the Navajo Tribal Council and its constitutional powers; and for the franchise to be restored to all Indians in Arizona and New Mexico, where it was denied them on the grounds that they didn't pay income tax.[58]

Yazza raised issues Reichard had long wanted the younger generation of returned Navajos to address. She responded with an editorial titled, "The Vote for the Navajo Indians," hoping to spur Yazza and his allies to do more than protest. To the uninformed onlooker, Reichard's editorial appeared to chide Yazza for wanting the vote. In reality, Reichard encouraged Yazza to refine and improve his line of argument. "I want you to

have the vote," she advised, "but I want to warn you of the danger in its
possession, to ask you to consider whether you are willing to pay the price
it entails." Access to the ballot, she explained, should not be viewed as a
bargaining chip. The issues Yazza raised each required careful research
and deliberation separately from the others to minimize the friction
among competing interests and factions.[59] Reichard pled with young
Navajo citizens to be realistic, self-sacrificing, self-aware, and relentless.
In the act of leading The People to the promised land, she warned, the
educated, worldly Navajo was more alone than he liked to think. He was
surrounded by "wolves" and "white dictators" shouting "fantastic ideals"
intended to distract from the real road to progress. She believed The
People had so far lacked the unity of purpose to keep "the Big Monster,"
state domination, at bay. "I summarize by advising you to work out some
constructive suggestions, plans you can yourselves administer, plans you
are willing to put your teeth into, to bring about a reorganization of the
Indian Service. Don't let the Federal Government give you up. Work for
reform and stay with it. Don't think you will accomplish anything by mere
beefing. When you lose, try again. Persistence is a marked Navajo trait;
use it for more important things than heretofore." White role models
like the late Fiorello La Guardia abounded, Reichard added, but should
Navajo activists study the mayor's methods of achieving reform in New
York avidly, ultimately they had to steer themselves out of the quicksands
they'd been left to die in.[60]

When the editor of the *Gallup Independent* did not publish Reichard's
nuanced editorial, she sent copies to friends, colleagues, and Peter
Yazza. Yazza may not have replied directly to Reichard, but John Adair
did, respectfully disagreeing with his elder on several grounds. Adair
subscribed to what he called the new "tenor of thinking of all anthropologists." Anthropologists were obliged to help minority people modernize, he asserted. "We must give up thinking about 'the Navajo' and
'the Pueblos' and the this and that tribe," Adair scolded Reichard. "A
philosophy of Nativism advances our science no more than it does the
primitive ethnic group. We must think in terms of a world wide situation,
a great period of transition of accelerated changed in which primitive
peoples all over the world are making a break with tribal custom and are
becoming willy nilly engulfed by western 'civilization.' . . . What we need
is a unified social science."[61] The Indian Bureau, according to Adair, was

certain to be abolished in the near future, and rightfully so. Without the
protection of the bureau, the vote was the Indian's only hope for progress.
"I know of no better way for the Indians to be trained, as painful and as
disruptful of the 'Navajo way' as it may be, as to have the Navajos learn the
democratic process from the vote getters whom they will have to face on
their reservation." He believed Navajo voters would hold state and county
politicians accountable for their actions, on the questionable assumption
that the individualistic Navajo would form a monolithic political bloc that
always voted in the best interests of their sixty thousand tribesmen.

Adair got particularly exercised at Reichard's suggestion that returned
Navajos had not yet done enough to show they were serious about
self-governance. He granted that too few Navajos like Yazza and Adolph
Bitanny were active in administering tribal life, but he believed criticism
might scare potential activists away.[62] Adair's paternalistic "temper" on
this point struck Reichard as the fly in the ointment of his argument.
Reichard had rejected the practice of treating Indians as perpetual wards
as early as 1934 when she saw how Collier's good intentions foundered
on his romantic projections. She persisted in sharing the opinion Erna
Fergusson expressed in 1940, that "Navajos, as a people, are never pitiful.
Tragic, yes, but their strength and cleverness preclude so soft an emotion
as pity."[63] Collier's folly was to believe he could rescue the Navajo from
their history without understanding it or them. As one Collier biographer
put it, the bureau chief "never worked out the inconsistencies inherent in
the use of social scientists to restore a sense of community [among Indi-
ans]. . . . [A] tendency always existed toward elitism, manipulation, and
repression."[64] Adair's belief that imperiled Native Americans needed "a
unified social science" rather than concerted, self-determining political
action was a disappointment to Reichard. The license Adair gave himself
to ignore the past prevented him from assimilating the critical lessons
taught by the failures of the Indian New Deal.

Others who received Reichard's political bulletin in the mail
approved. Clyde Kluckhohn responded cordially that he saw good hard
sense in "The Vote for the Navajo Indians" and hoped it would reach a
wide audience.[65] Museum of Northern Arizona board member and future
U.S. senator Barry Goldwater dashed off a similar note of assent. "Your
letter to Peter Yazza is one of the finest things I have seen written on this
particular Indian question or any Indian question," he wrote. "I wish that

millions of people could read this instead of the few who will."[66] Ethel
Cutler Freeman, a research anthropologist at the American Museum of
Natural History and a member of two American Civil Liberties Union
committees on Indian rights and affairs, went further. After reading
Reichard's editorial, she wanted Reichard by her side in the fight against
termination. "Your article is excellent, I think, and fundamentally sound.
I am so afraid that all this Navajo publicity will be used for selfish political
ends. . . . People who are not on the spot do not realize that these altru-
istic sounding procedures may have personal political ambitions behind
them. . . . I have just talked to the American Civil Liberties and [they] . . .
are calling a meeting of the Indian Committee shortly. I think you will
be here [in New York] and I want to talk to you before it takes place. I am
not sure I agree with you that you can be more valuable off of this active
committee."[67]

To Freeman's disappointment, Reichard declined to join the ACLU
Indian Committee. Instead, she wrote a second "Communication" titled
"Navajo Indian Problems," which she circulated privately just as she
had the first. To prompt discussion she listed "ten major administrative
realities" she believed the bureau had managed to ignore for too long,
among them the difficulty of communicating with a dispersed, largely
illiterate population and the staunch conservatism of tribal elders.[68] By
the time Reichard Communication No. 2 reach those on her mailing list,
President Truman had launched a task force under the Hoover Commission on the Organization of the Executive Branch that he charged
with relieving the Indian Bureau of its power to govern or protect Native
Americans. Hoping for the best, Reichard slipped copies of both her
communications and a letter of introduction into an envelope addressed
to John R. Nichols, president of New Mexico College of Agricultural
and Mechanical Arts and one of four men appointed to the Hoover
task force. "I am glad to see that you are doing something about the
Department of Indian Affairs," she began. "I hope your thoughts do
not run to liquidating it too soon." Reichard used most of her letter to
politely caution Nichols against throwing money at the problem before
he understood the facts as the Indians saw them. She recommended
The Changing Indian, edited by Oliver La Farge, and "Ella Deloria's little
book, *Speaking of Indians*," as reliable sources to consult for accurate
background information.[69]

In a long and thoughtful letter, Nichols took the time to thank Reichard for her counsel. He promised to forward her "most helpful communication" to others on his task force.[70] Reichard must have been less than thrilled by his admission that he believed the "Indian problem" was on par with that of "Spanish-Americans" in New Mexico and "Negroes" in the Deep South. After he was appointed Indian commissioner in 1949, it seemed to bode well that Nichols spent his first months in office touring Indian reservations to educate himself. Nevertheless, Nichols appears not to have taken Reichard up on her offer to "assist in any way."[71] Eleven months after being appointed commissioner, he was abruptly replaced by Dillon S. Meyer, a conservative ideologue so antipathetic toward America's First Nations that former Interior secretary Harold Ickes called him "a Hitler and Mussolini rolled into one."[72] In solidarity with the Navajo, Reichard braced for yet another high-level, low-information battle for the body and soul of Indian Country.

CHAPTER 10

CITIZENS CEMETERY

RETURNING FROM THE WEST IN FEBRUARY 1948, Reichard waltzed into a new chapter of Barnard's history. While she was away on sabbatical, Millicent Carey McIntosh, the director of the exclusive Brearley School and a PhD in literature from Johns Hopkins, had been installed as Virginia Gildersleeve's successor. It was a sign of the times that McIntosh was also the mother of five young children and happily married to a local pediatrician. Like her predecessor, McIntosh was highly intelligent, diplomatic, and thoroughly dedicated to the higher education and sound character development of college women. "Mrs. Mac" was in addition blessed with a round, apple-cheeked face framed by a soft wave of sandy blonde hair. Her effortless smile crinkled the pale skin around her eyes in a semaphore of maternal kindliness. McIntosh's overt femininity appealed to postwar Americans in a way that Gildersleeve's sexually ambiguous, blue-stocking formality had not. Tough-minded and efficient on the New York corporate, philanthropic, and activist boards she served on, Dr. McIntosh, was nevertheless perceived as a soothing presence, exactly the right woman to lead Barnard College at the dawn of the Cold War.

Reichard promptly complied when McIntosh, who was five years Reichard's junior and sincere in her desire to treat senior faculty with respect, asked for a copy of her bibliography as a get-acquainted gesture. The cover letter Reichard wrote gave her new dean a quick, perceptive resumé of the associate professor's priorities. Noting that her scholarly papers were "on very specialized subjects," Reichard hastened to explain that her general aim as an educator was to connect current anthropological scholarship to "the modern cultural scene." "I do not advocate more than a temporary ivory tower!" she exclaimed. To integrate technical knowledge into a liberal arts education, she had teamed with Modern

Language faculty to offer a major in linguistics in her department. "There are now three majors."[1] "Awareness of the weakness of our interracial and intercultural relationships accounts for my course Race Problems . . . and [underlies] my interest in . . . Indian education. . . . Unfortunately this last subject takes one into the lowest depths of politics where I am not at all at home," Reichard added. Ending on a brighter note, she wrote, "I put time left from teaching and research into writing: I have in mind tomes to contain scientific materials in hand; I have outlined numerous formal and informal articles; I toy with the idea of writing '*the* great American Indian movie script,' and even several novels!"[2]

In time, McIntosh would learn through her frequent contacts with the chair of her Anthropology Department that Barnard's first and only anthropologist loved outdoor sports and photography, wove occasionally on a Navajo loom that was a fixture in her apartment, and loved to drive and fly her way around the vastness of western states when possible. She came to understand that teaching, travel, writing "tomes," and running an academic program energized Reichard rather than drained her. As a first-time college administrator, McIntosh was encouraged to find in Reichard an ideal partner in harness: highly active and esteemed by her campus colleagues; imaginative in matters of curricular and program development; and caring where her students and Barnard's academic reputation were concerned.

McIntosh's steadfast advocacy for women who possessed "brains and tact and sympathy and interest in other people" ran counter to the zeitgeist, however.[3] After the war, the popular estimate of unmarried career women plummeted as a cult of motherhood and domesticity was caught up in the tangle of authoritarian ideologies that gripped her nation. By 1950, general ignorance of women's role in the cultural and political history of the United States meant emancipated, erudite, and childless women like Reichard (and Gildersleeve) were assumed to be sterile relics of the women's suffrage movement. A shiny new feminine stereotype became a hit on nightly television shows, the alternately wacky or saintly wife whose worldly-wise on-screen husband indulged her womanly misadventures as if she were a child.

For a retired Virginia Gildersleeve, the anti-feminist trend held worrisome portents for the gender-blind university, and therefore for the future of American democracy. "[T]here has arisen a particularly cruel and unwholesome discrimination against *unmarried* women for some teaching and administrative posts," she wrote as the Eisenhowers waited their turn to occupy the White House. "This is due in part to the attitude towards the unmarried of certain less responsible psychologists and psychiatrists of the day, which tends to voice disrespect for spinsters in the teaching profession as 'inhibited' and 'frustrated.'" Noting how few women held faculty positions in the nation's universities, Gildersleeve expressed concern that coeds taught "almost entirely by men professors" would develop "a kind of inferiority complex." She feared that a dangerous indifference to sexual inequality had already taken root in the minds of America's best women students. "A few days ago (December, 1952)," Gildersleeve related in her 1954 memoir, "I asked a young woman who was a junior with top marks at one of our best universities whether she had any woman professor. 'No,' she answered, 'I haven't. I never thought of a woman professor. I don't believe I should like to study under one.'"[4]

Reichard was shielded somewhat from the worst of the backlash against feminism and individual feminists during the censorious McCarthy era. Barnard had a long tradition of cultivating women faculty whose research or activism was openly feminist, a tradition McIntosh didn't shy away from.[5] Specifically, McIntosh wanted to reward meritorious women faculty of any age, married or single, with prompt or accelerated promotions in rank. Once she began to raise the funds to accomplish her goal, she put Reichard at the top of the list of those who deserved the rank of full professor for her stellar performance as a scholar, teacher, and administrator. In late 1949, McIntosh followed protocol and approached the chair of Columbia Anthropology, archeologist Duncan Strong, for his thoughts on her plan to promote Reichard. Nearly ten years earlier, Strong's predecessor, Ralph Linton, had submitted a glowing letter of recommendation in support of Reichard's previous promotion. Nothing that she knew of Reichard's professional history or of anthropology's disciplinary politics prepared McIntosh for Strong's ill-informed response. "[W]e in the Department of Anthropology have not found Dr. Reichard a very cooperative person," Strong wrote after a curt nod to the Reichard's undeniable productivity. "She has kept herself largely confined to Barnard and my deep regret is that she has not developed either an assistant professor or an instructor in the section of anthropology in her own college. We have had many excellent women who would have been wonderful in undergraduate teaching, but who cannot all be cared for through the graduate department of Columbia University. To the best of my knowledge there is no other professor in anthropology in Barnard beyond the status of temporary assistant."[6]

Clyde Kluckhohn's evaluation of Reichard made Strong's look almost gallant. "Gladys Reichard is devoted, sincere, and an extremely conscientious worker," Kluckhohn wrote in reply to McIntosh's query. "The total contribution of the data she has published is very impressive indeed. She is also outstanding among anthropologists because she writes well and has produced some excellent books addressed to general audiences." But, he continued, "On the theoretical side, some reservations must be entered. I believe that most of the profession feel that some of her work has been characterized by very strong convictions which, in part at least, were of extra-scientific and extra-logical derivation. I regret having to make these remarks, for Dr. Reichard is a personal friend, but it is my conviction that letters of this sort must be completely honest or the writer's testimony loses its value even when he speaks of persons about whose work he has no reservations. In sum, I think that professional opinion would agree in respecting Professor Reichard for her honesty and industry but in questioning her theoretical acumen."[7]

Kluckhohn's confidential letter to McIntosh had the power to offend Reichard with its gendered dismissals, though it wouldn't have shocked her. Since Kluckhohn betrayed Reichard in the early '40s, the two Navajo specialists had settled into a respectful détente, or so Reichard wanted to believe. During and after the war, Kluckhohn threw himself into proving anthropology was a "field of manipulation," a geopolitical enthusiasm Reichard was content to ignore in favor of keeping a trained eye on his output in Navajo studies.[8] To avoid any appearance of an ambush, Reichard acquired the habit of sending Kluckhohn draft reviews she was writing of his books. After he read her estimate of his 1947 book on Navajo witchcraft, he wrote her airily, "I like its spirit very much. . . . Will hope to see you in Flagstaff. . . . I very much want to get the benefit of all your criticisms of Witchcraft before I re-do it."[9] The following year, she sent him a draft of her review of *The Navaho*. With thanks and handwritten answers to the questions Reichard raised, Kluckhohn replied, "The review is more than fair and pleased me a lot."[10] By 1949 Kluckhohn had nothing to gain from attempting to block Reichard's long-overdue promotion to full professor. That he could not resist the temptation to undermine her progress confirmed that his intentions toward Reichard were, as usual, covertly hostile.

The response of McIntosh's third choice of referee in the matter of Reichard's promotion was a model of disinterested respect. David B. Stout, an associate professor of anthropology at Iowa State University and secretary of the AAA, wrote the dean, "It is a pleasure to comply with your request for an opinion of Professor Gladys Reichard." Stout continued, "Though I am not specialized in the same ethnographic area, I feel no hesitation in stating that Dr. Reichard has made fundamental contributions in social and cultural anthropology through her many years of fieldwork and many publications on the Navaho. Her field methods are of the very best and her written reports are of meticulous scholarship. . . . Her studies of myth and ritual are classic and required for study in most graduate anthropology departments." Stout approved not only of Reichard's enormous industry but also her style. He noted that her "rich knowledge and scholarly understandings of Southwestern Indians" was "not that of pedantry or intellectual isolation." She was an excellent teacher because she brought "the results of her own and other's researches into the classroom, much to the stimulation of students." He knew her teaching abilities firsthand, he said, because he had taken courses from her at Columbia "in the late '30's and early '40's."[11]

Unable to make the airtight case for promotion she'd expected, McIntosh delayed further action for nearly a year. Finally in late December 1950, McIntosh wrote Reichard, "the Dean's Advisory Committee has unanimously approved your promotion to full professorship. . . . This is a good Christmas present for me as well as for you, since I have been very anxious to have this happen."[12] On Valentine's Day 1951, the Board of Trustees unanimously approved Reichard's promotion, with a salary increase to $7,500 per annum to begin July 1. Soon afterward, Reichard used her raise to make an unrestricted donation of seven hundred dollars to Operation Bootstrap and the Barnard Fund, two new development campaigns McIntosh had earmarked for major campus improvement projects. Reichard's gift "stunned" the recipient.[13] "Don't take the donations too hard!" she advised McIntosh, who had been recently promoted herself to the position of president, Barnard's first. "The only 'stunning' part was the job I did for the U.S. Lines—it was extra-curricular and so extra for the Fund."[14]

The title of professor, though handy and welcome, changed Reichard's day-to-day life very little. At least as gratifying was the international acclaim *Navaho Religion* received soon after its publication. A reviewer for the British journal *Man* hailed it as "a monument of patient field observation undertaken with the utmost pains."[15] University of Arizona folklorist Frances Gillmor described Reichard's *capo lavoro* with the words, "Heavily documented, [*Navaho Religion*] organizes into pattern the vast body of material to which the author herself has so largely contributed. . . . [T]he book has substance for the specialist and the general reader in its intricate tracing of interlocking religious and aesthetic ideas, and in its revelation of the sense of paradox which keeps in balance a highly poetic culture."[16]

The valuation of *Navaho Religion* by Dartmouth professor of philosophy and literature Philip Wheelwright demonstrated that Reichard had succeeded in applying "her enviable knowledge of linguistics" to reach an eager audience of humanists and not merely a tiny elite within anthropology.[17] Wheelwright wrote for the *Sewanee Review*, "Gladys A. Reichard's *Navaho Religion: A Study of Symbolism* takes as its subject that ancient and honorable race of Americans toward whom our attitude as conquerors has usually wavered between patronizing curiosity and lethal neglect. . . . [She] has produced a two-volume report at once so comprehensive, so sensitively interpreted, and so enjoyably readable that it can be recommended with enthusiasm to anyone who wishes to become acquainted with Navaho thought and ways."[18] The philosopher seemed innocent of anthropology's postwar character when he called Reichard's approach "a model of anthropological fieldwork, in its combination of objectivity and sympathy, logical clarity and an acceptance of the mysterious and paradoxical as an irreducible part of any human data."

Reichard's colleagues in Navajo studies gave *Navaho Religion* the cold shoulder. Yet their collective silence did not prevent Reichard from keeping all the many irons she had in the fire hot.[19] In March 1952, Professor Reichard combined several of her favorite pastimes when she flew to Europe for a speaking tour sponsored by the International Federation of University Women. In Paris she spoke on the differences she perceived between the American style of education and that she'd observed among Native groups. Contesting the theories of "inevitability" that Americans learn to prop up their sense of cultural and mental superiority, Reichard noted that American pedagogy fell short of the Native approaches because white parents and educators "teach by words instead of by example," "rigidly divide men's and women's activities" that deprive them of "*esprit de corps*," and advocate a brand of "permissiveness" designed to ensure that youths are "having a good time" above all else.[20] After Paris Reichard flew to England to give a speech on education at the Royal Anthropological Institute in London. Ending her ten-day trip with a visit to Brussels, she flew back to the United States to finish teaching spring semester as if she had just stepped away for coffee and a smoke.[21]

Two recently graduated American anthropologists benefited from Reichard's unbroken commitment to mentoring the next generation of anthropologists in spite of her reduced involvement at Columbia. One was David Aberle, whose scholarship on Hopi life stories and psychoanalysis launched his rise through the ranks of academic anthropology, with Reichard serving as an attentive and stimulating sounding board behind the scenes. The other was Flora Bailey. Sixteen years younger than Reichard and also self-supporting, Bailey did fieldwork on the Navajo Reservation under Kluckhohn and Wyman during the war. After she completed her PhD in anthropology at New York University in 1947, she crossed paths with Reichard at the Museum of Northern Arizona every summer.

Back East, Bailey occasionally visited Reichard's apartment in Morningside Heights to talk more shop and close the circuit of their warm connection to the museum. "I have seen Dr. Reichard twice this past week," Bailey wrote Harold Colton in the spring of 1952, "as she is kindly lending me some myth manuscripts she has. She appears in the usual fine spirits and is working hard."[22] Gladys placed less emphasis on attending AAA annual meetings, which gave some AAA stalwarts the impression that she had withdrawn from the scholarly fray. Yet habitués of the American West knew that in summertime, Reichard was a regular at the Pecos Conference and the Gallup Inter-Tribal Ceremonial, where she was a judge, and rarely more than a day's drive from research universities in Arizona, Colorado, New Mexico, or Utah. She paid close attention to the publications of younger scholars, as she demonstrated when she alerted Harold Colton to a new paper University of New Mexico's Florence Hawley published relating ethnology to archeology.[23]

Reichard's best opportunity to groom an intellectual heir arose in 1952 when McIntosh succeeded in budgeting the funds that would allow Reichard to create a second faculty line in her department. Reichard had requested the new position after she learned that Barnard alumna and native Arizonan Nathalie (Sampson) Woodbury, one of her brightest, most serious students of the late 1930s, was in need of a job while she finished her doctorate at Columbia. Woodbury's husband, the Harvard-trained archeologist Richard Woodbury, had been asked to join the anthropology faculty at Columbia. A teaching job at Barnard for his wife seemed a win-win solution for all concerned. Reichard had invested heavily in Woodbury while she was at Barnard and even stayed in touch with her while Wood-bury earned her master's degree at Arizona State Teachers College in Flag-staff. Aside from wanting to promote a favorite alumna, Reichard viewed Nathalie's imminent arrival as an opportunity to have steady help with her heavy teaching load for the first time in thirty years. Consequently, Reichard enlisted President McIntosh in a benevolent conspiracy to hire Woodbury as a full-time instructor for the coming year. As Reichard was due to retire in 1958 per Barnard's mandatory retirement age of sixty-five, Nathalie Woodbury seemed a strong bet to replace Reichard as chair of Anthropology once she finished her degree at Columbia and had a few years of classroom teaching experience to her credit.[24]

In the meantime, Reichard intended to enjoy the perks of being beyond the reach of further promotion reviews. She found dispersing her latest salary bump, royalties, and savings to her favorite institutions particularly enjoyable. Two years after her promotion to full professor, Reichard wrote McIntosh, "Enclosed find my (anonymous) contribution to the Barnard Fund for 1953." "I reduced it a bit this year because of another interest I have adopted which seems at the moment a bit more pressing than Barnard's more or less permanent 'straits.'"[25] That competing interest was the Museum of Northern Arizona, where she was serving her first four-year term as a trustee on the museum's governing board.[26] The ground had been ceremonially broken for a new research center and library across the street from the museum's primary exhibition space, and Reichard was eager to speed construction along. Until 1952 Reichard had repaid the museum's intellectual largesse by teaching in Colton's Summer Seminar series. In exchange for informed discussions on Hopi art, Einstein's theory of relativity, bird banding, paleontology, tree-ring dating, and the prospects of life on Mars with other professional experts, Reichard taught seminars on subjects that were close to her heart. She led two summer seminars in the early 1940s, one on "The Interrelationship of Southwestern Cultures" and another on "The Navajo and Science." After her sabbatical at the museum in 1947, she became a fixture on the MNA Summer Seminar calendar. Over the next five summers she spoke on "The Present Navajo Situation," "Field Methods in Anthropology," "Anthropological Problems of the Southwest," "Language and Thought," and "Emotion and Cultural Pattern." Her audiences included natural historians, park rangers, astronomers, museum curators, archeologists, foresters, teachers, art lovers, and graduate students. Reluctant to see the wide-ranging discussions end each year, Reichard usually stayed on at the museum through August for the annual three-day Geology Symposium.

As a trustee at the museum, Reichard looked forward to reuniting each summer with lively and appreciative friends. One of Reichard's favorites, beloved by all, was L. F. "Major" Brady, a British-born geologist once described as "classicist, philosopher, gadgeteer, rock-hound, paleontologist-at-large, intimate of the Darwin family, humorist, raconteur, pipe-smoker extraordinaire, and motorist diabolique."[27] Another was Edwin "Eddie" McKee, longtime assistant summer director of the museum and chair of the University of Arizona Department of Geology before his 1953 transfer to the United States Geological Survey in Denver. Reichard's friendships within the Colton family grew to include Joseph Ferrell Colton, the Coltons' seafaring son, and Suzanne "Sue" Wilson, Harold's younger sister and wife of Texas oilman Robert Wilson. Other familiars tied to the Flagstaff museum were Milton Wetherill, the museum's archeological technician and handyman; C. B. Wilson Sr., a founding member of the museum's board and courtly attorney who had helped Reichard find accommodations at Hidden Hollow ranch for her first summer-long stay in Flagstaff in 1939; several faculty at Arizona State Teacher's College, including geographer Dr. Agnes Miller, head of the Science Department; and National Park Service brass John Aubuchon, superintendent of Canyon de Chelly National Monument.

Conveniently, summer stays in Flagstaff featured some of Reichard's "winter people" too. Among the easterners who held the title of research associate at the museum just as Reichard did were Leland Wyman, his protégé and co-author Flora Bailey, and Indiana University linguists

Carl and Florence Voegelin. Former students Frederica de Laguna, Kate (Peck) Kent, and Ruth Underhill were less often in town after the war, but when their research touched on Reichard's specialties, they knew just where to find their Arizona-loving friend from June through September.

Reichard openly expressed her appreciation for the museum's liberal, learned character in other venues. As a member of the Joint Committee on American Indian Languages, she advised that group to ponder the virtues of Harold Colton's Research Center as a model for their project to coordinate research on American languages nationally.[28] She sent a five-page memo to Carl Voegelin, the committee's chair, that said, in part: "To me the secret [of the MNA Research Center's success] seems to be a determination to emphasize achievement and ability of personnel, combined with extreme tolerance of personal ('personality' if you will!) and institutional idiosyncrasies. One of their most successful and expanding projects involves the cooperation of the Navajo Tribal Council, the Department of Indian Affairs of the U.S. Government, the Department of the Interior, the consent of the Geological Survey, and the University of Arizona. In this stupendous, almost miraculous achievement the Research Center of the Museum of Northern Arizona acted as a catalyst. The results grew out of goodwill, tolerance and cooperation. The Research Center is constructive, never destructive, but is nevertheless discriminating."[29] Reichard's enthusiasm for Colton's administrative vision landed her a spot as the spokeswoman for the center's Ethnology Department at the museum's twenty-fifth anniversary party. Speaking to a hometown crowd, Reichard drew attention to "the spirit of cooperation that has always been fostered here" by the Coltons. The moment was tailor-made for a personal tribute to the museum's chief patrons and Reichard gladly supplied one. "I think the efforts of Dr. and Mrs. Colton have been greatly understated in favor of the institution, which is probably the way they want it, the way things should be in science."[30]

Keen to act, Reichard saw the possibilities for honest good works through the museum as endless. Her first initiative as a trustee was to propose that the board sponsor a college scholarship fund for American Indian students.[31] Backed by Harold Colton's equal enthusiasm for her plan, Reichard brought together a team of people to launch the Fund for the Higher Education of American Indians in 1953. Philip Johnston, the catalyst for the Navajo Code Talkers program and a Flagstaff resident,

Speakers at the 25th Anniversary of the Museum of Northern Arizona
celebration. *Left to right*: Edwin H. Colbert, Arthur Strahler,
Harold S. Colton, Gladys Reichard, Edward D. McKee, and John C. McGregor.
Museum of Northern Arizona N-8C (1953).13.

was named president of the fund, with Colton as vice president. The new
foundation's board of twelve white and Native experts, including Reichard
and soon-to-be first-term senator Barry Goldwater, tasked Reichard with
advertising the program to offices that advised Native students on their
college options. Though she plied her East Coast contacts in government
and business for information and financial support, the private donations
needed to endow scholarships never materialized. The fund made just
three scholarships totaling less than a thousand dollars in its first year.
Board members were slow to respond with their evaluation of student
applications; Colton bemoaned the lack of time he could devote to the
project, given his other personal and professional obligations.[32] When the
Navajo Tribal Council began offering Navajo students scholarships made
possible by federal pass-through funding, the few private donors FHEAI
recruited to the cause withdrew their support in response. Ultimately
the fund had little impact in the region other than to make Reichard an
entrenched member of the MNA fold.[33]

As Reichard steeled herself for retirement, the prospect of making herself a permanent home in Arizona in 1958 considerably eased her dread of post-Barnard life. Flagstaff became her most logical and attractive option after the museum's board voted to give research associates and affiliates the chance to build homes directly on the MNA campus. As part of a long-range development strategy, the board proposed to develop four plots within walking distance of the research center for lease to researchers willing to build homes there at their own expense. After twenty years or the death of the homeowner-lessee, whichever came first, the houses were to become the exclusive property of the museum.[34] The initiative gave Reichard the perfect means of expressing her philanthropic and philosophical values through early estate planning. She had sold her Newtown cottage in 1947 and was waiting for the right opportunity to reinvest the proceeds. "It is really exciting!" she enthused to Harold Colton when he told her the terms of the board's proposal, "If I can fulfill [the conditions] satisfactorily I should be interested in starting [to build] next summer."[35]

·   ·   ·   ◈   ·   ·   ·

In the last five years of her life, Reichard ran her busy academic department as she had always done, like a well-oiled machine. Her preoccupation with managing all its interests to keep up with the fast pace of change at midcentury made her prone to overlook her own. "By some mistake," McIntosh wrote Reichard in the spring of 1954, "we had not noticed that you had put in your budget without an increase in salary for yourself. I am happy to inform you that the Advisory Committee is recommending . . . a salary increase for you of $500 beginning July 1."[36] "Dear Millicent," Reichard replied the next day, "thank you so much for looking after me! I cannot imagine asking for a raise for myself, but naturally I appreciate it greatly."[37] In June, just before she left New York for her third and final sabbatical, Reichard sent the president a summary of Anthropology's affairs. As she had done the previous year, Professor Reichard expressed gratitude for the breathing room having a permanent junior colleague in her department gave her. She praised Woodbury's performance as a teacher and hoped that though the younger woman would have additional duties as temporary chair in the fall, Woodbury would find a way to make greater progress on her dissertation. McIntosh responded sympathetically. "I was . . . interested to see how much work Natalie [*sic*] Woodbury is doing," the president replied. "She seems so able that I wish that it were possible for her to get her degree. Sometime after you get back, shall we talk this over? Yours affectionately, Millicent."[38]

Original, vigorous, and in demand, Reichard continued to make good copy for the *Barnard Bulletin,* A student reporting on Reichard's imminent seven-month stay at the Museum of Northern Arizona inquired about her personal history, hobbies, and plans for the future. Though Reichard was, as usual, reluctant to divulge personal details in lieu of discussing her research, the reporter succeeded in extracting a few tidbits. These included Reichard's mentioning that she had first met Ralph Linton in a biology class at Swarthmore; that after the war she had rewoven a swastika-like symbol into a cross on a German couple's Navajo rug at their request; that, like her grandmother, she was ready to "try her hand at anything" in the years ahead. Steering the conversation back to her work, Reichard admitted she was "energetically (and optimistically)" looking forward to writing a book on Native oral mythic literature once she finished the two books she planned to write during her sabbatical.[39]

There was little sense in overburdening the reporter with the details of the shorter projects that were also on her mind as well as in the boxes she had packed and sent ahead to Flagstaff. One was a comparative study of the Salishan linguistic family prompted by Boas's unpublished notes on Upper Chehalis, May Edel's grammar of Tillamook, Hans Vogt's *The Kalispel Language,* and her own *Coeur d'Alene.* She was confident that a combination of new and old analytical techniques would shed new light on the history of the large family, with intriguing consequences for phonological and morphological theory generally. "This comparison is based on the principle that the languages themselves must be the test of any theory," she wrote near the start of her draft, even if the results tended to contradict earlier findings of any single linguist, Boas included.[40]

The upbeat *Bulletin* profile seemed to suggest that Reichard was wrapping up "her study of the Navajos," but perhaps the student misunderstood her. Since the publication of *Navaho Religion* and *Navaho Grammar,* Reichard had trained her inquiring mind on the topic of Navajo values, attitudes, and emotional habits and their formation in childhood. She became convinced as she read her contemporaries' latest findings that in the name of taking a psychological approach to the study of culture focused on personality development, culture-and-personality anthropologists took liberties that allowed them to impose their own emotions, attitudes, and patterns of thought on their data. Psychological states such as anxiety, fear, mother-love, and disgust, Reichard believed, were universal but valued differently from culture to culture. Interpreting behavior through the lens of Western psychoanalytical models had the potential to blind investigators to other modes of being, especially when researchers failed to corroborate their conclusions with close studies of Native language, art, religion, oral tradition, and autobiography.[41] The most serious error an investigator could commit, in Reichard's view, was to fail to foreground the Native point of view over that required by the latest quasi-psychoanalytical fad. She would carry on her westbound plane drafts of two articles, "Permissiveness and Navaho Mothers" and "Cultural Influences on Behavior, Emotion, and Attitude," and the book-length manuscript "Another Look at the Navaho." If the coming summer and fall went as planned, Reichard intended to publish all three within the year.

Reichard also said nothing to indicate to the reporter that she was intimidated by the negative reviews written by Sapir loyalists of her *Navaho Grammar* (1951). She had made her motives for writing the grammar crystal clear in its opening pages. She aimed to present the linguistic patterns and principles underlying Navajo speech, she explained, in a way that invited learners, teachers, and ethnologists, professional or amateur, to join her in an exploration of what was required to speak and understand Navajo fluently. Adhering to the basic principles and procedures of structural linguistics, Reichard produced a rigorous portrait of Navajo in which she postulated major patterns in the language "on the basis of observed regularities, recurrencies, and reduction of redundancies."[42] Crucially, her postulates were "vulnerable" or subject to testing against spontaneous, native-speaker utterances and intuitions as well as the abundant texts at her disposal. The grammar was also extensive, treating the usual components of a formal reference grammar and including sections on usage, lexical verb classes, dialectal differences, and an exhaustively analyzed text given her by Nancy Woodman of Lukachukai in 1949. The primary value of the grammar, Reichard emphasized, lay in its ability to help students of the language acquire Navajo as "a means of communication."[43]

Navaho Grammar anticipated the savage criticism she'd come to expect from Sapirians with a brief excursus on "The Sapir School of Athabaskan." She measured her words carefully in an attempt to put her analytical differences with Sapir on a plane where they might be debated dispassionately. "The reports of the Sapir school indicate as a primary purpose the reconstruction of primitive Athabaskan; as another the demonstration of the method that has come to be called 'structural analysis,' purposes which are largely theoretical," Reichard noted evenly. "The interpretation of a particular language as a living, cultural phenomenon seems to be almost incidental." "In my brief papers on Navaho," she continued, "I have indicated that a major failing of the modern linguist is the overemphasis on phonetic-phonemic questions, an emphasis in many cases so exaggerated that one sometimes gets the idea that language is merely phonemics." The determination of phonemes was a necessary first analytical step, Reichard allowed, but the phonemicist should take care not to "obscure or eliminate a morphological process" in his eagerness to reduce the phonological inventory of a language to the smallest, tidiest set of abstractions. Given the inherent complexity of language as a symbolic system, even the most exhaustive investigation of a large and varied body of language data raised intriguing problems phonemic theory alone could not address. "The major question is not only what forms exist," she theorized, "but also where the lines are drawn within a single category of form—what is mechanical, what is morphological, and what is historical or genetic. Meaning seems to be the key that can open these doors. Not etymology, semantics, phonetics, phonemics, or morphology alone, but all in their fascinatingly intricate association."[44]

The reaction from Harry Hoijer and George Trager was swift and categorical. Trager thundered dismissively in a review for *AA*, "Reichard doesn't know how to do phonemics."[45] Hoijer flexed his muscle as book review editor at *IJAL* to flog *Navaho Grammar* as not worth the cost of printing it. Chiefly, he accused Reichard of disrespecting Sapir by having ideas of her own about Navajo. Her grammar, he fulminated, "displays an almost complete neglect, or misunderstanding, of the elementary principles of descriptive linguistics. . . . The result is a book that today . . . is wholly inadequate."[46] To less-emotional readers of *Navaho Grammar*, Hoijer's and Trager's disparagements were suspect. Their exercised tone implied that Reichard's ideas about Navajo were dangerous. Less threatened by a woman's competency in linguistics was Ruth Landes, a Columbia graduate who took classes from Reichard in the 1930s. Landes found Reichard's grammar a "finely worked" corrective to Sapirian analyses of Navajo. It was full of "new categories of grammatical thought" that usefully departed from narrow structuralist concerns.[47] From his vantage point in the Northwest, Melville Jacobs also viewed the grammar with a cool head. Counting Reichard among the "other three leading Nadéné students—Sapir, Li and Hoijer," he noted that *Navaho Grammar* was the lengthiest treatment of a language belonging to the Athabascan family yet to appear. Jacobs deemed it "likely to occupy a central role in descriptive and comparative Nadéné researches for some time to come."[48]

Only a human being, Reichard drafted a reply to her critics that she subsequently declined to publish. In it she addressed her remarks to the bulk of anthropologists who did not identify as linguists. "It seems to me only fair that the anthropologists should be directed to a summary of the purpose and results of my study *Navaho Grammar*, which was reviewed by linguists solely on the basis of a viewpoint hardly known by anthropologists or relevant to ethnology. I was interested primarily in learning the Navaho language; the reviews are concerned with my personality." She continued, "The linguists have introduced so much controversy in their subject that it has become an exercise in polemics rather than a useful tool. Many ethnologists have felt compelled by its very bulk, constantly changing terminology, and abstractness to throw up their hands and skip any attention to language whatsoever."[49]

Cultural study without detailed attention to language was tantamount to a devolution of anthropology's highest ideals, according to Reichard. "Language used to be defined as a means of articulate communication, a definition accepted by some even today," she advised. "In order to communicate attention to meaning seems inevitable. Some modern linguists consider the examination of meaning a form of activity to be avoided at any cost. They are sometimes obliged, of course, to resort to meaning in order to arrive at some of their conclusions, but they almost always apologize for doing so. At the outset therefore I was departing from the vogue as soon as I tried to learn the meaning of Navaho utterances for the sake of acquiring a vocabulary and a key to correct idiomatic usage. The linguists have pejoratives for investigators with habits of this kind! I deeply regret the controversial phase of the situation and would gladly avoid it if possible."[50]

Ultimately, Reichard had confidence that Trager's charge that she was "a school of one member" in linguistics would be seen by others for the lie that it was.[51] The list of scholars and helpers she acknowledged in *Navaho Grammar* proved that the grammar was the work of many sure hands over two decades, including George Herzog, Robert Young, and William Morgan beside Bitanny and her many named and unnamed Navajo informants. Among her most active and respected supporters at the time was Carl Voegelin, a student of Sapir's. Voegelin readily published Reichard's linguistic papers in *IJAL* and encouraged Florence Voegelin, Carl's second wife, student, and future founder of *Anthropological Linguistics*, to hold Reichard in high regard as well. Reichard was also a familiar figure at the New York Linguistics Circle, launched in 1943. A charter member, Reichard mingled with international emigrés Roman Jakobson, André Martinet, and Wolf Leslau as well as American linguists Morris Swadesh and Robert Fowkes. In 1945 Reichard helped launch the Circle's linguistics journal, *Word*, where she later published two articles under the editorship of Pauline Taylor.[52] Reichard had belonged to the Linguistic Society of America only briefly in the 1930s, but membership in that particular club wasn't central to her identity as a serious linguist.[53]

By the early 1950s, Reichard recognized that Sapirians were too intent on silencing her to engage with her novel ideas. She refused to back down. "The great weakness of work in Indian linguistics has been its negativism," Reichard wrote to the Joint Committee on American Indian Languages, which included Hoijer and Trager. "The tendency [has been] to discount even to the point of ignoring, work that has been done in the past—condemnation of methods, conclusions, and even of persons of those who have done it." The personnel who would dictate procedural norms in linguistics had changed since the committee was founded in 1927, but their techniques had not. "Linguists for many years have been so concerned with terminology that it has got out of hand," Reichard wrote. "It seems that as soon as a term takes on a comprehensible meaning a new word for it must be coined. The result is to obscure what went before, making the study of linguistics discontinuous. This tendency seems to me a mistaken notion of 'science' or 'scientific,' a spurious substitution that seems authentic because it is incomprehensible except to the word coiners. Science requires some residue of agreement if it is to go forward." The insistence of some on having the final say was a greater detriment to linguistic science than keeping an open mind. "The very development of linguistics (which I do not think yet rates the term 'linguistic science') has clearly shown that the study of no language is ever complete. It is a constantly growing interest, the more one knows about a language, the more one sees in it for continued study. We cannot wait until something is 'complete' in order to start or continue. Such idealism becomes circular so that progress is impossible.[54]

·   ·   ·   ◈   ·   ·   ·

As she had done many times before, Reichard spent the 1954 holiday season in Ganado with Roman and Dorothy Hubbell. Although they had returned to live at the trading post full-time, life there was a shadow of what it once was. Driving from Ganado to Winslow in October 1952, Roman had suffered the first of a series of life-altering strokes.[55] Most of the damage inflicted on his five-foot ten, 185-pound frame passed within days. But more than a few days of convalescence was all the trader felt he could afford. Four months earlier the Hubbells had filed for bankruptcy on behalf of the family business, the Lorenzo Hubbell Trading Company. Once a man for all seasons "busy as a centipede on a hot griddle," Roman took the failure of the business hard. A journalist had written approvingly of the trader as recently as 1949 that his "methods seem unbusinesslike and his charity unending."[56]

Indian trading as a whole became a more ordinary business in the 1940s but Roman, his father's son, continued to depended on personal loans, bank credit, and dumb luck to diversify his holdings. Carrying huge amounts of customer debt until the wool and lamb sales that anchored the reservation's economy went through was the norm for all the old-timers. "We cleaned up pretty good in the spring and in the fall," one man said of postwar trading, "but other than that, everything was just on paper."[57] Hoping to secure the family business for John and LaCharles, Roman and Dorothy plowed their savings and profits into new ventures rather than pay off the creditors they relied on to maintain cash flow between business cycles. While running Lorenzo Jr.'s wholesale house in Winslow, the couple took on substantial ill-advised debt. Eventually their paper empire was one severe snowstorm or a single stubborn price dip away from disaster. When the wool Roman bought on credit went unsold in 1951, the worst that could happen did.[58]

The unrest that roiled the Navajo Reservation after the war had an impact on the Hubbells' welfare as well. Out of the struggle for political and economic justice for veterans and their families, a movement to learn how the trading business was implicated in the oppression of The People turned ugly. Resentment toward unscrupulous white traders came to a head in March 1948 when the newly energized Navajo Tribal Council put the United Indian Traders Association on notice that the gentleman's agreement between trader and client had expired. The council intended to institute new terms that put the needs and values of Navajos first. Technically, the resolution called for price controls on goods, a tax on gross sales, and greater transparency in every trader's bookkeeping. White-owned trading posts could continue to serve as social and commercial hubs in remote reservation communities, but Indian-owned cooperatives were to be developed to replace them. The March resolution had no teeth without the approval of the Commissioner of Indian Affairs, yet as an expression of blanket distrust of white traders its intent was unambiguous.[59]

No enemy of tribal autonomy, Reichard's viewed the council's action against traders as misguided scapegoating. There were bad apples among reservation merchants but Reichard was adamant that the Hubbells were "unlike other traders."[60] She knew enough western history to see that economic inequality on the reservation had its roots in the racist assumptions of the reservation system itself. She concurred when representatives of the United Indian Traders Association asserted, "Rather than the Government it has been the trader, who has been doctor, lawyer, confidant, undertaker and relief agency for the Navajo Indians. . . . [Traders] have known the Navajo more intimately, speak their language and deal with them in everyday realities rather than in fanciful theories . . . [they] have done more than the Indian Service so far to give the Navajo his present economic independence."[61] Reichard appreciated with Roman Hubbell that the council's plan threatened to "knock the props out of the Navajo economy" by squeezing good white traders out with the bad. "[W]hen they are in need they will not have any where to go for help," Roman wrote a friend with genuine anguish.[62] Reichard seconded her friend's assessment when she wrote John Nichols, "The Indian Traders Association is doing a wonderful job. I have attended many of their meetings and their facts are *facts* not dreams. They try constantly to weed out the bad [traders]. . . . They differ from all other [non-Indian] groups in that they know the individual Indians and help them when they are most desperate, usually by taking the loss on the terrific amount of credit they give. I do not condemn any group of people; I find decent people among all classes, but I think the traders are the best as a whole."[63]

Reichard's opinion of white traders wasn't shared by all younger Navajos. Having fought and bled for America, they were eager to throw off the yoke of white guardianship at any cost. The angry responses she received from Indians to her "Communication" to Peter Yazza in January 1948 underscored the pent-up anger many Navajo felt toward whites after the war. Still, Reichard was convinced that an education in the history of the consistent failures of the Indian Bureau and other would-be reformers would relieve the pressure being put on honest Indian traders. "The Navajo can stand a lot of 'straight talk,' as a matter of fact they do a lot of it," she counseled Commissioner Nichols at the time. "But they speak without information and I think they ought to know."[64] In private she expressed her feelings in the matter to Harold Colton. "Did you see the Tribal Council action *in re* traders?" she wrote him that spring. "I think it one of the most shocking, lawless documents I have ever read."[65]

Because the holidays brought painful thoughts of missing loved ones, Gladys and Dorothy conspired in December 1954 to buoy Roman's flagging spirits. Frustrated by a series of recent strokes, the trader could no longer travel from camp to camp buying lambs or escorting tourists to sings. He tired easily and the only way to ward off future strokes was rest, damnable rest. As they sat around the oversized fireplace in the Hubbells' main hall, they chatted about their mutual friends, including those like Adolph Bitanny, who had seemed to vanish into the desert after returning from war. Rumors may have reached the trio that Bitanny was launching a second career as an artist, though the amount of acclaim he would later receive in the art world was likely unforeseen.

After returning to the reservation following World War II, Bitanny divorced his Jeanie and married Veah Pillsbury, a Polish American artist reputed to have studied at the Chicago Art Institute. Under Veah's tutelage, Bitanny spent several years in his hometown of Wheatfields, Arizona developing his signature style as a painter. Since the war, he was known as Adee Dodge, a moniker that allowed him to avoid sharing his given name with Adolf Hitler. "Dodge" replaced "Bitanny" in honor of his maternal grandfather, the late council chairman, Chee Dodge. In 1954 Bitanny began carting his tempera and watercolor paintings of curvilinear Navajo deities to the streets of Phoenix and Tucson, where he sold them from his car. By the end of the decade, Adee Dodge would earn a spot for his painting "So proud the blue stallion" on the cover of *Arizona Highways* and add the epithet "the best of the Navajo painters," to "successful artist." Arizona State University professor Harry Wood credited Adee with "natural talent, the inherent Navajo sense of color and form, patience, and the working of an incisively keen mind."[66]

Reichard would have enjoyed Bitanny's turn as a hero to white patrons. Dodge told his new contacts he held a BA from the University of New Mexico and a law degree from Columbia. He also claimed he'd spent some of World War II in the Pacific Theater as a code talker and fighter pilot, that is, until he was shot down, held prisoner by the Japanese, and escaped his captors by "decapitating a guard with a machete."[67] The amiable young nerd with a hole in his pocketbook became not only a commercially adept artist but a savvy entrepreneur.[68] Uncorrupted by worldly success, Bitanny did not end his allegiance to Navajo thinking. He would have made Reichard proud when in 1963 he was asked by a reporter from the *Arizona Republic* whether Navajo religion was "black magic." The yogi-like trickster replied, "The medicine man is not a worthless witch. . . . He is more commonly referred to as a holy man and he is an important contributor to the physical, mental, and spiritual well-being of the Navajo."[69]

Inevitably, the conversation in the Hubbell great room in 1954 turned to reservation politics. The headlines of the newspapers from Gallup and Albuquerque were filled with proof that Reichard's thinking on the issue of Navajo voting rights had been astute. In the crisis-riddled winter of 1948, she had concluded the tribe needed two tools more important than the right to vote in state and federal elections to defend themselves against cultural and political extermination: actionable information and a well-designed plan of political action. Only a democratically elected tribal council willing to represent Diné interests in statehouses and federal courts could prevail, she believed. Just as Reichard had warned, state legislators angled to prevent Navajos from acquiring the means to govern in their own interests. In the fall of 1949, a New Mexico congressman succeeded in adding an amendment to Truman's historic relief bill, the Navajo-Hopi Long Range Rehabilitation Act, that granted states jurisdiction over most Indian affairs. By that point many on the Tribal Council agreed with Reichard that state domination was a big monster that needed slaying. After a heated debate, the Tribal Council voted to withdraw support for the desperately needed legislation and demand President Truman veto it, which he reluctantly did.[70] Passage of the Long Range Rehabilitation Act minus the corrupting amendment six months later was a pivotal political victory for the Navajo council. The council's principled stance empowered The People to treat with their state and federal foes as equals for the first time since contact. Historians would later regard the victory as the moment the Navajo tribe began to transform themselves into the Navajo Nation.[71]

Much as it pleased Reichard to see the Navajo turn the tables on their antagonists, she didn't lose sight of the struggle ahead. With council chairman Sam Akeah and councilwoman Lilly Neil (the first woman elected to the modern Tribal Council), Reichard continued to believe the lasting success of the tribe depended on universal education. While council members favored vocational and professional training for the young, Reichard held out for a Navajo-taught literacy campaign that promoted "language tolerance" at the same time that it created bilingual access to the written information Navajos of all ages needed to become informed citizens.[72] She supported the efforts of the bureau, guided by linguist Robert Young, to produce readers, informational bulletins, Navajo language aids, and the monthly Navajo-language newspaper *Ádahooníłigíí*. With all the competing demands for improvements to social services on the reservation in the 1950s, Reichard's enthusiasm for universal bilingual literacy, like her support for tribal political independence, was not shared by everyone she met, Indian or white.[73] She could accept these differences of opinion as long as the paper trail led to the Navajos gaining the rights and privileges she herself enjoyed.

Dorothy Hubbell later recounted that the last days of 1954 were special to her simply because she'd spent them in the company of her rare friend, Gladys Reichard. "[Gladys] spent her last Thanksgiving with me, and her last Christmas with me," Dorothy told historian Frank McNitt in 1972.

> Well, when she came over for Thanksgiving vacation I'll never forget. She knocked on the front door and she had both arms full. She had a sack of, oh, fresh vegetables and stuff she'd brought from

Flagstaff. And I had the turkey, of course. And she said, "Dorothy, there's one thing I want to do. I want to make the gravy." And she said, "If you've got the turkey ready, I'd like to make the stuffing." I said, "All right, you'll do that." And so she was in the kitchen working with me, getting the turkey ready, and she had on a pair of riding pants, and a green leather jacket, and a red leather hunting cap. And she tied an apron over all of this to work in the kitchen. And when somebody wanted to see her . . . someone came over and said they wanted to see Miss Reichard . . . she went out [of] the kitchen, apron, green leather jacket, and red cap and all, and went out to talk to them. And I just, I never was so amused at an appearance of anybody. She didn't care much about . . .

McNitt finished Dorothy's sentence with "how she looked," then abruptly changed the subject. "And did [Gladys] learn to speak Navajo?" he asked her. "Yes, pretty well," Dorothy replied, "She knew it quite well. She had quite a number of papers on her work with the Navajo language. Have you seen any of them?" "No," McNitt answered, "I don't believe I have."[74]

March 1955 was half gone before Reichard wrote Hubbell to tell her she was back on the job in New York. Headlining her letter was the death of a mutual friend, the western painter, illustrator, and author William Robinson Leigh. Reichard tucked a copy of Leigh's obituary from the *Herald Tribune* into the envelope just in case Dorothy hadn't seen it. A second bit of sad news concerned a New Yorker Dorothy likely never met. "Ernst Boas died last week," Reichard informed her friend. "I did not see him often, but always depended a lot on his just being there. He became more and more like Papa Franz. He was 64, had been very ill for more than a year, probably cancer of pancreas and/or liver." Almost as an afterthought, Reichard admitted that winter had not been kind to her either. Soon after arriving home she'd suffered a "ten-day bout of pneumonia, very mild & peculiar." Her doctor threatened to hospitalize her if she didn't stay home in bed until it passed. "I was very good!" she swore, before adding, "I'm all right now." Fully recovered or not, Reichard didn't forget to gratify a mother's pride by mentioning that while she was laid up, John Hubbell had come south from his new home in Vermont to lend her a hand.[75]

Forced bed rest didn't keep Reichard from her writing but it did make her cranky. Her official portrait for the 1955 yearbook shows a pallid woman in a dark business suit grimly obliging her photographer against doctor's orders. Sometime that winter she reviewed Stanley Fishler's edition of a Navajo creation myth for *AA* at the request of book review editor David Aberle. When Aberle sent it back to her for revisions, she took it as a flat rejection and responded sarcastically with an unprintably telegraphic substitute. Aberle took the blame for setting too low a word count. "First, obviously I have annoyed you which is not my aim in life," he wrote Reichard entreating her to redo the piece. "It is obvious that whoever else I pick [to review Fishler's book] will not be nearly so qualified as you are."[76]

Reichard declined Aberle's invitation, thinking she would have her full say on Fishler and the current state of Navajo ethnography when her next monograph, "Another Look at the Navaho," was published. Most pressing was her intention to finish her paper on mental health and religion in Navajo society for the April meeting of the Committee for the Scientific Study of Religion. On the day, her talk on "Anthropology and Religion" engendered so much discussion and enthusiasm that afterward she was invited to submit a similar piece for a special issue of the *International Record of Medicine and General Practice Clinics*.

Next, Reichard sent "Permissiveness and Navaho Mothers" to *AA* editor Sol Tax and "Cultural Influences on Behavior, Emotion, and Attitude" to Leslie Spier at the *Southwest Journal of Anthropology*. Tax offered the opinion that "Permissiveness" should be split into two papers. The part of Reichard's paper he read as a "rejoinder" to Kluckhohn's article on modern parenting should go elsewhere, he opined. "[I]t seems to me you have given us a rather sensitive delineation of aspects of Navaho child rearing not ordinarily considered, and this is very worthwhile," Tax wrote to blunt the rejection.[77] Spier dangled the prospect of including "Cultural Influences" in the fall issue of his journal. He wanted to wait to see what other manuscripts landed on his desk by the end of the summer. "Are you willing to leave it with me on these necessarily uncertain terms?" he asked. He offered to meet with her in the spring as she made her way from Albuquerque to Flagstaff so they might discuss "a few minor matters of expression," if she had the time.[78]

At the Museum of Northern Arizona, the cabin named for Washington Matthews was readied for Reichard ahead of the summer of 1955.

She had stayed in the one-room log cabin during her sabbatical and liked "all those nice shelves" as well as its proximity to the new research center building.[79] Summer Seminars were scheduled to begin just after the Fourth, once the excitement of the annual rodeo and Indian powwow had subsided. The Pecos Conference was to be held outside Santa Fe at the end of the Laboratory of Anthropology field school starting August 15. She'd received an invitation to attend but hadn't yet made her mind up to go.[80] If it didn't conflict with her annual junket around the Southwest with Lilian, Reichard thought she might work it into her itinerary. Lilian was due in Flagstaff in early July. Their travel plans were vague, though as usual they would mark their birthdays quietly, together. Lilian would turn sixty-three on July 5, Gladys sixty-two on July 17.

Through June, Reichard put the ideal working conditions of the Arizona high country in summer to full use. Her top priority was finding homes in peer-reviewed journals for the articles she'd finished over the winter. She sensed that "Permissiveness" had ruffled more feathers at *AA* than Tax let on. She retitled it "Goals and Methods of Navajo Discipline" and submitted it to Wayne Dennis, a specialist in Hopi culture and editor of the American Psychological Association's *Psychological Bulletin*. She tinkered further with her paper for the *International Record of Medicine* based on suggestions she'd received from Werner Wolff, secretary-general of the InterAmerican Society of Psychology and a facilitator at the April conference. On June 29, she put a copy of it in the mail to Wolff in anticipation of further comments.

A week later she heard back from Dennis, with regrets. He didn't think "Goals and Methods" was a good fit for *Psychological Bulletin* because it lacked a "general marshaling of data concerning permissiveness." If he accepted a paper on Navajo child-training, he reasoned, consistency required him to "accept similar reviews relating to the Zuni, Kwoma, Alorese, etc." As Reichard feared he might, Dennis found her references to Kluckhohn's views too pointed. He recommended Reichard send the paper to *Child Development*, where Marian Smith had recently published an article "somewhat like yours."[81] The rejection was a setback that made it all the more urgent to get at "Another Look at the Navaho" again. The book format would allow her to advance her ideas on how to do ethnography effectively without being shushed by a male editor. August and September loomed as the time to put the finishing touches on her draft shrank. Reichard made final revisions to "Navajo Concepts of Well-being," her paper for the *International Record of Medicine*. On Thursday, July 14, she wrote separate letters to the two men overseeing publication of the special issue and enclosed a copy of her completed paper in each.

Hours after celebrating her birthday on Sunday, Reichard suffered a massive stroke. She was rushed from the Matthews cabin to Flagstaff Hospital, where her nurses and attending physician made their gravely ill patient as comfortable as possible. The damage to her brain was so severe that Lilian secretly began to wish for a coup de grâce. Minutes before 1:30 A.M. on Monday, July 25, Lilian's grim hope was realized. A second powerful stroke ended her sister's life. At daylight, Lilian wrote Millicent McIntosh two stricken lines: "Dear Dr. MacIntosh: Gladys died this A.M.! I don't know what to write you."[82]

Tuesday's edition of the *Arizona Daily Sun* announced that services would be held in Reichard's honor at 3 P.M., Wednesday, with burial to follow. The group that gathered at Flagstaff Citizens Cemetery for Reichard's funeral was modest in size. Lilian and a cousin, a Mrs. Ben Cox of Pittsburgh, were the only family members in attendance. Reichard's friends at the museum came out in force. Honorary and acting pallbearers included Harold Colton, Major Brady, John Aubuchon, Carl Voegelin, Milton Wetherill, and J. Ferrell Colton. Among others, Mary-Russell Colton, Sue Wilson, Katharine Bartlett, Flo Voegelin, and Richard and Nathalie Woodbury were at the gravesite as Reichard's coffin was laid in the ground. Lee Wyman and Flora Bailey were scheduled to arrive in Flagstaff for a month of research that day and may have begun their stay by attending Reichard's funeral.

Newspaper accounts did not record the presence of any of Reichard's many Navajo friends at the funeral. If they stayed away, the short notice given for the ritual was to blame. Missing from the graveside mourners were Dorothy and Roman Hubbell. On the morning of Reichard's funeral, they declined a ride from John and Ruth Aubuchon, who stopped by Ganado on their way from Canyon de Chelly to Flagstaff. Roman had suffered a recent series of strokes that left him paralyzed on the right side and unable to walk; Dorothy judged it impossible for her husband to withstand a five-hour drive without further jeopardizing his health. To attend the funeral on her own meant she would have to leave Roman home alone overnight, a risk she was not willing to take.

Perhaps Roman sent a message with the Aubuchons advising Lilian to place the tiny medicine bead Red-Point gave Gladys atop her sister's body, in the Navajo fashion. The symbolic nature of that gesture would not suggest that Roman had any illusions, as Dorothy did, that Reichard's spirit had moved on to a better place. There was no need of a talisman in an afterlife that did not exist. Gladys and Roman had a mutual understanding with Diné that "This life is what counts."[83] Reichard once wrote of a recently departed Navajo medicine man, "He has not gone to some other world where he retains his individuality and conceits. He came from we know not where, from the Earth which is the source of all things. His life and his ideals were of the earth . . . . He lived them all in order that he might, while breathing, follow the beautiful trail to the harmony which is above all things. He cannot now be in another world for he has gone back to the earth from which he originated. Now he needs no song for, having lost his identity, he is a part of it all, an indefinable part, he is not only of it he *is* it, the ultimate essence toward which man and all things earthly strive."[84]

Weak and careworn, Roman Hubbell had little time left on his own trail of beauty to waste on burying the dead. From any seat in his venerable house beside the Colorado Pueblo Wash, his imagination could travel effortlessly to the San Francisco Peaks towering in the distance above Reichard's gravesite. He could picture with his mind's eye the shawls of abalone shell draped on the slopes of the ancient black points pressing into the turquoise sky, the motes of yellow pollen drifting scarcely visible through the canyons and forests at their volcanic feet. Nothing he could say or do changed the fact that, excused for eternity from the disconcerting hush and the abominable quiet, Gladys Reichard, friend and scholar, was finished.

EPILOGUE

WITHIN DAYS OF RECEIVING LILIAN REICHARD'S STARTLING NOTE, a vacationing Millicent McIntosh set the wheels in motion for an official farewell to Barnard's first anthropologist. McIntosh soon had another letter, this time from Margaret Holland, one of Gladys's closest friends on campus, that convinced her to involve Lilian in the planning of the memorial. "I had a most wonderful letter from Gladys Reichard's sister which made me feel so very sad and sorry for her," the chair of Physical Education wrote the president. "Though I had never met her, Gladys spoke of her sister so often that I almost felt as though I had known her."[1] The condolences McIntosh sent Lilian included a proposal to hold a service in Columbia's St. Paul's chapel for her late sister, "Unless you personally have some objection to this type of memorial."[2] Surprising McIntosh for a second time, Lilian did object, and the idea for a memorial meeting, a mini-conference celebrating women's achievements in anthropology in Gladys's honor, was born.

While the Reichard Memorial Committee and not Lilian chose the speakers for the event, Lilian was more than pleased by the result. Two days after McIntosh, Frederica de Laguna, and Margaret Mead spoke to a crowd of Barnard students, alumna, trustees, and New York dignitaries, Lilian wrote McIntosh, "I want to congratulate you for the dignity and lack of sentimentality in the meeting. I know it was exactly the type which would have made Gladys very happy."[3] For those younger members of the audience attracted to a career in anthropology, the meeting was also informative. The tribute de Laguna read on the evening of December 5, 1955 was as lucid and well researched as something Reichard might have written herself. Through a combination of personal anecdote and sympathetic analysis of Reichard's career as a student, teacher, ethnologist, fieldworker, and writer, the Bryn Mawr archeologist gave members of the audience who hadn't known Reichard cause to wish that they had. To fully appreciate Reichard's abundant gifts, de Laguna advised, was to observe her in the warm light of her relations with the peoples and places of the American Southwest. De Laguna recalled the prewar summers she spent as Reichard's neighbor at the Museum of Arizona as "ones not to forget." "We were both working hard at our own writing," she said, "but found time to make trips together out onto the desert of the Navaho Reservation or into the mysterious forests of the San Francisco Peaks. These excursions were doubly delightful because of her sensitivity to the beauty of the woods, mountain, and plain, and her knowledge of the country. There was one especially memorable evening when she entertained almost 40 Indians and a few privileged pale-faces with a real Navaho dinner which she cooked on a camp fire under the stars."[4]

If McIntosh wondered at de Laguna's referring to her gregarious, perennially upbeat faculty member as "a lonely spirit," she decided de Laguna's talk, as expected, was perfectly suited to the occasion. Prior to the meeting, de Laguna had written McIntosh to emphasize that Reichard was no ordinary anthropologist. "Scholarly and valuable, even indispensable, are the contributions of other Navaho specialists, yet not one of them singly, or all added together, accomplish what Gladys Reichard has done—and that is to give you an inner understanding of this alien culture," de Laguna wrote the president. "She makes it alive, real and intelligible in a way that only a few ethnologists have succeeded in doing for a few peoples. [Alfred] Kroeber has said that this type of work calls for something more than scholarship and scientific methodology—and Gladys Reichard has that in full measure—but also requires the sympathetic appreciation of the artist, a rare combination. She makes the Navaho intelligible to us not through a process of translation from the Navaho, but rather in terms of the Navaho's own values, a translation into Navaho."[5]

McIntosh's thank-you note to de Laguna read, "Everyone seemed completely happy about the meeting and it was almost pathetic to see how relieved they were to have been interested and stimulated rather than bored!"[6] The similar message she sent Mead expressed a bit less warmth. There was something off in Mead's tribute to Reichard, though the event's host was too polite to mention it. Mead had an awkward start to the whole evening when she showed a rather too pointed interest in the faculty

position in Anthropology Reichard had vacated. At the pre-meeting dinner McIntosh held in the deanery, Mead recommended Rhoda Métraux,
the romantic partner Mead lived with after Benedict's death in 1948, as
Reichard's replacement. McIntosh responded by inviting de Laguna to
name a likely candidate. De Laguna mentioned Catharine McClellan,
a doctoral student in anthropology at the University of California, and
promised to contact Kroeber for his opinion on the matter. The conversation took a less than promising turn for Mead when McIntosh noted
that the search committee she had charged with filling the vice-Reichard
position was headed by Columbia anthropologist Charles Wagley, a loyal
personal friend of Métraux's ex-husband, Alfred.[7]

In her prepared remarks, Mead avoided crediting Reichard with
anything more laudable than being a dedicated fieldworker. Speaking of
"Commitment to Field Work," Mead addressed young women who wanted
to keep busy, liked a challenge, and didn't hope to make their living as
full-time anthropologists. "There is no burden of individual creativeness
laid upon the field worker, who works to discover what is there, assured of
results if she will only look and listen, observe and analyze her observations," she promised them. Anthropological fieldwork was an occupation
that required no "uncongenial narrowing of attention" or reading of "what
other scientists have written." Unlike a woman astronomer, Mead opined,
a fieldworker like Reichard satisfied her "immediate capacities" by taking
responsibility "for the whole round of life" as does a "housewife who gives
more time to jams and jellies, whose pies are better than her cakes, but
who still feeds her household day by day." Mead quoted Rudyard Kipling
to suggest that anthropology was the science of "Things as They are," and
that Reichard had done no more than what was expected of her.[8]

In the months between Reichard's death and Barnard's memorial
meeting, a flurry of obituaries appeared in newspapers and newsletters
across the nation. In early 1956, academic journals carried remembrances
written by Marian Smith, Reichard's former's executive assistant, and
Esther (Schiff) Goldfrank, her former Columbia classmate. Though well
intended, both articles were riddled with factual errors and damaging mis-
representations of Reichard's work. The gross inaccuracies in Goldfrank's
paper led Carl Voegelin to write Harold Colton, "I feel that we should
have a more insightful record of Gladys than this in one of the American
journals." He wondered if Colton "might consent to write an obituary of

Gladys Reichard for the issue of the International Journal of American Linguistics which goes to press early in March."[9] In the immediate wake of Reichard's death, Colton had posted a brief notice in *Plateau* regretting the loss of one of the museum's "most distinguished Research Associates" and a "warm, devoted friend."[10] At John Aubuchon's instigation, he helped raise money to mount a diorama at the Museum of Northern Arizona depicting "some scene from 'Desba' . . . showing the old and new way of life among the Navajo."[11] Yet Colton felt forced to decline Voegelin's request on the grounds that he wasn't trained to adequately summarize Reichard's contributions to North American Indian linguistics. "Although [Reichard] was associated with us summers for about twenty years, I have not followed her work very closely," Colton confessed to Voegelin, " . . . there must be someone more familiar with her work in that field."[12]

In fact, there was no living anthropologist with the same breadth of expertise in art, language, and culture "all in their fascinatingly intricate association" to write the kind of thorough, accurate appreciation Voegelin had in mind.[13] Reichard's detractors rushed into the void. In linguistics, Reichard's reputation began a sharp decline aided by the continuing scorn of prominent Sapirians and the silence of friends. The whisper campaign launched against Reichard by Ruth Benedict and Mead in the 1930s had spread during the postwar period through the Ivy League cliques of sociocultural anthropologists unchecked by scientific objectivity or a feminist's historical perspective. By 1960 Reichard was remembered in print by her critics as nothing more than a hide-bound if loyal intellectual appendage or "daughter" to Boas.[14]

Less predictable was the fate that befell Reichard's literary estate. Lilian Reichard and McIntosh were equally in the dark about anthropology's factionalism when naming Reichard's literary executor. Nathalie Woodbury appears to have been appointed by default in consideration of her role as acting chair of Anthropology. Woodbury might have emulated Reichard, who had shown herself to be a sincere and hard-working guardian of a colleague's legacy twice during her career. As one of several anthropologists tapped to manage Pliny Goddard's estate, Reichard was the most conscientious. As Elsie Parsons's literary executor, Reichard was exemplary. Not only did she prepare Parsons's 1941 AAA presidential address for publication in 1942, but she edited and published Parsons's unfinished *Folk-Lore of the Antilles, pt. 3* the same year. Through 1950

Reichard made time to organize a swath of Parsons's papers for deposit at the American Philosophical Society Library. Drawing attention to the Parsons collection in a published note, she reminded younger scholars that Parsons "did not simply dabble" in many projects "as a matter of mere entertainment, but followed them through, scenting out their ever widening significance and relationships."[15] One incomplete work was an edition showcasing a set of paintings by Isleta artist Joe B. Lente that Parsons had purchased in the 1920s. Stimulated by Reichard's vocal support of Parsons's legacy, Esther Goldfrank eventually succeeded in bringing *Isleta Paintings* to print in 1962. Goldfrank noted with regret in her memoirs that "Gladys was denied the happiness of seeing [the task] accomplished" despite having "worked so hard" to achieve it.[16]

Woodbury, by contrast, signaled her indifference to Reichard's reputation early when she declined to edit and resubmit "Cultural Influences on Behavior, Emotion, and Attitude," the paper Reichard had sent Leslie Spier the previous spring for the *Southwest Journal of Anthropology*, and which Spier had decided to reject before he learned Reichard had died. Woodbury's inaction set the stage for years of neglect of Reichard's unpublished materials, especially the original, nearly complete monograph on ethnographic method, "Another Look at the Navaho." More focused on her own struggle to complete her degree at Columbia than with valorizing a teacher, mentor, and friend she had come to view as unfriendly to new ideas, Woodbury interpreted her duty to her teacher and senior colleague as the obligation to disperse Reichard's intellectual property to other scholars to do with as they pleased. She released portions of Reichard's papers to the personal care of scholars at the University of California, Swarthmore College, the University of Arizona, and Indiana University on request. By not safeguarding the papers at Barnard until someone more in tune with Reichard's professional motives volunteered to curate them, Woodbury ensured that Reichard's papers would never be collected and placed beside those of Parsons and Boas at the American Philosophical Society Library. Finally, in 1961, Woodbury sent a selection of Reichard's writings and memorabilia related primarily to the Navajo to the Museum of Northern Arizona. The material, she wrote MNA director Edward Danson, had "its chief value in providing data for the few other specialists in the field."[17] The museum had no established manuscript collection or trained archivist at the time. Leland Wyman, Reichard's cordial but conflicted competitor, volunteered to organize Reichard's papers in the MNA library to suit his research priorities. Lilian's involvement was limited to her gift of more than three hundred of her sister's books to the MNA library, many of them annotated volumes from the Parsons estate that Parsons's children insisted Reichard accept for her work on their mother's behalf. What became of the bulk of Reichard's estate, including the large volume of audio recordings, films, slides, photographic negatives, and prints related to Reichard's decades of Navajo studies, remains a mystery.

·   ·   ·   ◈   ·   ·   ·

Once she had done all she knew to do with the detritus of her sister's brilliant career, Lilian Reichard melted back into her quiet life on the outskirts of Philadelphia. Given her scant direct contact with her sister's professional world, it is unlikely she was made aware of the occasional tributes to Gladys that appeared in print after 1956. Then in late 1959, Lilian received another request for assistance from McIntosh, who had faithfully maintained her intention to create a permanent on-campus monument to Reichard. Mrs. Mac's crusade to modernize the Barnard campus was realized in part by the construction of Adele Lehman Hall between 1957 and 1959. The first new building to be erected on the campus since 1925, Lehman Hall housed a new library, a state-of-the-art language laboratory, and all of the social science departments. McIntosh designated rooms on the fourth floor of Lehman Hall as the college's Social Science Center, with one classroom to be named for Gladys. Thanks to Lilian, word of the creation of the Gladys A. Reichard Anthropology Room reached Bangor, Pennsylvania. Gladys's childhood friend Dorothy Godshalk Flory alerted the local press. Bangor's *Daily News* reported in April 1960 that Flory and her husband had contributed to the preparation of the "Unique College Classroom" named for the "Former Bangorian" known in her hometown as Doc Reichard's daughter. The seminar room bearing her name at Barnard was fittingly decorated with "Navajo mementos" to "tempt students to push beyond their formal course requirements and explore the further delights of the subject that Miss Reichard made a life work."[18] Other donors to the project included Dr. Agnes Allen of Arizona State College at Flagstaff, Suzanne Wilson of Arizona's Williamson Valley, Dr. and Mrs. Clyde Kluckhohn, Esther Goldfrank, Dr. Frederica de Laguna, and Dr. and Mrs. Richard Woodbury.[19]

Professor Sylvia Broadbent lecturing in the Gladys Reichard Anthropopogy
Room, with rug woven by Navajo weaver Dintsosi in background, c. 1962.
Barnard College Archives Academic Photographs series (BC17.1).

In the spring of 1962, Lilian's last tie to Barnard College was severed
when President McIntosh retired.[20] Neither woman would have been
informed when little more than a year later the Reichard Anthropology
Room was dismantled and repurposed. At about the same time, the
Bollingen Foundation reissued *Navaho Religion* with a foreword by Oliver
La Farge. La Farge wrote,

> To the writing of [*Navaho Religion*] Gladys Reichard brought
> unusual equipment. She was a trained anthropologist who had
> spent more than thirty years in the study of the Navahos. She did
> not merely visit them; she lived with them and even mastered their
> art of weaving, after no little exasperation. Similarly, she did not
> only observe and study the ceremonies, she participated in them.
> Her books *Dezba* and *Spider Woman* testify to the warm, human
> understanding and affection that informed her studies. An able
> writer, aesthetically sensitive, she had the quality that enables some
> students to penetrate to the full values and beauties of an alien
> belief and ceremonial, as many anthropologists never do, and to
> communicate her findings.[21]

After seconding Reichard's preference for the term "chant" over "the meaningless but currently fashionable 'Way,'" La Farge confessed that he had meant to congratulate Reichard on *Navaho Religion* in person but had delayed too long. Her untimely departure in 1955, he said, left him unable to offer her more than a belated "sprinkling [of] a bit of pollen in tribute to her great work."[22]

Lilian Reichard was approaching her eighty-second birthday in July 1974 when Barnard College president Martha Peterson received notice that the New Mexico Folklore Society had added Gladys to their Folklore Honor Roll. The certificate the society sought to forward to Barnard recognized Reichard's "outstanding contributions to the study of the Navajo Indian language and ceremonials."[23] Peterson wrote Lilian to ask if she would like the certificate of the recognition sent to her. "It certainly is a fine honor," the president added. "I wish it had come before her death."[24] No reply in the Barnard College Archives confirms that Lilian received Peterson's letter or that the Folklore Society's certificate reached her before her body was buried in Bucks County, Pennsylvania in October 1975.

Well before the turn of the last century, memories of the Reichard Anthropology Room were erased by tide and time. Today faculty and staff at Barnard College credit the founding of the first anthropology department in a women's undergraduate college to Franz Boas rather than to Barnard's intrepid chair and professor of Anthropology, Gladys A. Reichard. In 2010 campus visitors could dine in the Millicent Carey McIntosh Student Dining Room or read about anthropology's most famous Barnard alumna, Margaret Mead, in a wide array of Barnard College media. In 2013 the college announced plans to demolish Lehman Hall to replace it with an academic complex nearly twice the size of McIntosh's edifice. Because she lacks a champion on her campus, the opening of the Milstein Center for Teaching and Learning Center in 2018 came and went without specific mention of Barnard's first anthropologist: not the ethical, reflexive, interactive-inductive framework Reichard brought to the study of non-Western art, language, and symbolism, nor the experiential, student-centered pedagogy she pioneered during her thirty-two years at Barnard. Vindicated by postmodern, poststructuralist scholars in each of her many disciplines, Reichard's name is rarely associated with the major developments in American studies for which Columbia is famous, despite the debt owed to her uncommon vision of anthropology as an inclusive, equalizing, and humanitarian endeavor.

The items once displayed in the long-forgotten Reichard Anthropology Room were and remain unaccounted for. Listed in the program distributed at the room's dedication ceremony on April 5, 1960 are "a vegetable-dye rug which took first prize at the Gallup Inter-Tribal Indian Ceremonial of 1958" depicting "five Navajo deities and the Rainbow Maiden . . . woven by Dintsosi"; a Navajo rug woven by Reichard and given to Charlotte Leavitt Dyer by her teacher; an original oil painting by "young Navajo artist" Harrison Begay donated by ten prominent associates of the Museum of Northern Arizona; and Hopi and Navajo objects donated by Cecil and Helene (Boas) Yampolsky and Richard and Nathalie Woodbury.[25] Along with these treasures, the unique classroom was for a short time the repository of some of Reichard's best-known books. One was a first-edition copy of *Navaho Religion*, donated by Dr. Catharine McClellan, Reichard's successor as chair of the Barnard Anthropology Department beginning in January 1957. Wherever the separate pieces of artwork that once graced the Reichard Anthropology Room currently reside, Reichard's voluminous writings may be found in libraries and archives scattered across North America, Europe, and the World Wide Web. In their understated way, they endure.

NOTES

ABBREVIATIONS USED IN THE NOTES

AA   *American Anthropologist*

AB   Adolph Dodge Bitanny (a.k.a. Adee Dodge)

BA   Faculty Archives, Barnard Archives and Special Collections, New York City

BB   *Barnard Bulletin*, Barnard Digital Collections, Barnard Archives and Special Collections, New York City

BH   Berard Haile

BHP   Berard Haile Papers, Special Collections at the University of Arizona Libraries, Tucson

DH   Dorothy Smith Hubbell

ECP   Elsie Clews Parsons

EPP   Elsie Clews Parsons Papers, Correspondence Series 1-4, American Philosophical Society Library, Philadelphia

ES   Edward Sapir

FB   Franz Boas

FBP   Franz Boas Papers, Correspondence, American Philosophical Society Library, Philadelphia

FN   Franc J. Newcomb

GR   Gladys A. Reichard

HCP   Harold S. Colton Collection, Museum of Northern Arizona Library and Archives, Easton Collection Center, Flagstaff

HFP   Roman Hubbell Family Papers 1899-1982, Special Collections at the University of Arizona Libraries, Tucson

HUTR   Hubbell Trading Post National Historic Site Oral History Collection, National Park Service Hubbell Trading Post National Historic Site Archives, Ganado, AZ

IJAL   *International Journal of American Linguistics*

JAF   *Journal of American Folklore*

KBP   Katharine Bartlett Collection, Museum of Northern Arizona Library
         and Archives, Easton Collection Center, Flagstaff

LCE   LaCharles Goodman Eckel

MM   Margaret Mead

RB   Ruth Benedict

RH   Roman Hubbell

RP   Gladys A. Reichard Collection, Museum of Northern Arizona Library
         and Archives, Easton Collection Center, Flagstaff

RUP   Ruth Underhill Papers, Denver Museum of Science and Nature

SC   Swarthmore Halcyons Collection, Friends Historical Library of
         Swarthmore College, Swarthmore, PA

WP   Leland S. Wyman Collection, Museum of Northern Arizona Library
         and Archives, Easton Collection Center, Flagstaff

PREFACE

1. Handler, "Vigorous Male," 129–30.
2. De Laguna, "Gladys Reichard," 17.
3. Clifford Geertz, foreword, in Witherspoon, *Language and Art in the Navajo Universe*, vii.
4. Lewis, "The Passion of Franz Boas," 450.
5. Wilson, "The Deeper Necessity," 156.

PROLOGUE

1. Dora Marsden, quoted in Deacon, *Elsie Clews Parsons*, 119.
2. GR to ECP, Nov. 4, 1926, EPP.
3. GR to FB, Oct. 3, 1926, FBP.
4. Ibid.
5. Cerveteri is now the accepted place name for the locale Reichard knew as Caere.
6. GR to FB, Oct. 3, 1926, FBP.
7. De Laguna, "Gladys Reichard," 11.
8. GR to ECP, June 27, 1927, EPP.

1. EQUALLY DESTINED FOR LIBERTY

1. De Laguna, "Gladys Reichard," 12.
2. GR to BH, Oct. 6, 1928, BHP Box 3a. It has been widely assumed that Reichard was raised a Quaker based on an erroneous assertion in one of Reichard's obituaries (see Smith, "Gladys Armanda [*sic*] Reichard," 913).
3. GR to DH and RH, May 28, 1940, HFP Box 3.3.
4. "Found His Wife Dead," *Easton Express*, Jan. 29, 1902.

5. "Death of a Respected Woman," *Easton Sunday Call*, Feb. 2, 1902.

6. Reichard's baptismal record is archived in the Henry F. Marx Local History Room at the Easton Area Public Library, Easton, Pennsylvania. The Reichard family's former place of worship is today Trinity Evangelical Church, which still stands at 404 Broadway a few blocks from the Reichards' former home.

7. Reichard, *Spider Woman*, 277.

8. Davis, *History of Bucks County*, 474–75.

9. Of the ethnic label "Pennsylvania Dutch" later applied to the Palatines, Melissa Hough writes, "[t]he term 'Dutch' is a transliteration of 'Deutsch,' meaning German, a term that the English have used since Elizabethan times to describe anyone who spoke a Germanic language" (Hough, "Pennsylvania Germans," 6).

10. Florey, "The Flory/Florey/Flora Families."

11. *History of Northampton County*, 33.

12. Frank, "Pennsylvania's Slate Belt," Hidden History [blog], Nov. 5, 2015, https://lflank.wordpress.com/2015/11/05/pennsylvanias-slate-belt/.

13. Ochsenford, *Quarter Centennial Memorial Volume*, 357–58.

14. "Bangor," *Census Directory of Northampton County*, 1890.

15. LaPenna, *Around Bangor*, 31.

16. Reichard was likely cared for after her mother's death by her septuagenarian paternal grandmother, Seraphina Reichard; Amanda Jordan, her maternal grandmother; Minerva's sister, Lillie, who married late in life and never had children; and Noah's unmarried sister, Frances. Neither of Gladys's grandmothers, both widows by 1900, lived to see Gladys graduate from college.

17. "Unique College Classroom Honors Former Bangorian," *Daily News*, April 1, 1960.

18. Gladys Reichard interview by Elsie McIlroy, (c. 1945), RP Box 5.2.

19. Mary was the daughter of English-born, middle-class immigrants. Because it was common practice for young widows to support themselves as house matrons, she may have been the housekeeper Noah hired in the wake of Minerva's death.

20. Ibid.

21. LaPenna, *Around Bangor*, 100.

22. This sketch of the Bangor of Reichard's childhood is owed to LaPenna's *Around Bangor*, especially the photographs in "Three: Bangor" (39–62).

23. Ibid., 111.

24. "Dr. Reichard Dies at Bangor," *Easton Express*, Jan. 27, 1925.

25. McBride, "Golden Age of Fraternalism," 4. If women weren't banned outright by important male orders like the Masons, their participation in fraternal clubs was confined to joining less potent ladies-only auxiliaries.

26. Lindsay et al., *Official History*, 11, 19. The Red Men's version of North American Indian history ends in 1830 with President Andrew Jackson's signing of the Indian Removal Act. Because the Order subscribed to the popular idea that Native Americans were a homogenous and vanquished "race," they claimed America's first peoples ceased to exist once they lost their liberty to the U.S. government.

27. McBride, "Golden Age of Fraternalism," 23–24. McBride summarizes the scholarly view that the fraternal movement was "a gendered response from American males to women's control of the institutions of morality, specifically the Christian Protestant church." Secret male clubs gave vent to a militaristic aesthetic threatened by peacetime. The demand for elaborate, costly regalia alone, McBride argues, spawned a specialized garment industry that valorized strict hierarchy, theatrical, virile display, and a shrill masculine mystique in reaction to an increasingly inclusive, "disorderly world."

28. William Penn quoted in Bacon, *Mothers of Feminism*, 2.

29. Jacoby, *Freethinkers*, 95.

30. Hull, "Swarthmore College," 41.

31. Palmer, "About Lucretia Mott."

32. Bacon, *Mothers of Feminism*, 108.

33. Spencer Trotter, "Swarthmore College: A Reminiscent History," *Halcyon of 1917.*

34. Bacon, *Mothers of Feminism*, 165.

35. GR to FN, Mar. 10, 1934, RP Box 3.9.

36. Sociologist Mary Roberts Coolidge attested to the "morbid embarrassment amounting to tragedy" the typical girl of Reichard's era experienced when she failed to attain "conventional prettiness" in her dress and person (*Why Women Are So*, 5). Coolidge's 1912 feminist critique also provides a sustained and trenchant analysis of the pervasive sexual conventions that attended Reichard's youth, including the pressure to accept motherhood as a career, domesticity as feminine vocation, and subservience to men at home and in public.

37. The Mortar Board Society, begun in 1915, was a women-only honor society until 1975.

38. *Halcyon of 1918*, 256.

39. "Prof. Reichard Plans Further Navajo Study," *BB*, June 1, 1954.

40. Robert Brooks, "Some Student Traits," *Halcyon of 1918.*

41. "Halcyon Days 1915–16," *Halcyon of 1917.*

42. *Halcyon of 1919*, 282.

43. Ibid., 8, 320.

44. "Classes," *Halcyon of 1919*, 100. Miss Clara Mabel Hogue, A.M., was an instructor in English.

45. Boas, "Aims of Ethnology," 638.

46. Degler, *Human Nature*, 72. Degler quotes Theodor Waitz, author of *On the Unity of the Human Species and the Natural Condition of Man*, a six-volume work published before the American Civil War. Boas frequently pointed to Waitz as the source of "his own commitment to cultural explanations of human social behavior."

47. Boas, "Aims of Ethnology," 638.

48. Dorothy Keur quoted in James, "Keur," 181.

49. "Prof. Reichard Plans Further Navajo Study," *BB*, June 1, 1954.

50. Ruth Lasalle, "Sidelights Given by Dr. Reichard," *Arizona Times*, Nov. 22, 1947.

51. GR to FB, May 18, 1919, FBP.

52. FB to GR, May 20, 1919, FBP.

53. GR to FB, May 27, 1919, FBP. Because Boas left New York for fieldwork in the Southwest with Parsons before Reichard's letter reached him, the meeting was postponed until fall.

54. Rosenberg, *Changing the Subject*, 130–31.

55. "Butler and Erskine Make Speeches at University's Opening Exercises," *Columbia Daily Spectator*, Sept. 26, 1919.

56. Rosenberg, "Woman Question."

57. Rossiter, *Women Scientists*, 35; Rosenberg, "Woman Question," table 1.

58. Gildersleeve, *Many a Good Crusade*, 70.

59. Rosenberg, *Changing the Subject*, 152.

60. Ibid.

61. Herskovits, *Franz Boas*, 22–23.

62. Kroeber, "Franz Boas," 15.

63. Ibid.; Boas quoted in Jacknis, "First Boasian," 528.

64. Mead, *Anthropologist at Work*, 10. Mead majored in psychology at Barnard. When she applied to Boas for admission to his department in 1923, he recommended she apply to the illustrious graduate program in psychology at Harvard instead. Benedict convinced Mead to pursue anthropology at Columbia and paid her tuition when Mead's father refused to (Lapsley, *Ruth Benedict and Margaret Mead*, 69–70).

65. Kroeber, "Franz Boas," 15.

66. Reichard, "Boas and Folklore," 55.

67. Lowie, "Franz Boas," 316.

68. Boas, "Scientists as Spies," *The Nation*, Dec. 20, 1919.

69. Kroeber, "Franz Boas," 19–20.

70. Goldfrank, *Notes*, 15. The AAA censure had little impact on Boas's progress as a scientist or political activist. The censure wasn't officially lifted until 2005.

71. Ibid.

72. Gildersleeve, *Many a Good Crusade*, 92, 50.

73. Kroeber, "Franz Boas," 22. A half-century of intense scrutiny of Boas's scholarly output has identified broad liberal biases that informed his work subconsciously but no evidence that he intentionally falsified his results.

74. Goldfrank, *Notes*, 4.

75. Deacon recounts Parsons's efforts to make Boas a partner to her fieldwork and the gratitude he expressed in return for the "stimulus" received (*Elsie Clews Parsons*, 248–50, 253–55).

76. For the length of Kroeber's Columbia dissertation, see Steward, "Alfred Louis Kroeber," 1043.

77. Reichard, "Boas and Folklore," 54.

78. Goldfrank, *Notes*, 17.

79. Reichard, "Boas and Folklore," 55–56.

80. Gunther and Spier left New York because Spier had a teaching appointment at the University of Washington. Gunther eventually found her scholarly niche in the Northwest coast region. With Boas's continued support, she received her PhD from Columbia in 1928.

81. Goldfrank, *Notes*, 18. Boas likely referred also to Martha Beckwith. Beckwith finished her PhD in anthropology in 1918. Afterward she embarked on a distinguished career in anthropology at Vassar College.

82. Ibid., 59. Schiff claims she began addressing Boas as "Papa Franz" before becoming his graduate student. "And it was not long," she adds, "before he and I began speaking of 'Mama Franz,' a mode of identification Mrs. Boas also soon adopted when referring to herself." (39–40).

83. Deacon, *Elsie Clews Parsons*, 234.

84. Mead, *Anthropologist at Work*, 9.

85. Richard Handler links Benedict's ambitions in poetry and ethnology to her "quest" for "the dignity of rich personality" ("Vigorous Male," 134–35). Benedict's biographers, including Mead, characterize Benedict as "very deeply troubled" during the 1920s (Lapsley, *Ruth Benedict and Margaret Mead*, 69–70, 262).

86. GR to FB, Sept. 29, 1921, FBP.

87. Degler, *Human Nature*, 49, 42–44. Madison Grant, author of the 1916 juggernaut *The Passing of the Great Race*, is credited with popularizing the term "Nordics" to denote a superior human race.

88. Boas, "Eugenics," 476.

89. "Want More Babies in Best Families," *New York Times*, Sept. 25, 1921.

90. Deacon, *Elsie Clews Parsons*, 129.

2. A BREATH OF FRESH AIR

1. *125th Anniversary Book, Bangor, PA 1875–2000*, 3.

2. *History of Northampton County*, 21, 31.

3. Boas, "The Aims of Ethnology," 638.

4. H. L. Mencken quoted in Deacon, *Elsie Clews Parsons*, 233. Mencken compared Parsons to Nietzsche as a canny truth seeker (449).

5. FB to GR, July 11, 1919, FBP.

6. Boas, "Herman Karl Haeberlin," 71–72.

7. Sapir's prejudice against women scholars is established fact, though one obscured by his general reputation for "crotchetiness" toward rivals of both sexes. His published correspondence reveals best that he did not limit himself to spreading "malevolent" gossip about "self-confident and prominent" women colleagues by word of mouth (Deacon, *Elsie Clews Parsons*, 260). When Sapir asked Kroeber for field assistant candidates, for example, Sapir emphasized the sort of "chap" he was looking for with the stark prohibition: "Ladies not wanted." (Golla, *Sapir-Kroeber Correspondence*, 386–87). Additional examples of Sapir's sexism as applied to Parsons, Benedict, Mead, and Reichard appears in Deacon (*Elsie Clews*

Parsons, 1997), Lapsley (*Ruth Benedict and Margaret Mead*, 1999), and Falk (*Women, Language, and Linguistics*, 1999).

8. Stocking Jr., "Boas Plan," 70, 69; GR, foreword to *Primitive Art"* (unpublished), 1950, RP Box 5.5.

9. Sapir, "Algonkin Languages of California: A Reply," 191–92. Sapir never published the data he claimed would conclude the "fruitless squabble" in his favor. (Sapir, "Epilogue," 198). Mary Haas provided additional comparative data in support of Sapir's claims in "Algonkian-Ritwan: End of a Controversy" in 1958. Despite Haas's triumphant title, consensus on portions of Sapir's original proposal was not achieved until the 1970s. "[D]eep differences" between the languages render some aspects of the controversy unresolved (Golla, *California Languages*, 62–63).

10. Boas, "Classification of American Languages," 369.

11. Unless otherwise noted, all direct quotes from Reichard's unpublished Wiyot field journals are from Volume 1.

12. There are two settlements named Indianola near Eureka. Reichard was directed to the predominantly white one in error.

13. Pliny Goddard did not accompany Reichard to the Humboldt Bay area in 1922 as claimed by Golla (*California Languages*, 40, 300, fn. 61). The couple didn't visit the area together until late summer 1924 (see GR to ECP, Sept. 21, 1924, EPP).

14. Loud quoted in Reichard, *Wiyot Grammar and Texts*, 5. Loud's archeological survey confirmed that the Wiyot had occupied their territory for at least a millennium before the arrival of white Europeans in the mid-1800s.

15. Loud, *Ethnogeography and Archeology*, 330. Rohde's "Genocide and Extortion" (2010) updates Loud's account with testimony from Wiyot survivors and other newly discovered documents. Far from exonerating the white assailants, Rohde's sources confirm the premeditated, racially motivated nature of the attack.

16. Rohde, *Both Sides*, 282. Mrs. Jane Sam, a survivor of the Indian Island Massacre and subsequent internment by the U.S. military, testified in 1921, "We were not treated well on [the Klamath River] reservation. We were not given enough clothes, shoes, hats nor any thing for the children. Sometimes on saturday they would issue about a hand full of flour on a shingle. . . . Men folks that would go out to hunt grub for a better living gets whipped by the Agent, with a black snake whip. Women and children were treated the same just for trying to get something to eat. . . . I would run away every chance I could get" (Sam interview with Warren Brainard, "Wiyot History Statements," a private collection made available to me by Jerry Rohde in 2013. The history of these testimonials is told in Rohde, *Both Sides*, 2–3).

17. Ibid.

18. Reichard, *Wiyot Grammar*, 5.

19. Golla, *California Languages*, 48, 42. Golla credits William E. Myers with collecting virtually all of the Wiyot-focused ethnographic and linguistic information that appears in Volume 13 of Curtis's magnum opus, which was not published until 1924.

20. Reichard alludes to an observation made by Loud that in the nineteenth century, Wiyot were known to reject beef in every form, considering it inferior and even disgusting compared to the proteins of their traditional diet. Loud adduces the Wiyots' disdain for beef as evidence that Wiyot men were unlikely to have stolen cattle from whites as was claimed by some of those who condoned the Indian Island Massacre (Loud, *Ethnogeography and Archeology*, 333–34).

21. Chin tattoos were common among Wiyot women born before 1900. Although Kroeber was told that chin tattoos distinguished women from men in old age, Mrs. Prince informed Reichard that they were a form of personal identification. When photographed in her eighties, Prince's tattoo was no longer visible (Lynnika Butler, personal communication, Jan. 31, 2014).

22. Golla, *Sapir-Kroeber Correspondence*, 395.

23. GR to FB, Sept. 26, 1922, FBP.

24. Golla, *Sapir-Kroeber Correspondence*, 405.

25. GR to FB, Nov. 26, 1922, FBP. "Gif" refers to Edward W. Gifford, then a curator at the Museum of Anthropology and Kroeber's eventual successor as museum director. Lucy S. Freeland, a UC graduate student concentrating in anthropological linguistics, is referred to by her nickname. While at Berkeley Reichard also interacted with Jaime de Angulo, a colorful, controversial figure who later became Freeland's husband.

26. Jacknis, "Artist Himself," 137, 140.

27. Reichard, "Complexity of Rhythm," 185, 199.

28. Ibid., 207.

29. GR to FB, Nov. 26, 1922, FBP.

30. GR to FB, Dec. 22, 1922, FBP.

31. FB to GR, Jan. 29, 1923, FBP.

32. GR to FB, Feb. 8, 1923, FBP. Rosenberg, *Changing the Subject*, 153–54.

33. Kroeber, "Pliny Earle Goddard," 3.

34. Golla, *Sapir-Kroeber Correspondence*, 36, fn. 2.

35. Goddard maintained a warm, close relationship with each of his children despite his estrangement from their mother.

36. Kroeber, "Pliny Earle Goddard," 6.

37. Golla, *California Languages*, fn. 60, 300.

38. ECP to GR, Aug. 16, 1923, RP Box 3.6.

39. Deacon, *Elsie Clews Parsons*, 260–61.

40. GR to ECP, Sept. 4, 1923, EPP.

41. Ibid.

42. Goddard, "Anthropologist Looks at Marriage," 24.

43. Reichard, *Social Life*, vii.

44. J. L. Hubbell, "Fifty Years An Indian Trader," (draft) HFP Box 1.1; Cottam, *Hubbell Trading*, 12.

45. Blue, *Indian Trader*, 261.

46. Ibid., 87; Cottam, *Hubbell Trading*, 97.

47. DH interview with Lawrence Kelly, 1979, HUTR #73.

48. LCE interview with Lawrence Kelly, 1979, HUTR #74.

49. DH interview with Lawrence Kelly, 1979, HUTR #73.

50. Ibid.

51. DH interview with Liz Bauer and Terry Nichols, 1977, HUTR #77.

52. DH interview with Frank McNitt, 1972, HUTR #72.

53. Ibid.

54. Reichard, "The Navajo Indians," *BB*, Dec. 4, 1925.

55. Jane Howard reported in *Margaret Mead: A Life* (1984, 104) that Gildersleeve threatened to fire and refused to promote Reichard after she learned of her extramarital relationship with Goddard. As Howard's claims have never been corroborated, they are likely unfounded rumors Mead exchanged with Benedict and others in her private correspondence. All positive evidence points to Reichard and Gildersleeve having had a cordial, mutually respectful relationship during their overlapping tenures at Barnard.

56. Underhill, *Anthropologist's Arrival*, 142.

57. FB to ECP, Oct. 22, 1924, FBP.

58. "Three Killed as Train Crashes Into Motor Car," *Brooklyn Daily Eagle*, Jan. 26, 1925.

59. "Dr. Reichard Dies at Bangor," *Easton Express*, Jan. 27, 1925.

60. FB to ECP, June 25, 1925, EPP.

61. GR to FB, Oct. 25, 1925, FBP.

62. FB to ECP, Mar. 28, 1926, EPP.

63. "History of the Fellowship," Guggenheim Foundation Seventy-fifth Anniversary Record, 32–34 (formerly at http://www.gf.org/system/assets/000%302/chronology.original.pdf?1226601170, archived since 2014).

64. Ibid.

65. Ibid. This ratio was an improvement over the noncompetitive round of 1925 in which fourteen men and one woman received awards.

66. GR to FB, July 3 or 10, 1926, FBP.

3. HER HAND ON A HIGH TRESTLE

1. GR to ECP, Nov. 4, 1926, EPP.

2. Panconcelli-Calzia was considered one of a handful of "pure" phoneticians in the world, someone who did not study phonology but the properties of speech production only. In 1933 he signed an oath of loyalty to Hitler.

3. GR to FB, Mar. 6, 1927, FBP.

4. Bing (1892–1964) drove an ambulance in London during German air raids until she was dismissed as an "enemy alien." After being passed over for decades, she was named director of the library (later renamed the Warburg Institute) in 1954.

5. GR to ECP, Nov. 4, 1926, EPP.

6. Mead, *Anthropologist at Work*, 139.

7. Benedict's failure to win a Guggenheim Fellowship for 1926–27 marked the third time she had fallen short in a grant competition in as many years (Lapsley, *Ruth Benedict and Margaret Mead*, 63). Sapir wrote her, "I was very sorry to hear that you did not get the fellowship after all. Did your being married have anything to do with it? . . . I suppose, my dear girl, that if you stay around Columbia long enough and learn the noble art of doing things Boas' way perfectly you may, in the fullness of time, look forward to getting a fellowship. . . . I hope, too, you may keep up the standard set by Gladys! (Mead, *Anthropologist at Work*, 183).

8. Underhill, *An Anthropologist's Arrival*, 152.

9. Benedict admitted to her diary that she knew she was never in contention for the job (Mead, *Anthropologist at Work*, 65). Although Mead was as yet an undergraduate student at the time of Reichard's hiring, she later claimed to know that Boas chose Reichard because she was not married and "did need a job," having no husband to support her (ibid., 342).

10. Lapsley, *Ruth Benedict and Margaret Mead*, 75.

11. Mead also disapproved of Boas's strong German accent and stern countenance. One of her biographers writes that Mead found Boas "monstrous in appearance" and possessed of a social manner distressing to the fast crowd of her preferred Greenwich Village set (Banner, *Intertwined Lives*, 189).

12. Mead, *Anthropologist at Work*, 343.

13. Lapsley, *Ruth Benedict and Margaret Mead*, 161.

14. Lapsley concludes Benedict had romantic feelings for Sapir (*Ruth Benedict and Margaret Mead*, 88).

15. Golla, *Sapir-Kroeber Correspondence*, 408.

16. GR to FB, June 19, 1923, FBP.

17. Reichard, *Wiyot Grammar and Texts*, 6.

18. Falk, *Women, Language, and Linguistics*, 140–41.

19. Darnell, *Edward Sapir*, 197.

20. Sapir's personal history and ideas are presented in Darnell, *Edward Sapir* (1990). For an impersonal appreciation of Sapir's scholarly contributions, see Boas, "Edward Sapir" (1939).

21. Golla, *Sapir-Kroeber Correspondence*, 350. Sapir was introduced to the possible ties between Athapaskan, Tlingit and Haida by Boas, who notice a resemblance before 1890. By 1920, Boas decided that areal diffusion better accounted for the similarities pending clearer proof of genetic relationship (I. Goddard, "Classification," 312). A remote relationship between Tlingit and Athapaskan is now accepted by most linguists, although through the 1990s it was still rated tentative.

22. Ibid., 355. Kroeber implored Sapir to recognize Goddard's "difficult position." "He says that he did not get everything in Athabascan and that you are doing it better," Kroeber told Sapir, "I think he would be quite affectionate if he could feel that you were not brushing him aside lightly or with scorn" (ibid., 399).

23. Ibid., 355.

24. Ibid., 401.

25. Ibid. Sapir's "critique" of Goddard echoes the derogatory sexual innuendo he aimed at Elsie Parsons. Sapir advised a student, Leslie White, that he might improve his relations with Parsons by having sex with her because, "[h]er interest in 'science' is some kind of erotic mechanism" (Deacon, *Elsie Clews Parsons*, 260). White later became a staunch admirer of Parsons's work.

26. The death of Kroeber's first wife, Henrietta Rothschild, from tuberculosis in 1913, gave him cause for despair. His rebound from personal tragedy and distinguished career in anthropology are reviewed in *Alfred Kroeber: A Personal Configuration* (1970), written by his second wife, Theodora Kroeber.

27. Golla, *Sapir-Kroeber Correspondence*, 76, 332.

28. Lapsley, *Ruth Benedict and Margaret Mead*, 98. Sapir claimed his first wife described him in the quoted terms.

29. Golla, *Sapir-Kroeber Correspondence*, 57.

30. Ibid., 410.

31. Sapir didn't object to the Committee's approving a grant to Reichard, the only woman grantee in their first grant cycle. He did register a private complaint with Kroeber. Linking his growing animosity towards Boas with his scorn for Reichard he wrote, "Boas still has a sublime faith in the adequacy of anybody that happens to have had a course or two with him to do anything from counting beads in Thompson River specimens to making a complete phonetic and morphological analysis of Navaho or Yurok" (Darnell, *Edward Sapir*, 279).

32. FB to GR, April 9, 1927, FBP.

33. GR to FB, April 25, 1927, FBP.

34. GR to ECP, Nov. 4, 1926, ECP.

35. GR to FB, May 10, 1927, FBP.

36. FB to GR, May 7, 1927, FBP.

37. FB to GR, June 9, 1927, FBP.

38. GR to FB, June 26, 1927, FBP.

39. GR to FB, July 12, 1927, FBP.

40. GR to FB, July 19, 1927, FBP.

41. GR to FB, Aug. 7, 1927, FBP. She adds, "Every stem in . . . Cd'A [may be] a verb."

42. GR to FB, July 21, 1927, FBP.

43. GR to FB, July 7, 1927, FBP.

44. Brinkman, "Etsmeystkhw," 14.

45. GR to FB, July 25, 1927, FBP.

46. Ibid.

47. GR to FB, Aug. 31, 1927, FBP.

48. The diarist for the De Smet expedition chose instead to flatter the Society of Jesus by describing the Schitschu'mush as "noted for dissimulations, egotism, and cruelty," and possessed as the Flathead and Blackfeet were of "an unrelenting spirit of independence, laziness, a passion for gambling, cruelty to the vanquished, very little regard for women, forgetfulness of the past and improvidence for the future" (Donnelly, *Wilderness Kingdom*, 12).

49. Diomedi, *Sketches*, 61.

50. Ibid., 64.

51. Williams, "American Imperialism," 233–34.

52. The once-popular slogan is attributed to Capt. Richard H. Pratt, founder of the Carlisle Indian residential school in 1892 (see http://historymatters.gmu.edu/d/4929/).

53. Williams, "American Imperialism," 237.

54. Cotroneo and Dozier, "A Time of Disintegration," 414.

55. Heiner, "Historical Demography," 65.

56. Ibid., 73–75.

57. GR to FB, July 19, 1927, FBP.

58. *Meriam Report*, ch. 4, para. 3–4.

59. Ibid.

60. GR to FB, Aug. 11, 1927, and July 25, 1927, FBP.

61. GR to FB, Aug. 24, 1927, FBP.

62. GR to FB, Aug. 31, 1927, FBP.

63. "Announce Promotion of Next Year Faculty," *BB*, April 20, 1928. Reichard was one of three faculty promoted to assistant professor for the year. As a point of comparison, Goddard was hired as an instructor in Berkeley's Anthropology Department in 1901 and promoted to assistant professor after five consecutive years in rank (Kroeber, "Pliny Earle Goddard," 2–3) while Reichard earned her first promotion after just three years of teaching at Barnard.

64. Reichard, *Social Life*, 162.

65. Aitken, "*Social Life of the Navajo Indians*," 118.

66. ECP to GR, Nov. 26, 1927, RP Box 3.6.

67. GR to FB, Oct. 3, 1926, FBP.

68. FB to ECP, July 18, 1928 EPP.

69. Ibid.

70. Ibid.

71. Boas, "Pliny Earle Goddard," 1–2.

72. Reichard, "Form and Interpretation," 462.

73. FB to H. F. Osborn, Jan. 18, 1929, EPP.

74. GR to ECP, Oct. 12, 1928, EPP.

75. Goddard, *Navajo Texts*, 5.

76. In 1954 Reichard reiterated that the texts in Goddard's *Navajo Texts* are "intelligible to one literate in Navajo . . . but unsatisfactorily recorded" ("Another Look," 35, RP Box 6.1).

77. GR to FB, July 13, 1932, FBP. Navajo chanter "Blue Eyes" was also known as "Grey Eyes" (Reichard, "Another Look," 5, RP Box 6.1).

78. GR to FB, June 12, 1929, FBP.

79. Ibid.

80. Ibid.

81. GR to FB, July 3, 1929, FBP.

82. Brinkman, "Etsmeystkhw," 24–25.

83. Ibid., 2.

84. GR to FB, July 26, 1929, FBP.

85. LCE interview with L. Kelly, 1979, HUTR #74.

86. GR to ECP, Aug. 25, 1929, EPP.

87. Mary-Russell Colton, "Letter to the Editor," *Coconino Sun*, Aug. 12, 1927.

88. GR to ECP, Aug. 25, 1929, EPP. Kidder and his co-instructors Sapir and Kroeber were disinclined to admit women students until Parsons was appointed a trustee and confronted their prejudice. Kidder held that young women were "an unreliable element" in professional anthropology because their careers ended abruptly once they married. In the name of "psychological honesty," Sapir warned of the "highly disturbing and embarrassing problems" a young woman created for men in the field (Deacon, *Elsie Clews Parsons*, 262–64). Kroeber dismissed Parsons's concerns as much ado about nothing. At Pecos he instructed Reichard, "Tell Elsie I never was a feminist, and I'm not anti-feminist now, appearances to the contrary notwithstanding." Of the three instructors, only Sapir failed to admit women to his field course.

89. Ibid.

90. GR to ECP, Feb. 24, 1930, EPP.

91. Mead, *Anthropologist at Work*, 95–96.

92. GR to ECP, Oct. 12, 1928 EPP.

93. Mead, *Anthropologist at Work*, 53.

94. Ibid., 180.

95. Ibid., 95–96; Reichard, *Spider Woman*, 143.

96. Parsons quoted in Deacon, *Elsie Clews Parsons*, 165.

97. Peter Gay quoted in Hymes, "Use of Anthropology," 14.

98. This sentence paraphrases the lines in Walt Whitman's "Song of Myself": "Do I contradict myself?/Very well then I contradict myself;/(I am large, I contain multitudes)." The full text of the 1855 poem may be viewed at https://whitmanarchive.org/published/LG/1891/poems/27.

4. WEAVING WOMAN AT WHITE SANDS

1. Early women anthropologists were often viewed as helpmeets who were useful for their ability to get closer to tribal women than could their male partners (Parezo, *Hidden Scholars*, 3–4). In *Spider Woman*, Reichard states that she described her larger purpose to members of the Red-Point family by explaining to them "how I teach girls in the winter, visit and learn from Indians in summer, and why I want to learn to weave" (8). In her last monograph, "Another Look at the Navaho," (never published) Reichard remembers that she engaged the Red-Point weavers "without divulging my real motive," which was to carry out a "protracted study of religion." If her motives were flexible, she set her sights on finding a very specific living situation. "I visualized the program [of research] as an acquaintanceship with a family, which ideally should include in its membership a singer (chanter) of

a major chant, an expert weaver, and at least one person who could speak English" The White Sands group met her ideal (Reichard, "Another Look," 4, 3).

2. Witherspoon, "Language in Culture," 2.

3. Reichard, "Another Look," 3; Hymes, "Use of Anthropology," 14.

4. GR to ECP, July 6, 1930, EPP.

5. Ibid.

6. Ibid.

7. Mrs. Ben Wilson interview with David M. Brugge and Roberta Tso, 1972, #14, HUTR.

8. Ibid.

9. Reichard, *Spider Woman*, 4.

10. GR to ECP, July 6, 1930, EPP.

11. Reichard, *Spider Woman*, 35.

12. Reichard, "Language and Cultural Pattern," 198.

13. Ibid., 175. Parsons was often charged with being domineering and insensitive to her informants' religious beliefs. Such criticism may have accrued to her because of her sex; men anthropologists were not accused of being too aggressive when they used similar field techniques. Parsons was forced to operate in the shadow cast over another determined woman anthropologist, Matilda Coxe Stevenson (1849–1915), by disapproving male rivals. Despite having "embraced a surprising number of practices valued by today's anthropologists," Stevenson's persecutors "invariably highlight[ed] perceived flaws in her character" to draw attention away from her valuable and sustained contributions to southwestern anthropology (Miller, *Matilda Coxe Stevenson*, xvii).

14. Reichard, "Another Look," 2, RP Box. 6.1.

15. GR to ECP, Aug. 13, 1930, EPP.

16. Reichard, *Spider Woman*, 211. Reichard labeled her open-ended, facts-first approach "inductive" to distinguish it from its putative opposite, the selective, hypothesis-driven or "deductive" approach favored by most of her contemporaries. She contended of the "theory-first" approach, "too often the student finds [only] what he is looking for" (Reichard, "Another Look," 7–8).

17. Reichard, *Dezba*, v.

18. Reichard, *Spider Woman*, 12, 27.

19. GR to ECP, Sept. 30, 1930, EPP.

20. Reichard, *Spider Woman*, 89.

21. GR to ECP, Aug. 13, 1930, EPP.

22. Ibid.

23. Reichard, *Spider Woman*, 13–15.

24. Mead, *Anthropologist at Work*, 209.

25. Reichard, "Elsie Clews Parsons," 46.

26. Mead, *Anthropologist at Work*, 204–5.

27. Mead, *Anthropologist*, 205–6; Handler, "Vigorous Male," 151.

28. Handler, "Vigorous Male," 147–48.

29. For Sapir's famous 1921 observation "All grammars leak," see Sapir, *Language*, 38.

30. Mead, *Anthropologist at Work*, 203.

31. Ibid., 202.

32. Handler, "Vigorous Male," 149.

33. GR to FB, July 2, 1933, FBP.

34. De Laguna, "Appreciation," 11.

35. GR to ECP, July 9, 1932 EPP.

36. GR to FB, July [illegible date], 1930, FBP.

37. GR to ECP, July 6, 1930, EPP.

38. Ibid.

39. GR to FB, June 27, 1931 FBP.

40. Reichard, "Another Look," 21, RP Box. 6.1.

41. Ibid., 18.

42. GR to ECP, July 13, 1931, EPP.

43. GR to FB, July13, 1932, FBP.

44. GR to FB, June 26, 1932, FBP.

45. Benedict quoted in Mead, *Anthropologist at Work*, 3.

46. The common title for a Navajo man is spelled variously as "haastiin," "haastin," "hosteen," or similar, with "hastiin" the more favored today. Reichard generally avoided using the title in reference to Klah.

47. Newcomb, *Hosteen Klah*, 126.

48. GR to ECP, July 6, 1930, EPP.

49. Parezo, *Hidden Scholars*, 24.

50. FN to GR, Nov. 10, 1932, RP Box 3.10.

51. The Museum of Navajo Ceremonial Art was later renamed the House of Religion before it became the Wheelwright Museum in the 1970s.

52. GR to ECP, July 6, 1930, EPP.

53. GR to FB, July 13, 1932 FBP.

54. Ibid.

55. GR to FN, Jan. 18, 1933, RP Box 3.5.

56. FN to GR, April 5, 1932, RP Box 3.10.

57. FN to GR, April 15, 1932 RP Box 3.10.

58. FN to GR, Jan. 22, 1932, RP Box 3.10.

59. FN to GR, Sept. 18, 1932, RP Box 3.10.

60. GR to ECP, July 13, 1931, EPP.

61. GR to FB, July 10, 1931, FBP.

62. GR to ECP, July 13, 1931, EPP.

63. See McMillen, *Making Indian Law* (2007) for an in-depth account of events leading to "the twentieth century's first major decision concerning Indian land rights" (165).

64. GR to FB, July 10, 1931, FBP.

65. Cottam, *Hubbell Trading Post*, 189.

66. Kelly, *Assault on Assimilation*, 120.

67. Schwartz, "Red Atlantis Revisited," 513–14.

68. Collier, *Indians of the Americas*, 313.

69. GR to FB, July 2, 1933, FBP.

70. GR to FB, July 11, 1933, FBP.

71. Philp, *John Collier's Crusade*, 121.

72. GR to FB, July 11, 1933, FBP.

73. Fergusson, *Dancing Gods*, 198.

74. GR to FB, July 11, 1933, FBP.

75. Philp, *John Collier's Crusade*, 120. Members of the brain trust included Ralph Linton, future chair of anthropology at Columbia, and Reichard's student at Columbia, Edward Kennard, who Philp describes as a "specialist on Indian languages." Reichard's name is not on Philp's list.

76. GR to ECP, Feb. 25, 1934, EPP.

77. Ibid.

78. GR to FN, Mar. 10, 1934, Box 3.9, RP.

79. GR to Collier, W. Zimmerman, and W. C. Ryan, Mar. 28, 1934 Box 3.5, RP.

80. GR to RH, April 13, 1934 Box 3.2, HFP.

81. GR to FB, July 17, 1934, FBP.

82. GR to ECP, July 29, 1934, EPP.

83. GR to ECP, Sept. 9, 1934, EPP.

84. Reichard, "Hogan School," Box 4.12, RP.

85. GR to Ryan, June 22, 1934 Box 3.5, RP.

86. John Collier [unsigned], "Report from the Navajo Written Language School," *Indians at Work*, Aug. 1934, 36.

87. See Louise Lockhard's "New Paper Words" (1995) for a history of Navajo literacy programs, 1852–1940.

88. Reichard, "Navajo Language and the Community Center," Fort Wingate, Aug. 28, 1934, RP Box 5.4.

89. Ibid.

90. GR to ECP, Feb. 25, 1934, EPP.

91. GR to ECP, Sept. 9, 1934, EPP.

92. ES to BH, June 6, 1934, BHP Box 3a.7.

93. GR to BH, April 13, 1934, RP Box 1.9.

94. ES to GR, April 30, 1934, RP Box 1.9. In the fall of 1934, Sapir published with others what he considered the definitive character set to be used in writing all American Indian languages phonemically (see Herzog et al., "Some Orthographical Recommendations").

95. Flyer advertising the reissue of *An Ethnological Dictionary of the Navajo Language*, BHP Box 3.4.

96. In correspondence between Sapir and Haile, Sapir implies that *AA* editors asked Haile to review the 1928 book (ES to BH, April 7, 1932 BHP Box 3a.6). Sapir may have used his pull at *AA* to ensure the untimely review was published.

Sapir was not above manipulating Haile to satisfy his own passions. In 1929 Sapir counseled Haile not to study for the PhD in anthropology, guaranteeing that the priest's superior knowledge of the Navajo country would not make him an academic rival. The unequal nature of the relationship between Haile and Sapir is revealed by the letters they exchanged, 1929–39, available in Haile Papers. See Lyon, "Ednishodi Yazhe," (1987) and Bodo, *Tales of an Endishodi* (1998) for overviews of Haile's professional history.

97. Haile, "Review of *Social Life of the Navajo Indians,*" 716.

98. FN to GR, Nov. 10, 1932, RP Box 3.10.

99. ES to BH, Nov. 7, 1932, BHP Box 3a.7.

100. Bodo, ed., *Tales of Endishodi,* 138.

101. "Franciscan Friars, Hospital Sisters and the Church in Lukachukai," *Voices of the Southwest,* Nov. 25, 2014, https://voiceofthesouthwest.org/2014/1½5/franciscan-fathers-hospital-sisters-and-the-church in Lukachukai. Accessed Jan. 15, 2015.

102. Bodo, ed., *Tales of Endishodi,* 138. Haile urged missionaries to apply "some anthropology" if they were to succeed in "uproot[ing]" Native traditions.

103. Msgr. Hughes to BH, Jan. 16, 1934, BHP Box 3.11.

104. Fr. Arnold Heinzmann to BH, Dec. 16, 1933, BHP Box 3.11.

105. BH to ES, July 4, 1934, BHP Box 3a.7.

106. BH to ES, Oct. 6, 1934, BHP Box 3a.7.

107. BH to John Collier, Nov. 16, 1934, BHP Box 3a.7.

108. ES to BH, Nov. 2, 1934, BHP Box 3a.7.

109. ES to BH, Nov. 2, 1934, BHP Box 3a.7.

110. ES to John Collier, Nov. 19, 1934, BHP Box 3a.7.

111. GR to ECP, Sept. 9, 1934, EPP.

112. GR to DH, Mar. 23, 1934, HFP Box 3.2.

113. GR to ECP, Aug. 26, 1935, EPP.

114. GR to ECP, Sept. 9, 1934, EPP.

5. NEITHER FISH NOR FOWL

1. GR to ECP, July 13, 1931, EPP.

2. McMahon, "Invisible Women."

3. Ware, "Women and the Great Depression."

4. McMahon, "Invisible Women."

5. Dora Marsden quoted in Deacon, *Elsie Clews Parsons,* 119.

6. GR to ECP, Mar. 7, 1933, EPP.

7. GR to ECP, July 20, 1940, EPP.

8. Zwergel, "Incomplete Portrait," 14.

9. Ibid., 14–15.

10. Dorothy Hubbell interview with Liz Bauer and Terry Nichols, 1977, HUTR #77. Reichard stayed at the home of Dorothy's sister, Lucille Vortruba, while she was in Chicago. Vortruba, who taught art for a living, and Reichard enjoyed horseback riding together when their visits to the Hubbells' Ganado ranch overlapped.

11. Reichard, *Melanesian Design*, vii.

12. GR to FB, July 26, 1929, FBP.

13. De Laguna, "Gladys Reichard," 13.

14. Jonaitis, *Wealth of Thought*, x–xi.

15. Reichard, *Melanesian Design*, 2.

16. Ibid., 7.

17. *Bulletin of New York Academy of Sciences and Affiliated Societies*, Dec. 26, 1932 [newspaper clipping] RP Box 3.4.

18. A. C. Haddon quoted in de Laguna, "Gladys Reichard," 13.

19. "Professor Reichard Wins Science Prize," *BB*, Jan. 17, 1933.

20. GR to ECP, Feb. 7, 1933, EPP.

21. Reichard worked on the galley proofs of Goddard's *Navajo Texts* and *Melanesian Design* at the same time. She completed both by early March 1933 (GR to ECP, Mar. 7, 1933).

22. Amsden, *Navaho Weaving*, 236–37.

23. GR to FB, July 2, 1933, FBP.

24. Reichard, *Spider Woman*, 252.

25. Reichard, Field notebook III (1932), 382, RP Box 12.1.

26. Reichard, *Spider Woman*, 258. Marie informed Reichard also that the mission doctors discovered that undiagnosed tuberculosis was a contributing factor in Maria Antonia's death.

27. GR to ECP, Jan. 20, 1934, EPP.

28. See, for example, Parsons, "Waiyautitsa of Zuni, New Mexico" and volume editor Barbara Babcock's introductory essay, in *Pueblo Mothers and Children*.

29. The onset of the "reflexive turn" in anthropology is often associated with the 1969 collection of papers edited by Dell Hymes in *Reinventing Anthropology*. Of the many key texts written before 1999 that urged ethnographers to abandon "value-free" ethnographic writing in favor of self-consciously collaborative, reflexive ethnography, none reference Reichard's prescient *Spider Woman* or its decentered episteme.

30. La Farge, *Laughing Boy*, xi. In a subsequent edition of the novel, La Farge expressed regret over this statement in his 1929 preface.

31. Reichard, "*Laughing Boy* by Oliver La Farge," 121.

32. The plot of *Joanna Godden* turns on Joanna's refusal to marry after her father, having no male heir, leaves his sheep farm to his eldest daughter. Several village men court Joanna to gain control of her estate but, determined to marry for love, she staves off the opportunists and becomes a successful businesswoman and property owner. After Joanna tries to marry for love, her story ends with her stoically facing her future as an unwed and therefore unmarriageable mother.

33. Reichard, "Understatement or Naivete," 200–201.

34. Ibid., 203, 202.

35. GR to ECP, Jan. 20, 1934, EPP.

36. Ibid.

37. GR to ECP, Aug. 26, 1935, EPP.

38. Leslie Spier to GR, Aug. 32, 1935, EPP.

39. GR to ECP, Aug. 26, 1935, EPP.

40. *Barnard Alumna* 24, no. 1 (Oct. 1934).

41. GR to ECP, Aug. 26, 1935, EPP.

42. Amsden, "*Spider Woman*," 497.

43. Fischer, "Reviewed Work: *Spider Woman*," 312–13.

44. Taylor, "Sisterhood, Solidarity," 280.

45. Ibid., 281.

46. Ibid.

47. GR to ECP, Mar. 17, 1931, Sept. 30, 1930, EPP.

48. FB to ECP, Feb. 28, 1931, FBP.

49. Benedict rejected an offer of a permanent faculty position at Smith College in 1927 (Lapsley, *Ruth Benedict and Margaret Mead*, 178).

50. FB to ECP, Feb. 28, 1931, FBP.

51. GR to ECP, Mar. 17, 1931, EPP.

52. Sapir quoted in Lapsley, *Ruth Benedict and Margaret Mead*, 200.

53. GR to ECP, Mar. 17, 1931, EPP.

54. Mead, *Anthropologist at Work*, 143.

55. Ibid., 142, 123.

56. FB to ECP, Jan. 1, 1930 [misdated 1929], FBP.

57. Ibid., 249, 261.

58. Reichard's handwritten note on "Scientific Program XXIII Session of the International Congress of Americanists, New York, September 17–22," 1928, RP Box 3.4. "Peggy" refers to Pliny Goddard.

59. Lapsley, *Ruth Benedict and Margaret Mead*, 190.

60. Handler, "Vigorous Male," 129.

61. FB to ECP, Feb. 10, 1931, FBP. Even Boas despaired of placing Bunzel because she was a woman. Bunzel's experience typified the bind most women PhDs faced during the Depression. In a review of Bunzel's 1929 monograph *Pueblo Potter,* Sapir praised Bunzel as "easily the most brilliant" anthropologist working in Native design ("*Pueblo Potter*," 243). Yet when Sapir might have used his influence to get Bunzel a permanent faculty appointment at Chicago, he was silent. Through the 1930s Bunzel held temporary teaching appointments at the University of Chicago, the National University of Mexico, and Barnard. None became permanent.

62. De Laguna, "Gladys Reichard," 9.

63. "History of Anthropology Interview with Frederica de Laguna."

64. De Laguna, "Gladys Reichard," 9. Dr. de Laguna (1906–2004) became a distinguished field anthropologist and archeologist with a professorship in anthropology at her alma mater. Boas warned de Laguna before she arrived at Columbia that it would be difficult for her earn a living as an anthropologist. She insisted that she didn't care, saying, "This is what I want to try, want to do" ("History of Anthropology Interview with Frederica de Laguna").

65. Green, "Ruth Underhill," 356–57. Underhill was interviewed by Green in November 1981.

66. When Underhill's *First Penthouse Dwellers of America* (1938) was republished in 1946, all of Lilian's photographs were replaced.

67. Underhill, *Anthropologist's Arrival*, 141, 152.

68. Underhill, *Anthropologist's Arrival*, 178; Nathalie Woodbury quoted in Lapsley, *Ruth Benedict and Margaret Mead*, 259–60. Woodbury remembered Benedict as "looking past or through you" and that working with her was "like dealing with plasma" (ibid.).

69. Tisdale, "Women on the Periphery," 316.

70. Joan Zeiger, "BWOC," *BB*, Dec. 18, 1944.

71. Underhill, *Anthropologist's Arrival*, 152.

72. Mead, *Anthropologist at Work*, 324.

73. "Reichard Explains Language and Thought," *BB*, Feb. 2, 1943.

74. Reichard, "Learning a Language vs. Being Taught," n.d. [c. 1945], RP Box 4.8.

75. "Unusual Technique Employed in 'Language and Thought' Class," *New York Times*, Feb. 14, 1937.

76. Reichard, "Social Life," 470–74.

77. Ibid.

78. "Prof. Reichard Writes on Auto 'Rackets,' " *BB*, Feb. 23, 1934.

79. "Professors Down Students in Tenikoit, But Tie in Tennis," *BB*, Oct. 29, 1937; "Barnard Teachers Quizzed by Students," *New York Times*, Mar. 29, 1939; "Tintypes, Photos and Snapshots All Reveal Faculty in Babyhood," *BB*, April 3, 1936.

80. Zwergel, "Incomplete Portrait," 14.

81. "Greet Reviews New Quarterly," *BB*, April 19, 1940.

82. Maxwell Perkins to Alfred Tozzer, Feb. 18, 1933, RP Box 5.10.

83. Bixler, *Winds of Freedom*, 44.

84. Philip Johnston to Robert Bridges, Nov. 5, 1932, RP Box 5.10.

85. Alfred Tozzer to GR, Feb. 21, 1932 RP Box 5.10.

86. GR to Maxwell Perkins, Feb. 24, 1933, RP Box 5.10.

87. Ibid.

88. Field instructors for the anthropology lab typically selected their students for their summer courses from a small pool of applicants. In 1931 Benedict chose one woman and four men for hers. Ruth Underhill, who was turned away from a summer course led by Ralph Linton, also elected to do solo fieldwork in Arizona that summer. She later portrayed her younger classmate as "trouble" despite admitting that she did not know Schmerler well (*Anthropologist's Arrival*, 154).

89. "Girl Killing Stirs Bureau," *Los Angeles Times*, July 28, 1931.

90. Schmerler's nephew, Gil, alleges that the lawmen, government officials, journalists, and anthropologists who were drawn into his aunt's murder investigation thoroughly mishandled the case while blaming and slandering the victim

(see G. Schmerler's 2017 *Henrietta Schmerler and the Murder That Put Anthropology on Trial*). My independent research into the case corroborates some of Schmerler's findings, except his understanding of Reichard's role in the affair, which he gleaned largely from unreliable secondary accounts.

91. GR to FB, July 26, [1931], FBP.

92. Ibid.

93. RB to MM, Dec. 27, 1931, in Lapsley, *Ruth Benedict and Margaret Mead*, 206.

94. Lapsley, *Ruth Benedict and Margaret Mead*, 207.

95. "Apache's 'Confession' Read at Murder Trial," *New York Times*, Mar. 18, 1932.

96. "Apache Gets Life for Slaying Girl," *New York Times*, Mar. 22, 1932.

97. GR to FB, n.d. [Dec. 1931], FBP.

98. "Indians Weep at Son's Fate," *Spokesman-Review*, Mar. 23, 1932.

99. GR to ECP, July 9, 1932, EPP. Gil Schmerler contends that the evidence used to characterize Henrietta as "loose" with sex and alcohol was planted or at best inconclusive (*Henrietta Schmerler*, 119–20). The brutal nature of her wounds was suppressed to minimize her innocence, as was Seymour's prior history as an alleged sexual predator. Assuming Donner to be an honest man, Reichard believed the claims he shared with her in 1932 had been proven in court. Schmerler's book casts serious doubt on the veracity of Donner's postmortem, via information Reichard had no access to.

100. GR to FB, June 26, 1932, FBP.

101. In addition to taking swipes at Reichard in their letters, Benedict and Mead belittled Reichard to their students and colleagues in person. Underhill unwittingly testifies to the effectiveness of the duo's smear campaign when she recounts that in New York in the early 1930s, "There was plenty of talk about the use of Gladys as a lecturer and Margaret as a museum worker when most people thought the positions should have been reversed." Office gossip portrayed Reichard as "simple" and "lusty," while Mead was described as "a true intellectual, a maker and investigator of theories" (*Anthropologist's Arrival*, 152).

102. Rossiter, *Women Scientists*, 289–96. Citing Cattell's *AMS* as "The chief source of data, numerical and biographical, on American scientists before 1950," Rossiter (*Women Scientists*, 25) exposes the irregularities that plagued Cattell's supervision of the *AMS* between 1903 and 1943. She concludes that the *AMS* star was but one sad token of the failures of the " 'reward system' of science" for women scientists before World War II. "Not only was good work by women very often not rewarded, but most women were weeded out long before they might have been considered eligible for top honors or most prestigious positions. . . . It was particularly blatant in honorary groups, especially the two major academies of science, where even the most highly qualified women of their generation were not taken realistically as candidates until the supply of not only first-rate men but also admittedly second-rate ones had been exhausted" (ibid., 295).

103. Rossiter, *Women Scientists*, 293. The first two women anthropologists to win stars in *AMS* were Alice Fletcher and Elsie Clews Parsons. Mead was awarded a star

in 1943 (Lapsley, *Ruth Benedict and Margaret Mead*, 233), about the time the *AMS* stars lost their luster.

104. Lapsley, *Ruth Benedict and Margaret Mead*, 233. Lapsley states that Benedict nominated Bunzel and Mead. Benedict's nominator is not known.

105. Ibid.

106. Anthropological historiographer George Stocking Jr. credits Kroeber with articulating the family conceit in his 1943 tribute to Boas. While Stocking warns that "the tenuous analogy should not be pushed too far" it has become a fixture in the historiographic literature (Stocking, *American Anthropologist*, 11–12).

107. Underhill, *Anthropologist's Arrival*, 142; Deacon, *Elsie Clews Parsons*, 132.

108. GR to ECP, Sept. 27, 1940, EPP.

109. ECP to Robert Lowie, Jan. 6, 1938 in Deacon, *Elsie Clews Parsons*, 358.

110. Mead, *Anthropologist at Work*, 348.

111. GR to ECP, Mar. 17, 1931, EPP.

112. Lowie, "Franz Boas," 318.

113. Underhill, *Anthropologist's Arrival*, 142.

114. GR to ECP, Mar. 17, 1931, EPP.

115. GR to FB, Aug. 16, 1932, FBP.

6. "SINGS, DARLING, SINGS!"

1. GR to FB, July 15, 1932, FBP.

2. Reichard, *Spider Woman*, 131.

3. Ibid., 146.

4. Reichard, *Navajo Medicine Man*, 5. Erika Bsumek provides an account of Adjiiba's death and burial in *Indian-Made: Navajo Culture in the Marketplace, 1868–1940* (2008). Bsumek contends, incorrectly, that Reichard was an employee of the Fred Harvey Company and intentionally misled the public about the circumstances of Adjiiba's death to protect her employer's reputation. Reichard reported what she was told in the 1930s by Red-Point's family and friends about a tragedy that had occurred twenty years earlier. She did not have access to the letters Bsumek cites that showed Harvey Company employees speaking callously about the Red-Point family's tragedy.

5. Reichard, *Navajo Medicine Man*, 6–7, 10.

6. Reichard, Field notebook III (1932), 307, RP Box 12.1.

7. Reichard, *Spider Woman*, 145.

8. Reichard, Field notebook III (1932), 382, RP Box 12.1.

9. Ibid., 319, 188.

10. Reichard, *Spider Woman*, 191.

11. Reichard, Field notebook III (1932), 345–46.

12. Reichard, *Spider Woman*, 162.

13. Reichard, Field notebook IV (1932), 413.

14. Ibid., 410, 417.

15. FN to GR, Nov. 10, 1932, RP Box 3.10.

16. GR to FN, Mar. 10, 1934, RP Box 3.9.
17. Reichard (with Newcomb), *Sandpaintings*, 3.
18. GR to FB, Sept. 6, 1936, FBP.
19. Ibid.
20. Kluckhohn quoted in "Biographical Introduction," *Navaho Witchcraft*, xi.
21. FN to GR, Nov. 14, 1936, RP Box 3.10.
22. Ibid.
23. FN to GR, n.d. [c. late 1937], RP Box 3.10.
24. Reichard, *Spider Woman*, 269.
25. GR to Katharine Bartlett, Jan. 14, 1945 [possibly 1946], HCP Series 1–240.
26. Kluckhohn and Wyman, *Navaho Classification*, 3.
27. Reichard, "Navajo Classification," 7.
28. Wyman quoted in Lyon, "Gladys Reichard," 145.
29. Reichard, "Distinctive Features of Navajo Religion," 210.
30. Reichard, "Linguistic Diversity," 168.
31. Kluckhohn and Wyman, *Navaho Classification*, 3.
32. Ibid., 38.
33. Lyon, "Gladys Reichard," 145–46.
34. GR to ECP, Oct. 2, 1936, EPP.
35. RH to GR, Oct. 11, 1936, RP Box 3.5.
36. GR to RH, Oct. 14, 1936, HFP (AZ375) Box 69.
37. FN to GR, Nov. 14, 1936, RP Box 3.9.
38. Reichard, "Individualism," 23.
39. Reichard (with Newcomb), *Sandpaintings*, 5.
40. Had Klah been working with Navajo initiates in training, his religious property would have passed to them on his death. Wheelwright's creating the museum-shrine in Santa Fe prevented Klah's effects from being sold to the highest bidder at auction and then scattered into private collections.
41. Reichard (with Newcomb), *Sandpaintings*, 5.
42. GR to RH, April 7, 1937 HFP (AZ375) Box 69.
43. Reichard, *Navaho Medicine Man*, 13.
44. FN to GR, May 23, 1937, RP Box 3.9.
45. Reichard, *Navaho Grammar*, vi.
46. Reichard, "Hogan School," Sept. 8, 1934, RP Box 4.12.
47. GR to ECP, July 9, 1937, EPP.
48. Ibid.
49. GR to FB, July 9, 1937, FBP.
50. Details of Nicodemus's time at Columbia are sketchy (see Brinkman, "Etsmeystkhw," 26–27 for Nicodemus's recollections). Reichard's statement in her foreword to *Coeur d'Alene* that Lawrence was in New York "in 1935 and 1936" refers to one academic year (521).
51. GR to RH, Nov. 17, 1937, HFP Box 3.2.
52. Reichard with Newcomb, *Sandpaintings*, 23.

53. Ibid., 87.

54. Elmore, "Review of *Sandpaintings*," 4. Mr. Elmore was an ethnobotanist whose research centered on the Navajo Reservation.

55. GR to DH, July 10, 1938, HFP Box. 3.2.

56. GR to FB, July 17, 1938, FBP.

57. Ibid.

58. GR to ECP, Jan. 7, 1939, EPP.

59. GR to FB, Oct. 11, 1938, FBP.

60. Reichard (with Newcomb), *Sandpaintings*, 15.

61. GR to FB, July 17, 1938, FBP.

62. Reichard, *Spider Woman*, 286–87. Reichard seems to have anticipated the concerns of some postmodern feminists who charge her with appropriating Navajo weaving technique. She asks Marie if she fears her pupil and the white women who read Reichard's books on Navajo weaving will become "competitors." Marie laughs and agrees that whites "don't stay with it." "Even though I have learned [to weave] she is sure I will not become a rival because it takes me too long to spin and weave. I could not earn my living at it."

63. Reichard, *Navajo Medicine Man*, 12.

64. Reichard, "Another Look," 19–20.

65. GR to ECP, Jan. 7, 1939, EPP.

66. De Laguna, "Gladys Reichard," 10.

67. GR to FB, Oct. 11, 1938, FBP.

68. GR to ECP, Jan. 7, 1939, EPP.

69. FN to GR, n.d. [1937], RP Box 3.7.

70. Ibid.

71. FN to GR, Oct. 25, 1938, RP Box 3.7.

72. GR to Herman Schweizer, Nov. 30, RP 1938, Box 3.7.

73. GR to DH and RH, n.d. [Feb. 1939], HFP Box 3.2.

74. GR to FB, Dec. 14, 1938, FBP.

75. Historian William Lyon claims Reichard "drove a pretty hard bargain with the Huckels" after treating Newcomb in "a somewhat arbitrary fashion." Relying on hearsay from an unidentified source, Lyon also asserts that Reichard's alleged mistreatment of Newcomb in the Harvey affair ended their friendship (Lyon, "Gladys Reichard," 141–42). Preserved in Reichard's MNA papers are several warm, collegial letters missed by Lyons that Reichard and Newcomb exchanged through the '40s and early '50s. I interpret these letters as solid evidence that Newcomb and Reichard remained friends until Reichard's death.

76. GR to DH and RH, n.d. [Feb. 1939], HFP Box 3.2.

77. Ibid.

78. GR to DH, Jan. 12, 1940, HFP Box 3.3.

79. GR to DH and RH, n.d. [Feb. 1939], HFP Box 3.2.

80. GR to DH, Jan. 12, 1940, HFP Box 3.3.

81. GR to H. A. Belt, Fred Harvey Company, Jan. 20, 1940, RP 3.10.

82. Erna Fergusson, "Old Wisdom and Beauty," *New York Herald Tribune Books,* June 30, 1940.

83. GR to DH, Jan. 12, 1940; Mar. 29, 1939, HFP Box 3.2.

84. GR to DH, Jan. 12, 1940, HFP Box 3.3. Reichard gives an ironic version of the opening words of "Endymion" by John Keats, "A thing of beauty is a joy for ever."

7. COOPERATION

1. GR to DH and RH, n.d. [c. Sept. 1937], HFP Box 3.2.
2. GR to DH and RH, July 30, 1939, HFP Box 3.2.
3. Reichard, "Another Look," 13.
4. Reichard, *Navaho Religion,* xxxvii–xxxviii.
5. La Farge, foreword to 2nd ed. of Reichard, *Navaho Religion,* xvi.
6. Reichard, *Navaho Religion,* xl.
7. La Farge, foreword to 2nd ed. of Reichard, *Navaho Religion,* xxi.
8. Reichard, *Navaho Religion,* xxxix.
9. De Laguna, "Gladys Reichard," 18.
10. Reichard, "Another Look," 18.
11. GR to FB, Dec. 28, 1938, FBP.
12. GR to DH and RH, May 28, 1940, HFP Box 3.2.
13. GR to FB, July 4, 1934, FBP.
14. GR to FB, Dec. 28, 1938, FBP.
15. "Faculty Sign Anti-Fascist Declaration: Four Members of Barnard Teaching Staff Join In Protest," *BB,* Dec. 13, 1938. Other Columbia signatories included Ralph Linton, Ruth Benedict, Ruth Bunzel, and Gene Weltfish. Boas headed the committee that organized the signature drive and wrote the manifesto. Neither Gildersleeve nor Columbia president Butler signed it.
16. GR to FB, Dec. 8, Nov. 30, Oct. 30, 1938, FBP.
17. "Prof. Reichard Defines 'Race,'" *BB,* Dec. 1, 1939.
18. Reichard, "Third Column," *BB,* Dec. 3, 1940.
19. "Conference United for Anti-War Struggle"; "Permanent Committee to Lead Future Action"; "11 Spokesmen Pledge Organized Support," *Columbia Spectator,* Nov. 2, 1933.
20. "ASU Convenes in Wisconsin," *BB,* Jan. 9, 1940.
21. Price, *Anthropological Intelligence,* 23.
22. Gildersleeve, *Many a Good Crusade,* 249, 256–57.
23. Reichard, "To the Members of the Swarthmore Alumni Committee on Policy," n.d. [c. 1944], RP Box 5.3. Barnard's enrollment hovered at about one thousand annually during this period.
24. Reichard, "On the Beam of a Song," 16.
25. Ibid., 16, 20.
26. Goodwin, *No Ordinary Time,* 319.
27. "Maps Sprout in Milbank Hall"; "Byrne Reveals All," *BB,* Mar. 20, 1942.

28. "Language Instructors Instigate Comparative Phonetics Study," *BB*, Mar. 25, 1943; "Reichard to Speak," *BB*, Feb. 25, 1943. The list of courses offered by Reichard during the war appears in "Anthropology—Studied, Taught, and Practiced," Barnard Alumna (1949), 5.

29. Eleanor Streichler, "Education for All," *BB*, Mar. 9, 1944.

30. Joan Raup, "The Negro: Viewed By An Anthropologist," *BB*, Feb. 24, 1944.

31. The promotion became effective in July 1941. The primary factor in Reichard's slow progress from assistant professor to associate was a lack of funds. Though Columbia University was the third-wealthiest institution of higher learning in the nation (behind Harvard and Yale), Barnard, "affiliated with Columbia on a purely educational basis," ran heavy deficits through the Depression ("Columbia is 3rd in Wealth," *BB*, Nov. 31, 1939). Complicating the financial straits Gildersleeve faced was her calculation that she must promote men more quickly than women or lose them. English professor Hoxie Fairchild, who became an assistant professor at Barnard the same year Reichard did (and with similar credentials), was promoted to associate professor in 1935, five years ahead of Reichard. Gildersleeve regretted having to "delay well-earned promotions," which "in some cases, ultimately caused grave hardship" (Gildersleeve, *Many a Good Crusade*, 77). One of the cases she alluded to was that of Dr. Emilie Hutchison, a beloved and eminent economist and one of Reichard's closest friends on the faculty. Hutchison taught at Barnard for twenty-five years, chaired her department, and died in early 1938 an associate professor. The promotion of assistant professor of English Dr. William Greet to associate professor in 1938 after twelve years in rank suggests that the Depression tied Gildersleeve's hands when making promotion decisions about men and women faculty. Barnard's finances did not recover fully in time for the 1939–40 round of promotions. Gildersleeve was planning for another slate of belt-tightening measures and was surprised when enrollment increased by 31 percent in fall 1939. That surge gave her the means to promote Reichard.

32. Ruth Lasalle, "Sidelights Given by Dr. Reichard," *Arizona Times*, Nov. 22, 1947.

33. Gildersleeve, *Many a Good Crusade*, 317, 391.

34. Ibid., 96.

35. J. L. Hubbell, "Fifty Years An Indian Trader" [draft], 1, n.d. [c. 1930], HFP Box 1.1.

36. Gary Witherspoon quoted in Blue, *Indian Trader*, 236.

37. Reichard, *Spider Woman*, 108.

38. GR to DH, May 7, 1937, HFP Box 3.2.

39. GR to DH, Jan. 12, 1940, HFP Box 3.2. John graduated with a BA in modern languages.

40. GR to Marj Trumbull, Sept. 8, 1938, HFP Box 3.2.

41. Reichard, "Assimilation or Extinction?" n.d. [c. 1934], RP Box 4.9.

42. GR to Gildersleeve, Dec. 6, 1938, HFP Box 3.2.

43. GR to RH, May 9, 1938, HFP Box 3.2.

44. Reichard, "Fifty Thousand Sign Posts," *New Mexico*, Mar. 19, 1939, 32–33.

45. The original broadcast, "Attractions around Gallup, New Mexico," took place on Sunday, April 30, 1939, 5:15 PM Eastern Time. A transcript appears in HFP Box 3.3.

46. GR to DH and RH, Feb. 28, 1939, HFP Box 3.2. No copy of the twenty-page scenario, which told of a Wiyot woman's experience of the Indian Island Massacre of 1860, survives.

47. GR to RH, May 8, 1939, HFP Box 3.2.

48. GR to RH, Mar. 9, 1937, HFP (AZ 375) Box 69.

49. GR to DH, July 10, 1938, HFP Box 3.2.

50. GR to FB, July 9, 1937, FBP.

51. GR to DH, July 10, 1938, HFP Box 3.2.

52. GR to DH and RH, Mar. 13, 1939, HFP Box 3.2. Reichard refers to Oliver La Farge and his successful attempts to dramatize Navajo concepts.

53. AB to GR, n.d. [c. 1940], RP Box 1.7.

54. GR to DH and RH, n.d. [c. Feb. 1939], HFP Box 3.2.

55. Reichard, *Dezba*, 142.

56. Ibid., 145–46.

57. GR to DH and RH, n.d. [c. Feb. 1939], HFP Box 3.2.

58. AB to GR, n.d. [c. 1940], RP Box 1.7.

59. RH to GR, May 5, 1939, HFP Box 3.2.

60. GR to RH, May 8, 1939, HFP Box 3.2.

61. DH and RH to GR, Mar. 18, 1939, HFP Box 3.2.

62. Reichard, "Parsons," 45.

63. Ibid., 47.

64. Reichard, "*Mitla, Town of Souls* by Elsie Clews Parsons."

65. Reichard, "Parsons," 48.

66. GR to ECP, May 9, 1939, EPP.

67. Reichard, "Parsons," 48.

68. Deacon, *Elsie Clews Parsons*, 352–53.

69. Zumwalt, *Wealth and Rebellion*, 164. Reichard makes scant reference to the search in her letters to Parsons. It may be a reflection of how happy she was at Barnard that there's no record of her expressing a desire to replace Boas herself.

70. Ibid., 163. Mead thought Benedict's personality unsuitable for such a high-profile position. She preferred her own husband, British anthropologist Gregory Bateson, for the post (Lapsley, *Ruth Benedict and Margaret Mead*, 257).

71. Lapsley, *Ruth Benedict and Margaret Mead*, 258–59.

72. GR to ECP, n.d. [June 1939], EPP.

73. GR to ECP, Aug. 3, 1939, EPP.

74. GR to DH and RH, Aug. 12, 1939, HFP Box 3.2.

75. Zumwalt, *Wealth and Rebellion*, 316. Of the sixteen memoir volumes Parsons funded, she wrote seven.

76. Ibid.

77. GR to ECP, Mar. 7, 1933, EPP.

78. Zumwalt, *Wealth and Rebellion*, 319.

79. GR to ECP, Feb. 25, 1934, EPP.

80. GR to FB, July 21, 1936, FBP.

81. GR to ECP, Aug. 11, 1940, EPP.

82. Caffrey, *Ruth Benedict*, 280.

83. Lapsley, *Ruth Benedict and Margaret Mead*, 257. Lapsley relates, pace Zumwalt (Wealth and Rebellion, 216), that Benedict handed the concordance off to Erna Gunther in the 1930s. Gunther then sat on it for several years before Boas demanded she send it back to Benedict for publication through the Folklore Society. Parsons spent more than $2,000 on the botched project, nearly $30,000 in 2015 terms. It was never published.

84. Archer Taylor quoted in Null et al., "Journal's Editors," 30–31.

85. ECP to Carl Voegelin, Feb. 25, 1940, EPP. Among those present to elect Reichard editor were then-secretary-treasurer George Herzog, Boas, Ann Gayton, Linton, Bunzel, Parsons, Herskovits, and AFS president A. Irving Hallowell. It is generally believed that Reichard was elected because Gayton declined the nomination (Zumwalt, *Wealth and Rebellion*, 317). Reichard's correspondence refutes that story. The journal's acronym was originally *JAFL*.

86. ECP to GR, Feb. 25, 1940, EPP.

87. Zumwalt, *Wealth and Rebellion*, 324.

88. GR to ECP, Sept. 13, 1940, EPP.

89. Null et al., "Journal's Editors," 29–30; GR to ECP, Oct. 2, 1940, EPP.

90. GR to ECP, June 26, 1941, EPP.

91. GR to ECP, July 14, 1941, EPP; GR to ECP, Aug. 2, 1941, EPP.

92. GR to DH and RH, April 3, 1938, HFP Box 3.2.

93. DH and RH to GR, May 6, 1938, HFP Box 3.2.

94. "An Adventurous Lady," *Abingtonian*, n.d. [c. 1938] (newspaper clipping), RP Box 3.4.

95. Mead quoted in Darnell, *Edward Sapir*, 395.

96. GR to DH and RH, May 28, 1940, HFP Box 3.3.

8. GHASTLY STUFF

1. Lapsley, *Ruth Benedict and Margaret Mead*, 272.

2. GR to FB, Dec. 28, 1938, FBP.

3. Reichard, *Spider Woman*, 274–75.

4. Lapsley, *Ruth Benedict and Margaret Mead*, 270; GR to ECP, Jan. 7, 1939, EPP.

5. GR to ECP, March 14, 1935, EPP.

6. Lapsley, *Ruth Benedict and Margaret Mead*, 271. Lapsley expresses disappointment at Mead's other reaction to Edward's death: relief. Though Mead and Sapir were briefly romantically involved in the mid-1920s, Sapir turned on Mead after she ended the affair. In 1929 Sapir wrote Benedict, "[Mead] is hardly a person to

me at all, . . . but a symbol of everything I detest most in American culture" (ibid., 193). In light of Sapir's volatility, Mead seems to have been justifiably afraid of him.

7. Zumwalt, *Wealth and Rebellion*, 330.

8. Deacon, *Elsie Clews Parsons*, 378.

9. Zumwalt, *Wealth and Rebellion*, 329–30. Reichard's letter to Kroeber, dated Dec. 19, 1941, once appeared in the A. L. Kroeber Papers at the Bancroft Library, UC Berkeley (CU 23 Box 125). An unsuccessful internal search for this letter in 2015–17 led to the conclusion that all previously archived correspondence between Reichard and Kroeber has been missing from the Kroeber Papers since at least the early 2000s.

10. Parsons, "Anthropology and Prediction," 339, 338.

11. Ibid., 343–44.

12. Boas, "Anthropologist's Credo," 203.

13. Zumwalt, *Wealth and Rebellion*, 330, 335.

14. Ibid., 330.

15. See Mead, *Culture and Commitment: A Study of the Generation Gap* (1970). Price provides a detailed picture of the 1941 AAA meetings, the personnel involved, and the arguments made in favor of the war resolution (*Anthropological Intelligence*, 20–22). Mead was not the only advocate of "weaponizing anthropology" at the meeting, but she was at the vanguard of nationalist anthropology from 1940 until the start of the Cold War (ibid., 220; See also Mandler, *Return From the Natives*).

16. Mead, *Culture and Commitment*, 61.

17. The posthumous publication of Mead's personal correspondence reveals she had an odd obsession with Reichard (see, for example, Lapsley's *Ruth Benedict and Margaret Mead* for dream sequences Mead recorded with Reichard as villain). Underhill reports Reichard was mum about her differences with Mead, although the two appeared to be "smeared with repellent" for one another at Columbia seminars where Mead demanded "reverence" from her hearers (*Anthropologist's Arrival*, 152, 141).

18. Addams, *Second Twenty Years*, 202.

19. Ibid., 220, 202.

20. Goldfrank, *Notes*, 151, 152–53.

21. Ibid., 123.

22. GR to DH and RH, Sept. 22, 1942, HFP Box 3.2.

23. Lewis, "Passion of Franz Boas," 456.

24. On the day Boas died, Reichard was living in her 116th Street apartment, a short walk from the Faculty Club. Though she is not listed as present at the luncheon in accounts written by the men who were, it seems likely she would have attended the meeting Boas arranged in honor of French anthropologist Paul Rivet.

25. Bunzel, "Gladys A. Reichard," 8.

26. Handler, "Vigorous Male," 150.

27. Benedict, *Patterns of Culture*, 53.

28. Given the intensely rivalrous atmosphere in Navajo studies during the '30s and '40s, it is probable that Bitanny was discredited by some as a linguistic informant and student at UNM and on the Navajo Reservation simply because he was Reichard's primary research partner.

29. AB to GR, Jan. 15, 1939, RP Box 1.4.

30. GR to DH, Jan. 12, 1940, HFP Box 3.3.

31. AB to GR, n.d. [1939/40], RP Box 1.7.

32. Young, "Written Navajo," 3–4.

33. AB to GR, April 18, 1940, RP Box 1.4.

34. Ibid.

35. GR to ECP, July 20, 1940, EPP.

36. AB to GR, Sept. 28, 1940, RP Box 1.4.

37. AB to GR, Oct. 12, 1942, RP Box 1.4.

38. Reichard was the only woman to make anthropological linguistics a primary focus of her academic career until Mary Haas earned a PhD in linguistics under Sapir at Yale in 1935.

39. Voegelin and Voegelin, "History of Structuralizing," 16, 15.

40. Falk, *Women, Language and Linguistics,* 5–6.

41. Stephen Murray quoted in Ibid., 7.

42. Ibid., 21–22. After serving in various executive offices, Hahn was elected president in 1946. Haas became LSA vice president in 1956 and president in 1963.

43. Murray, "Interview with Mary R. Haas," 702.

44. Falk, *Women, Language and Linguistics,* 21.

45. According to the Voegelins, the "eclipsing stance" holds that linguistic science advances by abandoning previous methods of analysis, while the "incremental stance" relies on "the gradual sharpening and differentiation of hitherto blurred notions" ("History of Structuralizing," 12–13).

46. Hockett, "Review of *Handbook of American Indian Languages 3,*" 54.

47. Jacobs, "Review of *Handbook of American Indian Languages 3,*" 97.

48. GR to DH and RH, Jan. 26, 1942, HFP Box 3.3.

49. Reichard, *Navaho Religion,* 14.

50. GR to DH and RH, Jan. 26, 1942, HFP Box 3.3.

51. Goodwin, *No Ordinary Time,* 339.

52. GR to ECP, June 23, 1941, EPP.

53. Goodwin, *No Ordinary Time,* 270.

54. Westerlund, *Arizona's War Town,* 27–28, 47.

55. For the important role Navajo women played in resisting the Indian Bureau's disastrous stock reduction program, see Martha Weisiger, "Gendered Injustice," 2007.

56. Roessel and Johnson, *Navajo Livestock Reduction,* 172, 153.

57. Philp, *Collier's Crusade,* 192, 194.

58. Westerlund, *Arizona's War Town,* 100–101.

59. Mandler, *Return From the Natives,* 199.

60. Price, *Anthropological Intelligence*, 25, 37.

61. Ibid., 35, 30.

62. Goldfrank, *Notes*, 197.

63. Price, *Anthropological Intelligence*, 143. Price notes as many as 110,000 Americans of Japanese descent were interned during World War II. The U.S. Supreme Court declared these internments legal in *Korematsu v. United States* on December 18, 1944.

64. See Price, *Anthropological Intelligence*, 147–54.

65. GR to FB, Aug. 10, 1939, FBP.

66. Reichard and Bitanny, "Agentive and Causative Elements in Navajo," 1–2.

67. Edward Sapir quoted in Dinwoodie, "Textuality and the Voice of Informants," 166.

68. Ibid., 185–86.

69. The last issue of *IJAL* Boas edited was that for 1939, volume 10, numbers 1–3. After a hiatus, volume 10, number 4 came out in 1944 under the editorship of Carl Voegelin.

70. GR to ECP, July 20, 1940, EPP. J. J. Augustin subsequently published "Agentive and Causative Elements in Navajo" as a pamphlet. Bitanny's last name was misspelled as "Bittany" on its baby-blue cover. No second edition was printed, and the error went uncorrected. Produced outside the peer-review process, the article was ignored until leading Athabascanist Michael Krauss deemed it "'significant'" and acknowledged it as "the only serious systematic attempt . . . [as of 1973] at describing the derivational prefix system of the [Navajo] verb . . . or for that matter, of any other Athapaskan language" (Krauss quoted in Falk, *Women, Languages, and Linguistics*, 153–54). Krauss is no admirer of Reichard or her Navajo linguistics. In a 1986 recap of Sapir's work on Athabascan, Krauss asserts that the "always jealous" Reichard was to blame for a "rift" over Navajo orthography that did "severe and long-lasting" damage to Athabascan linguistics (Krauss, "Edward Sapir," 165–66). Under Hoijer's influence, Krauss became the standard-bearer of his generation of Athabascanists for anti-Reichard propaganda.

71. Hoijer's later prominence combined with his relentless "condemnation of Reichard's linguistic work on Navajo" during her lifetime allowed him to "literally wr[i]te Gladys Reichard out of the history of the study of Native American languages" after her death (Falk, *Women, Languages, and Linguistics*, 150, 161).

72. Reichard, "Reply to Hoijer," 193, 195, 196.

73. Ibid., 195–96.

74. CK to GR, Feb. 24 [1947], RP Box 3.5. Perhaps as a response to Reichard's astute "Reply," Hoijer took a different tack when he reviewed her *Prayer the Compulsive Word* (1944). He refrained from making specific criticisms, but called Reichard's presentation "unsystematized and anecdotal." Hoijer's supercilious tone turned sarcastic when he closed with the "hope" that Reichard's "forthcoming treatise on Navaho religion will give to those of us who are amateurs" the background necessary to understand her analyses (Hoijer, *"Prayer the Compulsive Word,"* 97, 98).

75. GR to ECP, July 20, 1940, EPP.

76. Ibid.

77. Lyon, "Ednishodi Yazhe," 28–29. Sapir, puritanical about sex as he was, may have been alluding to rumors that Kluckhohn engaged in sexual relationships with Navajo men while conducting fieldwork on the reservation. The allegations found their way into a FBI file kept on Kluckhohn during and after the war (Mandler, *Return From the Natives*, 216).

78. Reichard, "Translation of Two Navaho Chant Words," 424.

79. Reichard, "Review of *Origin Legend of the Navaho Enemy Way*," 141.

80. In 1943 Reichard wrote a sharply critical review of Haile's *Origin Legend of the Navaho Flintway* in which she called his introduction "confused," "obscure" and out of date (Reichard, "*Navaho Flintway*," 384–85). Her objections lose the taint of retribution when they are compared to separate reviews of *Flintway* by Kluckhohn and Wyman. Both men take Haile to task for overlooking "innumerable" inexcusable typographic errors that "sometimes actually reverse the meaning" of his translations (Wyman, "*Navaho Flintway*," 365).

81. CK to BH, Oct. 3, 1942, BHP Box 3a.4.

82. Haile, "Navajo Upward Reaching Way," 308, 311; GR to Underhill, Feb. 19, 1945, BL. The "Way Boys" included Haile and other mythographers who preferred "way" to "chant" in the English translation of Navajo ceremonial names.

83. Reichard's assessment of Hoijer's modus operandi was later echoed by MIT graduate Richard Stanley, a specialist in the phonology of the Navajo verb, who criticized Hoijer's 1967 grammar of Navajo as "offering 'few new insights,' neither 'sophisticated' nor 'revealing,' and 'a disappointment'" (Falk, *Women, Languages, and Linguistics*, 150).

84. Reichard, "Review of *Language, Culture and Personality*," 505–6.

85. Ibid., 506.

86. Ibid., 507.

87. CK to GR, Nov. 12, 1943, RP Box 3.5.

88. GR to L. Wyman, n.d. [c. late 1943], RP Box 3.5.

89. Ibid.

90. GR to CK, Nov. 17, 1943, RP Box 3.5. Reichard wrote by hand on the letter in question, "written but not sent."

91. Reichard, *Prayer*, 10.

9. UNDERSTANDING

1. "Butler and Erskine Make Speeches at University's Opening Exercises," *Columbia Daily Spectator*, Sept. 26, 1919. The beauty of Erskine's speech masked his deep-seated male chauvinism, which excluded women from his utopian campus (Rosenberg, *Changing the Subject*, 159).

2. Marian Smith ("Reichard," 914) reports that Reichard was secretary of Section H (Anthropology) of the AAAS during 1945.

3. Alice Fletcher, Parsons, Louise Pound, and Martha Beckwith preceded Reichard as AFS president.

4. See "55th Annual Council Meeting," *JAF*.

5. "Prof. Reichard Tells of Life of Navahos," *BB*, Dec. 12, 1933.

6. Reichard, "Craftsmanship and Folklore," 195–96.

7. Paul Zolbrod to author, personal communication, April 9, 2014. Professor Zolbrod is the author-translator of *Diné bahane': The Navajo Creation Story* (1984). In the 1970s, Zolbrod drew on Reichard's Navajo papers at the Museum of Northern Arizona and typed his notes using the portable typewriter Reichard had altered to type Navajo and Salishan phonetic characters. Reichard's typewriter remains in its well-traveled case at the MNA library.

8. Reichard, *Prayer the Compulsive Word*, 56.

9. Ibid., 1.

10. RH to LCE, April 25, 1944, HFP Box 1.2.

11. GR to "Anyone interested in using linguistic texts," n.d. [summer 1944], HCP Series 1–240.

12. LCE to DH, Nov. 8, 1944, HFP Box 1.2.

13. William L. Laurence, "Eyewitness Account of Atomic Bomb Over Nagasaki," *New York Times*, Sept. 9, 1945. Laurence misidentified the plane carrying the Fat Man bomb as *The Great Artiste*. Instead it was *The Bockscar*.

14. Elsie McIlroy, "Dr. Gladys A. Reichard—The Pollen of Dawn Has Instructed Her," 1, RP Box 5.2. No published version of the interview has been found.

15. Ibid., 10. Reichard refers to Boas's 1908 paper "Decorative Designs of Alaskan Needle-cases: A Study in the History of Conventional Designs, Based on Materials in the U.S. National Museum," in which Boas argues that the artistic impulses and achievements of the best "primitive" artists are no different in kind from those of "civilized" western European virtuosos.

16. Mandler, *Return from the Natives*, 188, 190. Mandler quotes from a letter Mead wrote to husband Gregory Bateson dated Aug. 15, 1945.

17. Price, *Anthropological Intelligence*, 27.

18. MM to Caroline Kelly, Aug. 12, 1945, in Caffrey and Francis, eds., *Cherish the Life*, 300–301.

19. Price, *Anthropological Intelligence*, 265. The impulse to punish those like Reichard who refused to condone the AAA's wartime ambitions traveled in the opposite direction predicted by Mead. Reichard remained a member of the AAA for the rest of her life, but staunch war anthropologists with pull in the group like Mead, Alfred Kroeber, Fred Eggan, and Ralph Beals joined Sapirians in shaping Reichard's reputation as representative of everything they detested about Franz Boas: his self-restraint, his liberal social philosophy, and, most of all, his pacifism.

20. Ibid., 272.

21. Mead, *Anthropologist at Work*, 435. Benedict spent the war in Washington, D.C. at the Office of War Information's Division of Foreign Morale waging "white" or non-classified psychological warfare from her desk. Her success in that role

accounts for her receiving an ONR grant of $90,000 over three years to launch the Columbia Research Center.

22. Ibid., 434, 436.

23. Mandler, *Return from the Natives*, 198.

24. Benedict's abbreviated term in the AAA's highest office has been used as proof that she was the target of sexual discrimination even at the height of her career. Caffrey explains that Benedict's term ended after only six months only because the AAA reorganized itself and the duties of its officers at the start of 1947. Benedict had the option of running for a full term as president but declined to do so. She told Mead, "I was chosen as a person to fill a position of honor," while AAA offices after 1946 were intended to be filled by those "chosen to carry out a job" (Caffrey, *Ruth Benedict*, 332–33). Clyde Kluckhohn served out the last six months of Benedict's one-year term.

25. Reichard, *Coeur d'Alene Indian Myths*, 3.

26. Ibid., 1–2. For the beginnings of the "cultural revival" on the Coeur d'Alene Reservation in the 1930s, see Brinkman, *Etsmeystkhw* (chapter 3). Lawrence Nicodemus played a key role in the grassroots movement to revive use of Coeur d'Alene language, as did Pascal George.

27. Wilson, "Deeper Necessity," 157.

28. Reichard, *Coeur d'Alene Indian Myths*, 48–49, 53.

29. Ibid., 38–39. Another unusual feature of *Coeur d'Alene Indian Myths* is Reichard's inclusion of comparative notes made by her former student, Adele Froehlich (Barnard '31). Reichard credits Froehlich on the book's title page but does not indicate where Froehlich's text begins and ends relative to her own. Froehlich, a German major, assisted Reichard with the preparation of *Spider Woman* and Thelma Adamson with *Folk-tales of the Coast Salish*, both published in 1934. After graduation, Froehlich continued to reside in Brooklyn, where she founded and ran a children's sports program in Prospect Park. She became a local legend before her death in 1980. (All information about Froehlich's postgraduate life was kindly provided by William Seaburg in 2016.)

30. Reichard, *Navaho Religion*, 171–72.

31. Ibid., 406–7.

32. Ibid., 413, 408–9, 413, 411.

33. Reichard, "Human Nature," 360.

34. Mandler, *Return from the Natives*, 224–25.

35. Reichard, "*The Navaho* by Clyde Kluckhohn and Dorothea Leighton," 287.

36. Kluckhohn and Leighton, *The Navaho*, 293–94. Kluckhohn let it be widely known that he wrote *The Navaho*, while Leighton was merely a consulting research partner.

37. Ibid., 294.

38. Ibid., 179, 294.

39. Ibid., 303, 306–7.

40. Reichard, "Cultural Influences on Behavior," 8–9, RP Box 4.6.

41. Reichard, "Goals and Methods," 29, RP Box 4.1.

42. Ibid., 29–30

43. Reichard, "Elsie Clews Parsons," 46.

44. "Connolly to Discuss Discrimination Tuesday," *BB*, Feb. 24, 1947; "Reasons for Prejudice Subject of Forum Talk," *BB*, Mar. 4, 1947.

45. "Hidden Talents of Faculty Are Revealed at Hobby Show," *BB*, Mar. 10, 1947.

46. Katherine Harvey to GR, Nov. 18, 1946, RP Box 3.8. Reichard consulted with Clyde Kluckhohn and Roman Hubbell on the estimate. Backed by Hubbell's judgment, Reichard appraised the collection at $50,000 and signed affidavits to that effect in 1947 (Harvey to GR, Nov. 29, 1947, same location). Kluckhohn recommended a valuation of $5,000, which Reichard ignored.

47. AB to GR, May 13, 1947, RP Box 1.4.

48. "Sidelights Given by Dr. Reichard," *Arizona Times*, Nov. 22, 1947.

49. GR to DH, Sept. 7, 1940, HFP Box 3.3.

50. HC to GR, May 11, 1939, HCP Series 1–240.

51. H. Colton, "Museum of Northern Arizona," 61.

52. Reichard, "Protection in War: *Where the Two Came to Their Father: A Navaho War Ceremonial* by Maud Oakes, commentary by Joseph Campbell," *New York Herald Tribune Books*, June 18, 1944.

53. Adair, "*Dezba, Woman of the Desert*," 500.

54. John Adair to GR, Jan. 12, 1948, RP Box 3.1. The paper Adair mentions may have been one Reichard presented at a conference held at UNM that winter. As with most papers Reichard gave at conferences after 1940, no print version of the paper has been found.

55. See Iverson, *Diné: A History of the Navajos*, 188–94.

56. "Indian Assn. Head Urges Aid for Navajo Now," *Gallup Independent*, Dec. 2, 1947. Oklahoma District Judge and president of the National Congress of American Indians W. B. Johnson labeled the crisis "a national disgrace."

57. "President Seeks Winter Relief; Long Range Plan," *Gallup Independent*, Dec. 2, 1947.

58. "Communicated: Navajo Veteran Cites Discrimination Against Tribe, Lack of Progress," *Gallup Independent*, Dec. 30, 1947, 3. Collier resigned from a decimated Indian Bureau in 1946. During the war, all bureau offices but his were banished to Chicago to make room in D.C. for the white-collar war machine.

59. Reichard, "Reichard Communications No. 1, January 4, 1948: The Vote for the Navajo Indians," RP Box 3.11.

60. Ibid.

61. John Adair to GR, n.d. [c. Jan. 1948], RP Box 3.11.

62. Ibid.

63. Fergusson, *Our Southwest*, 214.

64. Philp, *John Collier's Crusade*, 238.

65. CK to GR, Jan. 12, 1948, RP Box 3.11.

66. Barry Goldwater to GR, Jan. 12, 1948, RP Box 3.11.

67. Ethel Cutler Freeman to GR, Jan. 12, 1948, RP Box 3.11.

68. No copy of Reichard's "Reichard Communication No. 2: Navajo Indian Problems" is preserved in her papers at the Museum of Northern Arizona.

69. GR to John R. Nichols, Mar. 12, 1948, RP Box 3.11.

70. Nichols to GR, Mar. 15, 1948, RP Box 3.11.

71. GR to Nichols, Mar. 12, 1948, RP Box 3.11.

72. Ickes, "'Justice' in a Deep Freeze," 17.

10. CITIZENS CEMETERY

1. Unable to meet student demand for the new major in addition to her other campus duties, Reichard shuttered the linguistics major after just two years.

2. GR to McIntosh, Feb. 21, 1948, BA.

3. McIntosh, "Today's Young Women," Nov. 14, 1953.

4. Gildersleeve, *Many a Good Crusade*, 108, 109.

5. For example, McIntosh aggressively promoted Mirra Komarovsky, author of the 1950 longitudinal study *Women in the Modern World*, through the Barnard ranks. Komarovsky's book revealed the deep discontentment expressed by Barnard alumnae who became full-time wives and mothers—feelings alien to women like Reichard, McIntosh, and Gildersleeve—more than a decade before Betty Friedan triggered widespread discussion of "the problem that has no name." Late-century feminists would judge that McIntosh was afflicted by "incomplete feminism" for, among other things, not intervening in the case of another younger scholar, Gene Weltfish, Reichard's former Barnard assistant. Weltfish's adjunct teaching position at Columbia was always tenuous owing to her open political activism. In 1953 Weltfish was not rehired at Columbia, ostensibly for lack of funds and allegedly for promoting "Red feminism," the archenemy of the House Un-American Activities Committee (Rosenberg, *Changing the Subject*, 5, 216, 203–4).

6. Duncan Strong to McIntosh, Jan. 20, 1950, BA.

7. CK to McIntosh, Feb. 23, 1950, BA.

8. Price, *Anthropological Intelligence*, 31.

9. CK to GR, May 9, 1947, RP Box 3.5.

10. CK to GR, Feb. 24 [1948], RP Box 3.5.

11. D. B. Stout to McIntosh, Feb. 23, 1950, BA.

12. McIntosh to GR, Dec. 20, 1950, BA.

13. McIntosh to GR, n.d. [c. Oct. 1952], BA.

14. GR to McIntosh, Oct. 7, 1952, BA. Reichard referred to the modest stipend she received for writing an interpretive brochure for a sandpainting-themed mural, "The Desert Goes to Sea," commissioned for the cocktail lounge of the *SS United States*.

15. Bouquet, "Review #226," 143.

16. Gillmor, "Review of *Navaho Religion*," 474.

17. Bailey, "Review of *Navaho Religion*," 436.

18. Wheelwright, "Symbol, Metaphor, and Myth," 697–98.

19. Wyman reviewed *Navaho Religion* tepidly. After reminding readers that Reichard was not the only noted student of the Navajo, Wyman conceded, "Dr. Reichard has written a book with the objectivity of a scientist, but not a cold objectivity, rather she writes with warm sympathy and often with humor." (Wyman, "*Navaho Religion*," 524). Flora Bailey's praise, though sober, was less muted. "The format of these volumes is most pleasing and because Dr. Reichard writes fluently, expressing herself accurately and colorfully with frequent touches of humor, there is pleasant as well as informative reading here." (Bailey, "Review of *Navaho Religion*," 436).

20. Reichard, Notes for "Education Among American Indians," read Mar. 9, 1952, RP Box 7.6.

21. "Reichard To Speak To College Women In Paris, England," *BB*, Mar. 6, 1952.

22. Flora Bailey to HC, Mar. 12, 1952, HCP Series 1–29.

23. GR to HC, Oct. 7, 1952, HCP Series 1–240.

24. As an archeology student in Duncan Strong's Anthropology Department at Columbia, Woodbury was encouraged to view Reichard as stubbornly out of touch with the latest trends in her discipline. Although Woodbury never completed her doctoral degree, she was known to be sharply critical of senior scholars like Reichard whose attitudes and work Woodbury deemed old-fashioned or uninformed (Katherine Bartlett interview by Sara Smith, Jan. 25, 1989, KBP Box 4.4).

25. GR to McIntosh, Oct. 27, 1953, BA.

26. Reichard was elected to the museum's board in 1949 and again in 1953.

27. Olberding, "Telling the Story," 21.

28. The Joint Committee was a revival of the Linguistic Committee headed by Boas, Sapir, and Bloomfeld. Postwar, it was under the auspices of the LSA, the AAA, and the American Council of Learned Societies. Leeds-Hurwitz, "Committee on Research," 154.

29. GR to HC, Oct. 23, 1952, HCP Series 2–272. Reichard included a copy of her memorandum with her letter.

30. Reichard, "Ethnology at the Museum of Northern Arizona," [transcript of speech given Aug. 22, 1953], RP Box 5.9.

31. HC to GR, Dec. 9, 1949, HCP Series 2–189.

32. See *The Life of Harold Sellers Colton*, by Jimmy H. Miller (1991), for a portrait of Colton as a thoroughly privileged "proper Philadelphian" who nevertheless opened his Arizona museum and research center to anyone with good moral character and sincere scientific interests. Harold was a serious scientist and administrator but he was also a devoted spouse and father. In the 1950s, his ability to pursue new initiatives at the museum was severely limited by the time needed to cope with Mrs. Colton's worsening dementia.

33. Largely inactive after 1954, the college fund was dissolved and its meager assets donated to Arizona State Teachers College at Flagstaff in 1957.

34. HC to GR, Feb. 3, 1953, HCP Series 1–240.

35. GR to HC, Jan. 12, 1953, HCP Series 1–240. The real estate scheme was later abandoned.

36. McIntosh to GR, Mar. 31, 1954, BA.

37. GR to McIntosh, April 1, 1954, BA.

38. McIntosh to GR, June 16, 1954, BA.

39. "Prof. Reichard Plans Further Navajo Study," *BB*, June 1, 1954.

40. Reichard, "A Comparison of Five Salish Languages I," 295.

41. Reichard, "Cultural Influences on Behavior," 1a, RP Box 4.6.

42. Voegelin and Voegelin, "History of Structuralizing," 14.

43. Reichard, *Navaho Grammar*, 2.

44. Ibid., 4, 5, 10–11.

45. Trager, "*Navaho Grammar*," 429.

46. Hoijer, "*Navaho Grammar*," 83.

47. Landes, "Review #175," 125.

48. Jacobs, "*Navaho Grammar*," 306.

49. Reichard, "Ethnology and the Navajo Language," n.d. [c. 1954], RP Box 4.2.

50. Ibid.

51. Trager, "*Navaho Grammar*," 429.

52. "History of the International Linguistics Association," http://hallidaycentre .cityu.edu.hk/ila/index.aspx.

53. Falk reports that Reichard gave a paper at the LSA annual meeting in 1944 (*Women, Language and Linguistics*, 167). There's no evidence that Reichard ever attended any of the LSA summer Linguistic Institutes, where younger linguists went to express their solidarity with "pure" linguistic structuralism and thus brand themselves "real" linguists.

54. GR to HC, Oct. 23, 1952, (excerpt from GR's letter to Joint Committee on American Linguistics, n.d., enclosed), HCP Series1–240.

55. DH interview by Lawrence Kelly, 1979, HUTR #73.

56. Hartwell, "White Brother of the Navajo," 64–65.

57. Powers, *Navajo Trading*, 116.

58. Cottam, *Hubbell Trading Post*, 216–19.

59. Iverson, *Diné*, 217.

60. Hartwell, "White Brother of the Navajo," 64.

61. M. L. Woodard, Secretary of the United Indian Traders Association to Nebraska Senator Burton K. Wheeler, Feb. 25, 1939 in Iverson, *Diné*, 171.

62. RH to R. G. Harris, April 2, 1948 in Cottam, *Hubbell Trading Post*, 214.

63. GR to John Nichols, Mar. 27, 1948, RP Box 3.11.

64. Ibid.

65. GR to HC, April 6, 1948, HCP Series 1–240.

66. Fillmore, *Shadows on the Mesa*, 223.

67. Ibid., 217.

68. The finding aid for the Adee Dodge Papers held at the Beinecke Rare Books

and Manuscripts Library states that Bitanny/Dodge (1912–92) opened a uranium prospecting company, Adee Dodge Enterprises, Inc., in the 1950s. I discovered the existence of the Dodge Papers too late to corroborate or refute Adee's claims about his post-1941 experiences. Dodge may have completed his undergraduate degree at UNM in the 1950s, but the Columbia law degree is almost certainly a fiction.

69. Donovan, "Adee Dodge Defends Medicine Men," *Navajo Times*, Jan. 2, 2014.

70. McNickle, *Indian Man*, 150–51.

71. Iverson, *Diné*, 188.

72. Reichard, "Reichard Communications No. 3, May 20, 1948: The Navajo and Their Language," RP Box. 3.11.

73. Young, "Written Navajo: A Brief History," 4. Young emphasizes that prior to Collier's appointment to the Indian Bureau, Navajo literacy efforts were not supported by the federal government. The shift away from "de-Indianization," a hallmark of the Indian New Deal, created an atmosphere more conducive to recognizing the links between literacy and self-governance, a connection Reichard made in her Hogan School in 1934. Appended to Young's report is the abstract of Wayne Stanley Holm's dissertation. The abstract begins, "Navajo has been written, in various forms, for more than a century." Holm's research was designed to determine if a standard practical orthography for Navajo might dispense with diacritics and symbols indicating length, tone, or nasality. Reichard's flexible attitude regarding a practical orthography for Navajo is vindicated by Holm's finding "that any phonemic contrast can be omitted in a practical orthography." Holm tested a non-phonemic spelling system with Navajo speakers and discovered that a simplified set of spelling characters increased learner interest and facility in written Navajo. The "ultimate test" of a non-phonemic orthography was, in Holm's view, "acceptance—or rejection—of such an orthography by Navajo decision-makers" (ibid., 13).

74. DH interview with Frank McNitt, 1972, HUTR #72.

75. GR to DH, Mar. 13, 1955, HFP Box 3.3.

76. David Aberle to GR, April 29, 1955, RP Box 3.5.

77. Sol Tax to GR, May 20, 1955, RP Box 4.7.

78. Leslie Spier to GR, May 16, 1955, RP Box 4.6.

79. GR to HC, Feb. 2, 1954, HCP Series 1–240.

80. R. Woodbury, *60 Years*, 231.

81. Wayne Dennis to GR, July 6, 1955, RP Box 4.1.

82. L. Reichard to McIntosh, July 25, 1955, BA.

83. Kluckhohn and Leighton, *The Navaho*, 314.

84. Reichard, *Dezba*, 127–28.

EPILOGUE

1. Margaret Holland to Mrs. Law [McIntosh's secretary], Aug. 23, 1955, BA.

2. McIntosh to L. Reichard, Sept. 13, 1955, BA.

3. L. Reichard to McIntosh, Dec. 7, 1955, BA.

4. De Laguna, "Gladys Reichard," 10.

5. De Laguna to McIntosh, Nov. 27, 1955, BA.

6. McIntosh to de Laguna, Jan. 3, 1956, BA.

7. Given Mead's disaffection for Reichard and her work, the opportunity the memorial gave her to promote her lover's career may explain why she agreed to speak at Reichard's memorial.

8. Mead, "Commitment," 26-27.

9. C. Voegelin to H. Colton, Feb. 13, 1956 HCP Series 1.

10. "Gladys A. Reichard, 1893–1955," *Plateau* 28 (1955): 48.

11. H. Colton to John Aubuchon, Aug. 29, 1955, HCP Series 1. MNA records do not confirm that the diorama was mounted.

12. H. Colton to C. Voegelin, Feb. 24, 1956, HCP Series 1. Colton did draft an obituary for *IJAL* anyway, but it was never published.

13. Reichard, *Navaho Grammar*, 11.

14. Mead's brief but dismissive caricature of Reichard in *An Anthropologist at Work: Writings of Ruth Benedict* (1959) became the cornerstone of the narrative that paints Reichard as an unoriginal thinker who subordinated herself blindly to Boas. The gendered, marginalizing accounts that populate the secondary literature on Reichard today often aim to restore Reichard's reputation in anthropology or linguistics. Uncritical as these accounts typically are of Mead's biases, they tend instead to repeat bad data and spread the malicious gossip offered by men hostile to Reichard's memory for extra-scientific reasons.

15. Reichard, "Parsons Collection," 308.

16. Goldfrank, *Notes*, 211.

17. N. Woodbury to Edward Danson, Oct. 11, 1961, WP MS 294-C-1. Flo Voegelin was the only colleague who ensured posthumous publication of a Reichard manuscript, "A Comparison of Five Salish Languages."

18. "Unique College Classroom Honors Former Bangorian," *Daily News*, April 1, 1960.

19. "Gladys A. Reichard Anthropology Room," [program pamphlet], April 5, 1960, BA.

20. McIntosh retired to her Massachusetts farm and lived to be 102. On her death in 2001 she was remembered in the *New York Times* as "ahead of her times" for urging Barnard students to balance family and career for the sake of a well-rounded life and a healthier society ("Millicent McIntosh, 102, Dies," *New York Times*, Jan. 5, 2001).

21. Reichard, *Navaho Religion* (2nd. ed.), xv–xxvi, xvii.

22. Ibid., xvi, xxvii.

23. T. M. Pierce, Historian-Archivist, New Mexico Folklore Society to Records Office, Barnard College, June 11, 1974, BA.

24. Martha Peterson to L. Reichard, June 20, 1974, BA.

25. "Gladys A. Reichard Anthropology Room," [program pamphlet], April 5, 1960, BA.

SELECTED WRITINGS
OF GLADYS A. REICHARD

"Literary Types and Dissemination of Myth." *JAF* 34, no. 133 (1921): 269–307.

"The Complexity of Rhythm in Decorative Art." *AA* 24, no. 2 (April–June 1922): 183–204.

Field Notebooks on Wiyot Indians 1922–23, Volumes 1–3. (Viewable through Bancroft Library Digital Manuscripts Collection, University of California).

Wiyot Grammar and Texts. In *University of California Publications in American Archeology and Ethnology* 22, no. 1 (Jan. 1925): 1–215.

"Wiyot: An Indian language of Northern California." *American Speech* 1, no. 12 (Sept. 1926): 654–58.

Social Life of the Navajo Indians. New York: Columbia University, 1928.

"Form and Interpretation in American Art." In *Proceedings of 23rd International Congress of Americanists,* 459–62. New York: Science Press Print, 1930.

"The Style of Coeur d'Alene Mythology." *Verhandlung de XXIV. Internationalen Amerikanisten-Kongresses, Hamburg* 7, no. 13 (Sept. 1930): 243–53.

"Review of *Laughing Boy* by Oliver La Farge." *JAF* 44, no. 171 (Jan.–Mar. 1931): 121–22.

Melanesian Design: A Study of Style in Wood and Tortoiseshell Carving, Vols. I-II. New York: Columbia University Contributions to Anthropology, Vol. 18, 1933. Reprint, New York: Hacker Art Books, 1969.

Spider Woman: A Story of Weavers and Chanters. New York: Macmillan, 1934.

"Understatement or Naivete." *American Speech* 9, no. 3 (Oct. 1934): 199–204.

Navajo Shepherd and Weaver. New York: J.J. Augustin, 1936. Reprinted as *Weaving a Navajo Blanket.* New York: Dover Publications, 1974.

"Attitudes Towards Avoidance: A Suggestion." In *Essays in Anthropology in Honor of A.L. Kroeber,* 265–72. Berkeley: University of California, 1936.

"Color in Navajo Weaving." *Arizona Historical Review* 7, no. 2 (1936): 19–30.

Sandpaintings of the Navajo Shooting Chant. With Franc J. Newcomb. New York: J.J. Augustin, 1937. Reprint, New York: Dover Publications, 1975.

"Review of *Mitla, Town of Souls* by Elsie Clews Parsons." *Barnard College Alumnae,* Feb. 1937.

"Social Life." In *General Anthropology,* edited by Franz Boas, 409–86. New York: D.C. Heath, 1938.

Coeur d'Alene. In *Handbook of American Indian Languages* 3, edited by Franz Boas, 517–707. New York: New York: J.J. Augustin, 1938.

"Fifty Thousand Sign Posts." *New Mexico*, Mar. 17, 1939, 18–19; 32–33.

Navajo Medicine Man: Sandpaintings and Legends of Miguelito. New York: J.J. Augustin, 1939. Reprinted as *Navajo Medicine Man Sandpaintings.* New York: Dover Publications, 1977.

Dezba, Woman of the Desert. New York: J.J. Augustin, 1939.

"Review of *Origin Legend of the Navaho Enemy Way* by Berard Haile and *Myths and Tales of the Jicarilla Apache Indians* by Morris E. Opler." *AA* 41, no. 1 (1939): 141–43.

"Stem-List of the Coeur d'Alene Language." *IJAL* 10, nos. 2–3 (1939): 92–108.

"On the Beam of a Song." *Barnard Quarterly* 14 (Spring 1940): 16–19, 20.

"Review of *Indians of the United States* by Clark Wissler." *New York Herald Tribune Books*, Mar. 17, 1940.

"*Pueblo Indian Religion* by Elsie Clews Parsons." *American Historical Review* 45, no. 3 (April 1940): 655–66.

Agentive and Causative Elements in Navajo. With Adolph Dodge Bittany [*sic*]. New York: J.J. Augustin, 1940.

"Craftsmanship and Folklore." *JAF* 56, no. 221 (1940): 195–96.

"Review of *Language Culture and Personality, Essays in Memory of Edward Sapir.*" *AA* 44, no. 3 (July–Sept. 1942): 503–7.

"Review of *A Bibliography of the Navaho Indians* by Clyde Kluckhohn and Katherine Spencer." *JAF* 55, no. 216 (1942): 105–6.

"Review of *Social Organization of the West Apache* by Grenville Goodwin." *AA* 44, no. 4 (Oct.–Dec. 1942): 693–96.

"The Translation of Two Navaho Chant Words." *AA* 44, no. 3 (1942): 421–24.

"Review of *Study of Society, Methods and Problems* (1939) by F.C. Bartlett and Others." *JAF* 55, no. 218 (Oct.–Dec. 1942): 259–60.

"Elsie Clews Parsons." *JAF* 56, no. 219, Elsie Clews Parsons Memorial Number (Jan.–Mar. 1943): 45–48.

"Franz Boas and Folklore." Memoirs of the American Anthropological Association 61. *AA* 45, no. 3, part 2 (July–Sept. 1943): 52–57.

"American Folklore Society." *JAF* 56, no. 221 (1943): 161–64.

"Intensive Language Study: Review of *Outline of Linguistic Analysis* by B. Bloch and G.L. Trager and *Outline Guide for the Practical Study of Foreign Languages* by Leonard Bloomfield." *American Speech* 18, no. 3 (1943): 226–28.

"Human Nature as Conceived by the Navajo Indians." *Review of Religion* 7 (1943): 353–60.

"Imagery in An Indian Vocabulary." *American Speech* 18, no. 2 (1943): 96–102.

Prayer the Compulsive Word. Monographs of the American Ethnological Society 7. New York: J.J. Augustin, 1944. Reprint, Seattle: University of Washington, 1966.

"Individualism and Mythical Style." Franz Boas Memorial Number. *JAF* 57, no. 223 (Jan.–Mar. 1944): 16–25.

"*Origin Legend of the Navaho Flintway* by Father Berard Haile." *Review of Religion* 8, no. 4 (1944): 384–86.

"Protection in War: *Where the Two Came to Their Father: A Navaho War Ceremonial* by Maud Oakes, Commentary by Joseph Campbell." *New York Herald Tribune Books*, June 18, 1944.

The Story of the Navajo Hail Chant. New York: Author/trans., 1944.

"Distinctive Features of Navaho Religion." *Southwestern Journal of Anthropology* 1, no. 2 (Summer 1945): 199–220.

Composition and Symbolism of Coeur d'Alene Verb-Stems. *IJAL* 11, no. 1 (1945): 47–63.

"Linguistic Diversity Among the Navaho Indians." *IJAL* 11, no. 3 (1945): 156–68.

"Reply to Hoijer Review: *The Story of the Navajo Hail Chant.*" *IJAL* 13, no. 3 (July 1947): 193–96.

An Analysis of Coeur d'Alene Indian Myths. With a Comparison by Adele Froehlich. Philadelphia: American Folk-Lore Society, 1947.

"Review of *Navaho Witchcraft* by Clyde Kluckhohn." *JAF* 60, no. 235 (Jan.–Mar. 1947): 90–92.

"Significance of Aspiration in Navaho." *IJAL* 14, no. 1 (Jan. 1948): 15–19.

"Navajo Classification of Natural Objects." *Plateau* 21, no.1 (July 1948): 7–12.

"Review of *The Navaho* by Clyde Kluckhohn and Dorothea Leighton." *Review of Religion* 10 (1948): 287–89.

"A Preliminary Analysis of Navajo Prefixes" and "Outline of Navajo Grammar." Unpublished manuscript [c. 1945–1950]. Harvard University, Peabody Museum Library, Cambridge, MA.

"The Character of the Navaho Verb Stem." *Word* 5, no. 1 (April 1949): 55–76.

"The Navaho and Christianity." *AA* 51 (1949): 66-71.

"Then and Now." (In Navajo with English translation). *Navajo Language Monthly* 4, no. 11 (1949): 8.

"Language and Synesthesia." With Roman Jakobson and Elizabeth Werth. *Word* 5, no. 2 (1949): 224–33.

"Language and Cultural Pattern." *AA* 52 (1950): 194–204.

Navaho Religion: A Study of Symbolism. New York: Pantheon Books, 1950. Reprinted with a foreword by Oliver La Farge, Princeton, NJ: Princeton University Press, 1977.

"Review of *The Indians of the Southwest* by Edward E. Dale." *Scientific Monthly* 70, no. 6 (1950): 291–93.

Foreword to 2nd. edition of *Primitive Art* by Franz Boas. Unpublished draft for 1955 Dover reprint of *Primitive Art* by Franz Boas [1950].

Navaho Grammar. Publications of the American Ethnological Society 21. New York: J.J. Augustin, 1951.

"Review of *Funk and Wagnall's Standard Dictionary of Folklore, Mythology and Legend, Vol.1 A–L,* edited by Maria Leach." *American Anthropology* 53, no. 1 (1951): 99–100.

"Review of *Legend of the Ghostway Ritual in the Male Branch of Shooting Way* by Berard
   Haile." Unpublished manuscript [1952].
Review of *Handbook of American Idioms and Idiomatic Usage* by H. C. Whitford and R.
   J. Dixon. *Word* 9, no. 3 (1953): 312–13.
"Ethnology and the Navajo Language." Unpublished manuscript [c. 1954].
"Permissiveness and Navaho Mothers." [Final draft of "Goals and Methods of
   Navajo Discipline."] Unpublished manuscript [c. 1954].
"Another Look at the Navaho." Unpublished manuscript [c. 1954–55].
"Review of *Conceptions of the Soul Among North American Indians* by Ake Hultkranz."
   AA 57, no. 1 (1955): 147–48.
Coeur d'Alene Language Materials 1927–1955. (Scanned copies of file slips and
   field notebooks viewable at http://meltr.org/Cr/CrMaterials).
"An Anthropological View of a Primitive Religion." *International Record of Medicine
   and G.P. Clinics* 168, no. 12 (1955): 768–73.
"A Comparison of Five Salish Languages: I–VI." *IJAL* 24 (1958): 293–300; 25
   (1959): 8–15; 90–96; 154–67; 239–53; 26 (1960): 50–61.

BIBLIOGRAPHY

ABBREVIATIONS USED IN THE BIBLIOGRAPHY

AA   *American Anthropologist*

IJAL   *International Journal of American Linguistics*

JAF   *Journal of American Folklore*

Adair, John. "*Dezba, Woman of the Desert*, by Gladys Reichard." *AA* 42, no. 1 (Jan.–Mar. 1940): 500–501.

Addams, Jane. *The Second Twenty Years at Hull-House: September 1909 to 1929.* New York: Macmillan, 1930.

Aitken, Barbara. "*Social Life of the Navajo Indians*, by Gladys A. Reichard." *JAF* 41, no. 1 (Mar. 1930): 117–20.

Amsden, Charles Avery. *Navajo Weaving: Its Technic and Its History.* Santa Ana, CA: Fine Arts Press, 1934. Reprint, Glorieta, NM: Rio Grande Press, 1969.

———. "*Spider Woman: A Story of Navajo Weavers and Chanters*, by Gladys A. Reichard." *AA* 37, no. 3 (Jul.–Sept. 1935): 497.

"Anthropology—Studied, Taught, and Practiced." *Barnard Alumna* (1949): 4–6.

Babcock, Barbara, ed. *Pueblo Mothers and Children: Essays by Elsie Clews Parsons 1915–1924.* Santa Fe: Ancient City Press, 1990.

Bacon, Margaret Hope. *Mothers of Feminism: The Story of Quaker Women in America.* San Francisco: Harper and Row, 1986.

Bailey, Flora L. "Review of *Navaho Religion*, by Gladys A. Reichard." *JAF* 64, no. 252 (Oct.–Dec. 1951): 434–36.

"Bangor." *Census Directory of Northampton County.* Easton, PA.: Joseph H. Werner, 1890.

Banner, Lois. *Intertwined Lives: Margaret Mead, Ruth Benedict and Their Circle.* New York: Knopf, 2003.

Benedict, Ruth. *Patterns of Culture.* New York: Houghton-Mifflin, 1934 [Mentor Book edition, 1960].

Blue, Martha. *Indian Trader: The Life and Times of J.L. Hubbell.* Walnut, CA: Kiva Press, 2000.

Boas, Franz. "Eugenics." *Scientific Monthly* 3, no. 5 (Nov. 1916): 471–78.

———. "In Memoriam: Herman Karl Haeberlin." *AA* 21, no. 1 (Jan.–Mar. 1919): 71–74.

———. "Scientists as Spies." *The Nation*, Dec. 20, 1919, 797.

———. "The Classification of American Languages." *AA* 22, no. 4 (Oct.–Dec. 1920): 367–76.

———. "Pliny Earle Goddard." *IJAL* 6, no. 1 (1930): 1–2.

———. "An Anthropologist's Credo." *The Nation*, Aug. 1938, 202–4.

———. "Edward Sapir." *IJAL* 10, no. 1 (May 1939): 58–63.

———. "The Aims of Ethnology." 1888. In *Race, Language, and Culture*, edited by Franz Boas, 626–38. New York: Free Press, 1940.

Bodo, Murray, ed./trans. *Tales of an Endishodi: Father Berard Haile and the Navajos 1900–1961*. Albuquerque: University of New Mexico Press, 1998.

Bouquet, A. C. "Review #226." *Man* 50 (Oct. 1950): 141–43.

Brinkman, Raymond. "Etsmeystkhw khwe snwiyepmshtsn: 'You Know How to Talk Like a Whiteman.'" PhD diss., University of Chicago, 2003.

Bunzel, Ruth. "Gladys A. Reichard—A Tribute." In *Gladys A. Reichard 1893–1955*, edited by Woodbury and McIntosh, 8. New York: Barnard College, 1956.

Caffrey, Margaret M. *Ruth Benedict: Stranger in This Land*. Austin: University of Texas Press, 1989.

Caffrey, Margaret M., and Patricia A. Francis, eds. *To Cherish the Life of the World: Selected Letters of Margaret Mead*. New York: Basic Books, 2006.

Collier, John. *The Indians of the Americas*. New York: W. W. Norton, 1947.

Colton, Harold S. "The Museum of Northern Arizona and the Post-war Period." *Plateau* 17, no. 4 (April 1945): 55–64.

Coolidge, Mary Roberts. *Why Women Are So*. New York: Henry Holt, 1912. Reprinted with an introduction by Mary Jo Deegan. New York: Humanity Books, 2004.

Cotroneo, Ross R., and Jack Dozier. "A Time of Disintegration: The Coeur d'Alene and the Dawes Act." *Western Historical Quarterly* 5, no. 4 (Oct. 1974): 405–19.

Cottam, Erica. *Hubbell Trading Post: Trade, Tourism, and the Navajo Southwest*. Norman: University of Oklahoma Press, 2015.

Darnell, Regna. *Edward Sapir: Linguist, Anthropologist, Humanist*. Lincoln: University of Nebraska Press, 1990/2000.

Davis, William W. H. *History of Bucks County Pennsylvania, from the Discovery of the Delaware to the Present Time*, 2nd ed. New York: Lewis Publishing, 1905. https://play.google.com/books/reader?id=-. Available at BUVAAAAYAAJ&printsec=frontcover&output=reader&authuser=0&hl=en&pg=GBS.PA474.

De Laguna, Frederica. "Gladys Reichard—Appreciation and Appraisal." In *Gladys A. Reichard 1893–1955*, edited by Woodbury and McIntosh, 9–21. New York: Barnard College, 1956.

Deacon, Desley. *Elsie Clews Parsons: Inventing Modern Life*. Chicago: University of Chicago Press, 1997.

Degler, Carl L. *In Search of Human Nature: The Decline and Revival of Social Darwinism in American Thought.* New York: Oxford University Press, 1991.

Dinwoodie, David. "Textuality and the Voice of Informants." *Anthropological Linguistics* 41, no. 2 (Summer 1999): 165–92.

Diomedi, Alexander. *Sketches of Modern Indian Life.* St. Ignatius, MT: Peter Decker, 1894.

Donnelly, Joseph P., trans. *Wilderness Kingdom: The Journals and Paintings of Father Nicolas Point.* Toronto: Holt, Rinehart and Winston, 1967.

Elmore, Francis H. "Review of *Sandpaintings of the Navajo Shooting Chant,* by Franc J. Newcomb and Gladys A. Reichard." *El Palacio* 44, no. 1 (1938): 4–8.

Falk, Julia S. *Women, Language, and Linguistics: Three American Stories from the First Half of the Twentieth Century.* New York: Routledge, 1999.

Fergusson, Erna. *Dancing Gods: Indian Ceremonials of New Mexico and Arizona.* New York: Knopf, 1936. Reprint, Albuquerque: University of New Mexico Press, 1988.

———. *Our Southwest.* New York: Knopf, 1940.

"Fifty-fifth Annual Council Meeting." *JAF* 57, no. 224 (1944): 136–38.

Fillmore, Gary. *Shadows on the Mesa: Artists of the Painted Desert and Beyond.* Atglen, PA: Schiffer Publishing, 2012.

Fischer, Lillian. "Reviewed Work: *Spider Woman: A Story of Navajo Weavers and Chanters,* by Gladys A. Reichard." *Mississippi Valley Historical Review* 22, no. 2 (Sept. 1935): 312–13.

Florey, Kenneth. "The Flory/Florey/Flora Families of Northampton County, Pennsylvania and Their German Ancestors," May 20, 1997. http://pages.swcp .com/~dhickman/articles/flory.html.

Gildersleeve, Virginia C. *Many a Good Crusade.* New York: Macmillan, 1954.

Gillmor, Frances. "Review of *Navaho Religion,* by Gladys A. Reichard." *Folklore* 62, no. 4 (Dec. 1951): 473–74.

"Gladys A. Reichard, 1893–1955." *Plateau* 28 (1955): 48.

Goddard, Ives. "The Classification of the Native Languages of North America." In *Languages,* edited by Ives Goddard, 290–322. Handbook of North American Indians 17. Washington, DC: Smithsonian Institution, 1996.

Goddard, Pliny Earle. "An Anthropologist Looks at Marriage." *New Yorker,* Sept. 8, 1928, 24–25.

———. *Navajo Texts.* New York: American Museum of Natural History, 1933.

Goldfrank, Esther. "Gladys Amanda Reichard, 1893–1955." *JAF* 69, no. 271 (Jan.–Mar. 1956): 53–54.

———. *Notes on An Undirected Life: As One Anthropologist Tells It.* Flushing, NY: Queens College, 1978.

Golla, Victor. *California Indian Languages.* Berkeley: University of California Press, 2011.

———, ed. *The Sapir-Kroeber Correspondence.* Survey of California and Other Indian Languages Report 6. Berkeley: University of California Press, 1984.

Goodwin, Doris Kearns. *No Ordinary Time: Franklin and Eleanor Roosevelt, The Home-front in World War II*. New York: Simon & Schuster, 1994.

Green, Joyce. "Ruth Underhill." In *Women Anthropologists: Selected Biographies*, edited by Ute Gacs, Aisha Khan, Jerrie McIntyre, and Ruth Weinberger, 355–60. Urbana: University of Illinois Press, 1989.

Haas, Mary R. "Algonkian-Ritwan: The End of a Controversy." *IJAL* 24, no. 3 (July 1958): 159–73.

Haile, Berard. "*Social Life of the Navajo Indians*, by Gladys Reichard." *AA* 4 (1932): 711–17.

———. "Navajo Upward Reaching Way and Emergence Place." *AA* 45, no. 2 (April–June 1943): 306–11.

Handler, Richard. "Vigorous Male and Aspiring Female: Poetry, Personality, and Culture in Edward Sapir and Ruth Benedict." In *Romantic Motives: Essays on Anthropological Sensibility*, edited by George Stocking Jr., 127–55. Madison: University of Wisconsin Press, 1989.

Hartwell, Dickson. "White Brother of the Navajo." *Collier's*, April 30, 1949, 30, 64–65.

Heiner, Christina Joy. "A Historical Demography of the Coeur d'Alene 1900–1930." MA thesis, University of Montana, 2006.

Herskovits, Melville J. *Franz Boas, The Science of Man in the Making*. Clifton, NJ: Augustus M. Kelly, 1953. Reprint, New York: Scribner, 1973.

Herzog, George, Stanley S. Newman, Edward Sapir, Mary Haas Swadesh, Morris Swadesh, and Charles F. Voegelin. "Some Orthographical Recommendations." *AA* 36, no. 4 (Oct.–Dec. 1934): 629–31.

"History of Anthropology Interview with Frederica de Laguna and Norman Markel." [videotape] 1984. University of Florida Department of Anthropology. UF Digital Collections at http://www.ufdc.ufl.edu/AA00007225/00001.

History of Northampton County, Pennsylvania. Philadelphia: Peter Fritts, 1877.

"History of the International Linguistics Association." http://hallidaycentre.cityu .edu.hk/ila/index.aspx.

Hockett, Charles. "Review of *Handbook of American Indian Languages 3*." *Language* 16, no. 1 (Jan.–Mar. 1940): 54–57.

Hoijer, Harry. "Review of *The Story of the Navajo Hail Chant*." *IJAL* 11, no. 2 (April 1945): 123–25.

———. "*Prayer the Compulsive Word*, by Gladys A. Reichard." *JAF* 60, no. 235 (Jan.–Mar. 1947): 96–98.

———. "*Navaho Grammar* by Gladys A. Reichard." *IJAL* 19, no. 1 (Jan. 1953): 78–83.

Hough, Melissa. "The Pennsylvania Germans: The Slate Belt's Quiet Giant." In *125th Anniversary Book, Bangor, PA 1875–2000: A Celebration of Our Heritage*. N.p., 2000.

Howard, Jane. *Margaret Mead: A Life*. New York: Simon & Schuster, 1984.

Hull, William Isaac. "A History of Swarthmore College Volume 1" [unpublished typescript] n.d. [c. 1939]. Hull Papers, Series 4 Box 30. Friends Historical Library of Swarthmore College.

————, ed. *An Anthropologist at Work: Writings of Ruth Benedict.* Boston: Houghton Mifflin, 1959.

————. *Culture and Commitment: A Study of the Generation Gap.* Garden City, NY: Natural History Press/Doubleday, 1970.

Meriam, Lewis, ed. *The Problem of Indian Administration Report.*1928. Facsimile posted at http://www.alaskool.org/native_ed/research_reports/IndianAdmin /Indian_Admin_Problms.html#transmit. Section numbers in references refer to online version.

Miller, Darlis A. *Matilda Coxe Stevenson: Pioneering Anthropologist.* Norman: University of Oklahoma Press, 2007.

Miller, Jimmy H. *The Life of Harold Sellers Colton: A Philadelphia Brahmin in Flagstaff.* Tsaile, AZ: Navajo Community College Press, 1991.

Murray, Stephen O. "A 1978 Interview with Mary R. Haas." *Anthropological Linguistics* 39, no. 4 (Winter 1997): 695–722.

Newcomb, Franc J. *Hosteen Klah: Navaho Medicine Man and Sand Painter.* Norman: University of Oklahoma Press, 1964.

Null, Elizabeth F., W. K. McNeil, and Lynn Pifer. "The Journal's Editors." *JAF* 101, no. 402 (Oct.–Dec. 1988): 20–49.

Ochsenford, Rev. S. E., ed. *A Quarter Centennial Memorial Volume, Being a History of the College and a Record of its Men.* Allentown, PA: Muhlenburg College, 1892.

Olberding, Susan Deaver. "Telling the Story: The Museum of Northern Arizona." *Plateau,* New Series, no. 2 (1997): 5–46.

Palmer, Beverly Wilson, ed. "About Lucretia Mott." The Lucretia Coffin Mott Papers Project. http://www.mott.pomona.edu/index.htm.

Parezo, Nancy, ed. *Hidden Scholars: Women Anthropologists and the Native American Southwest.* Albuquerque: University of New Mexico Press, 1993.

Parsons, Elsie Clews. "Anthropology and Prediction." *AA* 44, no. 3 (July–Sept. 1942): 337–44.

Philp, Kenneth R. *John Collier's Crusade for Indian Reform, 1920–1954.* Tucson: University of Arizona Press, 1977.

Powers, Willow Roberts. *Navajo Trading: The End of an Era.* Albuquerque: University of New Mexico Press, 2001.

Price, David H. *Anthropological Intelligence: The Deployment and Neglect of American Anthropology in the Second World War.* Durham, NC: Duke University Press, 2008.

Roessel, Ruth, and Broderick H. Johnson. *Navajo Livestock Reduction: A National Disgrace.* Chinle, AZ: Navajo Community College Press, 1974.

Rohde, Jerry. "Genocide and Extortion: 150 Years Later, the Hidden Motive for the Indian Island Massacre." *North Coast Journal,* Feb. 25, 2010. http://www.northcoastjournal.com/humboldt/genocide-and-extortion/Content ?oid=2130748.

————. *Both Sides of the Bluff: History of Humboldt County Places I.* Eureka, CA: MountainHome Books, 2014.

Rosenberg, Rosalind. "The Woman Question at Columbia: From John W. Burgess to Judith Shapiro." Paper delivered at the Columbia University Seminar on the History of the University, Feb. 17, 1999. http://web.archive.org/web/20080705143127/http://beatl.barnard.columbia.edu/cuhistory/archives/Rosenberg/woman_question.htm.

———. *Changing the Subject: How the Women of Columbia Shaped the Way We Think About Sex and Politics.* New York: Columbia University Press, 2004.

Rossiter, Margaret W. *Women Scientists in America: Struggles and Strategies to 1940.* Baltimore: Johns Hopkins University Press, 1982/1984.

Sapir, Edward. "Wiyot and Yurok, Algonkin Languages of California." *AA* 15, no. 4 (Oct.–Dec. 1913): 617–46.

———. "Algonkin Languages of California: A Reply" and "Epilogue." *AA* 17, no. 1 (Jan.–Mar. 1915): 188–94, 198.

———. *Language: An Introduction to the Study of Speech.* New York: Harcourt, Brace & World, 1921.

———. "The Unconscious Patterning of Behavior in Society." In *The Unconscious: A Symposium,* edited by E. S. Dummer, 114–42. New York: Knopf, 1929.

———. "Review of Ruth L. Bunzel, *The Pueblo Potter.*" 1929. In *Collected Works of Edward Sapir IV: Ethnology,* edited by Regna Darnell and Judith Irvine, 243–44. New York: Mouton de Gruyter, 1994.

Schmerler, Gil. *Henrietta Schmerler and the Murder That Put Anthropology On Trial.* Eugene, OR: Scrivana Press, 2017.

Schwartz, E. A. "Red Atlantis Revisited: Community and Culture in the Writings of John Collier." *American Indian Quarterly* 18, no. 4 (Autumn 1994): 507–31.

Smith, Marian W. "Gladys Armanda [sic] Reichard." *AA* 58, no. 5 (Oct. 1956): 913–16.

Steward, Julian H. "Alfred Louis Kroeber, 1876–1960." *AA* 63, vol. 5, no. 1 (Oct. 1961): 1038–87.

Stocking, George W., Jr. "The Boas Plan for the Study of American Indian Languages." In *The Ethnographer's Magic and Other Essays in the History of Anthropology,* edited by George Stocking Jr., 276–341. Madison: University of Wisconsin Press, 1992.

———, ed. *American Anthropology 1921–1945: Papers from the American Anthropologist.* Lincoln: University of Nebraska Press, 2002.

Taylor, Verta. "Sisterhood, Solidarity, and Modern Feminism." *Gender and Society* 3, no. 2 (1989): 277–86.

Tisdale, Shelby J. "Women on the Periphery of the Ivory Tower." In *Hidden Scholars,* edited by Nancy Parezo, 311–33. Albuquerque: University of New Mexico Press, 1993.

Trager, George. "*Navaho Grammar* by Gladys A. Reichard." *AA* 55, no. 3 (Aug. 1953): 428–29.

Underhill, Ruth. *An Anthropologist's Arrival: A Memoir,* edited by Chip Colwell-Chanthaphonh and Stephen E. Nash. Tucson: University of Arizona Press, 2014.

Voegelin, C. F., and F. M. Voegelin. "On the History of Structuralizing in 20th Century America." *Anthropological Linguistics* 5, no. 1 (Jan. 1963): 12–37.

Ware, Susan. "Women and the Great Depression." http://www.gilderlehrman .org/history-by-era/great-depression/essays/women-and-great-depression.

Weisiger, Martha. "Gendered Injustice: Navajo Livestock Reduction in the New Deal Era." *American Indian Quarterly* 38, no. 4 (Winter 2007): 437–55.

Westerlund, John S. *Arizona's War Town: Flagstaff, Navajo Ordnance Depot and World War II*. Tucson: University of Arizona, 2003.

Wheelwright, Philip. "Symbol, Metaphor, and Myth." *Sewanee Review* 58, no. 4 (Oct.–Dec. 1950): 678–98.

Williams, Walter. "American Imperialism and the Indians." In *Indians in American History*, edited by Frederic E. Hoxie, 231–49. Chicago: Newberry Library, 1988.

Wilson, William A. "The Deeper Necessity: Folklore and the Humanities." *JAF* 101, no. 400 (April–June 1988): 156–67.

Witherspoon, Gary. "Language in Culture and Culture in Language." Gladys A. Reichard Memorial Issue. *IJAL* 46, no. 1 (Jan. 1980): 1–13.

———. *Language and Art in the Navajo Universe*. With a foreword by Clifford Geertz. Ann Arbor: University of Michigan Press, 1977.

Woodbury, Nathalie F. S., and Millicent C. McIntosh, eds. *Gladys A. Reichard 1893–1955*. New York: Barnard College, 1956.

Woodbury, Richard B. *60 Years of Southwestern Archeology: A History of the Pecos Conference*. Albuquerque: University of New Mexico Press, 1993.

Wyman, Leland. C. "Origin Legend of the Navaho Flintway by Father Berard Haile." *American Antiquity* 9, no. 3 (Jan. 1944): 365.

———."Review of *Navaho Religion* by Gladys A. Reichard." *AA* 52, no. 4 (Part 1, Oct.–Dec. 1950): 524–26.

Young, Robert W. "Written Navajo: A Brief History." Navajo Reading Study Progress Report No. 19, Oct. 1972. Albuquerque: University of New Mexico Press. Facsimile at http://files.eric.ed.gov/fulltext/ED068229.pdf.

Zumwalt, Rosemary Levy. *Wealth and Rebellion: Elsie Clews Parsons, Anthropologist and Folklorist*. Urbana: University of Illinois Press, 1992.

Zwergel, Irma. "Incomplete Portrait." *Barnard College Quarterly*, Spring 1940, 14–15.

INDEX

Page numbers in italics refer to illustrations.

INDEX

330

Erskine, John, 213, 304n1
Eureka, Calif., 37, 42, 44, 279n12

Fergusson, Erna, 96, 103, 161–62, 234
Fischer, Lillian, 126
Flory, Dorothy Godshalk and family,
    12–13, 269
Freeman, Ethel Cutler, 235
Freeland, Lucy S. ("Nans"), 43,
    280n25
Froehlich, Adele, 306n29
Frazer, James George and Elisabeth
    "Lilly" Johanna de Boys
    Adelsdorfer, 66
Fred Harvey Company, 159, 160, 161,
    163, 294n4, 296n75; Albuquerque
    Indian Department, 142; Indian
    Detours, 172–73

Gallup Inter-tribal Indian
    Ceremonial, 173, 243, 272
Ganado, Ariz., 52, 77, 86–87, 137,
    152, 254, 292n88. See also Hubbell
    Trading Post
Gayton, Ann, 300n85
George, Pascal, 69, 73, 306n26
Gifford, Edward W., 43, 280n25
Gildersleeve, Virginia Cocheron:
    advocacy of university women, 23,
    127, 238–39, 308n5; as Barnard
    College dean, 23, 25–26, 56,
    58, 115, 237, 281n55, 298n31;
    internationalism of, 168, 170,
    297n15; support of Reichard, 46,
    73, 168–69, 170, 173
Gillmore, Frances, 242
Gladys A. Reichard Anthropology
    Room, 269, 270, 270–72
Goddard, Alice Rockwell, 47, 75–76
Goddard, Pliny Earle ("Peggy"): and
    Boas, 24, 30, 47, 63, 75; career of,
    46–48, 63–64, 73, 77, 82, 282n22,
    284n63; criticism of, 63–64,

282n22, 283n25, 284n76; death
    of, 74–76, 82, 109; family ties of,
    47, 57, 75, 77; and Navajo texts,
    76, 77, 86, 134, 284n76, 290n21;
    partnership with Reichard, 46–51,
    55, 58–59, 74, 80, 88, 267, 279n13,
    281n55, 291n58
Goldfrank, Esther Schiff, 30–31, 48,
    191–92, 202, 266, 268–69
Goldwater, Barry, 234, 274
Goodman, Barbara Hubbell ("Auntie
    Bob"), 51–52, 135, 217, 278n82
Great Depression, 81, 111, 115–16,
    126–27, 139, 147, 163, 180, 192,
    201, 291n61, 298n31
Guggenheim Memorial Fellowship for
    Advanced Study Abroad, 3, 58–59,
    61, 66, 282n7
Gunther, Erna, 29–30, 278n80,
    300n83

Haas, Mary, 198, 209, 226, 279n9,
    302n38, 302n42
Haeberlin, Herman Karl, 35, 65–66
Hagerman, Herbert, 100–101
Hahn, E. Adelaide, 198, 302n42
Haile, Berard ("Father Berard"):
    alliance with Sapir, 82–83,
    108–13, 148, 151, 207, 288n96;
    as anthropological linguist, 77,
    82, 109–10, 112, 204–5, 208–10,
    288n96, 304n82; criticisms of, 82,
    110, 176, 304n80; as Franciscan
    missionary, 111, 289n102
Hamburg Museum of Ethnology, 3,
    60, 73
Harrington, John P., 194
Heard Museum, 229, 230
Herskovits, Melville, 24, 300n85
Herzog, George, 253, 300n85
Hill, W. W. ("Nibs"), 176, 210
Hitler, Adolph, 166–67, 236, 256,
    281n2